FUNDAMENTALS
OF THE FAITH

Earlier volumes in the Series . . .

CONTEMPORARY EVANGELICAL THOUGHT (1957)

REVELATION AND THE BIBLE (1959)

BASIC CHRISTIAN DOCTRINES (1962)

CHRISTIAN FAITH AND MODERN THEOLOGY (1964)

JESUS OF NAZARETH: SAVIOUR AND LORD (1966)

CONTEMPORARY EVANGELICAL THOUGHT

FUNDAMENTALS OF THE FAITH

GORDON H. CLARK

HAROLD B. KUHN

SAMUEL J. MIKOLASKI

ADDISON H. LEITCH

JOHANNES SCHNEIDER

CALVIN D. LINTON

GEOFFREY W. BROMILEY

MARCUS L. LOANE

BILLY GRAHAM

CARY N. WEISIGER III

FRED CARL KUEHNER

WILBUR M. SMITH

MERRILL C. TENNEY

Edited by
CARL F. H. HENRY

ZONDERVAN PUBLISHING HOUSE
GRAND RAPIDS, MICHIGAN

INTRODUCTION

THIS IMPORTANT exposition of fundamentals of the Christian faith was four years in the making, from initial projection through final printing of these 13 essays in the fortnightly magazine *Christianity Today*. The articles were hopefully destined from the outset for reproduction in permanent book form, and their inclusion in this CONTEMPORARY EVANGELICAL THOUGHT series will assure their continuing availability to a wide company of readers.

The successive essays won cumulative interest as they appeared quarterly in pamphlet form, between September 1965 and August 1968, as a magazine bind-in. Expounded with scriptural fidelity for laymen and students, the volume will provide a high service to serious inquirers in an age when many increasingly wonder just what Christianity signifies.

Sharing in the effort are evangelical leaders of distinction in a wide variety of vocational callings. Philosophers, theologians and authors unite their energies in a common witness to crucial turning-points of Christian faith. The compilation is ecumenical in the best sense, since contributors from a wide variety of denominational affiliations present a remarkably homogeneous statement of basic Christian beliefs. The volume does not, of course, provide a complete systematic theology, nor was the pamphlet series originally intended to do so. But it provides a devout exposition of major facets of evangelical religion—in short, of the fundamentals of the faith.

Evangelist Billy Graham's contribution on the new birth is used by permission from his best-selling volume *World Aflame* published by Doubleday. Dr. Johannes Schneider's contribution on the life and ministry of Jesus Christ is a translation (by Helga Bender Henry) made with permission of Calwer Verlag in Stuttgart, Germany, of an article appearing in *Calwer Bibellexikon*. (Dr. Schneider will be remembered by delegates and observers attending the 1966 World Congress on Evangelism in Berlin for his ringing affirmation of New Testament theology and his driving criticism of current religious alternatives.) All other essays were specifically projected and prepared for the original series in *Christianity Today*, and the series appears here for the first time in convenient book form. This volume becomes the sixth in the CONTEMPORARY EVANGELICAL THOUGHT series. It merits, I think, as wide a reading as the significant volumes that have preceded it.

CARL F. H. HENRY

Arlington, Virginia

10,240

CONTENTS

INTRODUCTION

1. REVEALED RELIGION *Gordon H. Clark*   11

2. GOD: HIS NAMES AND NATURE *Harold B. Kuhn*   37

3. THE TRIUNE GOD *Samuel J. Mikolaski*   59

4. THE CREATION OF MATTER, LIFE, AND MAN
    Addison H. Leitch   79

5. JESUS CHRIST: HIS LIFE AND MINISTRY
    Johannes Schneider   95

6. JESUS CHRIST: THE DIVINE REDEEMER
    Calvin D. Linton   121

7. THE HOLY SPIRIT *Geoffrey W. Bromiley*   145

8. CHRIST AND HIS CHURCH *Marcus L. Loane*   169

9. THE NEW BIRTH *Billy Graham*   189

10. THE REFORMED DOCTRINE OF SANCTIFICATION
    Cary N. Weisiger III   211

11. HEAVEN OR HELL? *Fred Carl Kuehner*   233

12. THE SECOND ADVENT OF CHRIST *Wilbur M. Smith*   251

13. THE GLORIOUS DESTINY OF THE BELIEVER
    Merrill C. Tenney   273

REVEALED RELIGION

Gordon H. Clark

Gordon H. Clark is professor of philosophy at Butler University, In-dianapolis. The author of numerous books in the areas of philosophy and theology, he holds the A.B. and Ph.D. degrees from the University of Pennsylvania and taught philosophy in that university from 1924-36. Subsequently he taught at Wheaton College, from 1936-1944. Dr. Clark has been president of the Indiana Philosophical Society, and of Evangelical Theological Society. His published writings include Readings in Ethics *(1931),* Selections from Hellenistic Philosophy *(1940),* A History of Philosophy *(with Martin, et al) (1941),* A Christian Philosophy of Education *(1946),* A Christian View of Men and Things *(1953),* What Presbyterians Believe *(1956),* Thales to Dewey *(1946), and* Karl Barth's Theological Method *(1963).*

1.   *Gordon H. Clark*

REVEALED RELIGION

FEW QUESTIONS IF any are as important as the status of revealed religion. From an immediately practical point of view, revelation is the divide separating Bertrand Russell's unyielding atheistic despair from the Christian hope of eternal life.

Even such a positivist as Herbert Feigl, in the opening sentences of his important *Logical Empiricism*, writes, "Probably the most decisive division among philosophical attitudes is the one between the worldly and the other-worldly types of thought. . . . Very likely there is here an irreconcilable divergence. It goes deeper than disagreement in doctrine; at bottom it is a difference in basic aim and interest. . . . The very issue of the jurisdictive power of the appeal to logic and experience (and with it the question of just what empirical evidence can establish) is at stake."

Now, the hope of eternal life in another world depends on God; and to deny the existence of God is to reduce the universe to a pitiless inhuman machine, or, since scientific mechanism cannot in reality be sustained, to a purposeless chaos in which human life is a tragic futility.

From a more academic viewpoint, yet mediately just as practical, the status of revelation determines the specific nature of religion. In doing so, it not only sets the ethical standards of daily living but also modifies or controls the theory of psychology and of politics and the philosophy of history. For example, a good argument can be framed to show that in political theory atheism and even some forms of religion imply tyranny, whereas the justification of minority rights and the authority of a limited government depend on a specific type of revelation (see my *A Christian View of Men and Things,* chapters 3 and 4).

These few paragraphs are sufficient to indicate the importance of revealed religion. No effort will be made here to prove the existence of

11

God or the possibility of a divine revelation, though in so far as objections are removed, the following argument will have an indirect bearing upon these questions. What the contemporary situation requires is that the term *revelation* be explained. In good English the word is used in several senses. Each has more or less content. One meaning may prove to be virtually worthless; another may serve as the basis for a multitude of detailed conclusions; and a third may be placed midway between the two in fruitfulness.

What follows begins with this third type of meaning, a meaning, however, that is chronologically early. Then come some contemporary views of revelation that turn out to be logically sterile. And finally there will be an examination of one that is both chronologically early and satisfactorily productive both logically and practically.

That God reveals Himself to man in nature is a very early view of the mode of revelation. It is found in Aristotle and other pagan philosophers, with whom we shall not have much to do, and of course it is expressed in many parts of the Bible. But the acknowledgment that the heavens declare the glory of God has been developed in two rather different formulations.

STRICT NATURAL THEOLOGY

The first of these may be called natural theology in the strictest sense. Thomas Aquinas and the Roman Catholic Church hold, not merely that God can be known in nature, but that the existence of God can irrefragably be demonstrated, without any a priori equipment, from the data of sensory perception. To make good this claim, Thomas, following the lead of Aristotle, worked out an amazingly intricate system of philosophy.

This tremendous achievement merits professional and meticulous examination. The limits of the present argument, however, preclude any such elaborate analysis. In another volume (*Thales to Dewey,* pp. 274-78), I have tried to show that technical analysis can indicate several points (e.g., the concepts of potentiality and motion, the circular argument on infinite regress, the theory of analogy) at which the chain of Thomas' syllogisms breaks down. Surely it is extreme to claim, as the Thomists do, that the Apostle Paul in Romans 1:20 guarantees the validity of the complete argument. Now, if the Thomistic proofs are fallacious, as many non-Romanists are willing to admit, this would eliminate natural theology from any further consideration.

But for those who are suspicious of or unfamiliar with philosophy, there is a more obviously theological objection to Thomism. Karl Barth in our day has become well known for his stringent opposition to all natural theology; and a part of his argument, in the form of a destructive hypothetical syllogism, maintains that if the theistic proofs were in fact valid, they would quite demolish all Christianity.

Significant knowledge of God cannot be had, argues Barth, if "we reserve the question to which the doctrine of the Trinity is the answer (namely, Who God is) and deal first with his existence and his nature, as if this That and What could be determined otherwise than on the presupposition of the Who" (*Church Dogmatics,* I, 345). On the next page he continues, "If we do not know God in the way in which he reveals himself as the one, namely, *distincte in tribus personis,* the inevitable result is that *nudum et inane duntaxat Dei nomen sine vero Deo in cerebro nostro volitat"* (Calvin, *Institutes,* I, xiii, 2). Or, in English, if we do not know God as one substance in three Persons, the inevitable result is a blank, empty name floating in our brains without any idea of the true God.

A third reference to Barth, in which he quotes C. J. Nitsch with approval, takes us a step further. "So long as theism 'only distinguishes God and the world and never God from God, it is always caught in the reversion or transition to the pantheistic or other denial of absolute being. A perfect protection against atheism, polytheism, pantheism, or dualism there can only be with the doctrine of the Trinity' " (*Church Dogmatics,* I, 347).

If it seems strange to accuse St. Thomas of aiding and abetting atheism and pantheism, the direction of natural theology can better be seen as it worked itself out in Hegel and the theologians who followed him. The connection with St. Thomas lies in the fact that his terms denoting God are all neuters: *ens perfectissimum, primum movens,* and so on. This Aristotelian construction, essentially pagan, obscures the personality of God, with the result that an elevation of this neuter to the status of the Christian Trinity becomes an insuperable difficulty. With the advent of Hegelian absolutism, a person becomes an individual mode of the Absolute Spirit, while the Spirit, being Absolute, cannot be a person.

Theologians such as Siebeck, Lotze, Rothe, and Ritschl, who attempted to preserve the personality of God, found their principles unequal to the task. God became merely the content of the highest human values, so that in modernism the object of worship became man himself (cf. *Church Dogmatics,* I, 2, pp. 286-97).

At this point three conclusions may be drawn: (a) the theistic proofs are destructive of Christianity; (b) but fortunately they are invalid, so that Christianity escapes this danger; and (c) in so far as natural theology is an impossibility, the need of a revealed religion becomes clearer.

LESS AND MORE

Schleiermacher represents a type of theology that is less strict logically than Thomas' claimed to be but that at the same time hoped to extend itself to more doctrines. Thomas, of course, added biblical revelation to his natural theology, and only in that could he find the truth of the Trinity, Creation, Atonement, and so on. Schleiermacher turns from the Aristotelian apparatus of motion and prime mover and expects to uncover the whole of Christianity by an analysis of human nature, or, more accurately, the Christian consciousness.

Influenced by Pietism, Schleiermacher made emotion the essence of religion. Whereas the Reformers had based Christian experience on ideas and doctrine, for him theology is precisely the description of religious experience. The center of this experience is a feeling of absolute dependence, and God exists because we feel dependent on Him. It is not that the feeling is dependent on a prior knowledge of God but rather that the knowledge is dependent on the feeling. Doctrines, to say it again, are descriptions of this feeling.

Schleiermacher was in fact a pantheist, and his influence combined with that of Hegel to deny the personality of God, as explained above. Karl Barth showed how modernism developed from Schleiermacher, and why this type of religion substituted man for God as the object of worship. The empirical nature of his theology led away from the original "Christian" consciousness to a nondescript psychology of religion, and became the foundation of contemporary humanism. The story is interesting and complex (cf. Richard B. Brandt, *The Philosophy of Schleiermacher,* Harper and Brothers, 1941; Edwin A. Burtt, *Types of Religious Philosophy,* revised edition, chapter 2; and for a summary of Barth's criticisms, Gordon H. Clark, *Karl Barth's Theological Method,* Presbyterian and Reformed, 1963).

So far as logical status is concerned, however, the procedure of Schleiermacher, since it cannot be classed with the alleged irrefragable demonstrations of Thomas, must either be judged more glaringly fallacious or be classified with the loose form of natural theology in the next paragraph.

LOOSE NATURAL THEOLOGY

There is another and looser sense of natural theology to which the preceding arguments do not seem to apply. Instead of attempting an irrefragable demonstration of the existence of an *ens perfectissimum,* one might claim merely that the heavens declare the glory of God. Certainly this is natural, though perhaps it should not be labeled theology. Theology is commonly supposed to be somewhat systematic, and this is a most unsystematic knowledge of God.

Not only is it unsystematic; it is also quite inadequate and minimal at best. Without examining too closely the logic involved, let us ask what may be known of God by an examination of nature. First of all, it will be said that the planets as they move according to Kepler's three laws show that God is a great mathematician—at least as good a mathematician as Kepler, and perhaps even better.

Since this amount of knowledge does not equal omniscience, someone may claim that the creation of the planets and stars is evidence of omnipotence. This claim, however, must be disallowed, not because creation would be insufficient evidence of omnipotence but because we have no empirical evidence of creation. We do indeed see the stars, but we did not see God create them. If, now, instead of relying on observation, the claimant attempts to argue that the visible existence of the stars proves that they were created, we would have to return to an examination of natural theology in its strict sense. And we should save to do this with even less hope of success, for an argument that proves creation is considerably more difficult to construct than one that proves only the existence of some God. In fact, Thomas Aquinas himself, who worked out in such detail, laid such stress on, and was so certain of his theistic proofs, says explicitly, "That the world did not always exist, we hold by faith alone: it cannot be proved demonstratively" (*Summa Theologica,* I, Q. 46, Art. 2).

If, of course, we have some other source of knowledge, a bona fide revelation, that assures us of divine creation, we can then ascribe to the Creator the amount of power displayed in the heavens. But even so, and aside from the fact that we are now depending on special revelation, this amount of power, great as it is, cannot be omnipotence. Beyond the amount we observe, there can always be more.

Observation of nature is a very unsatisfactory method of obtaining knowledge of God. Christians are often unwilling to face the difficulties involved, and they sometimes try to ignore what their opponents see so clearly. The theory of evolution has described nature as red in tooth and claw. How can we see God in animal pain? Human beings are a part of nature, too; and the brutalities of Hitler and Stalin, the Red Chinese massacre of the Tibetans, and nearly all the rest of human history make a sorry picture. On such observations as these, Voltaire wrote this outlandish *Candide,* Hume his restrained *Dialogues on Natural Religion* (chapters 10 and 11), and Julian Huxley, with an air of superiority, his *Religion Without Revelation.*

Again, let us insist, if we have some source of information other than observation of nature, if God has revealed some parts of a philosophy of history, we can handle these unpleasant facts. Candid opponents of Christianity admit this possibility. But natural theology cannot handle them, and candid Christians ought to admit it.

To do the best for this loose form of natural theology, we may well say that the heavens make some display of God's power and glory; that the brutality of tyrants elicits a disaffection that attests the existence of a dim and feeble conscience that can serve as the ground of moral responsibility; but that nothing in the way of practical plans for amelioration is forthcoming.

Though dim and restricted, this natural knowledge of God is not to be denied. Romans 1:20 may not guarantee the validity of the theistic proofs, but it plainly asserts some knowledge of God derived from "the things that are made." Romans 2:15 shows a minimal a priori knowledge of moral principles. On such natural knowledge human responsibility depends. When Karl Barth argues that the heathen Paul has in view are not the heathen generally but only those to whom he preached the Gospel, so that all the others have no knowledge of God at all, we regret that his exegetical powers failed him (cf. *Church Dogmatics,* II, 1, pp. 119ff.). Yet this natural knowledge is minimal in extent and practically useless in communicating the way of salvation. Who can deny that the savage tribes of the jungles know very little about God?

In view of these considerations, the position of orthodox Protestantism seems soundly based, as expressed in the Westminster Confession, which, combining observation of nature with what I take to be a reference to innate moral ideas, pronounces this definitive judgment on natural theology in its opening sentence: "Although the light of nature, and the works of creation and providence, do so far manifest the goodness, wisdom, and power of God, as to leave men inexcusable; yet they are not sufficient to give that knowledge of God, and of his will, which is necessary unto salvation." It would seem therefore that some sort of revealed religion is a necessity.

ENCOUNTER

Such is the flexibility of the English language that there is nothing improper in a Thomist's or a modernist's assertion that nature, physical or human, is a "revelation" of God. This meaning of revelation, however, gives rise to a dry scholasticism and barren deism that, even if the validity of their arguments is not questioned, seem at best to enervate true and vital religion. Hence, without disallowing the usages of English, some devout writers prefer to indicate by the term revelation something more direct and personal. Having repudiated natural theology, they equate revelation with "encounter."

This contemporary idea of revelation, revelation as a living encounter, is foreshadowed in earlier movements. The Pietists sought a more personal religion than intellectual theology seemed to offer. The Quakers spoke of an inner light and waited for the Spirit to move them to speak in meeting. Even biblical terminology allows for a testimony of the Holy Spirit, which could be construed as a living revelation. There have always been individuals who sought God's immediate guidance both for the practical details of daily conduct and for the proper forms of divine worship. Some people saw visions and dreamed dreams while Joan of Arc heard voices.

Then there were the outright mystics who fell into trances. The droplets of their personality were poured out into the ocean of God's being. Like air, when it is so impregnated with light that it is more light than air, and like iron, which in the fire looks more like fire than iron, so the mystic soul becomes ineffably divine. No conceptual information is thus received, but it is a deeply satisfying experience.

This mystic or pietistic type of mind, exemplified in all ages, provides a fertile ground for the more recent developments. However, the contemporary movement that hangs its vital religion on event or encounter is not a lineal and direct descendant of mysticism or pietism. Certain modern complications must be taken into account. These will be considered later on. But first a most important point of similarity between the earlier and the current movements requires emphasis. The similarity is their anti-intellectualism. As St. Bernard was distressed by the "rationalism" of Abelard, so Sören Kierkegaard reacted against the omniscience of Hegel.

Hegelianism purports to furnish us with a completely rational explanation of all the universe. The philosopher had begun his system with the most empty and most general of all concepts. An analysis of this concept gave rise to its opposite or contradictory. Then Hegel's genius discovered how to harmonize the contradiction in a higher synthesis. The synthesis in turn gives rise to its contradictory, and these are then harmonized, and so on until the Concrete Absolute Universal synthesizes everything. In Hegelian philosophy, no problem escapes this dialectic solution.

Kierkegaard rejects the thesis-antithesis-synthesis scheme in favor of a two-term dialectic. Each concept has its contradictory, but no synthesis is possible. The final word is not Absolute, but Paradox.

The motivation for the attack against Hegel was supplied by the hypocrisy, the complacency, and the stupidity of the state church. Kierkegaard was fed up with the sawdust fare Hegelian pastors were feeding their parishioners. Literally and symbolically the pastors reduced Christ's miracle of the loaves and fishes to an ordinary picnic; and original sin became an inherited stomach disorder that was caused by Adam's eating some poisonous food. In such a theology, God and supernaturalism play no part. The spirit of the age had replaced the Holy Spirit and time had swallowed up eternity. One got his Christianity as one got his citizenship—by being born in Denmark. Piety was conformity to custom, and society had submerged the individual. It was in opposition to hypocrisy, citizen-Christianity, and socialism that Kierkegaard cried for a passionate individual decision. Hegelian philosophy had magnified conceptual abstract knowledge; but true religion, says Kierkegaard, does not consist in understanding anything: religion is a matter of feeling, of anti-intellectual passionateness. *What* one believes is of no importance; *how* one believes it makes all the difference in the world.

In one passage Kierkegaard describes two men at prayer. One is in a Lutheran church and entertains a true conception of God. But because he prays in a false spirit, he is in reality praying to an idol. The other man is in a heathen temple praying to idols; but since he prays with an infinite passion, he is in truth praying to God, for truth lies in the inward How, not in the external What.

Two quotations from Kierkegaard's *Concluding Unscientific Postscript* state the general position. "An objective uncertainty held fast in an appropriation process of the most passionate inwardness is the truth, the highest truth attainable for an existing individual." And, second, "If one asks subjectively about the truth, one is reflecting subjectively about the relation of the individual; if only the How of this relation is in truth, then the individual is in truth, even though he is thus related to untruth."

Kierkegaard spoke in vain to his generation. No one paid any attention. Everyone remained complacent and hypocritical. It took events of another character—events that had no parallel in the days when St. Bernard opposed the rationalism of Abelard—to force the meaning of Kierkegaard on the twentieth century. Today the modernistic optimism of the nineteenth century, a modernism that viewed original sin as a stomach disorder to be cured by the advances of medical science, has been shattered by the incredible devastation of two world wars. Complacency has given way to anxiety. Tragedy, torture, and death have been our lot, and a still worse World War III looms over us. Despairing of intellectual solutions in a world of insane chaos, the theologians of the twentieth century remembered the iconoclastic Dane.

The first of these was Karl Barth, who seized upon the notion of paradox and emphasized the opposition between time and eternity, but whose later writings toned down these themes. Emil Brunner was his early companion, though later there was a rift between them. Brunner made more of paradox and remained more outspoken against logic. Rudolf Bultmann, profoundly influenced by the philosopher Heidegger, is a still different color on the same spectrum. Bultmann may rather properly be called an existentialist, though Barth explicitly rejects existentialism. And finally one ought to mention Jean-Paul Sartre, who exemplifies the atheistic wing of this movement.

The differences among these men make it impossible to frame any summary that would apply accurately to them all. But there is a basic thesis that unites them. They are all anti-Hegelian; they all agree that intellectualism is superficial; they or their followers are apt to use the slogans of romanticism—such as, life is deeper than logic, and, experience is more real than thought; and finally they all more or less explicitly put paradox and contradiction at the heart of reality and assert that some problems are inherently insoluble.

This neo-orthodoxy, this neo-supernaturalism, or, in philosophic language, this existentialism, is not to be defined simply as an interest in matters of ultimate concern. Some existentialists try to do this and then claim that Augustine and Luther were existentialists. This is bad logic and bad scholarship. The important thing is that existentialism repudiates rational thought, as Augustine and Luther never did. Sometimes Pascal is called a forerunner of existentialism; but Pascal wrote, as Brunner and Sartre never could write, "All our dignity consists in thought." The essential point about these twentieth-century theologians is that they repudiate thought and extol non-intellectual experience.

Jean-Paul Sartre attempts to give a more positive and more techincal summary of existentialism. He asserts its common thesis to be "existence precedes essence." This anti-Platonic and anti-Hegelian phrase means that the Aristotelian *That* precedes the Aristotelian *What*. For example, if a carpenter wishes to make a cabinet, he must first know what a cabinet is and what particular size and shape of cabinet he intends to make. Here the What precedes the That: essence precedes existence. So too the Christian idea of God includes the notion that God knew what He was going to create before He created it. The doctrine of Providence ascribes to God a knowledge or plan of history that antedates the events. This is what Sartre denies. There is no pre-existent plan of history, nor even a determinate human nature that all men must have. Each man makes himself what he becomes. The What follows the That.

There are good reasons for selecting this as the definite principle of existentialism, even in its theological forms. These authors emphasize human freedom, an open universe, an indeterminate nature, in such a way that by implication at least God can have no plan. For example, Langdon Gilkey, although he is not a thoroughgoing existentialist, has absorbed enough of it to write: "Existence, while revealing an ultimate coherence and meaning, will not be completely reduced to any clear and precise sequence of relationships. There are depths of freedom, of creativity, and even of incoherence, within the mystery of being, which defy the attempt to organize life into simple rational patterns. Thus the very goal of philosophy is fatal to full understanding. . . . The insistent intuitions that our purposes are effective and our individuality is of value, belie systems in which all is determined from beyond ourselves . . ." (*Maker of Heaven and Earth,* p. 145). In spite of the phrase "an ultimate coherence," and the word "simple" in the phrase "simple rational patterns," the thought denies ultimate, all-inclusive order and refuses to acknowledge a God beyond us who has foreordained whatsoever comes to pass. Similar and perhaps even stronger denials of providence and predestination can be found in other writers.

Whereas Sartre sees clearly the atheistic implications of his definition of existentialism and his defense of freedom, the theologians attempt to escape them. To repeat, Karl Barth in particular asserts that he will have no part in "existential screaming and the like."

Yet Barth can hardly escape the charge of anti-intellectualism, and still less can Brunner. These men and those whom they have influenced argue that the intellect deals with abstractions and class concepts; it cannot handle the unique. But every individual, especially every human individual, is unique. We do not know persons the way we know things. There is an It-Truth and a Thou-Truth; there is knowledge about and there is knowledge by acquaintance. Now, God is a person. Therefore we cannot know about Him; we must encounter Him in a face-to-face confrontation. As Kierkegaard said, truth, non-intellectual truth, real truth is subjective. It is not knowledge, but a passionate experience.

These characterizations, though they give scant information on the details of Barth's twenty volumes of *Church Dogmatics* or on Sartre's long *Being and Nothingness,* are, I believe, about as accurate as possible. With them in mind it is now time to examine more closely the idea of revelation as encounter. First, let us return to Kierkegaard for a moment.

Kierkegaard's type of religion faces an obvious and inevitable question. If it makes no difference What one believes, if only the How is important, and if praying to idols is satisfactory, would not a passionate appropriation of the devil be as praiseworthy as a decision for Christ?

Kierkegaard notices this question and makes a feeble attempt to answer it. He tries to distinguish between the inwardness of infinity and the inwardness of the finite. The former is a Christian inwardness and is based on God; the latter relates to some other object.

This answer, however, is upside down. If there were a prior objective knowledge of God, a person could use this objective knowledge as a basis to judge that his passionate appropriation was infinite. But if there is no prior objective knowledge of God, and if therefore one is limited to the introspection of his own feelings, no qualitative difference between an idol is as satisfactory as God, why would not the socialism of Hegel and Marx be as acceptable as Kierkegaard and individualism? Communists are rather passionate, are they not?

It is this inability to justify one decision in contradistinction to the opposite decision, it is the equal value of encounter with God and encounter with an idol, it is the emphasis on the How and the rejection of the What, that has in one form and another plagued the existentialist movement down to the present. For example, the defects in Kierkegaard's subjectivism have not been removed in Emil Brunner's development of the same theme. Brunner doubtless improves upon Kierkegaard in that he interprets the passionate appropriation and moment of decision to be, what Kierkegaard did not clearly say, a personal encounter. Yet this religious experience gives no theological knowledge. It differs from ordinary cognition because of the distinction between It-Truth and Thou-Truth. In the religious field this bifurcation of knowledge was anticipated by Ferdinand Ebner and Martin Buber; while in secular philosophy Brunner strangely finds himself in the company of Maurice Schlick, who separated *Erleben* from *Erkennen,* and Bertrand Russell, who distinguished between knowledge by acquaintance and knowledge by description.

In fact the religious form of this bifurcation is more devastating to knowledge than the secular form. It prevents us from even thinking about God. Brunner writes, "God and the medium of conceptuality are mutually exclusive. God is personal and discloses himself only in the medium of personality, hence in a personal way, not through being thought. . . . One cannot be related to God by way of thinking. . . . To know about *God* does not mean merely to *know* about God, but to be personally encountered of him" (*Philosophie und Offenbarung,* p. 50).

How little of thought and knowledge Brunner leaves to religion can be seen in tracing through his argument in *The Divine-Human Encounter.* He opens with the lament that the early Church succumbed to the evil Greek influence that made revelation a communication of truth, and made faith an acceptance of these truths; then nearly a hundred pages later he concludes: "All words have only an instrumental value. Neither the spoken words *nor their conceptual content* are the Word itself, but only its frame" (pp. 19, 110, italics mine).

In this anti-intellectualism, faith, if there be such a thing, becomes a paradox. The paradoxes of faith, Brunner says, are not merely problems difficult to solve but are "necessary contradictions in themselves and therefore also contradictions against the fundamental law of all knowledge, the law of contradiction, *ergo* no knowledge" (*Philosophie und Offenbarung,*

p. 34). Specifically, he identifies the Trinity and the two natures of Christ as "logical monstrosities"—precious possessions of the Church, no doubt, but nonetheless logical monstrosities. Theology, that is, Brunner's theology, is not concerned with the univocal truth of reason; revelation must not be equated with a system of revealed doctrine; rather, theology has to do with incomprehensible personal unity that binds its contradictions together. (For a very thorough analysis and criticism see Paul K. Jewett, *Emil Brunner's Concept of Revelation,* James Clarke and Co., Ltd., 1954.)

In other words, namely, in my words, faith is insanity.

A criticism of the encounter theory of revelation need not spend much time on the philosophic intricacies of Heidegger or Sartre, because every detail is subject to the all-encompassing theory of knowledge and truth. The bifurcation of truth into It-Truth and Thou-Truth makes the term "truth" equivocal; and besides this, if it preserves anything at all on the side of encounter or *Erlebnis,* it preserves it as an unknowable *Ding an sich.* Confusion or deception then arises by talking about truth and by making believe that the talk, or the books published, are in some sense intelligible. They are not intelligible, for truth as encounter just is not truth at all.

In addition to the untenable and unresolved dualism, the evidence adduced actually tells against the conclusion. Phraseology such as, "We rationally analyze things, but we meet people," may be good rhetoric; but to deny that a person can be an object of thought flies in the face of our everyday procedures. Granted that our best knowledge of persons comes, not from our observation of them as physical objects, but from their voluntary self-disclosure, this self-disclosure is best made by speaking and by speaking intelligibly. If a person should refuse to talk, what good would it do to meet him? This is equally true in the case of God. Granted again, or, rather, demanded and insisted upon, that any knowledge a man may have of God depends on God's voluntary self-disclosure, what good would it be—for religion, for daily conduct, for theology or philosophy— to meet God if he disclosed nothing? Of course, persons should be met; but they should be met in order to converse with them.

For this reason the seemingly pious notion that Jesus Christ is God's revelation and that all our religion and theology derives from meeting Christ precludes systematic theology and all definite religion as well.

Of course, Jesus is the living Word of God. We do not for a moment deny it. Of course, God has in these last days revealed Himself to us in His Son. But if the person of Christ is divorced from what Jesus of Nazareth said, and if the person of Christ is divorced from what God said about Him through the apostles, how can we know what Christ has done for us? A mere encounter would leave the terms "regeneration," "imputation," and "justification" meaningless. Indeed, if there were no intelligible speech or thought, we could never know whether an encounter was an encounter with Christ the Son of God or whether it was Kierkegaard's encounter with an idol. The very identification of Jesus as the Son of God cannot possibly be made without intelligible thought.

Knowledge by acquaintance, in the anti-intellectual sense of encounter, *Begegnung,* or *Erlebnis,* will result in no religion other than some emotional entertainment. Theology there cannot be.

This point needs some emphasis and repetition. A meeting in which no conceptual knowledge or intellectual content was conveyed would not give the subject any reason for *thinking* he had met *God.* Nor could such an inarticulate experience point to anything definite beyond itself. Though the experience might still be stubbornly called religion by those who think or, better, feel that emotion is the essence of religion, it could never be identified as Christianity, Judaism, or Islam. These three require ideas, a What, and not merely a How.

That existentialism is a new religion, completely different from Christianity, is unwittingly made clear in *Pittsburgh Perspective,* a publication of the Pittsburgh Theological Seminary. In an article, "The Bible, Orthodoxy, and Karl Barth" (March, 1963), the author, after giving various detailed reasons in opposition to the orthodox doctrine of inspiration, brings his argument to its culmination by contrasting two types of religion. The one is "rationalistic"; its conception of "personal knowledge is painfully barren"; "the character of the revelatory word as an existential address is almost entirely overlooked in favor of the idea that the word provides true information"; one orthodox writer mentions the need for worship and for ethical conduct, and "these help to mitigate the intellectualism of his concept of theology. But they do not yet carry his thought into the range of problems that arise in the existentialistic-personalistic way of thinking." The author is obviously contrasting two types of religion; and the type he prefers is not historic Christianity.

The existentialistic phraseology about encounter and personality seems attractive to many who do not think beyond the language of propaganda. Examples of impressive but completely empty phrases abound. Another author insisted that religion is an "intensely personal" affair. No doubt it is. So is the study of calculus—no one can do it for you. And brushing your teeth. But no conclusions as to the nature, characteristics, value, or importance of the activity, or as to what we should properly do about it, can be drawn from the phrase "intensely personal." Such language is merely an emotional outburst. It is an empty phrase from an empty mind.

That existentialism and the personalistic way of thinking, or, better, the personalistic way of not thinking, is the antithesis of Christianity needs to be impressed upon all. The fact that Nietzsche was one of the forerunners of existentialism, the fact that Heidegger was a Nazi who ended his speeches with Heil Hitler, and the fact that Sartre is an atheist may fall short of full proof that existentialism is anti-Christian. But strictly theological considerations do not fall short of full proof.

The fundamental antagonism between existentialism and Christianity is substantiated by examining the relation between encounter and the belief in a future life. Existentialism, in its reaction against abstract, eternal truths, has emphasized death — my death — the death of the individual. Heidegger speaks of death as the end whereby a man's existence becomes complete. His capacity to anticipate death, not as a common phenomenon but his own death, is the basis of his ability to grasp his existence as a whole. So far as society is concerned, one man can be replaced by another. When a banker retires, another continues the same functions. But man is not a function; and I must do my own dying. Without anticipating death, a man cannot live "authentically."

But what can revelation as encounter tell us about death and a future life? Particularly, what can encounter tells us about a bodily resurrection from the dead? A non-conceptual, unintelligible encounter could never give us the information that Christ will return to raise the dead. It cannot even give us the minimum assurance of some sort of future life. Suppose with infinite passion I commit myself to freedom, or decide to live authentically instead of committing suicide or submerging myself in the masses: how could this emotional experience possibly inform me that I shall be conscious one hundred years from today, and what the quality of that consciousness will be? In the face of death, what we need is not infinite passion but definite information.

Other details of Christian theology and ecclesiology vanish. How does *Erlebnis* convince me of infant baptism or of the immersion of adults? By what standard do I determine the number of the sacraments and the forms of their administration? Apart from revealed information, can papacy, episcopacy, presbyterianism, or congregationalism be defended or attacked? Is it not rather clear that anti-intellectual religion can settle the nature of the Church only by an arbitrary decision on the part of its human officers?

And for a final point, the same difficulty is found in questions of morality also. That this should be true of Sartre's atheistic existentialism need not be surprising. What is surprising is Sartre's explicit recommendations of one type of life above another. If all is permitted, if man is the sole source of his values, if he is responsible even for his physio-psychological makeup and for the situation in which he finds himself (all of which Sartre apparently asserts), then how can Sartre implicitly require all men to choose freedom and live authentically?

The attenuated theism of the other neo-orthodox writers gives no better foundation for the distinction between right and wrong. It is true that Brunner says, "God . . . discloses himself . . . through actual address, summons, command." In fact, he says this in the very passage in which he asserts, "God and the medium of conceptuality are mutually exclusive," and where he also says, "One cannot be related to God by way of thinking." But thinking is required, if God is to address us by way of command. A God who speaks intelligibly can issue the Ten Commandments; but an encounter commands as little as it informs. Once more all the forms of worship are left to ecclesiastical politics, and all forms of morality too.

The great difficulty, as should now be clear, is the refusal to accept the law of contradiction. *Erlebnis,* faith, or encounter curbs logic. The result is inconsistency beyond excuse. Only the people Alice encountered in Wonderland can believe contradictions and logical monstrosities.

VERBAL REVELATION

It is now time to turn to something logical, consistent, and intelligible. The Christian view of revelation, while it admits to an empirical display of God's power in astronomy, and requires the a priori of the divine image in man, and while it above all makes possible an "encounter" with the mind of God, mainly identifies God's revelation with the words of Scripture. God has told us some things; He has spoken; He has given us information.

In several of the neo-orthodox writers there are statements that the idea of a verbal revelation, according to which God gives man true information, was an invention of a late Protestant scholasticism that had lost the original religious fervor of the Reformers.

Now, it is to be admitted, indeed it is to be insisted upon, that the later creeds, which, scholastic or not, represent the most authoritative and most mature conclusion of Reformation thought, teach the doctrine of biblical infallibility. Of all the creeds the Westminster Confession is the longest and the most carefully composed. The official doctrinal position of all Presbyterian denominations, it states that the Holy Scripture or Word of God, which it defines by naming the sixty-six books, is to be believed and obeyed because of the authority of God, its author. The Bible is to be received, continues the confession, because it is the Word of God, who is truth itself. Since the whole counsel of God is found in the Bible, nothing whatever is to be added to it. In all controversies the Church is to make its final appeal to the Bible, and the Supreme Judge by which all councils and opinions are to be examined is no other but the Holy Spirit speaking in the Scriptures. To avoid the hypocritical objection that the Spirit may speak in some parts of the Bible but not in others, the confession not only defines the Word of God as the sixty-six books but also later explains saving faith as follows: "By this faith a Christian believeth to be true *whatsoever* is revealed in the Word, for the authority of God himself speaketh therein."

An earlier confession, the Belgic Confession of 1561, states the same doctrine of Scripture: "We believe that the Holy Scriptures are contained in two books, namely, the Old and New Testaments, which are canonical, against which nothing can be alleged." This is an assertion of inerrancy; and to make it clear that inerrancy characterizes all the Bible and not just some portions, the Belgic Confession, after naming the sixty-six books, adds the words, "We receive all these books . . . believing, without any doubt, all things contained in them. . . ."

The Second Helvetic Confession reads: "Credimus et confitemur Scripturas Canonicas sanctorum Prophetarum et Apostolorum utriusque Testamenti ipsum verum esse verbum Dei. . . . Nam Deus ipse locutus est Patribus, Prophetis, et Apostolis, et loquitur adhuc nobis per Scripturas

Sanctas . . . ne ei aliquid vel addatur vel detrahatur." ("We believe and confess that the canonical Scriptures of the holy prophets and apostles of both Testaments are the very word of God. . . . For God himself spoke by the fathers, prophets and apostles, and still speaks to us through the Holy Scriptures . . . to which nothing may be added or subtracted.")

These credal positions are clearly and explicitly incompatible with the neo-orthodox view of the Bible. But is it true that this creedal position can be properly referred to by the derogatory term "scholasticism"? Do the creeds add artificial doctrines that differ from the preaching of Calvin and Luther? Did the Reformers deny that the Bible is the very Word of God? Did they deny the inerrancy of verbal inspiration?

First, let us look at Calvin. Since the truthfulness of Scripture was not formally denied by the Romanists, the subject is less thoroughly treated in the writings of the Reformers than is the doctrine of free grace. But Calvin's incidental remarks are clear enough. (For a fuller account of the matter see "Calvin and the Holy Scriptures," by Kenneth S. Kantzer, in *Inspiration and Interpretation,* edited by John W. Walvoord, Eerdmans, 1957.) In one place he says, "God is its Author. The principal proof therefore of the Scriptures is everywhere derived from the character of the Divine Speaker. The prophets . . . bring forth the sacred name of God to compel the submission of the whole world. . . . This use of the divine name is neither rash nor fallacious. . . . The Scripture exhibits the plainest evidences that it is God who speaks in it" (*Institutes,* I, vii, 4).

Indeed, instead of attributing to Calvin a looser view of Scripture than that of the Westminster Confession, it is easier to understand or misunderstand him as holding a more stringent view. In describing the method of inspiration Calvin uses the much maligned word "dictation." He says, "The Holy Spirit dictated to the prophets and the apostles" exactly what He wanted the finished writing to contain. And this is not a lone reference. Calvin's work abounds with references to the divine dictation of Scripture.

Some samples of Calvin's phraseology, which may be checked in Kantzer's work, are these: "God was pleased to commit his word to writing. . . . Historical details were added, which are also the composition of prophets but dictated by the Holy Spirit." "For the Word of God is not distinguished from the words of the prophet, as though the prophet had added anything of his own." Calvin refers to Scripture as the "sure and infallible record" and as the "unerring standard," "free from every stain or defect." With regard to the imprecatory Psalms, Calvin says, "David did not rashly or unadvisedly utter curses against his enemies, but strictly adhered to what the Spirit dictated."

Calvin's view of the nature of dictation and the orthodox doctrine of verbal inspiration have so frequently been misunderstood, and the misunderstanding has been so frequently pointed out, that one is forced to surmise that the misrepresentation is deliberate. Those who attack the orthodox Protestant doctrine try to reduce divine dictation to the so-called mechanical dictation of a business office. The liberals would have us think that orthodox theologians never even dreamed that God could use a prophet's personality. They, the liberals, constantly and mistakenly argue that verbal inspiration makes stylistic differences inexplicable. But this contention is historically false, as anyone can see by reading the orthodox theologians from Warfield in this century all the way back to Calvin himself.

Yet the misunderstanding would only go to show that the later confessions were not "scholastic additions" to the Reformation doctrines. Which way do the liberals want it? Did Calvin teach mechanical dictation or are the creeds scholastic? They cannot have both.

On the other hand, Calvin's acknowledgment of textual criticism and his remarks on canonicity have been used to attribute to him a looser view of inspiration. This might keep the creeds scholastic, but it flies in the face of all his emphasis on dictation. However, this attribution to Calvin of a looser view is also based on a misunderstanding. The type of passages from which the alleged evidence is taken show clearly that Calvin taught the verbal and plenary inspiration of God's Word.

The same is true of Luther. J. Theodore Mueller writes, "When church historians ascribe to Luther the merit of having established the *Schriftprinzip,* that is, the axiomatic truth that Holy Scripture is the sole principle by which divine truth is truly and unmistakably known, they do this in full justice to the Wittenberg Reformer, whose alleged 'liberal attitude' toward Scripture theological liberals, contrary to historical fact, in vain are trying to demonstrate" (*Inspiration and Interpretation,* p. 88; see all of Chapter 3 for justification of the following details).

Quenstedt, whom the liberals cite as a theologian who corrupted the freer Reformation doctrine of inspiration, wrote, "The canonical Holy Scriptures in the original text are the infallible truth and are free from every error; in other words, in the canonical sacred Scriptures there is found no lie, no falsity, no error, not even the least, whether in subject matter or expressions, but in all things and all the details that are handed down in them, they are most certainly true, whether they pertain to doctrine or morals, to history or chronology, to topography or nomenclature. No ignorance, no thoughtlessness, no forgetfulness, no lapse of memory can and dare be ascribed to the amanuenses of the Holy Ghost in their penning the Sacred Writings."

In spite of what the liberals say, these assertions of Quenstedt are not later corruptions. Everything in the above quotation can be found in Luther himself. For example, "The Scripures have never erred" and "It is impossible that Scripture should contradict itself; it appears so only to the senseless and obstinate hypocrites." Further examples are: "The Scriptures are divine; in them God speaks and they are his Word" and "Unless I am convinced by testimony from Scripture or evident reasons— for I believe neither the Pope nor the Councils alone, since it is established that they have often erred and contradicted themselves—I am conquered by the writings cited by me, and my conscience is captive to the Word of God. Therefore I will not and cannot recant anything since it is neither safe nor honest to do anything against conscience."

Detached from its context, this last quotation may seem to show that Luther could appeal to "evident reasons" in addition and out of relation to the Bible. An examination of the context and the historical situation requires us to acknowledge that "evident reasons" means correct deductions from Scripture, and that conscience means his conscience as bound by the Bible. The famous declaration therefore is an assertion of *Sola Scriptura.*

If this is sufficient to convince one of what the Reformers' position actually was, the next step is to see whether the doctrine was a new invention or whether it can be found earlier. Or, more pertinently, the next step is to see whether the doctrine of verbal inspiration is the teaching of the Bible itself. If the neo-orthodox claim to be biblical theologians, if their theology is called the theology of the Word, it is most important to see what the Word says about itself. Fortunately this is one of the easiest biblical doctrines to determine. Assertions or implications of plenary and verbal inspiration abound from Genesis to Revelation.

The best known, of course, is, "All Scripture is given by inspiration of God." A better and more literal translation would be, "All Scripture has been breathed out by God." It is to be noted, as orthodox theologians have repeatedly pointed out, that what God breathed forth were the words written on the manuscript. The verse does not say that God inspired the thoughts of the authors, nor even their speech. It is Scripture, the written words, that God breathed out.

Of course the verse does not deny that God inspired the thoughts of the authors. The point simply is that, whatever else God did, He also breathed out the written words. Because of the liberals' persistent misrepresentation of verbal inspiration as mechanical dictation, it might be well at this point to repeat that the prophets' mental processes remained normal throughout. The idea that verbal inspiration would conflict with a prophet's literary style depends on a deistic conception of God, which the liberals either hold for themselves or wrongly attribute to the orthodox theologians. This deistic conception of God pictures Him in the role of a business executive whose control over the stenographer is external and limited. He did not direct her education nor does he control her every thought. None of her personality is transferred to the typed wording. But the Christian view of God is of one in whom we live and move and have our being. He creates our personality and forms our literary style. He foreordains our education and guides our every thought. Hence God from all eternity decreed to lead the Jews out of slavery by the hand of Moses. To this end He determined the date of Moses' birth and arranged for his princely training and so on, until, when the time came, Moses' mentality and literary style were the instruments precisely fitted to speak and write God's words. Between Moses and God Omnipotent there was an inner union, an identity of purpose, a cooperation of will, such that the words Moses wrote were God's own words and Moses' own words at the same time.

Sometimes it is objected that the verse in Second Timothy applies only to the Old Testament. Perhaps it does, but it is amusing to see the liberals so determined to exalt the authority of the Old Testament in order to debase the New. At any rate, the New Testament repeatedly asserts the truth of the Old. One can examine our Lord's treatment of Scripture, i.e., the Old Testament. He defeats the devil, confounds the Sadducees, and reduces the Pharisees to angry silence by quoting Scripture.

The Old Testament also teaches its own infallibility, and this pushes the doctrine well into the past. In addition to many instances of phrases such as "The Lord hath spoken" and "The mouth of the Lord hath spoken it," a composite of Deuteronomy 18:18 and Jeremiah 1:9 will say, "I have put my words in thy mouth," and "whosoever will not hearken to my words which he [the prophet] shall speak in my name, I will require it of him."

So much for the Old Testament. The question now is whether the New Testament makes the same claims for itself. In the first place the New Testament pervasively presupposes its superiority to the Old. Explicitly, John the Baptist is said to be a greater prophet than those of the Old Testament, and the New Testament prophets are greater than John.

The superiority, of course, did not lie in a greater truthfulness, for this they could not have. However, had they been less truthful, they could not have been superior. Note that Peter says, ". . . our beloved brother Paul also according to the *wisdom given* unto him hath written unto you; as also in *all his epistles* . . . in which are some things hard to be understood, which they that are unlearned and unstable wrest, as they do also the *other scriptures,* unto their own destruction" (II Pet. 3:15, 16). Here Peter puts all of the epistles of Paul into the category of Holy Scripture. Paul himself claims to be a prophet: "When ye read [what he had written before in a few words], ye may understand my knowledge in the mystery of Christ . . . as it is now revealed unto his holy apostles and prophets by the Spirit" (Eph. 3:4, 5). The term "prophet" puts Paul on a level with Old Testament prophets; the term apostles puts him above them, for "God hath set some in the church, first apostles, secondarily prophets, thirdly teachers . . ." (I Cor. 12:28).

If an almost exhaustive list of similar claims for the Scripture is desired, one may read Louis Gaussen's *Theopneustia.* The small number quoted here only bespeaks confidence in the extremely large number easily located.

But if anyone would prefer to have a final quotation, let it be Second Peter 1:21, "The prophecy came not in old time by the will of man: but holy men of God spoke as they were moved by the Holy Ghost." Verbal and plenary inspiration, i.e., infallibility, inerrancy, is the claim the Bible makes for itself; and if the Bible does not correctly represent itself, there seems to be no good reason for taking it very seriously on any other subject.

Yet this doctrine on which all other doctrines depend is the one most viciously attacked of all. By a satanic instinct, the battle against Christianity is directed against its citadel. Barth writes, "The prophets and Apostles as such, even in their office . . . were . . . actually guilty of error in their spoken and written word" (*Church Dogmatics,* I, 2, pp. 528, 529). Brunner asserts that the Bible "is full of errors, contradiction, erroneous opinions concerning all kinds of human, natural, historical situations. It contains many contradictions in the report about Jesus' life, it is over-grown with legendary material even in the New Testament" (*Philosophy of Religion,* p. 155). Bultmann leaves even less uncontested than Brunner. With such a derogatory opinion of the Bible, their use of it for any religious purpose is another of their insoluble paradoxes.

But are their accusations true? Is the Bible really "full of errors, contradictions, erroneous opinions"? Is the Bible so utterly untrustworthy as Brunner and Bultmann say?

So far as accusations of doctrinal error are concerned, no general reply can be made. One would have to know on what philosophic ground the accusation was based. For example, the doctrines of original sin and total depravity were largely denied by modernism on the basis of an evolutionary optimism. The nineteeth-century theologians thought that evil was almost eradicated from the face of the earth and that socialism, per-haps national socialism, would usher in the Kingdom of God. The idea of original sin, therefore, and total depravity, was an error in doctrine. Likewise attempts are sometimes made to undermine the doctrine of pre-destination either through a particular interpretation of divine love or by an appeal to the principle of indeterminacy that Heisenberg tried to in-troduce into physics.

A full argument to show that these biblical doctrines are true and that the liberals are wrong cannot be included here. In the case of predestina-tion, surely no one wants at this spot a discussion of theoretical physics. So far as the liberals depend on their interpretation of divine love, it would be necessary to examine what source of information they use to obtain their concept of God. It is not the biblical concept. Do they then have another revelation? It ought to be a better one, since they consider the Scriptures so untrustworthy. In the case of total depravity versus the inherent goodness of human nature, an argument might try to disprove biological evolution, or it might deny that the principles of biological evolution can be extended to society and religion, or it might show that evolution, far from being optimistic, portrays nature red in tooth and claw. Since the backgrounds of the accusation are so varied, full argu-ments would be too long for the present purpose, and the matter of doc-trinal error must rest with these hints.

If, however, the Bible is charged with error on the basis that it contains accounts of miracles, a different reply would be required. Although the denial of miracles impugns omnipotence and returns us to the source of our knowledge of God, the more common argument against miracles is that science has disproved their possibility. Here is needed a philosophy of science to question the finality of Newtonian mechanics. Such an argument I have published elsewhere (*The Philosophy of Science and Belief in God,* The Craig Press, 1964).

When, next, Brunner claims that the New Testament is false because it is overgrown with legendary material, one can indicate that the early dates of the Gospels allow no time for legends to grow. If the Old Testament is criticized on this ground one may ask, What is a legend? If a legend is distinguished from history simply by reason of its fragmentary character, Brunner will have to prove that whatever is fragmentary must be false. Press this consistently and the result is that all history books are false because all are fragmentary. No book contains everything.

In the next place, destructive criticism of the Wellhausen type has been a still more popular basis for charging the Bible with error. The alleged errors are historical and cultural in nature, though they are sometimes loosely called contradictions.

In general, replies to these accusations are not difficult to make. Some of the "contradictions" clearly exist only in the critic's mind. For example, Edwin A. Burtt, professor of philosophy at Cornell University, in his *Types of Religious Philosophy* (second edition, p. 311)—a book that was acclaimed for its fairness of presentation—alleges the following contradiction: "In Ezekiel 26 the prophet proclaims as a divine revelation the message that the city of Tyre is to meet destruction at the hands of Nebuchadrezzar, King of Babylon . . . After a hard assault, however, Nebuchadrezzar failed to capture Tyre. . . . Accordingly, in Ezekiel 29 the prophet announces another revelation in which God promises the conquest of Egypt to Nebuchadrezzar as a recompense for his defeat by the Tyrians. There is no hint in the later of these passages that he now doubts the authenticity of the earlier revelation because the prophecy it contained failed to be verified as and when he expected. Apparently, what is essential to a divine revelation, in his mind, is not its factual infallibility, but the truth of the moral lesson it embodies."

If this is impartial scholarship, scholarship and impartiality are both in a bad way Burtt's charge is based on complete ignorance of what the Bible says. Ezekiel 26 nowhere prophesies that Nebuchadrezzar will conquer Tyre. In fact, it definitely implies that he will not, for Ezekiel 26:3 reads, "Behold I am against thee, O Tyrus, and will cause many nations to come up against thee." Then follows a description of the damage, considerable enough, that Nebuchadrezzar will inflict (verses 7-11), after which they, the many nations, will so complete the destruction that the site of Tyre will be a bare rock. Hence the contradiction between Ezekiel 26 and Ezekiel 29 exists only in Burtt's impartial and scholarly mind.

Or, again, the critics' assertion that the Hittite nation never existed, that camels were unknown in Egypt in the time of Abraham, that seven-stemmed lamps were first made in the late Persian empire, and numerous other denials of biblical statements have been so thoroughly refuted by archaeology that the liberals should hang their heads in shame.

Different in nature from these historical and cultural items are the cases where the term "contradiction" is used in its strictly logical sense. For example if one Gospel says there was one angel and no more at the tomb on Easter morning and another Gospel says there were two, this would be logical contradiction. Or, again, if two passages differ as to the exact number of Jacob's family that went down to Egypt, the two passages would produce a formal logical contradiction.

Such alleged contradictions, however, can be easily handled, even though in some cases we may not know which of two or three possibilities is the correct one. They are easily handled because in most instances the actual texts are not in formal contradiction. No Gospel says there was only one angel at the tomb all Easter morning.

Even the two genealogies of Christ can be shown not to be contradictory, however difficult it may be to reconstruct the actual history (see J. Gresham Machen, *The Virgin Birth,* Harper and Brothers, 1932).

These considerations and the several volumes referred to are sufficient to show good reason for accepting the Bible as true; they are conclusive against the plausibility of the liberal theory on these points.

We must now consider a different type of objection to the verbal inspiration of Scripture. Briefly the objection is that God cannot speak.

Once again this objection to verbal inspiration depends on a non-biblical concept of God. With its inheritance from Schleiermacher and Hegel, the older modernism denied that God could speak because it held an essentially pantheistic view of God. God was entirely immanent in or actually identified with the processes of nature. He was prohibited from interrupting these processes by any miracle, any intrusion into history, any once-for-all event, of which speaking would be an example.

The new liberals are not so fond of Hegel; they talk of God's transcendence; they try to find a divine action somewhere in history, even if only at an unexpected point. But they shy away from the idea that God can use words, such as, "Behold a virgin shall conceive," and "whom God set forth to be a propitiation through faith in his blood."

What they assert is that God produced some emotional or vaguely defined state of mind in the prophet and then the prophet relied on his own wisdom to talk about his experience.

Since this denial that God can use words is another denial of His omnipotence, the question of religious knowledge must again be raised with increasing emphasis. Where do these theologians obtain their information as to what God can or cannot do? Their ideas do not come from the Bible. Have they then another "revelation," or have they with Schleiermacher reduced "God" to a description of their own state of consciousness? Orthodox theologians do well to press this question and prevent the liberals from evading an answer. This orthodox strategy is sound because the liberal answers, when spelled out, are so obviously inadequate.

In addition to entailing a non-biblical concept of God, the thesis that God cannot speak depends on a theory of language. Human language on this theory is supposed to have evolved from the chirping of birds and the grunts of pigs, or at least to have had a totally sensory origin. Since therefore all terms derive from the visible and tangible things of the material universe, language is inadequate to express divine truth. When language is highly developed by figures of speech, metaphors, and analogy, words like "atonement" or "justification" can be used symbolically to suggest or point to something divine. But their literal meanings are spiritually false, because they can never be completely detached from their origin in sensation. William Marshall Urban has a most interesting 700-page volume along these lines; and E. L. Mascall is a noted English thinker who vigorously supports such views.

To defend the Bible as the Word of God, a reliance on God's omnipotence is sufficient. It takes a very brave man to deny that God *can* speak. But it is more persuasive if a conservative theologian also furnishes an alternate theory of linguistics. The Scriptures lay down the principles of such a theory. Instead of language being an evolutionary extension of the chattering of monkeys, Scripture teaches that man was created in the image of God. Basically this image is human reason. And language is its expression. No doubt God intended language to be applicable to the visible and tangible parts of nature; but there is also no doubt that God intended language to be used in worshiping Him, in conversing with Him, and in His conversing with Adam and the subsequent prophets. Naturally a non-theistic linguistic has difficulty with a verbal revelation. Naturally also there is no difficulty on a theistic basis. (See my *Religion, Reason, and Revelation,* chapter 3, "Inspiration and Language," Presbyterian and Reformed, 1961.)

Now, finally, the thesis that God cannot speak entails not only a non-Christian concept of God and of language but also a non-Christian form of religion. It is a religion without truth. The prophet had his emotional experience and he describes it to us. His description may be very much mistaken. But no matter, Brunner assures us that God can "speak" His word to man even through false doctrine. The only trouble is that the doctrine is false and God does not speak. In agreement with the theory of language just discussed Brunner writes, "All words have only an instrumental value. Neither the spoken words nor their conceptual content are the Word itself, but only its frame" (*The Divine-Human Encounter,* p. 110).

This type of religion is anti-intellectual and thoroughly irrational. It may consist of an emotional jag, an aesthetic experience, or a mystic trance. But it is totally devoid of knowledge. What Brunner calls the Word of God has no conceptual content. It despises logic, glories in contradictions, and deifies paradox.

But Christianity claims that God is the God of truth; that He is wisdom; that His Son is His Logos, the logic, the Word of God. Man was created a reasonable being so that he could understand God's message to him. And God gave him a message by breathing out all the Scripture, having foreordained the complete process, including the three stages of the thoughts of the prophet's mind, the words in his mouth, and the finished manuscript. Christianity is a rational religion. It has an intellectually apprehensible content. Its revelation can be understood. And because

God speaks in intelligible words, He can give and has given commands. We know what these commands mean, and therefore we should obey them.

If, now, anyone prefers a symbolism that points to some unknowable, if anyone takes pleasure in irrational paradox, if anyone enjoys wordless encounters, further words and ideas will not change his emotions.

A SELECT BIBLIOGRAPHY

1. REVEALED RELIGION

Karl Barth, *Church Dogmatics,* Volume I. New York: Harper & Row.

Richard B. Brandt, *The Philosophy of Schleiermacher.* New York: Harper & Brothers, 1941.

Emil Brunner, *Philosophy of Religion.* Naperville, Ill.: Allenson, 1958.

————, *The Divine-Human Encounter.*

John Calvin, *Institutes of the Christian Religion.* Philadelphia: Westminster Press, 1960.

Edwin A. Burtt, *Types of Religious Philosophy.* New York: Harper & Row, 1951.

Gordon H. Clark, *A Christian View of Men and Things.* Grand Rapids: Wm. B. Eerdmans Publishing Co., 1952.

————, *Karl Barth's Theological Method.* Nutley, New Jersey: Presbyterian and Reformed Publishing House, 1963.

————, *Religion, Reason and Revelation.* Nutley, New Jersey: Presbyterian and Reformed Publishing House, 1961.

————, *Thales to Dewey.* Boston: Houghton, Mifflin Co., 1957.

————, *The Philosophy of Science and Belief in God.* Nutley, New Jersey: The Craig Press, 1964.

Langdon Gilkey, *Maker of Heaven and Earth.* New York: Doubleday.

Sören Kierkegaard, *Concluding Unscientific Postscript.* Princeton: Princeton U. Press, 1948.

J. Gresham Machen, *The Virgin Birth of Christ.* New York: Harper & Brothers, 1932.

Jean-Paul Sartre, *Being and Nothingness.* New York: Citadel, 1964.

John W. Walvoord, *Inspiration and Interpretation.* Grand Rapids: Wm. B. Eerdmans Publishing Co., 1957.

GOD: HIS NAMES AND NATURE

Harold B. Kuhn

Harold B. Kuhn is professor of the philosophy of religion and chairman of the Division of Doctrine and the Philosophy of Religion at Asbury Theological Seminary, Wilmore, Kentucky. He received the A.B. degree from John Fletcher College and the S.T.B., S.T.M., and Ph.D. from Harvard University. He has also studied at the Universities of Munich, Mainz, and London, and the Free University of Berlin, and served as lecturer in theology at Emmanuel Bible College, Birkenhead, England. Dr. Kuhn, a recorded minister in the Ohio Yearly Meeting of Friends, has held various pastoral posts. He has been educational consultant to the United States Air Force in Germany and chaplain supply and missioner for the Air Force and Army in Europe, and has done extensive evangelistic and social work in Germany. During a recent sabbatical he taught in India.

2. *Harold B. Kuhn*

GOD: HIS NAMES
AND NATURE

ALTHOUGH, AS St. Augustine pointed out, the human spirit was made for God and finds no rest except as it finds it in Him, many moderns find it difficult or impossible to give serious regard to the existence of a living, personal, and loving God. The conception of such a Being as Scripture presents—the Creator of all things and the God and Father of our Lord Jesus Christ—has been misrepresented and often caricatured, until God seems to many people to be no more than a figment of the imagination, reflecting, perhaps, the condition of their immediate social environment. Whatever the reason, it is fashionable to regard faith as atavistic and to conclude that the educated person's philosophy of life must be built on a form of naturalism in which nature is regarded as self-explanatory and as exempt from the presence and direction of any Being transcending it or superior to it.

Not only so, but the conception of the Deity among the less sophisticated is frequently a parody of the biblical understanding of God. Some think of Him as little more than a celestial computer or transcendent Univac. Others see Him exclusively as a harsh and vindictive Judge, while many others regard Him as a genial and ancient grandfather, either too remote from human affairs to be worthy of notice or else too indulgent to be an all-wise Sovereign. There is, moreover, a general tendency to insist that God must conform to the demands of the human self and so be a sort of super-projection of it. Thus, apart from revelation, men usually form and hold a truncated or distorted notion of God.

Too frequently, theologians who call themselves Christian yield to the temptation to adapt and attenuate their definitions of God to suit the small dimensions of current thought. By some easy expedient, such as identifying God with something that indisputably exists, they feel they have "demonstrated" to the modern mind that God *is*. Too seldom are theologians of our times willing to listen with patient devotion to Holy Writ at this point.

It is the purpose of this essay to approach the subject in three ways. First, attention will be given to the typical forms of response that have in recent times been made to the question of the existence of a Supreme Being. Note will be taken of the outcome of modern denials of God's existence. Second, there will be a survey of the divine names, with special reference to the order of their appearance and the increasing insight they afford into the Being they reveal. Thus the groundwork will be laid for the third consideration, that of the nature and character of God as revealed in Holy Scripture.

The method will be to affirm the historic Christian understanding of God rather than to give a detailed refutation of inadequate views. Trends in contemporary mediating theology will be recognized, but the major emphasis will be upon the positive thrust of the Christian Scriptures on this all-important subject.

BELIEF IN GOD: ITS CRUCIAL SIGNIFICANCE

To define God as that with which man is ultimately concerned is currently fashionable. There is an element of truth in the definition. Certainly man should be concerned with ultimate issues and supremely concerned with the One we confess when saying, "I believe in God the Father Almighty, maker of heaven and earth." The evangelical's criticism of the definition noted above is that man's ultimate concern *ought* to be the God who is known to man in self-disclosure rather than that which man might, in a merely personal and idiosyncratic way, come to regard as a matter of ultimate interest.

Belief in God or in gods has been almost universal among all peoples. Some have concluded from this that in the earlier stages of his development man felt the need for the "idea of God" because of his limited understanding of the processes of the world and his inability to direct his own destiny. Whatever be the truth of this contention, the Christian cannot accept it as an explanation for the origin of belief in God. Nor can he admit that, with the advance of man's knowledge, the idea of God will become superfluous.

Assuming for the moment that belief in God or in gods is an observed fact of human experience, we should recognize that an apparent specialization of religious faith is also discernible. The Hebrew people seem from their earliest recorded beginnings to have had an understanding of God that was qualitatively unique among the belief-patterns of ancient peoples. This can be denied only by radically revising Hebrew religious literature. After some fifteen or twenty centuries (depending upon whether one reckons from Moses or from Abraham), there emerged from the matrix of the Hebrew religion a faith that presupposed the

Israelitish tradition and at the same time professed to carry it to its completion. Its center was the appearance of Jesus of Nazareth, one who impressed those who followed Him, both immediately and through the centuries, as unique in His origin and quality of life, in His death and rising again.

The Christian movement brought into the history of the Western world profound elements of belief. At its core lay belief in "God the Father Almighty." God's existence has been for the Christian a powerfully controlling motif. While some within the Christian movement have either distorted its central principles or drawn faulty implications from them, belief in God has always been a vital element in the thinking of Christians. As A. Seth Pringle-Pattison notes in his Gifford Lectures for 1912-1913, "To them it meant undoubtedly a doctrine which, if true, must profoundly affect our whole view of the universe and our conduct in it" (*The Idea of God,* 1917, p. 23).

That belief in God's existence has in recent times been a powerful and determinative motif finds oblique support in the extraordinary efforts put forth in the past two or three centuries either to eliminate belief in God or render it innocuous. After the movement known as the Enlightenment, in which the Deity was imagined to be so far above the world of men as to be irrelevant to them, there came the venomous attack upon belief in God in Voltaire's *Écrasez l'infâme!* ("Crush the infamous thing!"). On November 10, 1793, the leaders of the Commune of Paris marched into the Cathedral of Notre Dame and in the name of Reason declared the demise of Christianity, replacing the altar of the cathedral with an "altar of Reason." This so-called cult of Brumaire, mixing its anti-Christian animosity with its proclamation of liberty, was short-lived; but, as the historian Mathiez wrote in 1904, while the trappings of the revolutionary cults were things of the past, the spirit that impelled them lived on (M. Mathiez, *La Théophilanthropie et le Culte Décadaire,* p. 609).

Certainly this anti-Christian spirit was not confined to the Republic of France; Thomas Paine translated it into American terms, while David Hume gave it philosophical expression in the British Isles. Not only did Christianity, which was the basic religion of the West, undergo savage frontal attacks from her foes, but there was also substituted for Christian theistic belief the so-called religion of humanity (i.e., of humanity conceived in its ideal and collective aspect), which proclaimed "God" to be a projection of the human mind and thus irrelevant to man in an age of increasing scientific knowledge. Ludwig Feuerbach openly declared that belief in God was but an unconscious self-projection, and proposed that the time had come to recognize as subjective that which had formerly been thought to be objective.

This development paved the way for a second level of attack upon historic belief in God, the "death of God" movement. It was Friedrich Nietzsche who gave dramatic literary expression to this idea. In *The Joyful Wisdom* he causes his madman to appear in the town square and proclaim, "God is dead!" And man himself was God's executioner. It is

significant that this message was, in Nietzsche's view, to be proclaimed in
the marketplace to the masses, even though they appeared there, as also
at Zarathustra's public proclamation of the Superman, to be indifferent
to the news. But Nietzsche saw that the growing skepticism about God's
existence was reaching down from the philosophers and sages to the common man.

What was meant by the "death of God" was the death of human faith
in God's existence and almightiness. And it was an easy step from the
psychologism of Feuerbach and the nihilism of Nietzsche to Karl Marx's
assertion that belief in God was but an instrumental idea, invented by
the oppressing class to hold the oppressed masses in line. To him, the
"death of God" was an inevitable concomitant of the coming disappear-
ance of all religious faith, when the revolution he envisioned would sweep
away the capitalist regime and the existing class structure.

The net result has been neither the universalization of reason's attack
upon Christian faith nor the achievement of the goals set by Karl Marx.
It has been far more insidious. The foundations upon which Christian
faith rests have been systematically eroded until modern man feels himself an orphan. He no longer has a Father! Whereas his grandfather
peered into the heavens and beheld the eyes of God, modern man sees
only burnt-out holes. He looks out upon a horizon infinitely broader than
that known to his ancestors and discerns no God, only vastness. Beyond
the realm where the final shadow cast by Being disappears, he sees only
the eternal storm, raging over the trackless abyss and tamed by none.
Losing his view of God, man has lost himself in time. Having lost his
awareness of his own dependence upon the God of the universe, he is
left a victim of unnamed and intangible anxiety. For him, God *seems*
to be dead. Therefore, one looks out over the wasteland of modern man's
existence and asks himself, "Can this estranged creature find himself
again?" And the insistent answer cannot be evaded: He can find himself
only as he rediscovers for himself the living God.

It follows from the foregoing that the affirmation or denial of the existence and being of God is crucial for the whole of the human outlook.
No thinking person can afford to be neutral on this question. Despite
the contrary views of religious humanists, human character and human
purpose cannot be sustained apart from a vital belief in God as an exalted
Being, worthy of man's faith and worship. Even moral values cannot sustain themselves apart from reference to a Supreme Being in whom they
reside and from whom they proceed to inform the life of His creatures.
Nor can worship have meaning if it is based on anything short of the
devoted and loving relation of a willing human heart to a Sovereign Father.

Christian faith faces imposing and well-organized opposition in our day.
This opposition is entrenched in our institutions of higher learning and
is reinforced by the tremendous prestige science enjoys today. Without
minimizing the imposing achievements of scientific endeavor, we must
recognize that the contemporary "cult of science" has not added to man's
understanding of, or belief in, God. If He is to be made known, the

Church must renew her vision and her efforts to give out that which has been entrusted to her in revelation. Her task is, in the last analysis, to proclaim what she has received. The balance of this essay will sketch the outlines of this heritage and will endeavor to clarify it in relation to some of the currents of anti-theistic thought.

THE DIVINE NAMES

The Hebrew-Christian Scriptures are unique among the religious documents of the race in that their names for the Deity are not merely human constructs but divinely given designations. While philosophical systems name the Deity in terms of some central quality they may affirm of Him, the names for God given in the biblical record embody the features of His progressive self-revelation. Thus there may be seen in Holy Scripture a series of names of deepening significance, each expressing a more perfect manifestation of Him to His people.

The peoples of antiquity (and certainly the Hebrews among them) had a deeper feeling for names than men of our time. A person's name was regarded not merely as a possession but as something distinctively his, and often as an expression of his personal character. It is probable that some cultures have carried this idea too far. In some usages, the person seeks to conceal his real name; in others, persons are mentioned only by circumlocutions. The ancients seem at times to have believed that knowing the name of a person gave them a certain magical power over him. There was elaborate speculation over the importance of concealed and secret names of deities.

While there is no evidence that the peoples of the Old Testament shared the more extreme and superstitious of these common assumptions, it is clear that they did assign a deep significance to the names by which their God was called. The Hebrews regarded the names of the Deity, as, in and of themselves, self-revealing. God, in His adaptation of His revelation to man, respected this belief.

In some parts of Scripture, the name of God is regarded in a strictly singular sense, as in the Decalogue, "Thou shalt not take the *name* of the Lord thy God in vain" (Ex. 20:7). Here the term is generic and would exclude the frivolous or fraudulent use of any one of the appellations of the Deity. In other words, the entire pattern of words by which God is named was commanded to be held in respect and reverence. While the name of God may be diversified, so as to embody a number of personal designations and thus indicate progressive levels of self-disclosure, His Name is to be regarded as "excellent" in all the earth. No level of His revealed nature is to be taken lightly.

It is the use of the name, of course, and not merely its form or derivation, that is significant in Holy Scripture. While etymology is a legitimate study, its conclusions cannot by themselves determine the meaning of the divine names. There has been much discussion of the basic Semitic name for the Deity, *El,* which appears in the Old Testament in the plural form,

Elohim, and in such compounds as *El Shadday.* That the conceptions attached to *El* among other and earlier Semitic peoples are at times unworthy of the God of the Bible cannot obscure the fact that among this racial stock the term was common, and presumably very old. It is reasonable to infer that the name may reflect an original revelation, an *Uroffenbarung,* held and sustained with varying degrees of purity among the Phoenicians, Babylonians, Aramaeans, Arabs, and Hebrews. The name *El* seems to suggest power and authority. John P. Lange says in this connection:

> Power, greatness, vastness, height, according as they are represented by the *conceptions* of the day, carried to the fullest extent allowed by the *knowledge* of the day; this is the ideal of *El* and *Elohim,* as seen in the etymological congruity of the epithets joined to those in Genesis [John P. Lange, *Commentary on the Holy Scriptures,* I, 109n.].

Thus, the name *El* as applied to God is general and inclusive, reflecting a primeval monotheism from which the polytheism of the ancient world was a lapse. Its core of meaning is that of strength, authority, and majesty. The name *El* (in Babylonian *îlu,* in Arabic *'Allah*) is used frequently in the Old Testament, chiefly in Job and Psalms. It often appears with a coordinate noun or adjective, as *El 'Elyôn* or *El Rô'î,* such usages underscoring the Deity's excellent and lofty Person or his divine prerogatives.

It is significant that the plural form, *Elohim,* as applied to the one Deity occurs only in the usages of the Hebrews, and that it is the most frequent Old Testament noun for God. The usage appears to be definitely mathematical and collective. And while one must not press too far the element of plurality in the name, it seems valid to observe that the name suggests a diversity and richness within the Divine Life that both avoids the tendency toward undue abstractness and aloofness of the Deity and makes a place for the later disclosure of the triune nature of God. That is to say, in the light of the usage of this name among the Hebrew people, the New Testament revelation of the tripersonality within the one God did not appear as a complete innovation. Viewed grammatically, the name *Elohim,* plural in form, governs a singular verb or adjective when applied to the God of the Old Testament. It is occasionally applied to those who represent Him or to those who serve in His presence.

Observe also that beside the mathematical and collective quality of the plural usage, there is the possible understanding of the term in its intensive and emphatic quality. Franz Delitzsch calls attention to this usage in the Hebrew and suggests that it is employed here (Lange, *op. cit.,* I, 112). The stress falls upon the unique quality of God's being—a uniqueness that lays upon men the necessity of recognizing and serving Him. The call of Abraham was designed to teach the uniqueness of God and to provide for the transmission of monotheistic belief. It appears that even the immediate family of Abraham had fallen into polytheism (Josh. 24:2); thus the father of the faithful was called to a lonely walk, in spiritual isolation. It was the call to walk with God in a separate tradition that made Israel a race apart. And the ancient name of their Deity, stressing extension and dignity, emphasized the distinctness of His Person.

The compound name of *El Shadday* represents a progression in the self-disclosure of God to the men of the patriarchal period. Thus in revealing himself to Abraham as *El Shadday* or "the Almighty God," the Deity moved beyond the concept of Himself as mighty Creator and Sustainer of the cosmos to the view of His role as maker and keeper of covenant agreement. As such He moves actively into the human sphere, shaping the forces of nature to accomplish His purposes. The name itself is poetic; it is regarded, by some scholars at least, as the Hebrew form of a Babylonian word meaning "the mountain." Thus it suggests majestic stability, the strong refuge, the pillar that remains unmoved in the most turbulent times.

The disclosure of this name is most closely associated with the covenant with Abraham recorded in Genesis 17. Here the events chronicled are intimate, personal events, centering in the birth of Isaac, the institution of circumcision, and the provision for a place for Ishmael. It is clear that the disclosure of this name for the Deity was a clear advance in the revelation of His nature. It is not surprising that *El Shadday* became the major name for God during the partriarchal period, a period in which God's providences were made known in a unique way to the progenitors of the Hebrew race. This name was prominent in the pedagogy of the nation of Israel during this epoch. In a certain sense, its use formed a bridge in the thinking of the Hebrew mind, a means of transition from the period in which *Elohim* was the main designation of the Deity to the time of the revelation of the intensely redemptive name, *Yahweh* or *Jehovah.*

Another name that occurs frequently during this period is *Adhon* or *Âdhônāy,* usually transliterated *Adonai.* The term means, basically, master or lord. In the earliest usage it seems to have been a more transcendent term, suggesting God's role as high and over all things. But in later usage it came to suggest a more intimate and personal relation between Deity and people. The name is derived from the Hebrew word *Âdhôn,* which was also found in the Egyptian language and dates at least from the Hyksos period (i.e., the time of Joseph). The term denotes especially "a master of servants" and is used of Abram by one of his personal servants in Genesis 24:12, 14. Thus it denotes not only gradations of relationship but also obligations and duties (Melvin Grove Kyle, *Moses and the Monuments,* Oberlin, Ohio, 1920, pp. 14 f.).

The names *El Ôlām* and *El 'Elyôn,* both compounds of the original Semitic name for Deity, represent variant emphases. The former calls attention especially to God's eternal duration, his agelessness and perpetuity. The latter (*El 'Eliôn* or *El 'Elyôn*), a more poetic form, describes the Deity as "Most High" and suggests His quality as the Exalted One (Gen. 14:18; Ps. 78:35). The combination of *'Elyôn* with *Elohim* also occurs occasionally (Ps. 45:2; 78:56). That this name is employed early in the Old Testament points to the existence of monotheism at the beginning of Israel's history. This usage elaborates the more transcendent qualities suggested by the earlier name, *Elohim*.

During the patriarchal period, the names *El, Elohim, Adonai, El Ôlām, El 'Elyôn, and Elohim 'Elyôn* were employed as more general names for the Deity, while the name *El Shaddāy* was more personal and more specific in its designation of the divine activity among men. The entire usage of this period emphasizes the view that to the Hebrew the conception of Deity was concrete and specific, not abstract and metaphysical. Moreover, the nomenclature of this period affords no evidence that the Hebrew conceptions of Deity in the patriarchal era were abstracted from their experience with the powers of nature.

The most specific particularized name of the Deity in the history of Israel was, of course, that indicated by the tetragram YHWH, which when supplied with vowels is usually written *Yahweh* or *Jehovah* ("he who is"). It was by this name that God disclosed Himself specifically to Moses (Ex. 3:13-16; 6:2-8), although we are assured that with the birth of Enos, grandson of Adam, men began to proclaim the name of Jehovah (Gen. 4:26). And while Abraham knew the Deity by this name (Gen. 15:7), it seems that this level of God's disclosure was not sustained during the age of the patriarchs, whose deepest and most intimate name for God was *El Shaddāy* (Ex. 6:3).

The name *Yahweh* or *Jehovah* was given a larger interpretation and a deeper significance with the call of Moses. It was revealed as an intensely personal name, not merely a name that is generic or essential, as for example, the names *El, Elohim,* and *Shaddāy*. As such, its disclosure and use highlights the Old Testament insistence upon the possibility of the Deity's being known as a person. Thus the very name *Yahweh* became a channel of a special revelation. And while it did not appear as an innovation in Mosaic times, at that time it not only gained general currency and specific acceptance but also became intimately related to the life of Israel as a people. That is to say, it became the hallmark of a crucial and pivotal self-disclosure of God to His people—a disclosure that intertwined the mighty acts connected with the Exodus with the people's actual consciousness of the birth of their nation, and that at the same time wove into their national awareness the significance of the cataclysmic events associated with Sinai. This multiple-stranded revelation impressed upon the Hebrews their unique covenant relation with a Deity who took the initiative and stepped unmistakably into their national affairs.

It is also significant that the use of this name was unique with the Israelites. The other Semites seemingly did not know it, or at least did not use it to refer to Deity, save as forcible contacts with the Hebrews brought it to their attention. It was a particular possession of the Covenant People. The name gathered so much significance that the scribes had an almost superstitious fear of pronouncing it. Scribal usage inserted the vowels of the name *Adonai* into the tetragram YHWH (the Covenant Name) and read the name as *Yahweh*. In the Septuagint translation of the Old Testament, the combination was translated *Kurios,* the Greek equivalent of *Adonai.*

The grasp by the Hebrew people of the name *Yahweh* or *Jehovah* was, as has been noted, a landmark in their spiritual awareness and religious experience. With the Exodus, the Deity took upon Himself, in the minds of the Hebrews, a specifically redemptive role. His "mighty acts" were at the same time "saving acts" and were so understood. As thus revealed, Jehovah was the One who bent the forces of nature to the ends of grace, the One who brought the action of His power and personality to bear upon the Hebrews at a time of their historical emergency. Thus, to use contemporary terminology, there developed at the Exodus the proclamation (the *kerygma*) of the Israelites: "I am Jehovah your God that brought you up out of the land of Egypt, out of the house of bondage."

Here appears the specific and specialized direction of God's self-disclosure. We are not unaware of the charges leveled against the historic understanding of the election of Israel by such thinkers as Douglas Clyde Macintosh, who holds that for God to have revealed Himself especially and exclusively to the Hebrew people would have been an act unworthy of the nature of God, and ultimately an immoral act. Here, as much as at any point, the antithesis between mere human thought and the biblical insight appears.

The Christian is not moved by the objection just noted but rather sees God's choice of Israel as the glory of divine grace. Mankind in general has been estranged from God by sin. The knowledge-bond that held God and unfallen man together has been fractured. The knowledge of God in any clear and saving sense is no more a part of man's general endowment. It is not the common possession of the race. If that knowledge is to be restored, it must be restored at God's initiative. And in the exercise of that initiative, God saw fit to work from a specialized segment of the human race, into whose experience He moved at certain crucial points. Far from showing an errant partiality in His special self-disclosure to the Hebrew people, He began to demonstrate, in this form of revelation, an active desire to show mercy to all. And it was through His revelation to Israel of Himself under the name of *Yahweh* or *Jehovah* that the unfolding of saving history became effective and conspicuous. Few moments were as significant for the entire human race as those moments in which the Deity thus unveiled His nature by giving to Moses and the Chosen People this name (Ex. 6:3).

At this point, something needs to be said about the answer given by Jehovah to Moses' question, "What shall I say unto them?" (i.e., when the Israelites inquire who has sent him to them) in Exodus 3:14. Here the Deity speaks of Himself as the I AM THAT I AM. Some have found in these words little more than a statement of what was later given as a metaphysical abstraction by Aristotle and the Scholastics. While there may be deep philosophical implications in this self-designation by the Deity, it is more to our point to observe that God evidently intended the phrase to be interpretative of His nature as Jehovah. W. T. Davison suggests that the words I Am That I Am are "descriptive of the nature of God as then making Himself known—the one, true God, self-existent and self-sufficient, the cause and ground of all being faithful to His promise, and constant in all His relations with His people" ("God, Biblical and Christian," in *Encyclopedia of Religion and Ethics*, ed. by James Hastings, 1922, VI, 254).

Thus, Jehovah here emphasizes to Moses (and through him to Israel) that Jehovah as *their* God requires no explanation for His existence, suggests no prior source out of which He has come, and, above all, *will* perfectly fulfill His pledged word. It is significant that the term, I Am That I Am, has not in itself been preserved as a divine name in the Old Testament; but one is impressed by the fact that when our Lord used the emphatic form, *ego eimi* ("I am"), in the Gospels, particularly as a reply, unusual results sometimes followed (see John 18:6).

In addition to the major names for God that we have noted, there are several other designations that, though they occur less often, do reveal much of the nature of God as grasped by the Hebrew people. Several of these deserve brief attention.

The name *Elohim Tsebhā'ôth* (often written God of Sabaoth, occurring sometimes as Jehovah or Lord Sabaoth) is found in Jeremiah 11:20 and is transliterated in Romans 9:29 and James 5:4. The term means literally "God or Lord of Hosts" and indicates God's role as controller of all created agencies and beings. Thus it brings together the ideas of Divine Maker and Divine Controller.

The name *Tsûr* ("Rock") occurs five times in the Song of Moses (Deut. 32:4, 15, 18, 30, 31) and also in Psalms, Isaiah, and elsewhere. It is a richly figurative name, suggesting God's role as fortress or shield. The name *Qᵉdhôsh* ("Holy One") occurs in the Psalms and especially in Isaiah, where it is found some thirty-two times. It signifies the transcendence of God over the earth and, as well, His special relation to Israel. The name *Abhir* ("Mighty One") is used in connection with the names of Israel or of Jacob; it is, taken with a proper name, a poetic title. The name *Gibbôr* ("Mighty") bears the same significance and is found in connection with the names *El* and *Yahweh* (Isa. 9:6; Jer. 32:18; Isa. 42: 13). The name *El Rô'î* ("God of seeing") is used once (Gen. 16:13) by Hagar in connection with her flight from the persecution of Sarah. *Tsedeq* ("Righteous One") speaks of God's fidelity to Himself, and of His nature as Covenant-Keeper. It has thus much in common with the name *Yahweh*. Finally, the name *Qannâ* ("God of Righteous Zeal") suggests the demand of God for exclusive devotion. The name is, as in Exodus 34:14, translated "jealous," a term that in this usage is free from the unworthy qualities we ordinarily attach to it.

The names for the Deity in the New Testament continue and also simplify the nomenclature of the Old Covenant. The most common name is, of course, *Theos*, which occurs more than one thousand times. It corresponds, in general, to the names *El* and *Elohim* and their compounds and expresses essential Deity, with emphasis upon self-sufficiency, self-determination, and absolute righteousness (see Edward Mack, "God, Names of," in *International Standard Bible Encyclopedia,* 1915, II, 1268).

The name *Kurios* ("Lord") occurs very frequently. It seems to gather into itself the combined significance of *Adonai,* of which it is the equivalent and *Yahweh* or *Jehovah.* The name is applied with equal clarity to God the Father and to Jesus Christ. Thus in the unfolding of the redemptive message of the New Testament, the richness of Old Testament nomenclature for the Deity was presupposed. Not only is this richness gathered up in the wide range of usage of the names *Theos* and *Kurios,* but some of the attributive names for the Deity are also carried over. One recalls, for example, the names *Highest, Most High,* and *Almighty,* corresponding to *'Elyôn, Abhīr* and *Shaddāy.*

The most distinctive development in the use of divine names in the New Testament is the introduction of the name *Father.* The idea of "God as Father" was foreshadowed in the Old Testament, both in the relation between God and Israel and in the more intimate strains of the devotional literature between God and the devout among His people. It was made concrete by the usage of our Lord. To Him the term was natural, and as the Divine Son He used it often. It is noteworthy that His first recorded words (Luke 2:49) reveal His awareness of being about His Father's business, and that His last words on earth were concerned with "the promise of my Father" (Luke 24:49).

Our Lord's language is not philosophical but filial. He claimed that God was Father to Him in a unique sense (see John 5:18). But during His ministry He also proclaimed that God's Fatherhood was something to be shared (Matt. 7:11; Luke 11:13). In the parable of the Prodigal Son He extends the concept, showing by a moving human story the Heavenly Father's concern for all men. Throughout His ministry the perfect Son manifested the heart of the Father, laying bare before the eyes of men the redemptive desire that impelled the Incarnation of the Son. Thus the Christian community came very early to speak of God as "the Father of our Lord Jesus Christ." It is in terms such as this that the writers of the New Testament Epistles emphasize that God is the Father of all men in the sense of being the Creator and Sustainer of all, while noting specifically that there is an essentially Christian sense in which He is the Father of the twice-born. It is, of course, within the context of Christian redemption that the name *Father* comes to its fullest significance, a point that will be amplified in the next section.

THE DIVINE NATURE

Few tasks are more difficult than answering the simple question, "What is God like?" Yet this is a query which is frequently heard, and which merits some kind of intelligible reply. Asking the question presupposes that human beings are capable of some knowledge of God, and that this understanding can be put into intelligible verbal form. The existence of God is not argued in detail in Holy Scripture. The psalmist felt that God's existence was something so clearly seen that only "the fool" says in his heart, "There is no God" (Ps. 13:1). Later writers of the Bible recognized that God's existence is not so obvious that no one might legitimately question it.

There are several grades of atheism. First, there is the atheism of the casual scoffer who lives in disdain of "things sacred." The second type is the atheism that rises from the agnostic spirit, which, whatever its source, is by no means either simple or frivolous. Third, there is dogmatic atheism, typical of the man who has adopted, in advance of evidence, a position (often systematic materialism) that rules out any serious contemplation of God's existence. Finally, there is the practical type of atheism expressed in lives lived as if God did not exist.

This is not the place to set forth in detail the reasons for doubt of the divine existence. Men of our time often demand forms of evidence for the existence of God that are not likely to be found within the scope of scientific endeavor, particularly that endeavor oriented in naturalism. But the expanding quality of today's knowledge gives little logical support to the dogmatic denial that any evidence for the divine existence can or will be found. Such a denial contradicts the ideal of scientific inquiry and presupposes a sort of omniscience upon the part of the one making it.

But to return to our original line of thought, Scripture uniformly teaches not only that man can come to a knowledge that God is but also that concerning God's nature something may be known that is correct, at least so far as it goes. St. Paul takes it for granted in his writings (especially the Epistle to the Romans) that something may be known of God through the study of the created universe, namely, "his eternal power and Godhead." He goes further to note that the book of nature reveals enough of God's nature that men who peer into its pages are "without excuse" if they do not see Him (Rom. 1:20).

It is doubtless possible to attribute to "natural" knowledge of God much that has actually been derived from other sources. For the human mind is a very limited instrument, and those who take seriously the abiding effects of moral evil upon the human intellect recognize that the book of nature cannot be read easily and quickly by fallen men. This is not to agree with Immanuel Kant, who held that human knowledge (i.e., discursive knowledge) is limited in such a way that the mind cannot know whether or not God (or even a super-temporal realm) can exist. Rather, it is to point out that if man fails to see God in the light of the "things which are made," this failure is often due to a preassumed stance—a determination that the knower *will not* have God in his thoughts. And we are on good ground when we observe that at least some towering minds have, apart from special revelation, attained to some knowledge of God; namely that He exists, that He is related to the origin of the universe, and that He maintains some degree of control over it.

This is, to be sure, an exceedingly thin form of theology with which the Christian cannot remain satisfied. To the believer's desire for a more adequate knowledge of God's nature, the Christian revelation asserts its own form of reply. Its statements concerning the divine nature go beyond the conclusion of the observer of nature or those of the speculative thinker. It is, therefore, to the scriptural statements that the discussion must turn with the understanding that we shall cross-check revealed statements with the best of that which thinkers unaided by the biblical message have proposed.

The scriptural revelation begins by asserting the spirituality and personality of God. Already the Old Testament has implied these two qualities as most deeply characteristic of Jehovah. At times, the Old Testament conception appears excessively anthropomorphic; but in describing Him as a "jealous God" capable of wrath and anger and as having (in figurative expression) members like those of our bodies, the Old Testament writers are saying that He is a self-conscious, intelligent, and moral agent and thus are affirming His personality. Likewise there are clear indications of His spirituality, so that it comes to us as no surprise when our Lord announces that "God is spirit" (John 4:24). As such, He possesses a real substantive existence.

The twin qualities of spirituality and personality shine through very much that is said about other aspects of His being. It is to these we turn, and at the end of this discussion more will be said about them. For the present, let us remember that Scripture asserts uniformly that God exists without a mixture of what we know as matter, and that the qualities we commonly associate with personality exist in superlative quality in Him, so that He cannot be thought to consist in mere thought, force, or power.

The biblical revelation suggests, first, that God is sovereignly free; He is utterly above any determination from outside Himself. He existed before the world and is in no way dependent upon it for His existence. Thus the basic affirmation of the so-called Apostles' Creed is: "I believe in God, the Father almighty." Here the accent falls upon the absence of any extrinsic limitation in the being of God. He is unique in this freedom, being eternal and unchanging. Moreover, Scripture makes it abundantly clear that as He acts by free choice, He does so in conformity with the objectives He determines for Himself. Thus He is sovereign in both the means and the ends of the exercise of His will.

Again, His uniqueness has as its clear corollary the unitary quality of His Being. He answers to the *Shema* of Deuteronomy 6:4: "Hear, O Israel, the Lord thy God, the Lord is One." These words sum up the Jewish view of God, a truth that by the time of the birth of our Lord had been indelibly impressed upon the Hebrew mind. The core of meaning at this point is continued in the New Testament, being clearly proclaimed in such passages as Mark 12:29; Romans 3:30, and Ephesians 4:6. We are aware, of course, that God's unity is not static or monolithic. Aristotle perceived by the light of reason the unitary quality of God; but this was an abstract unity, whose highest characteristic was aloofness from the world. The Stoics also proclaimed the unity of God but immediately proceeded to announce that God was all and all was

God. Nothing is further from the biblical understanding of God than this form of pantheism, whether proclaimed by the Stoics or, in a more refined way, in the system of Baruch Spinoza.

As a unity, God is not composed of separate elements or attributes. These latter are properties essential to the nature of a Supreme Being and are part of our idea of God. Nor are His attributes transcendental "blurbs," all meaning the same thing and only separate as objects of our thought. His unity inheres in His majestic aloneness in the order of uncreated Being.

But God is not only sovereignly unique and exclusively unitary; He is also sovereign Father. At this point, the Christian understanding of Him towers supremely over the highest conceptions attained by the speculative philosophers. In the classical period of Greece, investigation plus speculation banished the old gods, one by one, into a far corner of the field of nature, largely as a result of the growing understanding of the universe as a harmonious whole. In place of the nature-gods of polytheism, there was posited a deity who was a first cause, and perhaps a general supervisor of the cosmos. But He was not necessarily an object of man's worship and could logically lay no obligation upon man's moral conduct. Thus a mere logically attained belief in God did not and could not satisfy the religious instinct and religious longings of men.

It is quite other with "God the Father almighty." Here sovereignty and Fatherhood are inseparably joined, something seemingly impossible in the non-revelatory systems. Although the concept of God's Fatherhood has been overworked in our century, particularly by those terming themselves "liberals," the careful reader of Scripture will not for this reason neglect the proper doctrine of God's Fatherhood, a doctrine that largely superseded the regal aspect of God stressed in the Old Testament in general, and particularly in the language of the Psalms.

The conception of God as Father was, as suggested earlier, implied in such Old Testament passages as Psalm 103:13: "Like as a father pitieth his children, so Jehovah pitieth them that fear him." However, the concept was not a determinative one in the Old Testament, this unfolding having been reserved for the revelation of the New Covenant. In the words of our Lord, God was pre-eminently revealed as Father. Thomas Rees reminds us:

> He meant that the essential nature of God, and His relation to men, is best expressed by the attitude and relation of a father to his children; but God is Father in an infinitely higher and more perfect degree than any man ["God," in *International Standard Bible Encyclopedia,* 1943, II, 1261].

God is most basically, of course, the God and Father of our Lord Jesus Christ. His Fatherhood has meaning for all men, in that He is creator of all and all are the objects of His gracious care. He does not will that any should perish (Matt. 18:14). Even if by evil choice men refuse to own Him as God, He still awaits to receive those who will return in penitence. There is reason to believe that even those who remain finally impenitent and who at length go into outer darkness forever will in doing so bring a pang to the Father's heart.

God does, of course, have an especial relation as Father to those who through faith in His Son become His adopted sons. These, as "heirs of God and joint heirs" with the Son, enjoy a relation that is morally based, and that goes infinitely beyond the relation of creatureliness and dependence which all men by nature sustain to Him.

The doctrines of the Sovereignty and the Fatherhood of God are further analyzable. That is to say, they have implication-doctrines that cast light upon them and serve to round out the basic elements just mentioned. Sovereign freedom implies the pattern of *omni*-attributes— omnipresence, omnipotence, and omniscience. The agnostic rejects every *all*-conception, while the humanist holds that a deity, even though He possessed these attributes, would not qualify as an object of worship. The Christian, however, believes that God's "everywhereness," all-capability, and all-knowingness enrich the doctrine of God as sovereign Lord; indeed, they are part of the conception of any Being who is really God.

God's omnipresence suggests that, while His power and presence may be somewhere localized, yet there is no part of the universe where His presence is not manifested. We are aware of the objections raised by Paul Tillich, Rudolf Bultmann, and others, and presented in popular fashion by Bishop Robinson, to the effect that modern scientific thought has rendered belief in a God "up there" or "out there" absurd, so that the only remaining alternative for the educated man is to believe in a "God" inside his own being. What advocates of this form of "theology" overlook is that dimensions outside our three-dimensional understanding may exist within which the power and presence of God may be localized, and from which He may express His "thereness" in every part of the universe He has made.

God's omnipotence implies that nothing lies outside His capability except, of course, the self-contradictory or the morally deleterious. His power, as distinct from the *exercise* of His power, knows no limitations. If it may be properly said that at a given moment He is not doing all He might do, then this comes from a self-imposed limitation upon the exercise of His ability. There is no hint in Scripture that He is subject to any necessary extrinsic limitation or restriction. And in the role of the omnipotent One, He is the Creator (i.e., the source of the absolute origination) of the universe and its mighty Sustainer as well. Thus as the all-capable One, He is "maker of heaven and earth."

His omniscience flows, not from any metaphysical consideration, but from His being as free from any restrictions of power or will. Whereas we know things, persons, and events seriatim, it seems clear that His knowledge is complete in an eternal *now*—that is, there is no point in the divine career in which all things are not immediately present to His mind. He knows the end from the beginning and is subject to no surprises. Thus He can view the whole unrolling drama of the universal (and human) enterprise with complete calm—and, we may add cautiously, even with a sense of humor.

Closely related to His omniscience is His wisdom. It is no accident that in one of the New Testament benedictions He is called the "all-wise God." This "wisdom" consists not merely in the ability to reproduce facts (a vast computer might do this) but in His ability to adapt, with perfect congruity, means to ends. In Him are, we are confident, no false starts, no lost motion, no tentativity. What He has promised, He is able also to perform. His will is being wrought, even amid the contrary winds of human perversity; and the "new heavens and the new earth" will proclaim with eternal eloquence the infinite wisdom of God.

It is clear from the foregoing that one cannot draw a completely neat line between God's "natural" qualities on the one hand and his "moral" attributes on the other. His nature and being are, at the deepest level, moral. It was this factor that differentiated Yahweh or Jehovah from the deities of the lands surrounding Israel. There is a discernible pattern of qualities within His Being that are more specifically exercised toward the moral needs of the race and form a special ingredient in God's specific relation to other personalities. Among these attributes there stand in a pre-eminent place holiness, love, and mercy.

In the Old Testament, holiness is a quality that shines forth with great intensity from God's self-revelation. In Leviticus, Moses quotes God as saying, "Ye shall be holy, for I am holy." It does not answer to the realities of Old Testament usage to contend that "holiness" was originally a morally neutral category, connoting some vague "numinous" or mysterious quality that elicited a sense of awe. Such a view as this, given classic form in Rudolf Otto's *Idea of the Holy,* rests upon a radical reinterpretation of the history of Israel's religion, a readjustment that is far from being evidently justified. With the prophets, the ideas of holiness and of righteousness were applied to Jehovah as virtually equivalent. While in places in the Old Testament record Jehovah was shown to be unapproachable in His "holiness," yet against the backdrop of human iniquity the prophets proclaimed Him to be holy in a deeply moral sense.

His holiness is also analyzable into components—i.e., as this quality is seen from our human point of view. First, holiness in action produces the twin categories of righteousness and justice. In other words, holiness when expressed in action implies both strict rectitude and an aggressive form of justice. Holiness in God was a permeate quality that gave direction, depth, and tone to all He did and does. In the extension of mercy or of grace, He will not violate the norms set by holiness. At this level, His justice appears as a closely related aspect of His holiness.

In the light of the inclusiveness of this category, many elements in the Bible, and especially in the Old Testament, fall into their proper place. Thomas Rees reminds us in this connection,

> Jehovah's rule is no longer limited to Israel, nor concerned only with the nation as a collective whole, but he deals impartially with every individual and nation alike. Other limitations also disappear. His anger and wrath,

that once appeared irrational and unjust, now become the intensity of his righteousness ["God," in *International Standard Bible Encyclopedia,* 1943, II, 1257].

Thus God's holiness shares and conditions every expression of His personality, every extension of His power. It does not cancel any other of His qualities or render any other attributes superfluous.

The simple statement, "God is love," tantalizes us as we seek to explore the nature of God. Here again the evangelical may tend to draw back in reaction to those who have set God's love in antithesis to His holiness and His justice. It is true that those calling themselves "liberals" have stressed love in such a way as to depreciate any expression of divine justice. But, as Carl F. H. Henry points out, it is not necessary to apply the attribute of love in such a manner as to cancel out the quality of holiness, or vice versa (*Notes on the Doctrine of God,* 1948, pp. 103 ff.). Actually, love and righteousness (or holiness) express differing aspects of the same quality in God's being.

Love in God approaches very nearly the definition given by Charles Hodge of God's quality of *goodness,* including "benevolence, love, mercy and grace" (*Systematic Theology,* 1871, p. 427). We would see love as the primary element in His being and see benevolence, mercy, and grace as derived from it. God's love moves Him to communicate with His creatures, to impart Himself to them for their highest good, and, in case of need, to use His fullest and best resources to redeem them.

This forms a suitable point of transition to a brief statement concerning God's triune or tri-personal nature. Other essays in this series will elaborate this theme, but it should be noted here that the richness of the Divine Life suggested by the Old Testament's use of the plural name *Elohim* is unfolded in the New Testament. There the one, unitary Divine Being is shown to exist in a union of three centers of self-conscious activity, each capable of proper designation by the singular personal pronouns. These "persons" are declared to be related in the most intimate fashion: as Father, as Son of the Father by generation from eternity, and as Holy Spirit proceeding from eternity from Father and Son. This teaching may be legitimately and clearly inferred from the events connected with the Incarnation. The doctrine is basically unfolded through direct revelation, since we have for the Trinity no precise analogue in nature.

The doctrine of the Trinity serves to round out and crown the New Testament understanding of God. It affords, we believe, the framework within which His personality may be understood with the greatest clarity possible to our finite minds. As One God (i.e., one in the deepest ground of His Being), He exists as the embodiment of three distinct and intimately interrelated Persons. In this, the Divine Life expresses to a degree impossible to us finite personalities the fullest manifestation of *the personal.* The doctrine of the Trinity is the great conserver of Christian theism. In the reverent contemplation and loving understanding of the Triune God, man attains to a full-orbed (though always limited in depth) grasp of the nature of Him with whom we have to do, God the Father Almighty.

CONCLUSION

Barbara Ward is correct in saying that "faith will not be restored in the West because people believe it to be useful. It will return only when they find that it is true" (*Faith and Freedom,* p. 265). This essay has not concerned itself largely with "the idea of God" or the mere "meaning of God for man's experience." No attempt has been made to survey the several arguments claiming to afford rational grounds for belief in His existence. These may have value in confirming belief in those already disposed to faith; but with the emergence of new scientific categories, "proofs for God" no longer have the force they exerted in the medieval and early modern periods. The emphasis in this study is upon the manner in which the Living God has taken the initiative in unveiling Himself to His creatures.

Belief in God has been a vital ingredient in the lives of those who have held it. The absence of faith has done its devastating work in human lives and human society. Restoration of biblical faith is, however, of pre-eminent importance because of *what God is,* and because all must ultimately stand before Him. Revelation has for its primary aim not the satisfaction of human curiosity but the healing of a fractured relationship between man and his Creator. This can become a reality only as God the Lord, as He has manifested His names and the qualities of His Being, becomes a relational reality in human lives.

Theoretical knowledge of God cannot in itself guarantee that this will occur. A profound pattern of insight is revealed in the words, "This is life eternal, that they might know thee, the only true God, and Jesus Christ whom thou hast sent" (John 17:3). There is a deeper knowledge of God that is realized only as the individual is confronted by the demanding claims of Emmanu-el, the Second Person of the Godhead, appearing among us in time and in a Sacred Land. In Him the depth of God's being and purpose are externalized in a manner comprehensible to us, and in His Cross there came to full view the love of God that will not let us go. At Golgotha the Father expressed His inner heart. Incarnation and Atonement crown our understanding of God and afford us unassailable ground for our hope.

A SELECT BIBLIOGRAPHY

2. GOD: HIS NAMES AND NATURE

Hubert S. Box, *God and the Modern Mind.* New York, 1937.

W. T. Davison, "God, Biblical and Christian," in James Hastings (ed.) *Encyclopedia of Religion and Ethics.* New York, 1922, VI, 252-69.

R. A. Finalayson, "The Holiness of God," in *G. Campbell Morgan Memorial Lectures* (No. VII). London, 1955.

Arthur C. Headlam, *Christian Theology: The Doctrine of God.* Oxford, 1934.

Carl F. H. Henry, *Notes on the Doctrine of God.* Boston, 1948.

J. R. Illingworth, *The Divine Transcendence.* London, 1911.

Charles W. Lowry, *The Trinity and Christian Devotion.* New York and London, 1946.

W. R. Matthews, *God in Christian Thought and Experience.* London, 1930.

A. Seth Pringle-Pattison, *The Idea of God.* Oxford, 1917.

Thomas Rees, "God," in James Orr *et al.* (eds.) *International Standard Bible Encyclopedia.* Grand Rapids, Michigan, 1955, II, 1250-64.

Daniel S. Robinson, *Christian Belief in God.* New Haven, 1918.

John I. Tigert, *Theism.* London, 1900.

THE TRIUNE GOD

Samuel J. Mikolaski

Samuel J. Mikolaski is now pastor of the Braemar Baptist Church, Edmonton, Alberta, Canada. He has served as professor of systematic theology at the International Baptist Theological Seminary, Rüschlikon-Zürich, Switzerland, and also professor of theology at New Orleans Baptist Theological Seminary. He holds the B.A. and M.A. (Phil.) from the University of Western Ontario (Canada), B.D. from the University of London, and the D.Phil. from the University of Oxford. Dr. Mikolaski is the author of many articles in religious periodicals and of a book entitled The Grace of God (1965). The subject of his dissertation at Oxford was the nature and place of human response in objective theories of the Atonement advanced by R. W. Dale, James Denney, and P. T. Forsyth.

3. *Samuel J. Mikolaski*

THE TRIUNE GOD

No ONE should suppose that the doctrine of the Trinity perches incongruously on the periphery of faith. Far from being nonsense, a fussy but obscure dogma, or an irreverent logical stumbling block, this doctrine is indispensable to the Christian understanding of God, Christ, salvation, and the divine purpose in creation. All that is Christian hinges on the truth of the biblical revelation that God is one, eternal, personal, and triune.

The cruciality of the trinitarian conception of God may be grasped by considering the inner structure of many primary doctrines. To begin with, scholars of every age have seen that it makes little sense to speak of God as personal and moral unless He is more than impersonal. What is personhood in isolation, whether of God or of man? Also, the doctrine of creation—that is, creation out of nothing *(creatio ex nihilo)*—which declares God's nondependence upon the world, points to the perfection of communal divine life prior to the creation (John 17:5). Even more crucial is the problem of how to fit in the Incarnation unless God is triune. Do not Christians confess the twin truths that God sent His Son into the world and that God is revealed incarnate in Jesus Christ? To contemplate the Incarnation in relation to the Cross is to see that the Son, not the Father, died on the Cross; that the Father raised the Son from the dead, thus vindicating both Father and Son (Rom. 1:1-4); and that the ascension, present session, and promised return of Christ mean little apart from trinitarian faith.

To beg the questions by reducing full trinitarian belief to unipersonal monotheism touches more than the doctrine that God is triune; it compels rephrasing the entire vocabulary of faith because the essential Christian realities have been jettisoned. In the Bible, trinitarian faith is not an intellectual conundrum but a vital spiritual datum.

THE ANCIENT CONFESSION

During the third and fourth centuries of the Christian era, formal doctrinal statements were developed to protect the Church from heretical opinion. (Note the carefully documented Bampton Lectures of H. E. W. Turner, *The Pattern of Christian Truth,* London, 1954.) This is not to say that the Bible was consciously eclipsed nor that doctrines such as the Trinity were post-apostolic innovations. The lines of biblical authority in the Father are clearly traceable in the extant literature from the beginning. To them the whole Bible was a Christian book, and by various interpretative procedures—many of which were surprisingly modern—they exhibited the truth of Scripture.

Far from suffering the burden of Hellenization (the view that original simple Christian faith became overlaid by the alien complexities of Greek philosophy, which produced the creedal statements), the Church strove to express Christian realities in the language of the times. They could not, nor can we, opt out of contemporary dialogue. Drawing upon their life and worship, nurtured by Scripture, hedged about by the rule of faith, baptismal, and catechetical formulas, Christian scholars, often under attack both from within and from outside the Church, shaped the creedal statements. Creedal formulation did not come as an alien force imposed from the outside; the creeds expressed the growing faith and understanding of Christians, sometimes apologetically oriented, sometimes polemically oriented, but usually grounded in the truth of Scripture. What Scripture says is what the Church believes, they said.

The most famous trinitarian formula derives from the Athanasian era of the fourth century. The first part of the confession commonly known as the Athanasian Creed declares: "We worship one God in Trinity, and Trinity in Unity; neither confounding the Persons, nor dividing the Substance." To comment on certain important terms in this statement is to see that the early Fathers knew very well what questions their beliefs and language raised in relation to the Bible and philosophy. Often this is not recognized now.

First, Christians employ the term "God" in more than one way. We believe in one God, we say. By this we mean God the Father and the Son and the Holy Spirit, or at times, God in the sense of the Father only (Rom. 15:6). But so astute a mind as the Cappadocian father Gregory of Nyssa said that the term "and" only joins the terms expressive of the persons of the Trinity, so that it is not a term that expresses the essence of God. We always use the term "God" in the singular with the name of each Person. By the term "God," therefore, Christians designate the essence or being of God, not the persons. The Godhead of the Father is not that which distinguishes Him from the Son. Similarly, the Spirit is not God because He is the Spirit, nor is the Son God because He is the

Son, but the Spirit and Son are God because their essential nature is what it is. We properly speak therefore of God the Father, God the Son, and God the Holy Spirit.

Secondly, no one should suppose that because the formulators of the Athanasian Creed used the term "substance," they meant materiality; rather, they meant reality. (See Part II of Austin Farrer's *Finite and Infinite*, Westminster, 1943.) We must not read back popular modern materialistic associations of the word "substance" into ancient times. The classical terminology was devised to express the distinctions between different kinds of reality, whether of God, of man, or of animal, and modern dynamic cosmologies must not obscure the truth of these distinctions. The Greek and Latin terms for substance, quality, and nature respectively are: *ousia, substantia; poiotetes, qualitas; physis, natura.* Each kind of being, they said, has its own qualities and nature. When we use the terms "substance" or "essence" we simply mean reality of a certain kind, whether of God, or of the created order.

Thirdly, the term "person" was devised to indicate that each particular instance of being has an individual reality of its own. In early trinitarian doctrine this individual reality was called *prosopon,* but later the term *hypostasis* in Greek and *persona* in Latin became equivalents, so that the formula of the Trinity read, "three persons in one substance" *(treis hypostaseis en mia ousia,* and *tres personae in una substantia).* These terms do not impose static concepts upon the doctrine. The Fathers, especially the Cappadocians, qualified their use significantly by the dynamic term *energeia.*

It is unrealistic to charge that all patristic writers fell short of our notions of personality because they lacked the modern term "person." Enough has been said to indicate that the works of the Fathers do stand up under modern critical analysis, and, as our argument proceeds, evidence will be adduced to show that the biblical writers thought of persons in fully modern ways.

Fourthly, the terms "one" and "unity" raised the question of number and the dangers of applying numeration to deity. The problems were fully apparent to earlier theologians. Opponents of trinitarian doctrine were quick to point to the tritheism implicit in the language, let us say, of "three in one." Orthodox Christians replied that number could be used of God only in a guarded, highly qualified way, because the indivisibility of the divine essence is axiomatic. Nyssa's brother Basil and their friend Gregory Nazianzus both urged caution in the use of number (Basil, *De Spiritu Sancto,* 41-45; Gregory of Nazianzus, *Fifth Oration: On the Spirit,* 7, 13-20, 31, 32; Gregory of Nyssa, *On "Not Three Gods").* Gregory of Nyssa said that number cannot strictly be applied to God because the personal distinctions cannot be enumerated by way of addition. Nevertheless, since we see no other way of preserving the distinctness of the persons, we must use number guardedly; but we must not transfer enumeration from the *hypostaseis* to the *ousia,* i.e., from the persons to the substance. The nature of God is altogether beyond our grasp. We can express it only as simple and indivisible.

What Christians can mean by "unity in trinity" will occupy our attention later. However, it is unambiguously clear to any student of the New Testament and of the Church Fathers that tritheism was never a threat to the Christian faith. Forms of modalism and subordinationism that attempted reduction of trinitarian faith were threats, but never tritheism. It is a point of some significance to observe that Christianity began as a sect of the Jews and that it was thoroughly monotheistic, yet the plethora of trinitarian language in the New Testament yielded not a trace of embarrassment from Jewish attack.

Our task must be, not to displace the full-fledged trinitarian language of the New Testament, nor to reduce it to other terms, but to try to understand it and to believe its truth. Only rarely has full trinitarian faith been achieved in the history of Christendom. Where it has, the vital redemptive, ecclesiastical, and eschatological realities that it communicates to Christians have generated a quality of life that reflects the holy fellowship of Father, Son, and Holy Spirit. Trinitarian religion yields a depth of theological insight that makes the truth grasped timeless, despite the language that clothes it. One may cite the quite remarkable statement of Evagrius, whose words bear striking resemblance to the exposition that follows:

> Against those who cast it in our teeth that we are Tritheists, let it be answered that we confess one God not in number but in nature. For everything which is called one in number is not one absolutely, not yet simple in nature; but God is universally confessed to be simple and not complex (Basil, *Epistles,* VIII, 2 [attributed to Evagrius Ponticus; cf. B. Altaner, *Patrology,* London, 1960, p. 307]).

REVEALED DOCTRINE

The truth that in the unity of God there is a trinity of persons can be affirmed only on the ground of revelation by God. On any other footing this audacious claim would be utter folly. Let him who approaches the thrice holy One (Isa. 6:3) do so out of reverent awe, for the deeper insights into the nature of God come only to the contrite in spirit.

For Christians, "the knowledge of God by revelation" means not less than "the historically revealed truth of God." This at once projects the Holy Scriptures to the center of the stage. To say anything about God is to say something about God; and to say something about God demands that what we say come under the judgment of Scripture. It is difficult, indeed impossible, to see what Christians can hope to say about God's nature and redemptive action unless the historical data of the Bible are taken seriously.

One might even concede that terms such as "being," "person," and "substance" are highly sophisticated mythology—if he is also prepared to be mythologized out of existence. Two points seem inescapable in the

Christian claim: First, the Christian narratives must be taken not just as illustrative stories or myths but as the actual forms that the universal principles have taken (cf. C. C. J. Webb, *The Historical Element in Religion,* London, 1935, pp. 31-51, 80-83, 89-91); and second, we must therefore grasp the truths that the language of the Bible conveys. If the biblical revelation does not tell us what is actually the case about God as one and triune, then we are left forever in ignorance of His true nature. Revelation involves truth, and truth is a function of language. We require devout, rational reflection upon the historical data of the divine self-disclosure, for this is the kind of evidence God has chosen to give us.

1. The Father is God. "Hear, O Israel: The Lord our God is one Lord" (Deut. 6:4). This much quoted kerygmatic utterance, the famous Hebrew *Sh'ma,* epitomizes the deeply embedded monotheism of the Old Testament. When joined to the equally firm monotheism of the New Testament (I Cor. 8:6; Jas. 2:19), such teaching is the foundation of the one biblical faith in the true God. There is but one God, the true, living God, who is Lord of creation, of life, and of destiny.

The truth that God is one can be documented voluminously from the Old Testament. ". . . the Lord he is God; there is none else beside him" (Deut. 4:35, cf. v. 39; Ex. 20:1-3; Isa. 45:5, 18, 22). (Note the famous passages that extol the unity and character of God and mercilessly satirize idolatry—Isa. 40:12-31; 44:6-20.) By nature He is righteous and holy (Deut. 4:24; 10:17, 18) and mighty to act on behalf of His people (Deut. 4:37, 38), and He keeps His covenant promises (Deut. 4:31; 7: 8, 9). By these attributes God is declared to be one, not many; personal, not impersonal; ethical, not morally neutral. As the Holy One He is high, transcendent, separate from the world He made; yet He condescends to us, especially to the humble in heart (Isa. 57:15; 46:4). His knowledge is infinite, His word is sure, His judgments are just, His works are perfect, and His mercy is everlasting (Deut. 32:4; Ps. 33:9; 102:26-28; 139:1-14; Lam. 3:22, 23). These truths demand from men utmost allegiance of mind, heart, and will (Deut. 6:5).

The signification of God as one, personal, moral, and self-revealing is made in Scripture through the terms of God's name. This is theologically profound and philosophically astute. In this way men learned of Him through the progressive unfolding of His person, character, and relations with them. God's names connote the truth about Him in His mighty acts (Gen. 17:1; Ex. 3:14, 15; 6:3).

The grammar of the names of God and the language of the designations of God have led many to conclude—albeit in the light of New Testament truth—that the Old Testament does yield important clues to plurality in God or even outright indications of it. At the least, the data that prompt Christian scholars to see trinitarian overtones in the Old Testament prove very troubling points indeed to those, whether Christian or Jew, who maintain that God is impersonal or is unipersonal.

The extent of this evidence is not small[1] but it can be only touched upon here. The *Sh'ma* itself poses such a question. "Hear, O Israel: YHWH our *Elohim* is YHWH a unity." Now *Yahweh,* or Jehovah, is singular, but *Elohim* is a plural noun. Despite various explanations of what this plural form means, no indisputable criterion for choosing one solution as against another has yet been found, including the offensive but grammatically correct translation, "Hear, O Israel: Jehovah our Gods is Jehovah a unity." If this plural form were an isolated instance, and if no other evidence remained, proponents of the unipersonal God theory could shrug it off; but this is not so.

Two instances may be cited in the creation narrative where the plural *Elohim* is joined to the singular verb *bara* (i.e., to create). Furthermore, the passages suggest communion in God, for angels do not seem to have been associated with God in the act of creation: "Let us make man in our image . . ." and "man is become as one of us . . ." (Gen. 1:26; 3:22). There is also the Babel passage, "Let us go down . . ." (Gen. 11:7). Parallels in the New Testament where plural subjects are combined with singular verbs are First Thessalonians 3:11 and Second Thessalonians 2:16.

The appearance of the angel to Hagar (Gen. 16:7-14) and to Abraham (Gen. 17:22; 18:1-22; cf. 19:1); the Captain of the Lord's Hosts who spoke to Joshua (Josh. 5:13-16; cf. 6:2); and the celestial visitor to Manoah and his wife, whose name was "full of wonder" (Judges 13: 2-23), have prompted some to see these as pre-Incarnation theophanies. The "Spirit of *Yahweh*" references, especially since Spirit in the Old Testament is seen to be life-giving power with a moral emphasis, are thought to signify the Spirit as the agent of *Yahweh* in the Old Testament (cf. Gen. 1:2; Isa. 40:13; 58:8-14). The personification of the divine wisdom in Proverbs 8 is tied by some to the *logos* doctrine of John 1 and the wisdom of God in First Corinthians 1:24. (In Scripture Christ is identified with the Word of God [*logos*] and the Wisdom of God [*sofia*], but never with the Spirit of God [*pneuma theou*].) The use of the threefold name of God in the benediction (Num. 6:24-27), in relation to the presence and activity of God (Ps. 29:3-5), and in the threefold invocation (Isa. 6:1-3) is significant also. (Note the striking words of Isaiah 48:16 [cf. Zech. 2:10-13], which seem to apply to *Yahweh's* redeeming Servant [cf. Keil and Delitzsch, and G. A. Smith, among others].) While such evidence as the foregoing is not strong, certainly not conclusive, it cannot be sloughed off if we regard the Bible—as Christians must—as a Christian book.

Historically, the doctrine of the Trinity originated in the necessity laid on the first Christians to distinguish Jesus from God, yet to identify Him

---

[1] See, for example, G. A. F. Knight, *A Biblical Approach to the Doctrine of the Trinity* (Edinburgh, 1956); D. L. Cooper, *The God of Israel* (Los Angeles, 1945); Edmond Jacob, *Theology of the Old Testament* (London, 1958); Th. C. Vriezen, *An Outline of Old Testament Theology* (Newton Centre, Mass., 1962); G. Vos, *Biblical Theology* (Grand Rapids, Mich., 1959).

with God. Through the incarnation of Christ and His teaching, Christians learned to distinguish the Father and the Son while maintaining the faith that both are God. That God is Father was no new doctrine (cf. Ps. 103:13; Isa. 9:6; Jer. 31:9; Mal. 1:6); but that the Father is God and that the Son is God became clear through the Incarnation in the truth that God is "the God and Father of our Lord Jesus Christ" (Rom. 15:6; II Cor. 1:3; Eph. 1:3; I Pet. 1:3; cf. John 20:17; Acts 4:24-30). Hence Christians test the truth of the doctrine of the Trinity by the truth of the doctrine of the Incarnation, and not vice versa. We do not assume a concept of unity by which to determine what the Incarnation can mean. Rather, because we confess unreserved faith in the Son as God Incarnate revealed for our salvation, and attested by the gift of the Holy Spirit, we affirm that God is triune.

The Old Testament revelation of God leads to the deepest insight of all, which is the truth of the New Testament that God is the Father of the Son and our personal heavenly Father. God the Father is defined in Scripture with reference to the redemptive work of the Son (John 14:9). Through Christ we cry "Abba," or "Father" (Rom. 8:15; Gal. 4:6). God is no abstraction, whether impersonal or suprapersonal, but the living, Holy Father. This truth eclipses doctrines of impersonal causation, or of a God who shows no concern, or of a finite God imprisoned in the world, or of a God identified with the world as in pantheism. Fatherhood means not only that God is the Creator but also that He exercises loving care of the world (Matt. 11:25-27). It is He whom the Son reveals and at whose behest the Son came to be sacrificed for sin (John 1:1, 18; 3:16; 17:1; Rom. 8:31-34; Col. 2:2; Phil. 2:5-11). Through His incarnation the Son declared the Father. Through the death and resurrection of the Son, the Father declared the boundless love, grace, and power of His Fatherhood. Therefore we pray, "Our Father, which art in heaven, hallowed be thy name" (cf. Matt. 6:8, 9; 7:21; 18:14; Luke 2:49; 23:34, 46; John 14:6; 16:16; 20:17; Col. 1:19; I John 1:3).

A word of warning on the doctrine of God and of the Father needs to be added. We must not suppose that the doctrine of the Trinity has been devised to solve the problem of creation—i.e., the problem of how to relate the infinite changeless God to the finite changing world—nor to solve the problem of revelation. The same applies to the Incarnation. Hence the Trinity is not merely an economic division of divine labor, nor do certain members of the Trinity simply bridge God's way to the world. The Trinity is the way God is essentially in Himself. The Trinity is immanent and eternal. Two viewpoints of which there are both ancient and modern examples err precisely at this point: they use the Trinity as a device to relate God, failing to see that God reveals Himself to be essentially triune and that all three persons are consubstantial to the Godhead.

First, the Christian doctrine is not derived from emanationist conceptions such as those of the ancient Gnostics and neo-Platonists, the former of whom related God to the world by sub-deities or aeons and the latter

·

of whom made the world out of the "overflow" of the divine being. Both these theories aimed at a logical unity behind what they considered the superficial multiplicity of experience. The Gnostic theories postulated intermediate divine beings to shield the ingenerate divine principle from the physical world, which they supposed to be evil because finite. The neo-Platonic schools concluded with three levels of existence: God, the world soul, and the physical universe. Thus, if the world is the way God is externalized, then one might speculate that the Father is God-in-relation-to-himself, and the Son is God-in-relation-to-creation. But the doctrine of creation denies that the world is the necessary expression of the being of God in space and time. The *creatio ex nihilo* declares that the world is the product of the will and act of God, that it is not derived from the being of God. Recent idealist approaches like the philosophy of E. S. Brightman reflect this same error. The views of Dr. Paul Tillich seem to reflect elements of the ancient neo-Platonic teaching in that God as Father is viewed as a relational name, as the ground of man's being, not as the revelation of a personal distinction in God (see his *Systematic Theology* [Chicago, 1951] I, 287-89).

Second, neither is the Trinity to be explained by modalistic monarchianism, which is an attempt to solve the problem of revelation. Deriving from the beginning of the third century through Noetus of Smyrna, Praxeas, and especially Sabellius, modalism declared that God is one in number, that the Father and the Son are one identical person. The Godhead is one individual monad, but the Father, Son, and Spirit express three operations of God, or are three modes of the divine activity. As Creator and Lawgiver, God is Father. As Redeemer, God is Son. As Inspirer and Bestower of grace, God is Spirit. Modalism, which was born of a legitimate passion to preserve the oneness of God and the deity of Christ, has persisted to the present time as the most active alternative to full trinitarian theology. It is small wonder that Tertullian made the famous jibe at Praxeas, "He drove out the Paraclete and crucified the Father" (Tertullian, *Adversus Praxeas,* I). Modalism cannot take adequate account of the personal distinctions that pervade the biblical teaching. The *prosopa* are not masks or modes but *hypostaseis.* They identify real personal distinctions in God; otherwise the complex pattern of Christian doctrines to which we alluded earlier is destroyed.

This debate is a live one today. Not a little contemporary theology is frankly modalistic, and much contemporary preaching and popular literature is implicitly modalistic by default, through fear of tritheism.[2]

---

[2] Dr. Leonard Hodgson, former Regius Professor of Divinity at the University of Oxford, has been openly critical of the theology of Karl Barth as modalistic (L. Hodgson, *The Doctrine of the Trinity,* 1955, p. 229; and "Trinitarian Theology: The Glory of the Eternal Trinity," CHRISTIANITY TODAY, May 25, 1962, p. 3). The dialogue extends to C. Welch, whom Professor Hodgson also charges with Sabellianism (L. Hodgson, *For Faith and Freedom,* 1957, II, 225-33; C. Welch, *The Trinity in Contemporary Theology,* 1953).

The key to the truth and the reply to both errors is the real incarnation of Jesus Christ. As a real historical event, the Incarnation sufficiently answers the Gnostic denigration of history and matter. As the real coming of the Son of God sent by the Father into space and time, it demands acknowledgment of the New Testament distinction between the Father and the Son. The early Christians were unable to deny either the unity of God or the Godhead of the Son, and neither can we (John 17:3).

2. *The Son is God.* Jesus Christ is the eternal second person of the holy Trinity who became incarnate at Bethlehem. Christian faith stands or falls with the truth that Jesus Christ is really God the Son and distinctly God the Son. Upon this the doctrine of the Trinity rests firmly. He is called God unambiguously by the New Testament writers (John 1:1, 18; 20:28; Col. 2:9; Titus 2:13; Heb. 1:8, 10).

First, the reality of Christ's divinity pervades all strata of New Testament teaching. It is impossible to understand the faith of the first Christians without the truth that they recognized Christ to be the Incarnate God. The titles of His deity especially harbor this deep-seated conviction of faith.

Christ is called the Son of God. Although this is used of His Sonship by incarnation (Luke 1:35; John 1:34; Rom. 1:4; Heb. 1:2), it is a mistake to limit the Sonship to the Incarnation, because the terms relate Him to the Father as His "own" Son in a special way (Matt. 11:27; John 5:18; Rom. 8:32). Especially in John, the terms "Father" and "Son" are correlatives, each being placed on the footing of eternity (John 1:1, 14, 18). Thus, God "sent" forth His Son (John 3:13; 17:5; I John 4:10). The term "Son of God" is certainly a title of deity, as was made clear when the Sanhedrin condemned Christ on the grounds of claims not to messiahship but to deity (Matt. 16:16; 26:63-65; Luke 22:70, 71; John 19:7; cf. John 8:58, 59; 10:32-38). The expression "only begotten Son" is to be understood in relation to Christ's pre-incarnate dignity and privilege (Rom. 8:29; Col. 1:15-18; Heb. 1:6) and in the special sense of "begotten from everlasting" or "begotten from eternity," i.e., from the being, not the will, of the Father. Therefore He is essentially one with the Father. This begetting is an eternal fact of the divine nature; otherwise, if there was a time when the Son was not the Son, then there was a time when the Father was not the Father.

Christ is called the Word of God. In the Prologue of John (1:1-18), the term *logos* is not explained but is simply used to declare the deity of Christ. "In the beginning was the Word" means that before creation the *logos* existed. The contrast between "was" and "became" in John (cf. 8:58; Ps. 90:2) clearly establishes the distinction between Abraham's finite "becoming" and Christ's eternal "being" (cf. John 6:20; 8:24, 28; 9:9; 18:6). Lacking the definite article, the construction of the phrase "the Word was God" marks "God" as the predicate, which means that the Word is identified with the being of God (cf. Rom. 9:5), or the essential nature of God. No other English translation will suffice save "and the

Word was God." (Greek does not have the indefinite article, but this anarthrous [used without the article] construction does not mean what the indefinite article "a" means in English. It is monstrous to translate the phrase "the Word was a God." For a perceptive discussion of this, see Victor Perry, "Jehovah's Witnesses and the Deity of Christ," *The Evangelical Quarterly,* Jan.-Mar., 1963.) These phrases state the eternal substance of the Word, and the eternal oneness of the Word with God. The phrase "and the Word became flesh" (John 1:14) identifies Christ with the Word. Thereby the mystery of the Incarnation is proclaimed and we are led on to the climactic utterance, "God no one has seen at any time; the only begotten, who is God, who dwells in the Father's bosom, this is he who revealed God" (John 1:18).

In numerous other ways our Lord is proclaimed to be true God. Old Testament titles are ascribed to Him that, in the light of strict Jewish monotheism, are inexplicable unless Christ is being identified with the nature of *Yahweh* (cf. Matt. 3:3 with Isa. 40:3; John 12:41 with Isa. 6:1; Acts 13:33 with Ps. 2:7; and Eph. 4:6-8 with Ps. 68:18). The works and attributes of God are ascribed to Christ (John 1:3, 4; 8:58; 14:6; Col. 1:17; Heb. 13:8; 7:26). He is honored and worshiped as God (John 20:28; 5:23; Acts 2:36; 7:59; Rom. 10:9; Phil. 2:10, 11; Rev. 5:12-14). His name is associated with the Father and the Spirit on equal terms in the baptismal formula (Matt. 28:19), in the benediction (II Cor. 13:14), and in the bestowal of eternal life (John 5:23; 14:1; 17:3). Finally, the whole biblical structure rests on the claim that redemption belongs to God alone (I Tim. 2:5; II Cor. 5:19). If Christ were not God, then regardless of how great a being He might be, there would really be no contact with God through Him. This is the heart of Athanasius' great argument against Arius: only God can redeem and reconcile.

Secondly, the foregoing data establish equally well the personal distinctness of the Son from the Father. This is precisely the meaning of the middle clause of John 1:1, "and the Word was with God." The thought is reiterated in verse 2. The sense is relational, and the divine nature of the subjects of the clauses conveys the sense that the relationship is eternal. Thus the emphatic "he" in verse 18 is consistent with the theological climax that this concluding verse registers: the Son from the bosom of the Father—specifically He alone—interprets or declares the Father. It is impossible to avoid the distinct interpersonal relationships of which this and other passages speak (cf. John 17:1-5, 18, 21; Acts 2:33; 3:13, 26; 9:20, 22; I John 5:20).

Unless the Son is viewed as distinctly personal, we fail to grasp the theology of the New Testament when it builds upon and freely assumes the reality of this distinction. The Son, not the Father, is made incarnate (I John 1:1-4). The Son, not the Father, suffered the Cross (Mark 14:36; 15:34; Rom. 5:8-11). The Father raised the Son from the dead (Acts 2:22-32). In His glorified state the Son ascended to the right hand of the Father (Acts 1:11; 2:33), where He acts as our great High Priest (Heb. 3:1; 6:20; 7:24, 25). The Son will return in power and glory to gather the Kingdom unto the Father's hands (Heb. 9:24-28; I Cor. 15: 24). The interpenetration of these doctrines in the whole that constitutes biblical teaching cannot be brushed aside. When one part is touched, the whole is affected. Thus, if our doctrine falls short of full trinitarian faith (cf. Rom. 15:30; I Pet. 1:2), we are left with the problem of reinterpreting, not only isolated concepts, but the entire body of theology.

Nevertheless, attempts to account for the language of the Son on other than a trinitarian basis have always comprised active, polemically minded alternatives. There are two of these: subordinationism and adoptionism. Both are attempts to account for Jesus Christ in view of the impassibility of God. In my judgment both fail, but both have their modern exponents. Subordinationism and adoptionism derive from attempts to preserve a concept of the unity of God that is supposed to be indispensable to faith. However, as noted earlier, we must start from the truth of the Incarnation rather than from a presupposition concerning the meaning of "one."

Subordinationism is represented chiefly in the ancient doctrine of Arius of Alexandria and in the heretical opinions of the Jehovah's Witnesses today, though any doctrine that reduces Christ to less than God is subordinationist. Virtually nothing has been added to the terms of this debate since Athanasius opposed Arius at Nicea in A.D. 325. The subtlety of Arius' opinion is that he threw the derivation of the Son back to the preincarnate state. Beginning with the premise of the mathematically single unoriginate divine being, Arius agreed that Christ existed before Bethlehem, that He was the agent of creation, and that as the foremost of created beings He should be worshiped. But, Arius said, Christ had a beginning. There was [a time] when the Son was not. Therefore Christ cannot be called God in the sense in which we apply this designation to the Supreme Being. He is like God *(homoiousios)* but not of one substance with the Father *(homoousios)*. Out of this distinction there sprang the famous Nicene Symbol, the first great formal doctrinal confession in defense of Christ's deity.

On the basis of a certain logic of terms, Arius' contention is consistent. If God is indivisible and not subject to change, then, on one reading of "begotten," whatever is begotten of God must derive from a creative act, not from the being of God. Hence it has a beginning of existence. Therefore, the Son is not co-eternal with the Father. Fastening upon the term "begotten," Arius said that because He is begotten He must have had a beginning; Athanasius countered that because Christ is begotten of the Father, He could not have had a beginning. To say that a father begets a child is one thing, but to say that the Father begat the Son is another. The one is temporal, the other eternal. The one is of the will, the other from the being of the Father; hence the Nicene Creed insisted that Christ is of the substance of the Father, thereby sacrificing neither the impassibility of God nor the deity of the Son. To say that the Son is begotten from the Father from eternity is not to divide the indivisible God but to accept the testimony of the apostles.

Adoptionism derives from a unitarian view of God as not only one being but also one person. (Adoptionism is of two types: adoptionist monarchianism, the attempt to preserve the *monarchia* or primacy of the one divine principle; and dynamic monarchianism, the view that Jesus *became* the Son of God as a Spirit-energized man after His baptism.) This doctrine has elements common to the Cerinthian aberration of the first century but was articulated clearly at the end of the second century by Theodotus at Rome, and later by Paul of Samosata. To them Jesus was a particularly virtuous Galilean but not God incarnate. Rather, He was chosen by God for a special mission and endowed with the Spirit at His baptism, or "adopted" as the Son of God. He did not pre-exist; nor is He essentially of the nature of God. Usually a sharp distinction was drawn between Jesus and the Christ, as is commonly done in contemporary existentialist theology.

Adoptionism is advocated today under the guise of the teaching that Jesus was a man of such goodness that God exalted Him to divine status. This view holds that Jesus is divine because He lived a perfect life, not that He lived a perfect life because He was true God and true man. Biblical Christianity makes the Incarnation dependent not upon the earthly choices of Jesus but upon the coming of the eternal Second Person of the Trinity into actual human existence.

3. The Holy Spirit is God. It is universally acknowledged by Christians that the Holy Spirit is God. There is no reluctance to see the activity of the Spirit as the activity of God, but some are reluctant to acknowledge the personal distinctness of the Spirit. To distinguish the Father and the Son but not the Spirit is to maintain in practice, if not in theory, a binitarian rather than a trinitarian conception of God.

There is a consensus that early uses of spirit in the Old Testament mean the active power, or invasive force, of God (cf. H. Wheeler Robinson, *The Christian Experience of the Holy Spirit* [London, 1930, p. 8]: "The primitive and fundamental idea of spirit [*ruach*] in the Old Testament is that of active power or energy [*energeia,* not *dynamis*], power superhuman, mysterious, elusive, of which the *ruach* or wind of the desert was not so much the symbol as the familiar example"). Crucial to this concept is the idea of energetic action, not immanence; of invasive, not pervasive, power. No one wishes to make the Spirit impersonal force; rather, the Spirit is the personal God acting, or the personal activity of God. We are left therefore with two levels of difficulty: namely, is the Spirit personal, and is the Spirit distinctly personal?

The fact remains that no Christian scholar is content to make of the Spirit simply divine invasive power. It is widely recognized that an idea other than the apparent controlling idea of the Old Testament must control interpretation of the New Testament data. The moral character and life-giving prerogatives of the Spirit demand definition couched in some form of personal language. The question is, Do the new controlling ideas that emerge in the course of revelation history compel thinking of the Spirit in more personal or fully personal terms?[3]

The Christological revelation of the New Testament and the new life in the body of Christ are such a significant advance over Old Testament thought that new revelational ideas that control the meaning of Spirit in the New Testament are commonly assumed to exist. (For example, Professor Eduard Schweizer says that the Lukan materials pass beyond the Matthean and Markan emphasis on the "man of the spirit" Christology to the "Lord of the Spirit" conception. In other words, Luke [including Acts] and presumably subsequent writers [including Paul] go beyond the conception of divine power possessing a man.) What are these, and how do they handle the data of the new covenant? We may consider the data in the following way:

Two strands of New Testament evidence are noteworthy. First, there are those passages where the personal pronoun is distinctly used of the Holy Spirit, i.e., the "he" passages (e.g., Mark 3:22-30; Luke 12:12; John 14:26; 15:26; 16:7-15; Acts 8:29; 10:19, 20; 13:2; 15:28; 16:6, 7; 20:28; Rom. 5:5). Second, there are other passages, i.e., the "it" passages, that may allow of a personal reading but do not demand it (e.g., Matt. 1:18; 4:1; 12:28; Luke 1:15; John 7:39b; Acts 1:8; Rom. 8:26, 27).

After carefully considering the data, one must conclude that reluctance to assign full personhood to the Spirit is unwarranted. The main current of New Testament interpretation is in the line of the "he" passages. These compel us to think equally of the Spirit as God with the Father and Son. One can account for the "it" passages in terms of the "he" passages, but it is simply impossible to account for the "he" passages in terms of the "it" passages. Otherwise, language fails of sense, for, as in the Johannine texts on the Spirit, we are left without meaningful denotation of terms if we impersonalize the pronouns referring to the Spirit but retain the pronouns referring to the Father and to ourselves as personal. There are other kinds of spirits also referred to that cannot be accounted for on an impersonal reading (cf. Matt. 8:16, 29; John 4:24;

---

[3] The fact that the Greek noun for Spirit (*pneuma*) is neuter need have little bearing on this, no more than, let us say, the fact that the German word for young lady (*das Mädchen*) is neuter should cause us to think that a young lady is not of the female sex. I must dissent from the view of Professor Eduard Schweizer (*Theologisches Wörterbuch Zum Neuen Testament*, VI, 432), who says that the question of how far the Spirit is personal may be a false one because the word "personal" does not exist in either Greek or Hebrew. Neither do such words as "monotheism," "existential," and "confrontation," occur, but this does not prevent our asking whether what these terms denote is in Scripture. Are we to suppose that Abraham and Moses were not persons, and did not think of themselves as persons? The question is, What evidence compels us to conclude full personhood in any given case, or prevents us from doing so? Professor Schweizer himself is reluctant to understand Spirit as impersonal power but rather understands the Spirit as the way the personal Lord is present in His Church.

Heb. 1:14; 12:23). In the light of the evidence, the real question seems to be the Spirit's distinctness, not His personhood.

Even if we should reduce the Spirit to the indwelling Christ in the New Testament, the problem of persons in the Godhead is not relieved (saved by Christological subordinationism or adoptionism) unless we move from a trinitarian to a binitarian formula. This is logically no less severe. While the risen Christ is not sharply distinguished in the New Testament, He is not identified with the Spirit. The New Testament never says that Christ is the Spirit of God; and if the distinction between Christ and the Spirit is made before the resurrection, why not maintain it after the resurrection?[4]

It is very difficult to know what to do with the personal language of the New Testament unless the Spirit is personally distinct. Not only in formulas such as that used at the baptism of Jesus, the benedictions, the salutations, and the baptismal symbol is the Spirit put on an equal footing with the Father and the Son, but numerous trinitarian passages join His work to the one work of the Godhead (I Cor. 12:4-6; Eph. 1:3-5, 6-12, 13; 4:4-6; I Peter 1:2, 3). In particular, our Lord clearly indicates that He will send the Spirit from the Father (John 15:26) and that the Spirit will not attest Himself but Christ (16:13). A further point of some importance is the parallel established theologically between Christ's relation to the Spirit and our own.

TRINITY IN UNITY

In the light of the foregoing data, it should be clear that for Christians the incarnation of the Son at Bethlehem and the descent of the Spirit at Pentecost compel radical revision of unipersonal monotheistic belief. God is not a person; there are persons in God. The immanent, eternal Trinity, known by divine self-disclosure, means that God is not the lonely God whose world becomes the logical "over-against-himself" to make Him personal. Nor does the Trinity suggest that God is "coming-to-be" in the world through the modalities of Son and Spirit. The eternal Son and Spirit are God. They have their reality on the other side of the gulf that

---

[4] The only doubtful exception is Second Corinthians 3:17, where the term "Lord" has been understood in both extremes, as Christ and as the Holy Spirit. The sense of the passage is probably the "spirit of freedom" as against the "spirit of bondage" of Judaism (cf. Alan Richardson, *New Testament Theology*, 1958, pp. 105, 120; and A. Plummer, *Second Corinthians* in the *International Critical Commentary*, 1948, p. 103). If, as Professor Schweizer says (*op. cit.*, pp. 402, 403), the Lukan conception is crucial to New Testament theology, then the remark by Alan Richardson that among the gospel records Luke alone itemizes and dates the resurrection and ascension of Christ and the coming of the Spirit as separate historical events, assumes distinct significance. Lionel Thornton states the truth of the matter: "Both Christ and the Spirit dwell in the Christian soul, but not in the same way. Christ is the indwelling content of the Christian life. . . . The Spirit is the quickening cause; and the indwelling of Christ is the effect of the quickening" (*The Incarnate Lord*, 1938, p. 322).

separates the infinite being of God from the finite world. The triune God is infinite, changeless, eternal, the glorious Creator, Sustainer, and Redeemer, who has full resources within Himself for the perfection of His inner life.

Nevertheless, the early Christians affirmed faith in the Son of God on the basis of unflinching monotheism. We cannot grasp the theology of the Gospel unless we see that New Testament Christians believed in both the eternality of the Son and the unity of God. The theological struggles from the second to the fourth centuries are best understood as attempts to articulate this faith in the face of the difficulty of utilizing terms and categories unsuited to the inner realities of the Gospel. It is false, therefore, to say that the simplicities of early Judean faith in Jesus were corrupted by alien Greek metaphysical speculation. Rather, through the Christian Gospel that proclaimed the self-revelation of God there was injected into the intellectual climate of the time evidence about the nature of God that the existing categories could not assimilate. The Church was compelled to decide whether to jettison the evidence or to revise the categories. Christians chose to do the latter. The choice we confront is very much the same.

We must think of unity in terms of persons and interpersonal relations, rather than in terms of a certain kind of logical abstraction. (An excellent discussion of this point which has influenced my thinking is that of Leonard Hodgson, *The Doctrine of the Trinity,* London, 1955, pp. 89-96, 104, 105, 183.) There is more than one way of speaking about unity; more, that is, than the undifferentiated abstraction "one," or the absence of multiplicity. There are inclusive as against exclusive conceptions of unity, such as the unity of personal life in the complexity of being a thinking, feeling, and acting creature; the unity of husband and wife; the unity of the Church; the unity of Christ and the Church; and the unity of the Godhead.

Further, the question is greater than simply exclusive or inclusive, or simple or complex conceptions of unity. We must ask also whether analogies that are personal or impersonal, dynamic or static, living being or abstraction are more suited to the case in point. The revelation of God as living and acting is something other than a conclusion derived by subtracting away elements of multiplicity (i.e., the *via negationis*).

Professor Hodgson's point therefore is a good one. That internal complexity is a sign of imperfect unity could be said only if all approximations to unity were to be measured by a scale of degrees of absence of internal multiplicity. But this is not so, if the degree of unity achieved is to be measured instead in proportion to the intensity of the unifying power in the life of the whole.

Even a monadic conception of God must cope with the problem of the duality of thought and thinker. If God is revealed as tripersonal, then it may be best to think that the unity of the Godhead is more intense than any finite unity known to us. In human personality, the degree of normality achieved depends upon how intense the unification of the elements of personality is. In God, the revealed elements unified are each fully personal. The fact is that so far as we know, no one can be personal in isolation; God is revealed not as the lonely God but as tripersonal.

Should we fall back upon a conception of unity that is undifferentiated, the problem remains that we have no actual experience of such a thing. At least it is doubtful that we do, and I can think of no instance of such a thing's existing. Such abstract unities cannot approximate the internal complexity of living beings. The higher up we go on the scale of living beings, the more complex they are, and the more intense must be the power of their inner unification.

From personal experience we know what inclusive types of unity are. In Scripture the comparisons between the divine life and human life, especially in the body of the Church, suggest that more than mere analogy is involved. We believe that the essential realities of divine and human life are revealed by God in terms of the complex unity of persons in interpersonal relations.

TRINITARIAN FAITH

By accepting at face value the evidence that demands thinking of the full personhood of Father, Son, and Holy Spirit, we can give a rational, though partial, account of the personal God. As indicated earlier, the doctrine of the *creatio ex nihilo* tells us not only that the world had a beginning by the will of God but also that the world is of such and such a kind. This means that God's personhood is self-sufficient in the perfection of His inner life. The relations of the Trinity are inscrutable to us, but the doctrine that God is love and the doctrine of the *creatio ex nihilo* are fully consistent with the doctrine that God is triune. In God there is the mutuality of perfect communion. What is love to an unipersonal being? The doctrine of the Trinity is therefore the high point of revelation about the nature of God. It declares that no matter how vast or how important the universe is, none of it is necessary to the perfection of the inner life of God.

The completeness of revelation in the doctrine that God is triune leads us to say that tripersonal monotheism is more intelligible than unipersonal monotheism. When we see that in the Incarnation the eternal second person of the Trinity actually became man, then we arrive at an apprehension of the essential nature of God. Christians cannot avoid the primacy of Christological interpretation for the whole range of their theological ideas.

Because of faith in the finality of the Christological revelation, Christians affirm with confidence that God is not seven or twelve or fifty-one but triune. That God is triune rests not upon inherent natural trinities in logic or nature but upon the faith that God has fully revealed Himself in Jesus Christ and the descent of the Spirit. When we share this life in the Father by the Son and through the Holy Spirit, we are convinced that the biblical revelation is terminal and complete.

Thereby also we perceive the significance of the truths that God sent

His Son to the Cross and that God was in Christ reconciling the world to Himself. As the author of redemption, God is not only the object of sacrifice but also the subject of sacrifice.

Finally, the distinctness of tripersonal life in God is fully consistent with the doctrine of the resurrection and eternal life for the individual. Contrary to views that reject the continuance of discrete personal life, Christian belief in the future life as perfect, personal, and distinct rests on the doctrine that it will be essentially of persons in interpersonal relations.

TRINITARIAN LIFE

Christians should enter more fully into the significance of the Trinity as a way of life and not only as a theological dogma. The foregoing data should encourage us to do so without hesitation. Historically, trinitarian theology simply attempted to express the new way of trinitarian religion that the New Testament Christians knew in Christ. The doctrine is not metaphysical obscurity hung on a skyhook. It declares God to be more than numinous mystique.

Trinitarian worship enriches Christian experience. We are helped best if we grasp the biblical truth of the unity of interpersonal relations that characterizes not only the life of Father, Son, and Holy Spirit but also our lives in God and in one another. The crucial passage, rarely seen in this light, is John 17. In fact, the entire Gospel can be subtitled "the Gospel of the Trinity." If we wish to discover the biblical definition of unity, then it stands in the significance of these words,

> I do not pray for these only, but also for those who are to believe in me through their word, that they may all be one; even as thou, Father, art in me, and I in thee, that they also may be in us, so that the world may believe that thou hast sent me. The glory which thou hast given me I have given to them, that they may be one even as we are one, I in them and thou in me, that they may become perfectly one, so that the world may know that thou hast sent me and hast loved them even as thou hast loved me (John 17:20-23, RSV).

"I in thee," "thou in me," "that they may be one in us"—these phrases indicate integrity of discrete personal life and unity of interpersonal life. Love is the bond of perfect union (Col. 3:14) that joins us to God in the redeeming work of Father, Son, and Holy Spirit (Eph. 4:2-6).

The perfection of our Lord's humanity is the revelatory historical instance of this. In Scripture His life is the parallel to our lives. One may note passages like Romans 8:4-11, and especially verse 11, for this truth. While the phrases "Spirit of Christ" and "Spirit of God" are used interchangeably, this is done in a special sense. As Jesus received the Spirit, so we receive the Spirit from Jesus. As the Spirit who came upon the Messiah was God's Spirit, so the Spirit who indwells us is God's Spirit. We are partakers of His humanity as members of a new race and body by the same Spirit.

Paul says that the Father who raised up Jesus from the dead quickens us also because the Spirit who quickens us is the Spirit of Him who raised up Jesus Christ from the dead. Our God is the Lord of life and death, of time and eternity, of past, present, and future. What He did for Christ He will do for us because we share the same indwelling Spirit. By this Spirit we are made partakers of Christ and joint heirs with Christ. By this same Spirit we cry, "Abba, Father" (Rom. 8:14-17) and look to the day of glory when we shall know as we are known, giving praise that is justly due to Father, Son, and Holy Spirit, one God, blessed forever.

A SELECT BIBLIOGRAPHY

3. THE TRIUNE GOD

Athanasius, *The Incarnation of the Word of God.* New York: Macmillan, 1946.

Augustine, *On the Holy Trinity,* in Volume III of "The Nicene and Post-Nicene Fathers," Series I. Grand Rapids, Mich.: Eerdmans, 1956.

D. M. Baillie, *God Was in Christ.* London: Faber and Faber, 1948.

H. Bavinck, *The Doctrine of God.* Grand Rapids, Mich.: Eerdmans, 1951.

H. Bettenson, *Documents of the Christian Church.* Oxford: University Press, 1946.

John Calvin, *Institutes of the Christian Religion.* London: James Clarke, 1949.

Gregory of Nyssa, *On "Not Three Gods,"* in Volume V of "The Nicene and Post-Nicene Fathers," Series II. Grand Rapids, Mich.: Eerdmans, 1952-54.

L. Hodgson, *The Doctrine of the Trinity.* London: Nisbet, 1955.

J. N. D. Kelly, *Early Christian Doctrines.* New York: Harper and Brothers, 1958.

G. A. F. Knight, *A Biblical Approach to the Doctrine of the Trinity.* Edinburgh: Oliver and Boyd, 1957

A. H. Strong, *Systematic Theology.* Philadelphia: Judson Press, 1947.

C. Welch, *The Trinity in Contemporary Thought.* London: SCM Press, 1953.

THE CREATION OF MATTER, LIFE, AND MAN

Addison H. Leitch

Addison H. Leitch is professor of theology, Gordon Divinity School, Wexham, Massachusetts. He holds the degrees of B.A. (Muskingum College), B.D. and Th.M. (Pittsburgh-Xenia Seminary), and Ph.D. Cantab. (Cambridge University, England). His honorary degrees are D.D. (Muskingum College) and D.D. and Litt.D. (Grove City College). Before the merger of the Presbyterian U.S.A. and United Presbyterian churches, Dr. Leitch was president of Pittsburgh-Xenia Theological Seminary; after the merger he served as professor of systematic theology at Pittsburgh Seminary. His other posts include teaching at Assuit (Egypt) College, Pikeville (Kentucky) College, and Grove City (Pennsylvania) College, where he was dean of men and college pastor. He has written Meet Dr. Luke, Beginnings in Theology, Interpreting Basic Theology *and* Winds of Doctrine.

4. *Addison H. Leitch*

THE CREATION OF
MATTER, LIFE, AND MAN

FOR ABOUT a century the lines of debate have been drawn between the Darwinian theory, with its variants and outcomes, and the different kinds of creationism. And from time to time thought has been given to how these two positions interlock or overlap.

A complete acceptance of evolution pushes toward a mechanistic interpretation of the universe, and so of mankind. Creationism, on the other hand, demands the introduction of the supernatural (that which is beyond nature); this is abhorrent to anyone who accepts only scientific data.

The scientists, as scientists, must work out processes and cannot allow the confusion of any *deus ex machina*. It is unfair, they feel, to bring God in from the wings of the stage whenever He seems needed. Conversely, the creationist is protecting the idea of an eternal God who works in eternity as well as in time, who is personal and who deals with men personally, and who is not therefore only the "I am" but also the God of Abraham, Isaac, and Jacob. The scientists while practicing science cannot utilize purpose or design, while the religionists cannot escape it.

Darwinian evolution insists that what has now come to pass in life on the earth is the result of processes that grew out of the nature of things themselves. (In *The Origin of Species,* however, Darwin allowed for God as creator of the first living forms or form.) The word "evolution" demands that what now appears is already in the systems of potential out of which it evolves. Nothing else is demanded; anything more than this leads to confusion.

Darwin saw the process basically as one of "natural selection" resulting in "survival of the fittest." He meant by this that certain variations happen to appear in individuals of a species, and that some variations persist and others do not. Those variations that persist do so because they fit the individuals of the species for survival over against other individuals, or over against the environment. (Modern evolutionists emphasize, however, that the carriers of the variations may have outbred and hence outnumbered the ancestral types.) Shifts in environment, such as the coming and going of the Ice Age, meant the survival of some species that were fitted for survival and the elimination of others that were unfitted.

The data Darwin profferred and the evolutionary theory to which they led him demanded that the existence of the earth itself and some form of life on the earth be postulated. But the mind of man, naturally wedded to the cause-and-effect relationship, had to ask questions not only about our planet and its possibilities of life but also about how the planet arrived here in the first place.

This longer perspective shifted thinking to chemistry and then to astronomy. A considerable body of data in both chemistry and astronomy led to numerous speculations; for the scientist in this century cannot of course, examine scientifically what is supposed to have happened, by his own speculation, billions of years ago.

In general, scientists in our day hold two main views of the beginnings of what we know as our earth. One view is called the superdense-state theory and the other is called the steady-state theory. (For a helpful discussion of these, see George K. Schweitzer's contribution to *Evolution and Christian Thought Today,* edited by Russell L. Mixter [Grand Rapids, Michigan: William B. Eerdmans Publishing Company, 1959], pp. 42 ff.)

The superdense-state theory holds that six billion years ago, all the matter and energy of the universe was gathered together in one mass with extremely high temperature. At some point in time this mass exploded (and there are astronomical reasons for holding that at present we are inhabiting an expanding universe). As the explosion continued, there was a cooling process, which meant that the various masses that had blown off from the center core began to shrink. Thus they became more dense. This increased the speed of their whirling motion. And this increase in speed led to a flying-off again of certain of their parts, because of centrifugal force, until equilibrium was set up between the forces driving away and gravity pulling together. The universe as we now know it is the result of that equilibrium. Astronomers believe that some of the same process is still going on.

Over against this superdense-state theory is the steady-state theory. Astronomers who hold this theory maintain that the limits of our observation of the universe reach out three billion light years. They hold that clusters of galaxies are constantly crossing this observational barrier, and thus an area is lost to sight. Meanwhile creation is going on inside the observable area. According to George K. Schweitzer's summary of the theory in the volume previously mentioned:

> The Steady State Theory says that hydrogen atmospheres are being created out in space at the rate of one atom per year in the volume about

the size of a skyscraper. This amounts to about 1,000,000,000,000,000,-000,000,000,000,000 tons per second in the observable universe. As this matter is created, it begins to form clouds; these then condense into planets, stars, galaxies, and galaxial clusters. The clusters recede from all other clusters and finally pass beyond the limit of observation. Thus while clusters of galaxies are continually reaching the horizon of observation, other clusters are being created within the observable unit and starting to recede toward the horizon. It is said that this process has been going on for an infinite time. This means that the picture of the universe is the same regardless of when one observes it. . . . Hence, the name of Steady State Theory is applied to this idea (pp. 43, 44).

Now it is highly significant that Fred Hoyle, who has been the leading proponent of the steady-state theory, recently abandoned it (see *Christianity Today,* December 3, 1965, p. 31). Apparently the superdense theory has more to be said for it and less against it than the steady-state.

Whether we accept the superdense or the steady-state theory, it is time to "come back to earth." In biblical language, "the earth was without form, and void." In either theory we have our own planet cooling off and shrinking. There were tremendous upheavals and crackings on the surface of the earth and great clouds of steam surrounding the earth. This steam eventually cooled and condensed. The waters of condensation then filled the seas. Equilibrium was set up between the clouds and their condensing, and atmosphere reached its balance. Finally, with time, the surface of the earth eroded sufficiently to give us topsoil that could sustain life. The same process is still reflected in earthquakes and volcanic action, and the core of the earth is apparently a molten mass.

According to evolution, out of the primordial ooze and over millions of centuries, there came the union of elements that made a complex molecule which could reproduce itself and be called alive. The odds against this happening by chance, if it had to happen all at once, have been estimated as something of the order of 10 to the 72nd power. Hence scientists now assume the process was a gradual increase in complexity from gases and water to amino acids and proteins (necessary to life) that require proper temperature and pressure to persist.

Since an evolutionist can talk in terms of billions of years, the question of time is irrelevant; but our minds naturally hesitate to picture this kind of unguided process. It is amazing that some scientists think a Christian is gullible to believe in God but do not think themselves gullible for believing in this kind of accident. They hold to the objectivity of what they would like to call proof and criticize the Christian because he is only a "believer" who openly confesses that his faith turns not on what he has seen but on what he is told on higher authority. Yet there is scarcely any difference in the amount of belief necessary to accept either one or the other of these views.

Evolutionists tell us that with the appearance of the first living cells, where no clear distinction existed between plant and animal (such as among the bacteria), natural selection began to work. In time plant life became distinguishable as the possessor of chlorophyll and animals as freely moving types without chlorophyll. Plants continued to diversify until the major groups of algae, mosses, ferns, evergreens, and flowering plants eventually appeared.

If we move along the other life line, we move through the stages of two-layered animals (now represented by jellyfish) and three-layered animals (such as flatworms and primitive echinoderms like starfish) to the first animals with skeletal supports in their backs instead of undersides. These are presumed to have evolved into fish, followed by amphibians and reptiles. The reptiles are considered ancestral to both mammals and birds. The first mammals had descendants as varied as kangaroos, shrews, rodents, carnivores, and ultimately apes and men. All of this occurred because species are altered by changes in their hereditary makeup.

We still have the question of how hereditary differences arose within the plants or the animals. These hereditary changes, called mutations, had to happen in the genes. From what we can understand of DNA, which is the essential nucleic acid of the genes, an alteration in sequence of its bases will cause a mutation. The bases are adenine (A), cytosine (C), guanine (G), and thymine (T). If the sequence of bases in a gene is ATC and A is replaced by T, a mutation occurs.

If one grants that some mutations are beneficial, one can imagine natural selection increasing the offspring of the owners of the good genes. And eventually, as enough mutations accumulate, a species will be sufficiently altered to be considered a different species from its ancestors.

A pressing question, however, is how a mutation has any survival value unless it produces a major change. Take, for example, the structure of the wax in a beehive. This structure is amazingly strong and space-saving, so much so that we cannot think of a better storage structure. But if this structure is the end product of a series of minute steps or mutations leading eventually to this perfection, what was the advantage or survival value of the first minute move in this direction?

THE 'EVIDENCE' FOR EVOLUTION

Phillip Wheelwright of the University of California, in his good introduction to philosophy entitled *The Way of Philosophy* (New York: The Odyssey Press, 1954, 1960), refers to "the *hypothesis* of evolution" (p. 158). At the outset of his discussion, he declares, "It may be said without fear of serious rebuttal that the hypothesis in this limited form has been established beyond reasonable doubt." (By "this limited form" he means what he has set forth in a previous discussion of empirical evidence.) He raises serious questions, however, about the "how" of the process and about the further question of "how life originated."

Then he turns to what he calls "the evidence for evolution" but makes the very careful statement that "of the several kinds of evidence adduced in the support of the hypothesis not a single one would be accepted by all investigators as conclusive. Taken collectively, however, the evidential value accumulates." He cites six areas of evidence:

1. *From fossil remains.* Wheelwright says "this argument strongly suggests . . . ." but that is as far as he will go. We must remind ourselves that the fossil record is incomplete. Because there are large deficiencies in the record—that is, many missing links—clearly fossils cannot be said to show gradual transitions from a few early living organisms into all the varied forms now in existence. For example, there are no fossils bridging the considerable anatomical gap between four-footed beasts and bipedal man.

2. *From geographical distribution.* Some land masses now separated by water are thought to have once been continuous stretches. They are also thought to have had a common flora and fauna, although since the separation of continents different kinds of animals and plants have appeared. However, such differences indicate only a limited amount of change from common ancestors and not total evolution. Again Wheelwright is cautious. He says that the observable phenomena are "supposed to be" the "result of an ancient common ancestry."

3. *From comparative anatomy.* It takes only common observation to see likenesses in the anatomy of widely diversified individuals and species, such as the relationship of nail, hoof, and claw, or of scales and feathers. The likenesses are assumed to have resulted from common ancestry. This is a strong argument for evolution until we raise a very simple question. Does likeness necessarily imply relationship? Consider an analogy. A ship, a bridge, and an office building may all contain steel girders. Yet this does not prove that they have any relationship, except in the creative mind of an architect who needs a certain structure for a certain function. They are "related" only in a common creative mind. To quote Wheelwright on anatomical likenesses: "They may be considered as strengthening the evolutionary hypothesis when it has been set up, but they do not necessarily suggest it by themselves."

4. *From embryology.* In embryology there is growth from the single fertilized cell to the fully formed individual ready for birth. The embryos of many animals, including man, are indistinguishable from one another at early stages. It was formerly alleged that the human embryo passes through all the stages mankind must have passed through in evolution. But actually the human embryo merely resembles the embryos of other animals. It is never like a mature fish, but in an early stage it resembles a fish embryo. Wheelwright put it in these words, "It supports that hypothesis if the additional assumption is made that an organism in embryo tends to recapitulate the main states through which its ancestors have passed. . . ." Notice: ". . . if the additional assumption is made."

5. *From vestigial remains.* Here one observes certain parts of the anatomy of man (the appendix, for example) that appear to be reduced from a former larger structure and whose function may not be known. These can be observed also in many other members of the animal kingdom. But the question may be raised whether these so-called vestigial

remains are actual "overhangs" from some creational past or whether they are simply parts of the organism for which no use is now understood. Tonsils have been coming into their own recently as being more useful in than out, because their cells produce antibodies (see *Life,* Feb. 18, 1966). The appendix also is packed with these same antibody-forming cells. Wheelwright says that the presence of these vestigial remains is understandable "if they can be supposed to have served a useful function in some ancestral animal of a different type." But one may say that, if they are really vestigial, they are merely vestiges of one's own former better anatomy and not a hangover from a different species.

6. *From artificial breeding.* Dogs are evidence of what man was able to do in domesticating the wolf. Luther Burbank introduced improved varieties of plant life. Some argue therefore, that what we do now may well have happened in eons past. Two things, however, must be kept in mind. First, these things happen now because of the purpose of a creative mind. Second, those things that are creatively improved go back to parental type when the creative mind is no longer applied to them; their natural tendency seems to be "devolution" rather than evolution. (It would be interesting to analyze how many of the arguments for evolution might apply equally to "devolution." Perhaps the higher levels of animals are like us because of man's disintegration, for example, rather than because of the animal's progress. Turn 1,000 men loose on a desert island and watch them slide away from control; then turn one woman loose on that island and see whether civilization is something that "happens" or something that is maintained because of ideals that do not "arrive" by natural selection but are fed in from some other source.)

Here are the words of Wheelwright again: "How much does this evidence present? It is a useful intellectual discipline to examine each separate time of evidence by itself and reflect how far it would suggest and logically support the hypothesis of evolution to a person who had no other ground for believing in it." The argument is *cumulative* and *evidential.* The question remains whether a series of doubts can give us a firm assurance. All Wheelwright in his argument is willing to say is this: "The hypothesis of evolution has been proved not by absolute finality but as immeasurably more probable than any competing explanation that has been offered." On the grounds of the epistemology that science demands, will this kind of thinking be accepted as proof?

(The writer has leaned heavily on Wheelwright, not because he is the only source for this kind of argument, but because he illustrates so clearly how the argument moves and has the added virtue of being a careful thinker. He makes no conclusions about creationism or God or values. He is a trained philosopher engaged in the philosophy of science.)

Here are some words from John Oman, an extremely liberal philosopher and theologian:

> But I knew at the time of writing of no biologist who had given serious
> thought to the problems of his science whose views were not regarded by

most biologists as heresies. . . . Mr. Woodger says (J. H. Woodger, *Biologist Principles,* 1929) that in comparison with physics the principles of biology are still in the middle ages and that we have at this moment no theory of evolution . . . . a main criticism is the persistent question: what is really proved? Many years ago, after I had read several books on reproduction, I went to Professor Alexander Macalester and asked him if he could tell me what is fact and what theory, or in other words, what does one see in a germ with a powerful microscope. "A great deal," was the reply, "but mostly with the eye of one's theory." Most observers affirm this suspicion about almost all biology . . . (John Oman, *The Natural and the Supernatural,* Cambridge, England: Cambridge University Press, 1931, p. 480).

THE BIBLICAL VIEW

Turning now from a consideration of the evolutionary interpretation of beginnings and processes, we must clarify our approach before taking the biblical and Christian view of things. In so brief a treatment as this, we shall have to pass over without discussion the idea of the eternity of pantheism. While these create their own problems in philosophy and comparative religion, the real area of agreement or disagreement lies necessarily between the evolutionary hypothesis and the biblical record.

Christian apologetic can have several starting places. Yet at some time or other, authority rests in the words of Christ and with the analysis and synthesis of the New Testament writers, especially Paul. In our day, with the prevalence of modernistic and existential theology, we must take a clear position on the authority of Scripture and particularly the "words" of the New Testament.

Moreover, we must turn aside from any argument on demythologizing and assume for the purposes of our discussion that we may trust the New Testament and, on the basis of what it says, the Old Testament also. There are other lines of evidence supporting the genuineness and authenticity of the Bible record, but for a Christian the line generally runs through the authority of the New Testament to the Old. Thus any problem that arises between evolution and the Bible can best be faced when the Bible is accepted as authority. And one would conclude that for anyone who does not accept the Bible, the problem is mitigated or eliminated.

It is important to notice, also, that even a "Bible-believing" Christian is left with questions of interpretation. These questions may find differing answers among those who accept the authority of Scripture.

There are in Scripture very many unsolved problems regarding the creation of matter, life, and man. The writer to the Hebrews gives a clear word on beginnings: "Through faith we understand that the worlds were framed by the word of God, so that things which are seen were not made of things which do appear" (Heb. 11:3). This is creation *ex nihilo.* But once we admit that creation is "out of nothing," we have accepted an area of discussion that cannot in the very nature of things be discussed, although some would dispute this. The Hebrew *bara* used in the first chapter of Genesis also sustains the weight of this same idea—

namely, "creation out of nothing." However, when we move from the world as now observed and understood to creation by divine fiat, we have moved into an area where nothing we know gives us any analogy or parallel from which to work.

To put it in other words, we are moving from time into eternity. And what we know outside time and before the creation of matter has to be known by faith. By definition metaphysics is beyond physics. This presents some real difficulties, because to argue in the area of physics requires an approach somewhat different from that used in metaphysical argument. To this extent, the scientist as scientist and the religionist as religionist do not meet on the same ground. To test this out, consider what must be done with the statement in Hebrews, "the worlds were framed by the word of God," in order to give a scientist a scientific ground for the beginnings of things.

Yet at the same time we must point out that the scientist, as scientist, is nevertheless actually beginning with assumptions. He *has* to assume all sorts of things to make a start. However, he dismisses this as being outside the realm of science. And it is quite all right for him to do this, so long as he knows what his assumptions are and is not overly critical of the religionist, who also makes his assumptions.

At the very opening of the first chapter of Genesis, there is a line that in the Hebrew says literally, "In the beginning he created, God did." By that sentence we move from eternity into time and from Spirit into matter. As we move on through this chapter, certain problems in interpretation appear. Among the problem areas are these:

1. How much time can be postulated between verses one and two? The first verse tells us that "God created the heaven and the earth." Then verse two moves to a discussion of the earth. Some hold that this creation of heaven and earth could have taken the billions of years scientists require.

2. The acts of creation are listed according to "days." There are still those who would argue for a twenty-four-hour day, because, as they see it, if God can create at all, He can create with immediacy as well as by processes. But if He can, one may ask why He needed twenty-four hours. Furthermore, it would be easy for an Eskimo to argue for a six-month day instead of a twenty-four-hour day. Other passages of Scripture tell us that "a day in God's sight is as a thousand years," or a "day" may be defined as an "age."

If we aim to stick with the Scriptures, however, the text itself gives us our definition (verse 5): "And God called the light Day and the darkness he called Night." The Genesis definition of day is simply light as against darkness. Astronomers assure us that our own planet is as light as day, if observed from the right point in space. Obviously, our normal use of the word "day" will not fit here, because the heavenly bodies by which we measure day and night do not appear in the Genesis account until the fourth "day." Thus whatever the word "day" means, it does not mean a division of time governed by the heavenly bodies.

3. What do we mean by light? Surely it must mean "cosmic light," light in itself, not the bodies by which light is made known to our light-receiving organs, the eyes. Here again "lights" that appeared in the firmament *had* this light. They did not give it or create it.

4. What do we mean by firmament? At the time this is being written, those who have ventured farthest into space and those marvelous pieces of equipment by which we have been able to observe things in space have told us virtually nothing about life on the moon or on Mars, although we are reasonably certain that there is life in neither place. Life as we know it seems to be possible only because of the precarious arrangement of our air mixture and our air pressure—what we call the atmosphere. That our atmosphere is a wonder in itself will become increasingly evident as we learn more of other planets. The insight of the revelation whereby this very early Genesis record speaks of the "firmament" deserves our most profound pondering.

5. Is there any support for process as well as creation in the Genesis record? Consider such phrases as these: "Let the earth bring forth grass" (v. 11); "Let the waters bring forth abundantly" (v. 20); "Let the earth bring forth the living creature" (v. 24). When one adds to these the repetition of the phrase "after its kind," the door seems to be open for process as well as creation. And when such details as these are identified in the chapter, the Bible-believing Christian ought to have an open mind regarding at least two things: (a) the process of evolution may have something to tell us; and (b) questions that still plague us are of the same order of difficulty as those that plague the scientist as he attempts to control his information by way of a strict scientific method.

One other interesting fact emerges from this chapter. It is the quite remarkable parallel between the creation account in Genesis and the evolutionary account. Take, for example, what happens on each creation day: (1) light; (2) separation of the heavens and the earth, with the firmament (atmosphere?) between; (3) land and sea separated and the appearance of plant life; (4) the heavenly bodies; (5) fish and fowl; (6) animals and man. Observe that in the Genesis account man appears in the same creation "day" with animals.

Now read the list backwards and follow the probing of the evolutionists back toward their beginnings: man, animals, fowl, fish, plants, land and sea, heaven and earth, the nebular mass in white heat. While this is not the kind of parallel listing that can be pressed at every point, the order of events is too close to be coincidental. The only awkwardness lies in the appearance of the sun and the moon and the stars on the fourth "day," and Albertus Pieters in his *Notes on Genesis* has suggested that this is understandable if the viewpoint of the writer is that of one standing on the earth. (The intention here is not to press this matter but merely to point out its suggestiveness.)

The parallels between the Genesis account and the evolutionary account may give some Bible-believing Christians a sense of support in what the scentists have found; and those whose sympathies are with the scientists may well take some satisfaction in discovering how closely the scientific account touches that of Holy Writ. In any case, in the constant flux of both scientific discovery and biblical interpretation today, these two parallel accounts appear to indicate that Genesis and science are closer together than is generally believed.

If we look at the whole picture now from the standpoint of the evolutionist, and if we remember what we said earlier about humility in these matters, it would seem that science in this decade of the twentieth century ought to make such allowances as these:

1. Science is unable to say anything definitive about beginnings.

2. The facts available are used by many to support evolution but can be construed to imply creation of basic types and variations since creation. The facts are quite incomplete. Indeed in many areas they are amazingly incomplete, when one considers the wide acceptance of evolution. Much in the evolutionist's position is speculative, and speculation is not proof.

3. There is about man some kind of a transcendence that objective science has so far been unable to explain or explain away. In the case of man, something beyond the natural order seems to be at work, something that is subjective rather than objective.

4. The evolutionary scientist has actually established a philosophical position. So long as he is working with a hypothesis and not a body of conclusive evidence, he must also see that he is projecting this philosophical position in such a way as to answer further questions. It is right for him to do this, for this is the way any hypothesis survives while further evidence is awaited. But we must insist that a hypothesis is nothing more than an attempt to state a position that best seems to cover the available (not the final) evidence. Would the scientist then admit that the religionist, by taking a broader view that includes such unscientific things as loyalty, courage, creativity, and self-consciousness, also has a very valid hypothesis (apart from any acceptance of the record) when he insists on the idea of an almighty God who is personal and living? As a matter of fact, does not the theistic hypothesis coordinate the answers to all our queries better than the evolutionary hypothesis? This is the question.

When we ask for humility in the scientist, we must also ask for humility in the religionist. He too must accept some questions about his own position: (1) Can he argue his belief in the break from eternity into time in any other way than as an acceptance by faith? Observe again what the writer to the Hebrews says (Heb. 11:3): "Through faith we understand . . . ." (2) Does not the Bible record allow all the time the evolutionist wants? (3) Does not the Bible record allow for process as well as creation?

One of three positions can be taken regarding the two major lines of belief about the beginnings of matter, life, and man. The first position is to continue to pursue the evolutionary hypothesis, digging up meanwhile all the facts that seem in line with the hypothesis. (And most scientists now believe that the hypothesis has been strengthened to the point where no reasonable man can question it.) The second position is to dismiss the findings of the scientists and in a great exercise of faith continue to insist that the whole question is an unresolvable mystery for which there can be no satisfactory explanation short of the acceptance of God as Initiator and Sustainer of everything that now appears.

A MIDDLE ANSWER

Most adult theists find it difficult to dismiss the findings of the scientists. Living as we do in an atmosphere of science, we cannot simply discount all science as scientism and then ignore it. The effort, then, is to hold to both the findings of science and the fact of the Creator God.

There is a middle answer that is generally called "theistic evolution," the belief that God guides the process of evolution in all its phases. Some think that in terms of process one may follow the teachings of evolution but that at those periods in the evolutionary process where we are faced with great gaps, or questions for which there are no scientific data, it is allowable to posit the God who is behind all things as intervening directly. (This view is perhaps more accurately described as "threshold evolution.") For example, if there is no scientific evidence for the crossing-over from plant to animal life or for moving from one species to another (many biologists consider the latter probable), we can assume that these are places where God moved in creatively.

Keeping in mind the striking parallels between the Genesis account and the evolutionary account, one could then see that God acted as "Creator" in the beginning of each "creative age." At the end of that period when plant life was established, God then acted to create animal life; and at that break between animal and man, God "inbreathed" the soul into some highly developed form of the animal kingdom and "man became a living soul." (This term "living soul" was used of the animals in Genesis 1. What we now call soul or spirit is the image of God; the inbreathing [Gen. 2:7] made man a physiological being and not just dust. A living soul in the Genesis usage is a living creature.)

There are two basic arguments against this middle position. First of all, we have nothing in the nature of "proof" that theistic evolution (or threshold evolution) ever happened. It is a sensible and rational hypothesis because it gives us an answer at those periods in the process where we have the most difficult questions. But what we do not know is whether this answer is, after all, *the* answer. If we want to be true to the findings of science and also true to our belief in God, we may find that our minds rest easy in a solution of this sort. But that proves nothing.

The second criticism of theistic evolution is that it is a contradiction in terms. "Evolving" means that what comes out at the end of a process had to be in some way in the process at its inception. If we believe that life as we know it now evolves from a single living cell (and this apart from the question of how the living cell came into existence), evolution *qua* evolution means that both actually and potentially the myriad changes that now appear were already involved in that single cell and its environment and in the laws that surrounded it before the multiplicity of living things could evolve out of it. If we use the word "evolution" at all, we cannot allow something or somebody to break in from the outside, because such breaking-in is really just another and more complex way of describing creationism.

If we have trouble believing in evolution, or if we have trouble believing in creationism, the answer is not necessarily some halfway house. In other words, we cannot have it both ways. It is possible for a good Christian who wants to believe the Bible to be happy in this solution called theistic evolution, but he needs to reconsider the terms he is using. He certainly must present a different definition of "evolution," if this is the term he wants to use.

It seems evident, also, that any such solutions will not satisfy scientists, who, insofar as they are working scientifically, cannot allow in their definition and understanding, God is Spirit or God is Creator breaking in from eternity into time and thus cannot possibly be the object of scientific study.

The real crux of the matter for Bible-believing Christians rests finally in the creation of man. If the evolutionary hypothesis is accepted, then man appears on the scene as the most highly developed animal, even though he comes on the scene with amazing powers such as creativity, self-consciousness, the power to think abstractly, a sense of humor, and the like. When man arrives, however, he still carries with him some of his "ancestral overhangs." He appears as the starting place of further evolutionary progress and is observed progressing step by step from what we call primitive man to civilized man.

Thus we move from the cave man or even from the last of the missing links to the level of Bach or Einstein. Such front-runners are still to be thought of as the end products of a process that began with the one-celled animal. But of course, this implies that the end is not yet, even in terms of Jesus Christ, and that man will continue evolving toward a standard introduced by such a mutation as Christ might have been.

If, however, one takes the Bible account seriously, he is faced with what is called the spirit of man. Adam and Eve may be thought of as simple folk (in the best sense of the word "simple") who yet were made in the "image of God," who were actually in communion with God, and who *fell* from this high estate. The Bible believer must also insist that man fell into "sin," which is basically a rebellion against his Creator. He must also hold that man's sinful condition is the sort of thing that is passed on, as the catechism says, by "ordinary generation."

This may well be "ordinary generation," but at the present level of biological research there is nothing apparent in the chromosomes that would justify calling this "ordinary" at all. We can speak theoretically about original sin and ordinary generation and the imputation of sin and guilt, as well as about the imputation of righteousness; but in doing so we have by necessity moved far afield from biological research. When we recall that for centuries a theological debate has been carried on between creationists and traducianists as to whether sin and guilt are carried from generation to generation or are "created" at the time of conception, we must conclude that the theologians, even when they believe the Bible, are not agreed.

Furthermore, this problem is not confined to the opening chapters of Genesis. It is also built into Paul's theology. "As in Adam all died . . ." says Paul; the debate continues as to whether "Adam" is to be thought of as a single person or as a term descriptive of "mankind" as such.

In any case, the Bible teaches the fall of man and the necessity of new creation in Christ Jesus. And surely one must admit in such matters that we have moved away from anything that can be studied biologically. Now we are well over into the area of belief and are working in the area of "proof" only insofar as we have in some way accepted the authority of the Scriptures and only as we accept the fall of man and his need for a new birth because this is what "the Bible says." We need not argue here whether this kind of authority will do; we need only argue that, if we accept this kind of authority, we know what we are doing in relation to scientific research.

It seems, then, that at the present there is no way to find any parallels between evolution and the scriptural doctrine of the fall of man.

Perhaps the words of Samuel Chadwick, Methodist divine, will be illuminating. "Evolution," he said, "is neither proved by science" nor "denied by Scripture." The answers offered by "theistic evolution" need reassessment in our day, in relation to what can be clearly said about the biblical view of creation and what can be clearly said about the meaning of the word "evolution." Having determined this, we can question whether theistic evolution is possible as a solution and do so with a new understanding of the word "evolution." And whether the religionist can say anything convincing here to the biologist is a pertinent question.

But the theological question that will not be put down in this and many other areas of discussion is: How does God who is a Spirit relate to matter? Creation "out of nothing" is a mystery. Creative process working on matter is also a deep mystery. We repeat that this is *the* theological question and in no way an answer. If God creates, He creates out of nothing. The incarnation means that Christ "according to the flesh" reveals God who is Spirit. The question becomes very pressing in the relationship between divine sovereignty and human freedom. How may a man pray for things to happen in a world governed to some extent by what we call natural law?

To say that such areas are shrouded in mystery is in no way to deny their reality. Rather, it is to assert that if scientific evidence is derived from a study of the material world according to law and order (both of which can be analyzed and stated), then there is no scientific answer to the theological question and the theologian is forced again and again into belief rather than "evidence." The evidence may be forthcoming by implication or by results in the areas of matter; but this is not to say that we are talking about the grounds of being, the nature of creative power, or the way in which spiritual things and material things interact.

A long time ago Descartes faced the same problem of the interaction of mind and body. In trying to come up with a rational answer (and who has ever been more rational than Descartes?), he made the wild guess that spirit and matter have their meeting in the pineal gland. But no one believes this any more, and certainly no one could possibly figure out how to prove it. We cannot imagine, even in our wildest speculation, what the nature of such a gland would be, if at one end it were mind and at the other end matter.

Epistemologically, we must insist that beginnings for the scientist (is there an uncaused cause at the beginning of the causal sequence?) have to be an assumption or a presupposition—or, if you like, an acceptance in faith or belief. Much of what follows with the scientist does so because he believes in the strength of his hypothesis; and much of what follows for the religionist does so because he believes that there is a God who not only is able to act on the matter he created but also does so act.

The overall thrust of this essay might lead one to believe that the writer is an agnostic. He is not. He is simply saying that, in the present state of scientific evidence and biblical interpretation, we have a stand-off. Truth is not divided. But while we are approaching ultimate truth, we are necessarily divided by the inadequacies of our thinking and the inadequacies of our evidence.

Therefore, both the scientist and religionist ought to be hesitant to dogmatize about the beginnings of matter, life, and man. The findings of science need not unsettle belief in the Bible. What one must see, however, is that while he holds his belief, he cannot use science as proof nor even as a crutch. We see through a glass darkly, and it is time that we face that cloudy fact.

A SELECT BIBLIOGRAPHY

4. THE CREATION OF MATTER, LIFE, AND MAN

Russell L. Mixter, *Evolution and Christian Thought.* Grand Rapids: Wm. B. Eerdmans Publishing Co., 1959.

Albertus Pieters, *Notes on Genesis.* Grand Rapids: Wm. B. Eerdmans Publishing Co., 1947.

Phillip Wheelwright, *The Way of Philosophy.* New York: The Odyssey Press, 1954 and 1960.

JESUS CHRIST:
HIS LIFE AND MINISTRY

Johannes Schneider

Johannes Schneider was professor of New Testament in East Berlin's Humboldt University, which was the University of Berlin in the undivided city. He taught in Breslau and Berlin universities 1933-38 and contributed many articles to Kittel's famous Theologisches Wörterbuch. *Returning to Germany after a visiting professorship in Ottawa University, he found that the Nazis had deprived him of his chair. He was restored in 1945 and became dean of the theological faculty, the only Baptist in an Evangelical Lutheran divinity school in Germany. One of his books, the commentary,* The Letter to the Hebrews, *has been translated by W. A. Mueller and published in the United States. He is now retired and lives in West Berlin, where he is preparing a commentary on the Gospel of John. Dr. Schneider's essay is a translation of his article on the life of Jesus appearing in* Calwer Bibellexikon, *published in 1960 by Calwer Verlag in Stuttgart, and is used by permission of the publishers.*

JESUS CHRIST:
HIS LIFE AND MINISTRY

I. SOURCES FOR THE LIFE OF JESUS

THE GOSPELS are our most important source of information about Jesus Christ. They are primarily testimonies of faith used in early Christian preaching. Their purpose is not to give a complete picture of the life of Jesus; these records of His words and acts are designed, rather, to demonstrate as well founded the apostolic proclamation that Jesus is Christ and Lord. They propose to show that the faith of the Church and its comprehension of the person of Jesus go back to Jesus Himself.

Since the Gospels deal with the revelation of God in history, they are historical records of unique significance. They rest upon the testimony of the disciples, who heard Jesus' words and saw His mighty deeds. The account in John's Gospel differs in many respects from that in the Synoptic Gospels. But this does not entitle us to question the historical value of the Johannine record. No doubt Jesus' ministry was more extensive than what is related by the Synoptic writers, whose presentation follows a specific pattern. John could not have made up the events that he alone of the gospel writers shares with his readers; they are a part of the tradition that he is repeating.

Outside the Gospels there are relatively few New Testament references to the historical Jesus. This is true of Acts, where the "Petrine passages" trace the life of Jesus but briefly from the arrest of John the Baptist to Easter and also of Paul's letters, of Hebrews, and of First Peter. Acts 20:35 quotes a saying of the "Lord Jesus"—"It is more blessed to give than to receive"—that is not found in the Gospels.

Of doubtful value are the *Agrapha* (isolated sayings of Jesus) that were transmitted by the Church Fathers. Their authenticity cannot be established with certainty, and they contribute nothing essential to Jesus' message and teaching. Nor do the "Fragments of the Lost Gospels" (the Gospel of Peter, among others) add reliably to our knowledge of the life and sayings of Jesus.

There is very little extrabiblical source material. Although ancient historians do mention Jesus, they supply little concrete information. Tacitus (Ann. XV:44) in his account of the sack of Rome states that the persecution of the Christians under Nero goes back to a "devastating superstition" whose author was "Christ." Suetonius (Claud. 25:4) maintains that Claudius expelled the Jews from Rome because they created disturbances at the instigation of one "Chrestus"; the reference is probably to Christ. More important are two passages in Josephus. In the "Testimonium Flavianum" (Ant. XVIII:63 f.) Josephus states that Jesus was a wise man, a doer of wondrous works, a teacher of men; that He was the Messiah whom Pilate punished by crucifixion and who after three days reappeared alive to His disciples. But this passage may have been inserted later by Christians, or at least edited by Christians. Elsewhere Josephus mentions James, who was executed in A.D. 62, and calls him a brother of Jesus who is called "Christ" (Ant. XX:200).

The Talmud also testifies to the existence of Jesus, but all of its statements are full of ugly polemic. It is said, for example, that Jesus practiced magic, led Israel astray, held in derision the words of the wise, and was the illegitimate child of a Roman soldier named Panthera.

II. CHRONOLOGY

Just how long Jesus lived or how long His public ministry lasted is uncertain. The Synoptic writers mention only the one Passover at the time of the crucifixion and provide no other basis for calculating the period of time that preceded it. But from statements in Mark (1:14; 2:23; 14:1), one gains the impression that Jesus' ministry lasted a year and a half. The Gospel of John, on the other hand, mentions three Passover feasts that Jesus attended (2:13, 23; 6:4; 11:55); also mentioned are a feast of tabernacles (7:2) and a feast of dedication (10:22). John, in other words, covers a period of three years or—if John 5:1 alludes to another Passover feast—of more than three years. Matthew 23:37 and Luke 13:34 also seem to indicate that Jesus sojourned in Jerusalem several times. In any case, John shows greater interest in precise dates than do the Synoptic writers.

According to Luke 3:23, Jesus was about thirty when He began His public ministry. John 2:20 states that forty-six years had elapsed since the beginning of the building of Herod's temple. This computation would point to the year 27 or 28. According to the Gospels and all other sources, Jesus was crucified under Pontius Pilate, who was governor between 26 and 36. Jesus died on a Friday. According to the Synoptic writers this was the fifteenth, and according to John the fourteenth, day of the Passover month of Nisan. Here, too, John is probably correct rather than the Synoptic writers, who were concerned that the record show Jesus' last meal to have been a Passover feast. The year in which the fourteenth of Nisan fell on a Friday seems to have been A.D. 30 (cf. J. Jeremias, *Die Abendmahlsworte Jesu,* 1959). April 7 of that year was therefore the day of Jesus' death.

The only specific reference in the Gospels to a particular year — the fifteenth year of Tiberius Caesar—is in Luke 3:1. Although the passage concerns John the Baptist, unquestionably it is also intended to point to the beginning of Jesus' public ministry. Thus we may say that His ministry covered the years 28 to 30.

III. BIRTH AND CHILDHOOD OF JESUS

Jesus was born when Augustus was the Roman Caesar and Herod the Great was king of the Jews (Luke 2:1; Matt. 2:1; Luke 1:5). Herod died in 4 B.C., and so Jesus' birth must have occurred before that date. Therefore the calculations made in Rome in the sixth century by Abbot Dionysius Exiguus are incorrect, for they place the birth of Jesus in the year 1. The story of the Star of Bethlehem (Matt. 2:1 ff.) and reports of the census taken in Palestine (Luke 2:1) indicate that Jesus was born in 7 B.C. On the basis of more recent findings (the "Berlin table of the planets" and the "Star Calendar of Sippar"), the Star of Bethlehem is thought to be the conjunction in that year of Jupiter and Saturn in the constellation of Pisces. The astrology of that time seems to have thought of Jupiter as the star of the ruler of the world and of Pisces as the sign of the end time; the Magi concluded, therefore, that the ruler of the end time would appear in Palestine in the year 7 (Stauffer). The Roman census mentioned in Luke that involved a "systematic survey of all taxable subjects and objects" is to be understood as the "initial phase of the census-taking operation that began in the year 7" (Stauffer). That the first census took place in Judea is also indicated by Josephus (Ant. XVII: 13.5; XVIII:1.2; XX:5.2; Bell. Jud. VII:8.1).

Jesus was a Nazarene, but He was born in Bethlehem, Luke tells us. According to the prologues of Matthew and Luke, Jesus was the Son of David and the son of a virgin. That He was the "son" of David was expressed very early in testimonial-like statements (Rom. 1:3; cf. II Tim. 2:8; Rev. 5:5). Jesus Himself did not reject the appellation "Son of David" (Mark 10:48; 11:10); He made it clear, however, that as the Messiah He was more than merely a descendant of David—as "Lord" He ranked above David (Mark 12:35-37).

The genealogies of Matthew and Luke (Matt. 1:1 ff.; Luke 3:23 ff.), which go back, respectively, to Abraham and to Adam, seek to show that Jesus is indeed descended from the family of David. They point to Joseph, who "as was supposed" (Luke 3:23) was the father of Jesus; they are combined, however, with the account of virgin birth (Matt. 1:18-

25; cf. Luke 1:30 ff.). The two genealogies differ greatly. That Luke intended to present the genealogy of Mary is quite unlikely. For the Jews it was sufficient if Joseph—into whose family Jesus was born, despite His supernatural procreation—was a descendant of David.

The virgin birth brings to expression the fact that Jesus' true origin is in God. By the combining of the two paradoxical statements, that Jesus was both the Son of David and the son of a virgin, the mystery of Jesus' divine sonship is intimated, though it defies human comprehension. From Mark's Gospel one might get the impression that Jesus was not declared the Son of God until His baptism. Matthew and Luke, however, connect Jesus' divine Sonship to an act of God that established His earthly existence in a unique way. Other than this, the New Testament says nothing about the miraculous birth of Jesus. During His lifetime He was considered to be the son of Joseph and Mary (Luke 3:23; 4:22; John 6:42). While the name Jesus (Jeshua, shortened from Johoshua, meaning "Jahweh is salvation") is not uncommon in Judaism, it is a uniquely apt designation for the person and work of Jesus of Nazareth.

We are told very little about the childhood and youth of Jesus. He was reared in a modest home whose piety reflected the impact of the law and of the eschatological hope of Israel. Pharisaic zeal for the law probably exercised as little influence in Nazareth as did Greek thought. The most important channel of education was the Old Testament, whose basic truths were no doubt familiar to Jesus from early youth, for it was through the synagogues that a substantial knowledge of the Scriptures was brought into the Jewish home. At age five a Jewish boy was allowed to enter the synagogue in his own right; here, in every worship service, he heard the Torah and the lesson from the Prophets. Presumably, Jesus also attended the school in Nazareth, where instruction in the law occupied a central place in the curriculum. We may safely assume, then, that Jesus not only knew Aramaic, the everyday language of the people, but could also read the Hebrew Bible. What, if any, knowledge He had of Greek, we do not know. The story of the twelve-year-old Jesus in the temple shows how fully versed He was in the sacred writings of His people; it also gives us a glimpse into His personal relationship to God (Luke 2:41-52).

Concerning His inner development in the years that followed, only Luke gives us any information, and that in just one very general sentence: "Jesus increased in wisdom and stature, and in favour with God and man" (Luke 2:52). What was actually going on inside Jesus is hidden from us. But the silent years in Nazareth were very significant for Jesus' later work. No remarkable events attended the external course of His life. He worked with Joseph and, like him, became a carpenter. Information about His family is limited. We learn that Jesus had brothers and sisters (Mark 6:1 ff.; cf. Matt. 13:55 f.). What role His mother played in this period of His life is unknown; we can make certain deductions, however, from Luke 2:19 and 2:51.

IV. THE BAPTISM OF JESUS

The determinative event in Jesus' life was His baptism. He was already a mature man when the news reached Nazareth of John the Baptist's ministry and of the movement that grew up around Him. Thereupon Jesus went to the Jordan and was baptized (John understood baptism to be "of repentance unto the remission of sins"). More significant than the baptism itself was what immediately followed. That Jesus possessed God's Spirit became visibly apparent; moreover, a divine voice called Him the Son of God. He was the Messiah to whom John had pointed in his proclamation. The Baptizer was fully aware of the place he occupied in the unfolding pattern of redemption: he was only the forerunner of the coming eschatological bringer of salvation. In Jesus, John saw the fulfillment of his prophetic message.

The temptation followed hard upon Jesus' baptism. He was led by the Spirit of God into the wilderness and for forty days was subjected to severe testing. Throughout the temptation He stood His ground against all Satanic suggestions and enticements. From God's Word Jesus gained full understanding of His task. He was not to rule the world but to establish the sovereignty of God.

V. THE PUBLIC MINISTRY OF JESUS

A. *Setting of the Ministry*

Mark's account is arranged as follows: (1) Jesus' ministry in Galilee, and (2) the passion in Jerusalem. Between these parts is a brief account of Jesus' journey into Judea. Both Matthew and Luke uses this same geographical setting. Luke, however, also gives a detailed travel account (9:51; 19:27); in it he includes material that is unique to his Gospel. Characteristic of this travel account is Luke's constant reiteration that Jerusalem is the destination of the long journey (Luke 9:51; 13:22, 32 f.; 17:11). Unlike Mark and Matthew, Luke emphasizes that Jesus went also to Samaria. John likewise reports this, describing one scene in Samaria in detail, namely, Jesus' encounter with the Samaritan woman at Jacob's well (chapter 4). Luke and John thus show that the ministry to the Samaritans was established by Jesus. Mark records nothing about Jesus' association with the Samaritans, and Matthew includes a statement by Jesus that expressly forbade the disciples to minister among them (Matt. 10:5). In distinction to the Synoptic writers, John tells of repeated visits Jesus made to Jerusalem on the occasion of feast days. John also speaks of Jesus' ministry in Judea and Perea before the Galilean period (3:22– 4:3; cf. 10:40; 11:54) Jesus had been in the country's capital city several times before His last trip there (Matt. 21:17; cf. Luke 10:38 ff.; Matt. 23:37); the Synoptic writers make several references to this fact without giving specific details.

The Synoptics indicate that Jesus did not begin His ministry in Galilee until after the arrest of John the Baptist (Mark 1:14; Matt. 4:12; Luke

3:20; 4:14). They say nothing, however, about the period between Jesus' baptism and the beginning of His work in Galilee. John, on the other hand, emphasizes that Jesus was active already before John the Baptist's imprisonment, and that, in fact, His disciples were baptizing during this period (John 4:2). According to this, Jesus and John the Baptist worked side by side for a while. Jesus did not leave Judea until after John's death. This would suggest that not until this time did He separate Himself fully from the movement associated with John. One point in favor of this view is that Jesus then completely dispensed with baptism as an eschatological "sacrament of redemption." From then on, forgiveness of sins would come solely through His Word.

John and the Synoptic writers agree that most of Jesus' public ministry occurred in Galilee; they differ, however, in their presentation of the various events. It must be kept in mind that here, as elsewhere, John and the Synoptic writers relate only fragmentary portions of Jesus' ministry. This is especially evident in the epilogue of the Fourth Gospel (John 21: 25). It is characteristic of John to view many reports kerygmatically, as, for example, the account of the feeding of the five thousand.

There is no doubt that Jesus' activity in Jerusalem was extensive. The first three Gospels are concerned exclusively with Jesus' activity in Galilee and His passion in Jerusalem. John, however, gives a much more comprehensive picture. It is likewise apparent that his account of the events follows a definite plan. His purpose in writing the Gospel is stated at the close—that his readers might believe on Christ Jesus, the Son of God (20:31). John also gives a fuller account of Jesus' last visit to the country east of the Jordan and in Judea than do the Synoptic writers. Mark 10:1 and Matthew 19:1 do state, however, that Jesus left Galilee and came to Judea.

During the Galilean period, and first of all in the area of the Lake of Gennesaret, Jesus began fulfilling His God-appointed task. The starting point was clearly Capernaum, where, it seems, He sometimes dwelt (Matt. 4:13). Later He also visited more distant regions, the country of the Gadarenes on the other side of the lake, for example (Mark 5:1 ff.). Occasionally He crossed the border of Palestine and came to the region of Tyre and Sidon (Mark 7:24). His travels took Him still further north to Caesarea Philippi (Mark 8:27). As He traveled throughout the country, men from all its areas came to Him.

B. *Jesus' Preaching*

Jesus developed no doctrinal system. He was no scribe in the usual sense. He never attended the School of the Torah in Jerusalem. What He said was derived directly through divine authority. Jesus preached and taught in private homes (Mark 2:2) as well as in the synagogues, where any capable member of the congregation, after reading a passage from the prophets, was at liberty to bring a message (Mark 1:39). When crowds followed Him, He preached in the open air, He spoke from a mountain top (Matt. 5:1) or from a fishing boat along the lakeshore

(Mark 4:1). His ministry differed from that of John the Baptist in that He did not summon people to Himself but rather sought them out to share His message with them and to minister to their specific needs. He taught the people and worked miracles; we have no reports of John performing miracles. Jesus not only announced the message of salvation; to the lost multitudes He also brought God's salvation in word and in deed, for He was, in truth, the bearer of divine powers of redemption and healing. On journeys with His disciples He gave them special teaching, unlocking the mysteries of the Kingdom of God to them and giving them instruction for their life and service.

1. *The Proclamation of the Kingdom of God.* Jesus took up and carried forward John the Baptist's preaching of repentance and of the Kingdom of God. His coming in messianic authority gave it deeper meaning, however. Central to Jesus' preaching and teaching was the imminent coming of the Kingdom of God. God Himself will establish His dominion at a time He ordains and will make an end of all the kingdoms of the world. God's Kingdom will come without man's assistance. It will not result from human effort or endeavor. It will come suddenly, "as the lightning, that lighteneth out of the one part under heaven, shineth unto the other part" (Luke 17:24). At the same time there will be signs that the Kingdom of God is near; these signs should be heeded. From them men are to recognize "that summer is near" (Mark 13:28 f.). But knowledge of the day and hour of this great cosmic event is reserved unto God alone.

Jesus said that the coming of the Kingdom was imminent (Mark 9:1; Matt. 10:23; 24:34). This explains the dynamic urgency of the call He issued at the beginning of His ministry. Moreover, His great eschatological discourses of Mark 13, Matthew 24, and Luke 21 contain statements that tie in with traditional apocalyptic concepts and speak of specific events that will precede the coming of the Kingdom. There is no contradiction involved here, and there is no need to ascribe the second group of statements to the theology of the early Church. No doubt Jesus grew increasingly certain that His death was to be the Father's ordained consummation of His work. That the great eschatological discourses follow the foretelling of His passion is significant. They were given after Jesus' entry into Jerusalem, and were intended to familiarize the disciples with the idea that God's dominion would not truly become a reality until He Himself returned in power and glory as the Son of Man. Here, too, He said that no one but God knows the time of the last event (Mark 13:32 f.).

Besides the purely eschatological passages, however, there are statements by Jesus that refer to the Kingdom of God as a present great reality. They stress that God's Kingdom is already dawning. God's dominion is an active force that is manifesting its power in the present time. It was evident in the ministry of Jesus. Through Him God was establishing His Kingdom in the midst of a doomed world. Jesus knew He had ushered in the age of redemption in which the promise of Isaiah 35:5 was beginning to be fulfilled. The message of salvation was proclaimed, and unprecedented deeds were done (Matt. 11:5 f.). Jesus testified concerning Himself, "If I cast out devils by the Spirit of God, then the kingdom of God is come unto you" (Matt. 12:28; cf. Luke 11:20). To the extent that the power of Satan is driven back, God's dominion asserts itself and gains ground. As the mightier one, Jesus invaded the kingdom of God's adversary. By wresting the spoil from Satan, He showed that in the power of divine authority He was more than a match for the enemy (Mark 3:27). He was therefore the representative of the Kingdom of God on earth. The disciples He sent forth acted in His name. When the Seventy returned, Jesus was overjoyed at their sucess and said, "I beheld Satan as lightning fall from heaven" (Luke 10:18). How strongly Jesus felt this Satanic power He indicated by the words, "And from the days of John the Baptist until now the kingdom of heaven suffereth violence, and the violent take it by force" (Matt. 11:12).

Of supreme significance are Jesus' words in Luke 17:21. Responding to the Pharisees' question about when the Kingdom of God would come, He said, "The kingdom of God is in the midst of you." To translate these words as ". . . is within you" is senseless, inasmuch as Jesus was speaking to the Pharisees, who wanted nothing to do with the lordship of God He proclaimed and manifested in His works. Advocates of "consistent eschatology," who believe that all of Jesus' statements about the Kingdom of God refer to the future, translate Luke 17:21, "The kingdom of God *will be* in the midst of you, and that suddenly, at one stroke." Although this is linguistically possible, it does not fit the context.

Finally, there are references by Jesus to the gradually unfolding power of God's sovereignty. This is expressed in several parables, primarily those of the sower, the mustard seed, and the leaven. Here the Kingdom of God is conceived as what R. Otto has termed the "sphere of salvation and power" that continually extends its borders and embraces more and more people. The power of the Kingdom of God works both extensively and intensively. Through the Word proclaimed by Jesus, a mysterious process takes place in those who are receptive to His message. In the parables of the treasure in the field and the pearl of great price, the Kingdom of God is seen as the blessing of salvation that men strive to obtain. If they seek it earnestly, it becomes theirs as a gift of divine grace. "He that seeketh findeth; and to him that knocketh it shall be opened" (Matt. 7:8).

In other words, Jesus spoke of the Kingdom of God in three ways: (1) as the future Kingdom that God would bring about at a time concealed from men; (2) as the Kingdom that was already a present reality in the ministry of Jesus; (3) as the power of almighty God, increasingly apparent, that lays hold of men and molds their whole existence.

Jesus also related the conditions that must be met by anyone who would "enter the Kingdom of God." He demands an unequivocal decision. The call to decision is the call to repentance. Participation in the Kingdom of God is impossible without a complete about-face. Man must break completely with his old life; he must turn wholly to God and allow his thinking and doing to be controlled by God alone. But repentance must be more than merely an inner experience; its purpose has not been truly achieved until it bears fruit and leads the repentant one to fulfill the will of God. Making a decision for God includes complete obedience to Him. "Not everyone that saith unto me, Lord, Lord, shall enter into the kingdom of heaven; but he that doeth the will of my Father which is in heaven" (Matt. 7:21). Jesus requires of His disciples that their righteousness— that is, their ethical life—surpass that of the scribes and Pharisees (Matt. 5:20). Once made, a decision for God must be determinative for all of life: "No man, having put his hand to the plough, and looking back, is fit for the kingdom of God" (Luke 9:62).

Jesus also associated decision for God with decision for Himself. Belief in the message of God's sovereignty includes following Jesus. Here, too, an either-or situation is involved. A person who has decided to follow Jesus must allow no obligations to hinder him, not even sacred ones (Matt. 8:22). Jesus even goes so far as to require a break with parents and family where this is necessary (Luke 14:26). He Himself, for the sake of His task, severed Himself from His family and designated the people of God—those yielded to the sovereignty of God—as His true kinsmen (Mark 3:35). As He saw it, the greatest hindrance to total decision for God is bondage to this world's goods. Crucial to a man's destiny is what he sets his heart on: God or mammon. Jesus requires, therefore, that those who follow Him not gather treasure on earth but rather find their wealth in God, for no man can serve two masters. There is only one requirement: to seek first the Kingdom of God and His righteousness (Matt. 6:33). This sets up a new system of values. He who lives by it will lack for nothing, including the earthly necessities of life.

Anyone who chooses the lordship of God and the discipleship required by Jesus must understand what he is undertaking. Just as one estimates the cost before building a tower or starting a military expedition, so one must seriously consider what is involved in total commitment to God (Luke 14:28 ff.). Anyone who desires to share in the Kingdom of God must be ready to make any and every sacrifice. As Jesus graphically put it, "It is better . . . to enter into life [the Kingdom of God] halt or maimed, rather than having two hands or two feet, to be cast into everlasting fire" (Matt. 18:9). Narrow is the gate that leads into the Kingdom of God, and few there are who find it (Matt. 7:13 f.; Luke 13:24). Only a minority can meet the conditions of repentant and obedient attachment to Jesus that opens the door to the Kingdom of God. It is to the small band of His followers that Jesus says, "It is [God] your Father's good pleasure to give you the kingdom" (Luke 12:32).

But besides the stern requirements that come with total commitment, Jesus utters also tender and gracious words. They deal with the inner requisites for entrance into the Kingdom of God. Foremost are references to a childlike spirit: "Whosoever shall not receive the kingdom of God as a little child, he shall not enter therein" (Mark 10:15). The message of salvation is to be grasped intuitively, with, as R. Otto says, "humble,

undeliberate forthrightness, in simplicity and unconditional surrender of
the heart." Believing trust is determinative. The way of salvation revealed
by Jesus contrasts with that of the scribes and Pharisees, whose sophistry,
casuistry, and legalism erect barriers to entering the Kingdom of God.
Against them Jesus leveled the serious charge that they lock people out of
the kingdom of heaven; they themselves do not enter in, and they hinder
those entrusted to them from doing so (Matt. 23:13; Luke 11:52). The
Beatitudes and their promises point in the same direction. The poor (according to Matthew 5:3 the poor in spirit), the meek, the suffering, the
merciful, the peacemakers, all who hunger and thirst after righteousness
and are pure in heart—that is, all who are inwardly prepared—are promised a share in God's Kingdom. Jesus addresses the penitent sinner *and*
the weary and burdened.

2. *The Kingdom of God, Israel, and the Nations of the World.* The
Kingdom of God is composed of the eschatological people of God. They
are the sons of God who will "inherit" the Kingdom. Jesus addressed Himself first of all to His people, to the "lost sheep of the house of Israel"
(Matt. 15:24; cf. Matt. 10:5 f.). But He declared from the very start
that the people chosen of God had no special claim on the Kingdom.
Abrahamic lineage, the covenant-sign of circumcision, and efforts to fulfill the law do not assure eternal salvation. He who hardens his heart
against Jesus' call to repentance will have no part in the Kingdom of God.
Election is the gift of divine grace toward those who unreservedly choose
God and who by faith receive the proclamation of the Gospel of salvation. Jesus' proclamation is selective. Many are called, but few are
chosen (Matt. 22:14).

In the parable of the great supper (Luke 14:16 ff.) Jesus makes it
clear that the Jews are indeed the first-invited guests; their prerogative is
forfeited, however, if they do not respond to the King's invitation. Then
the call to share in the glory of God's Kingdom will be extended to those
who were not originally invited. The Synoptic record shows that the
heathen did not come within range of Jesus' message until the vast majority of the Jews had either rejected it or shown hostility toward it. Even
if, at first, only isolated experiences showed Jesus that the heathen, too,
were open to the message of salvation, the certainty that God would gather
His people out of *all* nations was already a part of the prophetic vision
of salvation for all mankind: "They shall come from the east, and from
the west, and from the north, and from the south, and shall sit down in
the kingdom of God" (Luke 13:29; Matt. 8:11). It was Jesus' awareness that the Jews would lay hands on Him and kill Him that caused Him
to utter the harsh words: "The kingdom of God shall be taken from you,
and given to a nation bringing forth the fruits thereof" (Matt. 21:43).

To the Jews who reject every invitation He extends to the Kingdom of
God, Jesus proclaims judgment. Preaching judgment is the other side of
proclaiming the Gospel of the Kingdom. Luke considers Jesus' rejection
at Nazareth at the very beginning of His ministry as portentous and significant (Luke 4:16 ff.). The ominous references to the future judgment

are directed against Israel as a whole or against representative groups. Jesus speaks primarily against the leaders of the law-reverencing nation, against the scribes and Pharisees, who decline His call to repentance and reject the way of salvation He requires. Several of the pronouncements apply specifically to Jerusalem and its inhabitants. In the last judgment, especially severe punishment will befall the Galilean cities of Chorazin, Bethsaida, and Capernaum (Matt. 11:20 ff.). Finally, Jesus bewails the rich; sated with their wealth they have no desire for the treasures of the coming Kingdom of God. They are like the farmer whose trust is in his overflowing granaries and who is not rich toward God (Luke 12:16 ff).

Jesus' words of judgment show that God is not obliged to Israel if she rejects Jesus' prophetic-eschatological proclamation and shows no comprehension of the new situation in redemptive history that has come with the appearance of the Messiah sent from God.

But the final judgment will not affect Israel alone. When the Son of Man comes in His glory, all nations will be gathered before Him, and He will divide all people as a shepherd separates sheep from goats. Then final sentence will be pronounced upon all men. Jews and Gentiles will be on both sides. On the basis of their relationship to their fellow men, their eternal destiny will be decided by the verdict of the Son of Man, who considers every deed of love as done unto Him. One group will go to "eternal punishment," the other into "eternal life." The latter will hear the words, "Receive as your inheritance the kingdom prepared for you from the foundation of the world" (Matt. 25:31 ff., especially vv. 31, 34, 46).

Entrance into the future Kingdom of God presupposes, therefore, the judgment and final separation of the "righteous" from the "unrighteous," the "good" from the "bad" (cf. the parables of the wheat and the tares and of the net, Matt. 13:24ff., 47ff.). When the end of the world comes, the "tares" will be gathered and burned, but the "wheat" will be put into God's storehouses (Matt. 13:30).

Eternal life is the essential characteristic of the new existence. Jesus uses metaphors almost exclusively in referring to the state of blessedness in the Kingdom of God; the prime example is the traditional representation of the messianic feast. The sons of the Kingdom will sit down to eat with the patriarchs (Matt. 8:11). Jesus promises the disciples, "Ye may eat and drink at my table in my kingdom" (Luke 22:30; cf. Matt. 26:29). Or there is the illustration of the wedding feast that the king prepares for his son (Matt. 22:2 ff.). Jesus demands total preparation of heart for the day when the "bridegroom" will appear (Matt. 25:1 ff.). There will also be a new order of existence in the Kingdom of God. Differences between the sexes will end, and men will be "as the angels of heaven" (Mark 12:25). The state of blessedness in the Kingdom of God is one of perfection, of eternal joy, of eternal life, of unclouded fellowship with God. There is no more opposition to the will of God, for He has established His Kingdom.

3. *The Kingdom of God and the Disciples.* From among those who

came to believe in the redemption-message of the Kingdom of God, Jesus gathered about Him a select group of twelve disciples. No doubt the number twelve is symbolic. The disciples were representatives of the nation with its twelve tribes, and at the same time representatives of the new nation of God that is being gathered together through the preaching of the Kingdom of God. They were the foundation on which would be raised the structure of the eschatological fellowship of the redeemed, the people of the New Covenant. Since they were especially close to Jesus, they were the "friends of the bridegroom," the "elect," the "sons of the kingdom." Jesus called them "the light of the world" and "the salt of the earth" (Matt. 5:13 f.)—designations in keeping with Israel's position and status. He promised them, in fact, that they would one day sit on twelve thrones and together with the Messiah would judge the people of Israel (Matt. 19:28).

Jesus solemnized the establishment of this inner circle by a formal ceremony (Mark 3:13 f.), sent the disciples as His representatives to the towns and villages of Palestine (Mark 6:7 ff.), and invested them with the authority He Himself possessed: authority to proclaim the Gospel, to heal the sick, and to cast out devils. At the end of His earthly ministry He appointed the Kingdom to them (Luke 22:29) and gave them the power to bind and to loose (Matt. 18:18), thus putting into their hands the determination of entrance into the Kingdom of God.

Jesus bound the twelve to Himself. As their Master He was their teacher and Lord, one who pledged them to unconditional discipleship. For His sake they left everything and openly confessed Him, even when they did not understand His way. Jesus established an intimate relation between Himself and His disciples; He called them His "friends" (John 15:14). And He also made it clear that they would share not only His work and His authority, but also His lot. They could expect the same persecution He expected, especially by those in authority. "The disciple is not above his master, nor the servant above his lord" (Matt. 10:24).

In the twelve Jesus saw the nucleus of the messianic fellowship of the redeemed, destined and equipped for the Kingdom of God; but He gave this fellowship no fixed organizational form. Not until Jesus' resurrection appearances and the event of Pentecost did the "Church" come into being; it presupposes His death, His resurrection, and the outpouring of the Holy Spirit. Jesus' disciples formed no "special synagogue." Jesus did, however, establish the *foundation* for the certain confirmation of the family of God that came into being through His ministry and through the colaborship of His disciples. Peter was designated as the rock upon which this building would rise. This is a prophetic statement that indicates how Jesus intended His work on earth to be carried forward. Since we have no reason to think this word of Jesus is spurious, it is not to be thought of as a later formulation of the Church; on the contrary, Jesus Himself, toward the end of His ministry, took care to ensure that His earthly work would be continued until His return. As the Risen and Ascended One, He is still the "master builder" of His Church. Just as the temple of the Old Covenant in Jerusalem was raised upon a rock, so the building that

Jesus would erect would be founded upon a rock, but with this differ-ence: The foundation of the messianic fellowship of the redeemed was to be no earthly stone; rather, it would be Simon Peter, the disciple of His choosing. Him Jesus particularly invested with the power of binding and loosing (Matt. 16:19)—"didactic and disciplinary authority"—thereby conferring on him what corresponded to the spiritual and pastoral au-thority of the highest officialdom in the Jewish theocracy. We can de-scribe the relation between the Kingdom of God and the eschatological fellowship of the redeemed by saying that the Church of Christ is com-posed of those who confess Jesus, who yield to the sovereignty of God, and who, finally, will share in the Kingdom of God when it comes in power and glory.

C. The Moral Imperative of Jesus

1. *The Basic Requirement.* The ethical proclamation of Jesus is closely related to His eschatological message. At the heart of both is the con-cept of the Kingdom of God. Anyone who has heard and responded to the call to repentance encounters the claims of God in everyday life. The claims that confront him originate in the will of God as it is revealed in His commands. To act ethically, therefore, is to do what God wills in concrete life situations. But God does not want some *thing* from man; He wants *man himself*—not only his heart and mind but also his deeds. Jesus demands not a formal but rather a radical kind of obedience. But man can respond in this way only if he has experienced a complete trans-formation of his being. Only a good tree can bring forth good fruit (Matt. 7:16).

Jesus reduced all laws and stipulations to one single requirement: love of God and neighbor (Mark 12:28 ff.). This embraces all man's obliga-tions. Basically no further guidelines are needed for ethical conduct. Where more are given, they serve only to explain the one basic require-ment. By making the commandment of love central, Jesus frees men from the bonds of legalism.

The command to love has no limits. It includes even love of one's enemies, for as soon as my enemy needs my help, he becomes my neigh-bor. Jesus brought this home with the story of the good Samaritan (Luke 10:30-37). Love demands a conquest of self that is willing to leave un-just treatment unrequited. It must be capable of unlimited forgiveness (Matt. 18:21 ff). And God will forgive only him who has forgiven his brother from the heart (Matt. 18:35; cf. Matt. 6:12, 14 f.). Jesus also pointed out that forgiveness is to be preferred to religious observance (Matt. 5:23 ff.). At any rate, religious observance without ethical con-duct is not in keeping with God's will. Man can stand before God only if he has met the requirement of neighbor love.

2. *Instruction in Discipleship.* Jesus taught His people, but particu-larly He taught His disciples. The Gospels are full of teachings that were intended only for them. Prominent among these is the Sermon on the

Mount, which presents in concise form Jesus' most important moral requirements. The Sermon is closely related to His kingdom preaching, and one can properly understand it only by realizing that it was intended as instruction for the disciples (Matt. 5:1 f.; Luke 6:20). The Sermon on the Mount gives guidelines for the proper conduct of the disciples, who by becoming Jesus' followers have yielded to the sovereignty of God and who through Him become doers of His will. The Sermon on the Mount demands a life lived in utter obedience to the decrees of the Kingdom of God. It deals with the ethical conduct of Jesus' disciples in the period between the proclamation of the Kingdom of God and its consummation. The Sermon on the Mount requires of the disciples, therefore, a manner of life during this world age that is in keeping with the Kingdom of God. Obviously, then, the Sermon on the Mount is not to be considered normative for the world.

In the Sermon on the Mount Jesus speaks as the new teacher of the law. This does not mean that He came as a new lawgiver; it does mean, however, that by virtue of His messianic authority, He claims to be the proper, the only true interpreter of the law. Unlike the rabbinical teachers, He so interprets the commandments that they completely and unmistakably reveal and express the true and deepest purposes of God. Unlike the scribes, Jesus did not govern the lives of His disciples by legalistic principles; instead He used illustrations to show how God's will is to be carried out in various life situations.

Jesus took the Sermon on the Mount seriously. He did not give it to crush man with its unattainability; He gave it to be followed. Discipleship is prerequisite to doing the will of God. This relation brings obligation for a specific kind of life. Matthew 7:21 expressly says, "Not every one that saith unto me, Lord, Lord, shall enter into the kingdom of heaven; but he that *doeth* the will of my Father which is in heaven." Thus the Sermon on the Mount is not merely a set of ethical principles; it teaches, rather, that right conduct comes from having a right relationship to God. This is how in the Sermon on the Mount Jesus describes the new man who is motivated by the principles, the spirit, and the order of the Kingdom of God, and whose goal is ethical perfection (Matt. 5:48). Jesus' disciple is a fanatic, not about what is right for right's sake, but rather about exercising love, even sacrificial love.

3. *Claims of Jesus in the Realm of Social Ethics.* Jesus developed no comprehensive system of social ethics, nor indeed of any kind of ethics. But He did give specific precepts on marriage, the family, and the state.

Although Jesus Himself did not marry, He considered marriage a divinely established institution. He required absolute purity in marriage; even looking at another man's wife "to lust after her" is adultery. Once contracted, the marriage bond is indissoluble. According to Matthew 5: 32, only immorality is justified grounds for divorce. Unlike the rabbis, Jesus did not teach that marriage was obligatory for all; He presupposed, rather, that some persons would voluntarily forgo marriage and sexual intercourse (Matt. 19:12). Marriage belongs to this world; in the world to come it will have no validity (Matt. 22:25 ff.).

Like marriage, the family is also a divine institution. Jesus blessed the children and preached obedience to the fourth commandment. The moral obligation of children to care for their parents if they are unable to support themselves, or if they are in financial need, supersedes the ceremonial obligation of keeping a vow made to God (Mark 7:10 ff.). Jesus, however, separated Himself from His family for the sake of His mission. The family must not stand in the way of doing the will of God. In addition to family relationships—and superseding them if necessary—is the higher bond of the children of God, that of the *familia dei.* In case of conflict, the order of the Kingdom of God takes priority over the order of creation.

Jesus' attitude toward the state can be inferred from a few passages. He developed no comprehensive political philosophy, however. His opinion of world rulers is clear from Matthew 20:25, "You know that the rulers of the Gentiles lord it over them, and their great men exercise authority over them." But "it shall not be so among you": a wholly different situation is exhibited by the community of disciples, who have subordinated their wills to the sovereignty of God. Their essential characteristic is service. "Whoever would be great among you must be your servant" (Matt. 20:26). The state and the eschatological community of the redeemed differ completely from each other; so also do world dominion and God's dominion. Jesus' life on earth is characterized also by service—service that leads Him not to an earthly throne but to the cross and, finally, after His ascension, to the throne of God. His kingdom is not of this world (John 18:36). One day He will reign as King over a kingdom where there will be no more violence or demonic power. In the discussion of tribute money (Mark 12:13 ff.) Jesus looked beyond the factional disputes of the day. Just as the state (in this case the hated foreign state of Rome) is to receive the money that belongs to it, so God is to be given what belongs to Him.

Jesus established no new social order, nor any new system of property ownership; He did not incite to social revolution. The Kingdom of God will be the just social order. Although Jesus did not wholly condemn material possessions, He did point out the danger of riches: they make entrance into the Kingdom difficult, if not impossible. Even in the parable of the rich man whose barns were overflowing, Jesus did not condemn riches in themselves; rather He condemned the folly of trusting in possessions and not in God (Luke 12:16 ff.). In one case—that of the rich young man (Mark 10:17 ff.)—Jesus required complete renunciation of material possessions, for He was extending him the opportunity of becoming a disciple. Once while addressing the disciples, Jesus blessed the poor and offered them the prospect of participation in the Kingdom of God (Luke 6:20; Matt. 5:3). The beatitudes, the parable of the rich man and Lazarus (Luke 16:19ff.) and the statement about reward for discipleship (Mark 10:29 ff.) all contain the thought of a future justice that will balance the scales.

4. *The Idea of Reward in the Moral Teaching of Jesus.* Jesus made it clear that man can lay no claim for reward from God; he can only do his duty (Luke 17:10). It is God's prerogative to reward as He wills. This is especially evident in the parable of the workers in the vineyard (Matt. 20:1-16). Despite their varying hours of labor, all received the same wages. This arrangement contradicts the idea of social justice. But that is not Jesus' concern here; He wishes to show that God's reward is of grace. He thus categorically rejects the Jewish concept of demanding fixed recompense from God on the basis of personal moral achievement. He also rejects the idea of reward as a compelling motive for ethical behavior. Jesus' disciple endeavors to do the will of God not because he expects to be rewarded but because he is constrained to such action by love of God and neighbor. God rewards men because He honors all service done unto Him. For Jesus' disciples, the most compelling motive for ethical conduct is the ethical imperative that stems from the very nature of God (Luke 6:36).

God rewards *every* good deed. Even the smallest good deed done unto the poor, unto the very least and needy, is not overlooked (Matt. 10:42; cf. Luke 14:12 ff.). Sacrifices made in the course of discipleship for the sake of God's Kingdom will also be richly rewarded (Mark 10:29 f.). He who dedicates himself wholly to God and to serving his neighbor obtains true and abundant life; for "whosoever shall seek to save his life shall lose it; and whosoever shall lose his life shall preserve it" (Luke 17:33).

5. *Jesus and Jewish Legalism.* For Jesus, the Scriptures (the Old Testament) were a record of divine revelation to Israel—the determinative authority for thought, life, and action. From this followed His basic attitude toward the law: He affirmed it, and considered fulfilling of the law and the prophets to be His mission (Matt. 5:17). But He attacked the legalistic interpretation of the law and the plethora of ordinances imposed by the scribes. The law, in which the will of God finds expression, is after all understandable in and of itself. When, despite this fact, Jesus came as the new interpreter of the law, He did so because He was reestablishing the *original* significance of the divine commandments. He demanded a "righteousness" exceeding that of the scribes and Pharisees (Matt. 5:20). Proper conduct is possible only, however, where the whole counsel of God is recognized (5:21 ff.). This awareness may sometimes lead to violation of the letter of the law. For example, Jesus set Himself above the Sabbath commandment and ignored its legalistic observance when the saving of human life was involved. For "the sabbath was made for man, and not man for the sabbath" (Mark 2:27). In controversies over healing on the Sabbath, Jesus held forth the principle that the obligation to do good takes precedence over perfunctory observance of the Sabbath commandment.

But Jesus reserved His strongest criticism for legalistic ritualism. The ceremonial laws of purification mean nothing unless one is concerned with purity of heart. For "there is nothing from without a man, that entering into him can defile him: but the things which come out of him, those are they that defile the man" (Mark 7:15). Jesus criticizes the scribes and Pharisees for keeping the outside of the cups and vessels clean while they neglect inner purity (Matt. 23:25 f.). Further, more important than proper payment of the tithe is keeping justice, mercy; and good faith (Matt. 23:23). That is the essential heart of the law.

Jesus did not abolish the Jewish practices of fasting, almsgiving, and praying. He did, however, fight against the hypocrisy that so often was associated with them (Matt. 6:1 ff.). He showed His disciples how to fast, to pray, and to do good in a manner pleasing to God. In the Lord's prayer He taught them the true manner of praying (Matt. 6:9-13; Luke 11:2-4; cf. also Luke 18:9-14).

By virtue of His sovereign and unique authority, Jesus went so far in one case as to annul a legal provision (Mark 10:3 ff.). Mosaic law permitted divorce initiated by the husband. This provision, said Jesus, was made only because of the hardness of men's hearts; as verified in the plan of creation, it is not in keeping with the Creator's original intent. For "from the beginning of creation God made them male and female." That is why marriage bonds are indissoluble. "What . . . God hath joined together, let not man put asunder" (Mark 10:9).

D. *Jesus' Intuitive Knowledge of God*

Underlying all the declarations of Jesus is the intuitive knowledge of God that was His as the Son. Jesus brought no new teaching about God; He did, however, bring a deeper meaning to Judaism's concept of God. It is apparent from the eschatological character of His proclamation that for Him, God was primarily the God who reveals His sovereignty. Jesus was concerned, therefore, that men come into a right relationship with God.

But Jesus was also aware of the redemptio-historical significance of revelation. The God whom Jesus proclaimed is the God who testified of Himself in Israel through Moses and the prophets (Matt. 5:17), the God of Abraham, Isaac, and Jacob (Mark 12:26). He is the one God, beside whom there is none other (Mark 12:32). Firm and absolute monotheism was the basis of Jesus' faith in God. God is the Creator of heaven and earth. He is the God who rules in the world in history, the God who manifests concern for all creatures (Matt. 6:25 ff). He is full of goodness and mercy, and knows men's needs. People's lives are completely in His control. Therefore they must always recognize their dependence upon Him. Above all, Jesus proclaimed the God who is nigh; in God He saw the heavenly Father who is interested in His children in all their circumstances (Matt. 6:34). Jesus Himself spoke of God as His Father (Matt. 10:32 and elsewhere) and taught His disciples to say "Father" in praying to God (Matt. 6:9; Luke 11:2). God understands the requests that come to Him and hears the prayers of His own (Matt. 7:7); He gives good things to those who ask Him (Matt. 7:11).

God is love in His essential being, and He revealed Himself as this in all that Jesus said and did. God's forgiveness stems from His mercy

(Mark 11:25; Matt. 6:14). He who comes to God as a penitent sinner receives His grace (Luke 18:14). God grants forgiveness, however, not just to those who come back to Him after having turned away (Luke 15:11 ff.), but also to the disciples who repeatedly stand guilty and needy before Him (Matt. 6:12).

But Jesus saw God not only as the God who gives but also as the God who expects. In man's encounter with God, the God who also confronts him in his neighbor relations, man learns what God requires of him.

As sovereign Lord, God will be man's judge in the last judgment. Everyone must then give an account of all he has said and done. God, therefore—even in His revelation in Jesus Christ—is to be not only loved but also feared. He is able to destroy body and soul in hell (Matt. 10:28).

E. The Miracles of Jesus

Miracles are not understood to be, as modern thought would say, disruptions of natural law or of the "normal cosmic order"; rather, they are divine acts of power that serve to attest Jesus' messianic office. They are a revelation of His glory and signify the dawning of the Kingdom of God. They are closely related, therefore, to Jesus' preaching ministry. In the miracles, Jesus' proclamation of the sovereignty of God now manifested in Him takes actual form. What will be true in the future is present reality in the works of Jesus: the sick are healed, evil spirits are driven out, the dead are raised (Luke 7:21 ff.). Through the miracles, which to Jesus' contemporaries seemed monstrous, paradoxical manifestations that defied rational explanation, the power of the coming age breaks in upon a doomed world. The miracles prefigured the messianic order of redemption, which will be fully realized in the return of Christ; at the same time they are also a restoration of the original order of creation. For the miracles of Jesus liberate men from the powers that bring ruin and destruction. As Jesus explains in Matthew 12:28: "If I cast out devils by the Spirit of God, then the kingdom of God is [already] come unto you."

Jesus was aware that He was a miracle-worker in the service of God. He acted through the "Spirit of God" or "with the finger of God" (Luke 11:20). From Him issued a supernatural power of healing (Mark 5:30). According to Luke 5:17, He performed miracles of healing because the "power of the Lord" operated in Him. Often He healed by laying His hands upon the sick (Luke 4:40). The decisive thing always, however, was His word (Mark 1:41 f. and elsewhere). This word was so powerful that it could heal people even at a distance (Matt. 8:13). Jesus defended Himself vigorously against the accusation of the Pharisees that He cast out devils by Beelzebub, the prince of the devils (Matt. 12:24). He did not underestimate the formidable strength of these powers; He knew, however, that the authority granted Him was stronger than the demons of the world. The prerequisite to healing was belief in Jesus' mighty power. He challenged people to believe on Him also because of His miracles (Matt. 11:20 ff.; John 10:38; 14:11); He set little value, however, on belief that rested merely on miracles (John 4:48). In no case did He force His miracles upon people; on the contrary, He often warded off crowds of the sick and ailing who pressed around Him, and withdrew from them (Mark 1:38 and elsewhere). He harshly opposed demands for spectacular miracles to prove His claims, for these were usually prompted by wrong motives (Matt. 12:38 ff.; 16:1 ff.; John 2:18; 6:30). The miracles Jesus performed stood wholly in the service of His proclamation of the Kingdom of God.

VI. THE PERSON OF JESUS

One cannot answer the question of Jesus' consciousness of His identity and mission by stating—as modern critics tend to do—that He believed Himself to be merely a rabbi, prophet, miracle-worker, and no more. To be sure, He was an authoritative teacher: He disputed with His opponents in the manner of Jewish legal debaters; words of wisdom that He spoke have been recorded. As prophet He proclaimed the dawning of the Kingdom of God and, with apocalyptic vision, foretold the course of last things. There is no question but that He performed miracles. But one does not do Him justice by merely characterizing Him as the "last herald," whose significance is "unique" because "nothing more comes after him but God himself" (Conzelmann). To assert that the "Christological appellations" attributed to Jesus originated in the faith of the Church robs Jesus of the exalted position and the majesty that He claimed for Himself. In other words, the person and work of Jesus can be understood only if He actually considered Himself to be the Messiah and applied the Jewish messianic titles to Himself with a new depth of understanding.

A. *Jesus' Consciousness of Mission*

From the time of His baptism, Jesus declared Himself to be the One sent from God. This He expressed in His very first public appearance in the synagogue at Nazareth with quotations from Isaiah (Isa. 61:1 f.; 58: 6; cf. Luke 4:18 ff.). Especially chosen by God, He is the favored Charismatic One who possesses the gifts of healing, of exorcism, and of forgiveness of sins (Mark 2:10; Luke 5:24; Matt. 9:6). He is the eschatological Redeemer, sent to fulfill God's plan of redemption for His people. Therefore He is greater than Jonah, the preacher of repentance, and greater than Solomon, the sage of antiquity (Matt. 12:41 f.). How Jesus comprehended the task for which He was sent He revealed by using the first person when speaking of His advent. He came to call sinners to repentance (Mark 2:17; Luke 5:32), to seek and to save that which is lost (Luke 19:10), to send fire on the earth (Luke 12:49), to establish a new order of life for His disciples (Matt. 5:17), to minister, and to give His life a ransom for many (Mark 10:45; Matt. 20:28). The devils acknowledge that Jesus came to destroy them (Mark 1:24; Luke 4:34). Jesus' words about His coming showed that with Him the time had dawned when all messianic-eschatological promises would be fulfilled. To John the Baptist, who sent the anxious message, "Art thou he who is come?," Jesus replied that with His works the time of salvation had begun (Matt.

11:4 f.; Luke 7:22). As the One sent from God, Jesus summons men not only into the Kingdom of God but also to Himself. He will restore the weary and heavy-laden (Matt. 11:28 f.).

B. *Jesus' Messianic Consciousness*

Jesus' awareness of His mission presumes certainty of His Messiahship. The Church's faith in the Messiah was not an outgrowth of Easter; it originated, rather, in Jesus' own preaching. It is true that the title "Christ" does not often occur in the Synoptics. Jesus Himself used this title of honor very little (but cf. Mark 9:41; 12:35 ff.; 13:21). In Mark 12:35 ff. He responds to the scribes' assertion that Christ is the son of David. Jesus obviously did not parade and emphasize His position as the son of David. Important only is the fact that as the Messiah He is greater than David— He is David's Lord.

The name Christ is found chiefly in testimonies (by the disciples and by demons) given to Christ's identity and redemptive work. Most significant is Peter's confession made near Caesarea Philippi (Mark 8:29; Matt. 16:16), which leads Jesus to inform the disciples of His coming passion and resurrection.

Undoubtedly Jesus knew that He was the Messiah. He was anointed in His baptism as the Saviour-King of the endtime. This knowledge He kept to Himself until Caesarea Philippi. Of the demon-possessed—who knew Him to be the Messiah—He demanded silence (Mark 3:11 f. and elsewhere); after Peter's confession and the transfiguration He gave His disciples strict instructions not to reveal His messiahship (Mark 8:30; 9:9). At the same time, Jesus spoke and acted as the Messiah from the very beginning of His ministry. It is quite likely, then, that Mark's writing his Gospel from the viewpoint of messianic secrecy was wholly in keeping with Jesus' intention. And therefore it is impossible to say, as do such scholars as Wrede and Conzelmann, that Mark reflects some subsequently developed theory. It is true, of course that the Gospel of John gives a different presentation. Here immediately after their call the disciples bear witness to Jesus as the Christ and Jesus reveals Himself through the "I am's" as the Messiah sent from God. This is related to the unique purpose of the Fourth Gospel.

C. *The Son of Man*

"Son of Man" is the phrase that most strongly expresses Jesus' messianic consciousness. This is especially true in the Synoptic Gospels, less so in John's Gospel. It is striking that others never use the title "Son of Man" in addressing Jesus; it is used only by Jesus Himself. By it He indicates His role in the story of redemption and in eschatological history. The name goes back to Daniel 7:13 and to apocalyptic traditions (the Book of Enoch and others).

References to the Son of Man in the Synoptic Gospels fall into three categories. They refer, first, to the promised Son of God; second, to the One who is presently at work; and third, to the suffering and risen Son of Man. Even when He speaks of the Son of Man in the third person, Jesus does not mean another Messiah, someone other than Himself (as Bultmann contends); He means Himself. The theory that the early Church invented the "Son-of-Man dogmatics" and first applied it to Jesus is untenable. If one accepts this theory, the person and work of Jesus becomes totally incomprehensible.

References to the future *parousia* of the Son of Man are "veiled words of revelation" that speak of the appearance of Christ in power and glory (Mark 8:38; 9:1; 13:26; 14:62). In His earthly existence, Jesus is the Lowly Son of Man; that is, His glory is veiled. As the One sent from God, He leads a transient, restless existence: He has no place to lay His head (Matt. 8:20), and He is destined to minister to mankind (Luke 19: 10); on the other hand, as the Son of Man He is Lord of the Sabbath (Mark 2:28), has power to forgive sins, and is called to establish a new dispensation of salvation. Man's destiny in time and eternity is determined by His attitude toward this Son of Man (Luke 12:8 f.). Moreover, statements about the suffering dying Son of Man who would rise again were not formulated by the early Church after these things occurred; rather, they were prophecies made by Jesus Himself, in which He perceived the fulfillment of Old Testament prophecies (Mark 9:12; 14:21; Luke 18: 31 ff.); they grow out of a clear recognition of the path that God had ordained for Him (Mark 8:31; 9:31; 10:33f.). Jesus taught these prophecies concerning His passion to the disciples (Mark 9:31 f.); His disciples, however, did not fully understand them at first.

The title "Servant of God" (from the Ebed-Jahweh songs, particularly from Isaiah 53) Jesus used of Himself only rarely, and then with diffidence (Mark 10:45; Luke 22:37; cf. John 10:11, 17 f., and especially Jesus' words at the last supper: Mark 14:24; Matt. 26:28; Luke 22:20). But Jesus revealed awareness of His identity by applying to Himself and to His redemptive work the concepts involved in the terms "Son of Man" and "Servant of God," closely associated with each other, and thus gave the deepest possible meaning and significance to His suffering and death. Matthew (in 8:7 and 12:18ff.) cites Isaiah 53:4 and 42:1-4 to show that in Jesus' healing of the sick Isaiah's prophecy concerning the servant of God is fulfilled. In the testimony he gave his disciples about Jesus, John the Baptist (John 1:29, 36) presented Jesus as the "Lamb of God" (Isa. 53:4, 7).

D. *The Son of God*

In Judaism the title "Son of God" is rarely used of the Messiah. In the Gospels it occurs more frequently, as in the accounts of Jesus' baptism, temptation, and transfiguration, in the cries of the demon-possessed (Mark 3:11; Luke 4:41), in the parable of the evil husbandman (Mark 12:6), and in Jesus' interrogation before the high priest (Mark 14:61). Jesus Himself refers to Himself as the "Son," who stands in a peculiar relationship to God; He is vested with absolute authority by His Father and is the Revealer of God; for "neither knoweth any man the Father, save the Son, and he to whomsoever the Son will reveal him" (Matt. 11:27; Luke 10:22). In an exclusive manner He speaks of God as *His* Father (Matt. 7:21) and does not include Himself in the expression "our Father" (Matt. 6:9). But there are things that He does not know, for God has reserved them unto Himself. The Son, for example, does not know the hour of the *parousia* of the Son of Man (Mark 13:32). John's Gospel makes greater use of the title "the Son of God" than do the Synoptic Gospels.

The prologues of Matthew and Luke answer the question about the origin of Jesus' identity as the Son of God. In the account of the virgin birth, it is emphasized that Jesus was begotten by the power of the Holy Spirit. "Therefore," the angel says to Mary (Luke 1:35), "that holy thing which shall be born of thee shall be called the Son of God." From the very beginning a divine mystery surrounds Jesus; He comes directly from God. This acknowledgment is given special delineation in the Fourth Gospel.

VII. PASSION, DEATH, AND RESURRECTION OF JESUS

After an extended ministry in Galilee, interrupted by several trips to Jerusalem for feast-day observances, Jesus' path led Him through suffering to death. Those faithful to the law—scribes and Pharisees—were ready with accusations, including political accusations (Mark 3:6; 8:15; 12:13). John reports a steadily growing succession of threats and attacks upon Jesus' life (John 5:16, 18; 7:1, 25, 30, 32; 8:59; 10:31, 39), behind which stood the Council. Shortly before the last Passover, the highest Jewish officialdom formally resolved to put Jesus to death (John 11:47 ff.). Twice orders were issued for His arrest (John 7:32; 11:57). These first plans to kill Jesus failed. But the triumphal entry into Jerusalem, coupled with the stir caused by the raising of Lazarus (John 11:45 f.), and also Jesus' own increasingly biting attacks (Matt. 12:12, 38 ff.), drove the Council to decisive action. Judas' betrayal eliminated the doubts that stood in the way of arresting Jesus during the feast.

After Jesus had observed the Passover with His disciples and had instituted the observance of Communion, He was taken prisoner in the garden of Gethsemane and brought to Annas, the high priest (who was no longer in office), where He was subjected to a preliminary interrogation (John 18:19 ff.). In the same night Jesus was taken to the high priest Caiaphas, who had convened the Council (John 18:24; Mark 14:53). This was the decisive judicial proceeding that led to Jesus' conviction on the charge of blasphemy. Since the Council could not carry out the death penalty, Jesus was brought before Pilate, the Roman governor, who tried to evade making a decision. Finally, however, he yielded to pressures from the Jewish accusers and surrendered Jesus into their hands. The charge that Jesus was politically dangerous decided the issue (Matt. 15:2 f.; Luke 23:1 f.; John 18:33); Pilate confirmed and thus validated the death sentence of the Jewish authorities. Crucifixion was a method of execution frequently used by the Romans.

Jesus died on a Friday, according to John, whose chronology is probably to be preferred to that of the Synoptic writers (see section II); the execution took place on the fourteenth day of the Passover month of Nisan. Jesus' words on the cross once again show the depth of His capacity for suffering, and His greatness as the Son of God. The body of Jesus was buried in the garden of Joseph of Arimathea (Matt. 27:60; John 19:41). The resurrection occurred on the third day after Jesus' crucifixion and burial (Mark 16:1ff.; Matt. 27:62ff.; 28:1ff.; Luke 24:1ff.; John 20:1ff.). Jesus appeared to His disciples for forty days in transfigured form. The ascension concludes His earthly ministry; it brings about His exaltation to the right hand of God (i.e., His "accession to the throne"), thus making Him Lord of the universe and of His Church (Phil. 2:9).

The Christology of early Christianity comprises the person and work of Christ. There are differences in terminology and emphasis (for example, in Paul and in the letter to the Hebrews), but the entire New Testament bears the same witness to God's acting in Jesus Christ. The basic confession is: Jesus Christ the Lord. From this foundation, the various Christological declarations developed: Christ is the Son of God, the one whose origin is in God, who proceeded from God, who completed His redemptive work on earth, who as the Exalted One exercises sovereign power, and who one day, at His return, will bring about the perfecting of the Church and of the cosmos.

JESUS CHRIST
THE DIVINE REDEEMER

Calvin D. Linton

Calvin D. Linton is professor of English literature and dean of Columbian College, The George Washington University, Washington, D.C. He holds the A.B. degree from George Washington and the A.M. and Ph.D. from Johns Hopkins University. Dr. Linton has served various government agencies as a consultant in report writing. He is author of How to Write Reports *and* Effective Writing.

6. *Calvin D. Linton*

JESUS CHRIST
THE DIVINE REDEEMER
Our Lord's Teaching and Works

INTRODUCTION

ONE OF THE most desperate quests of our time is for personal identity. Beneath the weight of countless millions of souls, behind the faceless façade of statistics, sociological categories, and psychological "types," the individual feels himself lost, totally absorbed and insignificant. By joining a "group," he may feel for a few moments an illusory sense of reality, of at least corporate identity, as if a single soul had taken possession of alienated individual fragments and formed a robot, a death-in-life machine. Separate from his fellows he finds the loneliness intolerable, and he fears the infinite void, the dark endlessness of non-being.

To millions, the inevitability of individual death demonstrates irrefutably the ultimate absurdity of the universe. That which is inescapably doomed to nothingness can make no valid claim to significance, meaning, or identity. The materialistic existentialist may try to make anxiety itself, the fear of non-being, become the basis of being; and the mystic may try to conceive of nothingness as the ultimate good. But neither can touch the unassuageable yearning of the human consciousness for redemption and continuation, for illumination and fulfillment, for purposeful being and timelessness—for, in short, an abundant life.

Over the millennia, men have tried to explain on natural grounds this strange tension in man, this discontented self-scrutiny that finds no peace and no end. Some say it results from the discrepancy between what man is, after (in this view) his long rise upward from the mud, and what he may become. But in what does this awareness of what he "may become" reside? How can natural forces, always seeking their own level, "naturally" produce that which is dissatisfied with itself? Others attribute the tension

121

to the malignancy of imagined Dark Powers in the universe, which hate man. But then how is man also capable of happiness? Natural (biological) man is neither so miserable as infinite malice could accomplish, nor so happy as infinite beneficence could cause. There must be another ingredient, another dimension, where the secret lies.

The Bible tells us what it is: man's own greatest gift, his freedom. Without freedom, happiness would be un-self-conscious and hence compatible only with a lower nature than man's. Moral responsibility is a power, an element of greatness, an aspect of being dependent upon a spiritual nature, permitting man to commune with God. And the Bible tells us the reason for man's predicament. It is moral (spiritual) rebellion and its consequence, alienation—not merely separation, for man cannot find that place in the universe where God is not, but alienation, with offense. Man has initiated antagonism between himself and the only wise God, between himself as creature and God the Creator, between himself and Truth, Goodness, Beauty, Order, and Meaning. "Your iniquities have separated between you and your God, and your sins have hid his face from you, that he will not hear" (Isa. 59:2).

This is the hardest truth man confronts, to say with Job, "Behold, I am vile; what shall I answer thee? I will lay mine hand upon my mouth" (Job 40:4); to know that, apart from God's grace, "ye will revolt more and more: the whole head is sick, and the whole heart faint. From the sole of the foot even unto the head there is no soundness in it; but wounds, and bruises, and putrifying sores . . ." (Isa. 1:5, 6).

The consequence of this alienation is spiritual death. Since the fall of Adam, all men have been born into a doomed life, in which the desires of the body and of the mind are felt and gratified (Eph. 2:3) but in which the spiritual capacity is dead because of sin (rebellion).

In this condition of spiritual death, no hope can come from ideas, or from ethics, or from metaphysics, or from social structures. Only He who first gave the spirit life, God, can, by another act of creation, restore life to it. "I, even I, am the LORD; and beside me there is no saviour" (Isa. 43:11).

So every page of the Bible speaks of the Person of God our Saviour, every promise of salvation tells of a Person. Every gracious offer is of healing for personal alienation. "Look unto me, and be ye saved, all the ends of the earth: for I am God, and there is none else" (Isa. 45:22). "Acquaint now thyself with him, and be at peace" (Job 22:21a).

And the great light emanating from the Person of God, shining throughout the Old Testament, becomes focused with brilliant intensity on the Person of that God, in the form of Son and Servant, revealed in the New Testament, whose name is Jesus. "These things have I written unto you that believe on the name of the Son of God; that ye may know that ye have eternal life . . ." (I John 5:13). "Not by works of righteousness which we have done, but according to his mercy he saved us, by the washing of regeneration, and renewing of the Holy Ghost; which he shed on us abundantly through Jesus Christ our Saviour" (Titus 3:5, 6).

From beginning to end, the matter is one of personal relationship, of identity, of a love relationship between God and man, broken by man, and healed by God, who took the form of sinful flesh to redeem all who call upon His name in faith. Without a personal encounter, there is no restoration, "for other foundation can no man lay than that is laid, which is Jesus Christ" (I Cor. 3:11).

This essay is written within these convictions and certain others: first, that the Old and New Testaments are our sole infallible source of information about God and His salvation, and are written for our instruction, not for our argument and refutation; second, that the scriptural view of history and man is valid in reason and faith, compatible with all true knowledge and man's nature and need; and third, that the historical Jesus of the New Testament is He of whom the prophets spake, the Ancient of Days, known to Abraham and Isaac and Jacob, the "Alpha and Omega, the beginning and the ending, . . . which was, and which is to come, the Almighty" whose words to His redeemed, as to John, are, "Fear not; I am the first and the last: I am he that liveth, and was dead; and behold, I am alive for evermore, Amen; and have the keys of hell and of death" (Rev. 1:8c, 17, 18).

"BOTH TO DO AND TO TEACH"

Man-made religions so uniformly consist only or chiefly of a set of teachings, of formulas for living, of principles of conduct, that many (even many Christians) mistakenly believe that the central significance of Jesus is that He gave us moral instruction. But if that were true, the Incarnation need not have taken place, for there is no inadequacy in the moral instruction of the law recorded in the Old Testament. The same Lord who spoke to Moses on the mountain could have spoken again to expand, emphasize, or clarify any aspect of the moral code given to the nation of Israel. He need not have humbled Himself and taken on the form of a servant; He need not have left the courts of everlasting glory and been born of a Jewish virgin; He need not have hungered and thirsted, or been tempted and smitten; He need not have died on the cross, or risen from the dead, or ascended to the Father. If teaching were all that were required, the Scriptures would end with Malachi. Actually, all these events took place that the Scriptures might be fulfilled.

No, it is not that the teaching is inadequate and needs improvement; it is that man is inadequate—dead, spiritually, indeed—and needs a Saviour. "By the deeds of the law there shall no flesh be justified in his sight: for by the law is the knowledge of sin" (Rom. 3:20).

It is, therefore, only on the basis of what Jesus *did,* and of *who He is,* that His perfect teaching is authoritative, available, and meaningful. Luke is quite clear on this point when he describes the nature of his own earlier writing: "The former treatise have I made, O Theophilus, of all that Jesus began both to do and teach, until the day in which he was taken up, after that he through the Holy Ghost had given commandments unto the apostles whom he had chosen: to whom also he showed himself alive after his passion by many infallible proofs, . . . speaking of the things pertaining to the kingdom of God" (Acts 1:1-3). "Both to *do* and to teach"—and these doings and teachings are to be received because of who Jesus is, He by whom the worlds were made, the only Lord.

Wise men in all ages have uttered profound words, but none but the God-man Jesus Christ has been able to say, "Lazarus, come forth," as well as to teach about eternal life; or to say truly, "For as the Father hath life in himself; so hath he given to the son to have life in himself"; or "I am the resurrection and the life"; or "I lay down my life, that I might take it again. No man taketh it from me, but I lay it down of myself. I have power to lay it down, and I have power to take it again."

From the first, therefore, we must recognize that Jesus the Redeemer is He who has *acted* to redeem us; His teachings are authenticated by His deeds and may be received only by those who have accepted the work of redemption in their own lives. The king's laws apply only to citizens of the kingdom. To those who reject the king, He has only judgment, not instruction, for "he that believeth not is condemned already, because he hath not believed in the name of the only begotten Son of God" (John 3:18). This Nicodemus had to learn painfully when he tried to engage in an ethical dialogue with a king into whose kingdom he had never been born. God is a God of the living (spiritually), not the dead; the teaching of the Sermon on the Mount is for the redeemed.

Let us, therefore, always observe both what Jesus did and what He taught in the same context, that of His Lordship. And let us also have in mind another and infinite dimension of His teachings, namely, that He *is* the Word made flesh. His teachings are not merely helpful counsel but divine truth itself, incarnate (embodied). "The sayings that I have spoken unto you are spirit, and are life" (John 6:63). "If a man keep my saying, he shall never see death" (John 8:51). "Heaven and earth shall pass away, but my words shall not pass away" (Matt. 24:35). Here is a unique and marvelous dimension of reality, the only unalterable reality, the reality that is with God from eternity, and that is God, and that was made flesh and dwelt among us, full of grace and truth.

All this, then, is a wholeness, a perfect unity—teachings, doings, being.

JESUS AND HIS KINGDOM

The centrality of the Kingdom in Jesus' ministry, both His teaching and His works, is a matter some overlook and others find confusing. Many think of the Kingdom as being peculiarly of the Old Testament, and of the Church as being in some way a substitute for it in the New Testament. Others think of the Kingdom as that which is promised exclusively to national Israel; still others as a magnificent but rather vague condition of heaven; yet others as a condition that gradually improving man will ultimately set up for himself on this earth by ever more closely obeying the social teachings of Jesus.

The topic is vast, and no pretense is made here of dealing with it in any complete or definitive way. There are endless books on the subject, some useful.

The present purpose, rather, is to underscore certain plain and key assertions about the Kingdom, as we find Jesus Himself uttering them, and also to note how they are relevant to the larger picture of Jesus as Redeemer and King.

We must clearly understand that though Jesus' human activities had little or nothing of the outward marks of earthly kingship, yet His every deed is an assertion of His royal rights and of His kingly powers. We must understand, too (and here we touch on a subject of great interest and almost limitless opportunities for biblical study), that the concept of the Kingdom of God is inscrutable unless we view it from the perspective of the Old Testament. Surely all those who first came to Jesus understood it in this light and strove to comprehend it in terms of all that Moses and the prophets had written, precisely as Jesus instructed. In other words, the coming of Jesus was not the intervention of a newly devised plan of God, unexpectedly inserted into the stream of history because of the imperfection of an earlier plan, namely, the law. Rather, it was the perfectly harmonious, immutably planned working out of the Gospel of redemption that began to operate the instant after Adam and Eve fell and corrupted the heritage of mankind.

We cannot begin to read the New Testament without having this continuity thrust upon us. The first verse of the chapter of the first book of the New Testament insists upon it: "The book of the generation of Jesus Christ, *the son of David, the son of Abraham*" (Matt. 1:1). John takes us back to the ultimate beginning and tells us of Jesus before time began—"In the beginning was the Word, . . ."

The Kingdom of which Jesus taught will have no end. It is timeless, perfect, blessed, and it is the heritage of the redeemed. It is that unimaginably glorious rule from which Satan rebelled and in natural enmity to which every man since Adam has been born. (The glorious fact that for the redeemed, God is not only sovereign but also Father, that the Son Himself is Elder Brother, and that believers are joint-heirs with Him, is an immense truth, but not the aspect of the Kingdom now being considered.)

The announcement of this Kingdom by the inspired writers of the Old Testament was sufficient in every dimension for any Jew in Jesus' day to accept Him as the promised king, provided the wholeness of scriptural delineation was studied and believed. For the majority of Jews, however, misled by their religious leaders ("Let them alone: they be blind leaders . . ."—Matt. 15:14), only those prophecies speaking of the power and visible rule of the promised king were remembered. Those about Jehovah's Suffering Servant were ignored or spiritualized away. Whenever Jesus' role was questioned by a Jew, Jesus never replied by directing attention away from the Scriptures. Rather, He opened them up more fully, as He did to the disciples on the road to Emmaus. And so the modern Christian who would better understand Jesus' teaching of the Kingdom must study *all* His teaching, including the words He gave Moses and the prophets to speak, as recorded in the Old Testament.

At the moment, however, our attention must be directed almost entirely to the words from His own lips during His earthly ministry, and to His works.

A basic truth to be learned is that Jesus' teaching of the kingdom *is* the Gospel. It is not a peripheral matter; it is what He came to announce. "From that time Jesus began to preach, and to say, Repent: for the kingdom of heaven is at hand" (Matt. 4:17). The primacy of the teaching is put beyond question: "Seek ye *first* the kingdom . . ." (Matt. 6:33).

It was man's rebellion from the sovereignty of God that, in Eden, brought death and all its woes—"Of man's first disobedience, and the fruit of that forbidden tree. . . ." The doom of disobedience is to be cast out of the Kingdom, as Adam and Eve out of Eden, and then discover that only in God's eternal realm is there order, or meaning, or light, or peace, or joy.

It is also the doom of disobedience to truth that the rebel wanders in self-induced disorder, progressively less capable of knowing the difference between truth and error, righteousness and sin, wisdom and folly. He is utterly self-slain, without all hope of self-restoration, depraved (corrupted) in his every capacity. Hence, had not God in His grace maintained, through His Chosen People, Israel, a line of communication of truth and teaching (just as He maintained a living seed-line from Eve to Mary), the heraldic announcements of John the Baptist and the royal proclamation of Jesus would have fallen on ears as totally bewildered as Pilate's. Jesus came to His brethren, to the children of Israel, because He was their promised Messiah, of course, that the Scriptures might be fulfilled ("to the Jew first"); but He also presented Himself to them because in all the rebellious world only the Jew had any idea of the meaning of the Kingdom of God. Only He was familiar with such words as, "Behold my servant, whom I uphold; mine elect, in whom my soul delighteth; I have put my spirit upon him: he shall bring forth judgment to the Gentiles. . . . I the Lord have called thee in righteousness, and will hold thine hand, and will keep thee, and give thee for a covenant of the people, for a light of the Gentiles" (Isa. 42:1, 6). No recorded apostolic sermon of the New Testament fails to relate Jesus' mission to the promises given to Israel, that is, promises of a kingdom.

The Nature of the Kingdom

This, too, is a large and complex topic. Jesus taught much about the nature of the kingdom, mostly in parables—"Therefore is the kingdom of heaven likened unto . . . ." Although biblical scholars do not agree on every detail of the interpretation of the parables, the major points of the teaching can be asserted with confidence.

First, the Kingdom of Heaven is not now visible on earth; nor is it of this world. "If my kingdom were of this world, then would my servants fight . . ." (John 18:36). The rulers of world power, the centers of human authority, the citadels of world thought, the patterns of the world's political structure, the nature of the world's philosophy — these are all foreign. They are all set up in enmity against the Kingdom of Heaven, under, indeed, the ultimate rule of Satan, who "was a murderer from the beginning, and abode not in the truth, because there is no truth in him . . ." (John 8:44). Therefore Jesus came not as a welcome king visiting, after long absence, His loyal citizens, but as a rejected monarch. "Think not that I am come to send peace on earth: I came not to send peace, but a sword" (Matt. 10:34).

When the Almighty unsheathes His sword, there is no doubt of victory; so we know, also, that the heavenly Kingdom will conquer the world. "Be of good cheer; I have overcome the world" (John 16:33c). The final and visible victory will be the consequence, not a gradual leavening of the kingdom of the world by the influence of the Kingdom of Heaven (indeed, it is not provable that leaven is ever used in Scripture as a symbol of good influence), but of the appearing of the King Himself, coming in power and in terrible judgment. "For the Son of Man shall come in the glory of his Father with his angels" (Matt. 16:27a).

Second, therefore, we learn that until that Day of the Lord, promised throughout Scripture, the Kingdom of Heaven is within, for the kingdom is wherever the true King reigns; wherever the individual heart has surrendered, in repentance and faith, becoming as a little child (Matt. 18:3), accepting without question the gracious words, "Fear not, little flock; for it is your Father's good pleasure to give you the kingdom" (Luke 12:32). Every group of believers compose, as it were, a "cell" of loyalty to the true king in the midst of treason, a part of the great secret underground. Although they live in the Satanic world system, they are not of it. They serve as ambassadors to the true King and are assured of a perfect means of communication at any instant with the throne, through prayer. And they are equally assured of the ultimate control of all history by the King, who withholds His judgment only that souls may hear about and accept His offer of amnesty, and be saved, before the doors of time forever close and eternity resumes its changeless sway over the universe. "Behold, I send you forth as sheep in the midst of wolves: be ye therefore wise as serpents, and harmless as doves" (Matt. 10:16).

We learn, third, that perfect obedience is a condition of the Kingdom. Just as disobedience—disbelief, rebellion—shattered the perfect existence of Adam and Eve in communion with God, so must a perfect obedience (beyond the capability of fallen man) restore the union. Here, centrally, is our God both King and Saviour; for it is the King who accomplishes the perfect and atoning obedience in our behalf, creating something far better than merely a restored Edenic relationship. "I came down from heaven not to do mine own will, but the will of him that sent me" (John 6:38). A psalm is echoed: "Then said I, Lo, I come: in the volume of the book it is written of me, I delight to do thy will, O my God: yea, thy law is within my heart" (Ps. 40:7, 8). "And being found in fashion as a man he humbled himself, and became obedient unto death, even the death of the cross" (Phil. 2:8). And the promise: "Though he were a Son, yet learned he obedience by the things which he suffered, and being made perfect, he became the author of eternal salvation unto all them that obey him" (Heb. 5:8, 9). The principle is enunciated first in Genesis, in the promise to Abraham: "In thy seed shall all the nations of the earth be blessed; because thou hast obeyed my voice" (22:18). Without this obedience, the kingdom may not be entered, nor are "good works" possible. "Then said they unto him, What shall we do, that we might work the works of God? Jesus answered and said unto them, This is the work of God, that ye believe on him whom he hath sent. . . . And this is the will of him that sent me, that every one which seeth the Son, and believeth in him, may have everlasting life: and I will raise him up at the last day" (John 6:28, 29, 40).

Fourth, Jesus teaches of the Kingdom that it is both a present possession of the believer and a future condition; that the Kingdom is a matter of progressive revelation and final manifestation, of stages of fulfillment and climactic emergence. Just as the first coming of the Lord Jesus Himself was anticipated by a succession of foretypes, until He Himself was born in Bethlehem, so the Kingdom was foreshadowed, under various foretypical kings (David, most notably), until the King Himself appeared and declared Himself: "The time is fulfilled, and the kingdom of God is at hand: repent ye, and believe the gospel" (Mark 1:15). "The law and the prophets were until John: since that time the kingdom of God is preached, and every man presseth into it" (or ". . . presses his way into it with violence," that is, by the drastic action of repentance, self-condemnation, the exercise of faith—all empowered by grace) (Luke 16:16).

When Jesus walked the earth, the Kingdom was literally present on earth, even though Caesar remained on his throne and Satan continued to rule the world. For the Kingdom is where the King is. Wherever Jesus sat or walked with His disciples, there was the true Kingdom—the King, the authority, the rule, the laws, the citizens, the environment. "Neither shall they say, Lo here! or Lo there! for, behold the kingdom of God is within you" (Luke 17:21). The external kingdom of Israel, set up to reflect the rule of God, had failed through disobedience. Its outward power had vanished, and its spiritual center was dead. "Therefore say I unto you, The kingdom of God shall be taken from you . . ." (Matt. 21:43). And to the disciples, "It is your Father's good pleasure to give you the kingdom" (Luke 12:32*b*).

Since the resurrection and ascension of the Lord, the Kingdom is set up in every believing heart, under the rule of the Holy Spirit. "For as many as are led by the Spirit of God, they are the sons of God" (Rom. 8:14). The body is the realm: "Know ye not that ye are the temple of God, and that the Spirit of God dwelleth in you?" (I Cor. 3:16). Until the Lord comes, the kingdom is of the spirit, for "that which is born of the flesh is flesh, and that which is born of the Spirit is spirit" (John 3:6);

"and I will pray the Father, and he shall give you another Comforter, that he may abide with you for ever; even the Spirit of truth, whom the world cannot receive, because it seeth him not, neither knoweth him: but ye know him; for he dwelleth with you, and shall be in you" (John 14:16, 17). The kingdom is thus the immediate inward possession of the believer. Released from servitude to Satan (". . . because greater is he that is in you, than he that is in the world"—I John 4:4) and to sin ("for sin shall not have dominion over you: for ye are not under the law, but under grace"—Rom. 6:14), the believer spiritually dwells in the peace of the everlasting Kingdom. "For our citizenship is in heaven; from whence also we look for the Saviour, the Lord Jesus Christ" (Phil. 3:20).

Outside is the world, which hates the Kingdom. "If ye were of the world, the world would love his own: but because ye are not of the world, but I have chosen you out of the world, therefore the world hateth you" (John 15:19). With his inner citadel of the spirit "kept by the power of God through faith unto salvation ready to be revealed in the last time" (I Pet. 1:5), the believer assumes the high honor of serving as ambassador of the kingdom. "Ye have not chosen me, but I have chosen you, and ordained you, that ye should go and bring forth fruit, and that your fruit should remain . . ." (John 15:16).

Fifth, we learn that if the Kingdom is a present spiritual possession of the redeemeed, it is also unmistakably, in its ultimate manifestation, a climactic event in future history.

Although there is disagreement among modern biblical scholars as to whether Jesus taught such a future event, to anyone who reads the Bible trustingly, the issue seems beyond question. (For a useful summary of the positions of a dozen or more contemporary scholars, see Norman Perrin's *The Kingdom of God in the Teaching of Jesus* [Philadelphia: The Westminster Press, 1963].) As a matter of fact, few who deny the futurity of the Kingdom deny that Jesus taught it, or that His disciples and the early Church expected it; rather, the concept is dismissed as a misunderstanding on the part of both Jesus and His followers, consequent upon their over-confident and "materialistic" reading of the promises of the Old Testament. Needless to say, such a view does not accept Jesus Himself as Lord and King, nor as the Incarnate Word, but only as a gifted prophet, subject to error and misunderstanding.

Jesus' words are quite direct: "The Son of Man shall come in the glory of his Father with his angels" (Matt. 16:27*a*). (One must remember Daniel 7:13, 14: "I saw in the night visions, and, behold, one like the Son of man came with the clouds of heaven, and came to the Ancient of days, and they brought him near before him. And there was given him dominion, and glory, and a kingdom, that all people, nations, and languages, should serve him: his dominion is an everlasting dominion, which shall not pass away, and his kingdom that which shall not be destroyed.") "The Son of man shall send forth his angels, and they shall gather out of his kingdom all things that offend, and them which do iniquity; and shall cast them into a furnace of fire: there shall be wailing and gnashing of teeth" (Matt. 13:41, 42). "Immediately after the tribulation of those days shall the sun be darkened, and the moon shall not give her light, and the stars shall fall from heaven, and the powers of the heavens shall be shaken: and then shall appear the sign of the Son of man in heaven: and then shall all the tribes of the earth mourn, and they shall see the Son of man coming in the clouds of heaven with power and great glory. And he shall send his angels with a great sound of a trumpet, and they shall gather together his elect from the four winds, from one end of heaven to the other" (Matt. 24:29-31). "Heaven and earth shall pass away, but my words shall not pass away" (Matt. 24:36).

To many who believingly await the return of the King, the quietest words are somehow the best: "I go to prepare a place for you. And if I go and prepare a place for you, I will come again, and receive you unto myself; that where I am, there ye may be also" (John 14:2b, 3). Just before His ascension, His disciples asked Him again: "Lord, wilt thou at this time restore again the kingdom to Israel? And he said unto them, It is not for you to know the times or the seasons, which the Father hath put in his own power" (Acts 1:6, 7). But two angels (of what must have been a mighty host unseen by the disciples), who had received the high honor of attending the Lord on this occasion of His victorious departure from the earth He had redeemed, left us an explicit word: "This same Jesus, which is taken up from you into heaven, shall so come in like manner as ye have seen him go into heaven" (Acts 1:11b). There are really only two attitudes toward these things: either "Amen," or "Not so, Lord"—though Satan would like us to consider a third, one of hesitant, debilitating, Prufrockian doubt: "Yea, hath God said . . . ?"

Jesus' "hard sayings" about the Kingdom must be understood in the light of the finality of the Kingdom, of its absolute ultimate judgment and its universal sway. It is not a realm in which it would be rather pleasant to be; it is the only environment of salvation, outside of which is eternal condemnation. . . . "He will throughly purge his floor, and will gather the wheat into his garner; but the chaff he will burn with fire unquenchable" (Luke 3:17). "And I saw a great white throne, and him that sat on it, from whose face the earth and the heaven fled away; and there was found no place for them. . . . And whosoever was not found written in the book of life was cast into the lake of fire" (Rev. 20:11, 15). "Therefore hell hath enlarged herself, and opened her mouth without measure: and their glory, and their multitude, and their pomp, and he that rejoiceth, shall descend into it" (Isa. 5:14).

Jesus employs every power of parable, metaphor, and direct injunction to shock His listeners into a realization of the urgency, the overwhelming importance, and the immutability of each individual's choice in regard to the Kingdom. Anything is better than living and dying outside the Kingdom—any maiming, any loss, any sacrifice. "It is better for thee to enter into the kingdom of God with one eye, rather than having two eyes to be cast into hell fire" (Mark 9:47b).

Hence, too, the terrible "Woes" pronounced on the religious leaders of Israel, ". . . for ye shut up the kingdom of heaven against men: for ye neither go in yourselves, neither suffer ye them that are entering to go in" (Matt. 23:13). It would be better for a man that a millstone be tied about his neck and that he be cast into the midst of the sea, than he should cause the least seeker of the Kingdom to stumble in his search.

Lastly, under this heading of Jesus and His Kingdom, note the significance of His mighty acts of power, His miracles. It is all well and good to have one claim a status for himself, but does he have the identity and the power that the status demands? The acts of Jesus were "signs," performed not primarily to diminish immediate human suffering in Palestine but to attest to Himself. For every blind man who received his sight, thousands remained in darkness; for one Lazarus raised from the dead, thousands who died that day remained in the tomb; for every man released from demons' possession, legion remained enslaved. If the works of Jesus were intended to alter the balance of suffering and well-being in the world of His day, they utterly failed.

But this was not their purpose. When John the Baptist, in prison, heard of the works of Jesus but saw no visible, worldly evidence of a growing power, "he sent two of his disciples, and said unto him, Art thou he that should come, or do we look for another?" (Matt. 11:2, 3). Jesus' answer was to remind John of the prophecies about the redemptive work of the promised Messiah, and to point to their fulfillment in His own works. "Go and show John again those things which ye do hear and see: the blind receive their sight, and the lame walk, the lepers are cleansed, and the deaf hear, the dead are raised up, and the poor have the gospel preached to them. And blessed is he, whosoever shall not be offended in me" (Matt. 11:4-6). This truth is confirmed in the actions and words of Jesus immediately after His defeat of Satan in the wilderness. Returning "in the power of the Spirit" into Galilee, and going into the synagogue to teach, He heralded His own arrival by reading from the Prophet Isaiah (61:1, 2): "The Spirit of the Lord is upon me, because he hath anointed me to preach the gospel to the poor; he hath sent me to heal the broken-hearted, to preach deliverance to the captives, and recovering of sight of the blind, to set at liberty them that are bruised, to preach the acceptable year of the Lord. And he closed the book . . ." (Luke 4:18-20). The beautiful propriety of "closing the book" at that precise point (in the middle of Isaiah's sentence) is that the next phrase has to do with the second coming of the King, in judgment: ". . . and the day of vengeance of our God" (Isa. 61:2).

So, from us as from John the Baptist, the Lord commands attention to and belief in His works, for in them He proved His identity and His kingship. "For as the Father raiseth up the dead, and quickeneth them; even so the Son quickeneth whom he will. For the Father . . . hath committed all judgment unto the Son: that all men should honour the Son, even as they honour the Father. He that honoureth not the Son honoureth not the Father which hath sent him" (John 5:21-23). Throughout all history, unbelievers have denied His miracles; but it is a peculiarity of our times that denial is now an accepted position within some areas of the Church itself, and some of its seminaries. As always, the heart of the problem is not a matter of adequate evidence, or of satisfying the intellectual processes, but of the will, set in natural enmity against belief. Jesus, knowing the heart, perceived no sincerity in those scribes and Pharisees who came to Him, saying, "Master, we should see a sign from thee." "An evil and adulterous generation seeketh after a sign; and there shall no sign be given to it . . ." (Matt. 12:39). Ample evidence for the sincere seeker of truth is provided; the pretense of needing more evidence on the part of those already predetermined not to believe cannot stand before the eye of Jesus. Saving belief is impossible without repentance, and to repent is to do violence to one's own self-esteem (hence Luke 16:16), achieving "repentance toward God, and faith toward our Lord Jesus Christ" (Acts 20:21). The two go together. Mere intellectual assent without repentance and faith is a condition of the devils, who also believe, and tremble (Jas. 2:19). Jesus does not break through the door of the heart; it must be opened from the inside. And in a deeply significant statement, He declares: "If any man will to do his will, he shall know of the doctrine, whether it be of God, or whether I speak of myself" (John 7:17).

As "signs," Jesus' miraculous works were to demonstrate much more than sovereignty and power over the natural universe and the world of physical things. Each act also demonstrated spiritual sovereignty. Bodily disease He cured, but never without spiritual significance. ". . . the Son of man hath power on earth to forgive sins . . ." (Matt. 9:6), and to the skeptical bystanders He demonstrated His power by healing the sick of the palsy. The fact that all bodily illness, all pain and suffering, and death itself are the consequences of sin is the clear teaching of the Bible. Therefore, the relation between the physical acts of healing and the spiritual power to save from sin is demonstrable.

So when the blind were made to see, we find the power to heal the physical disability of blindness a demonstration of the power to make the spiritually blind perceive the truth of God, and the death to hear, both physically and spiritually, and the lame to walk, and the leprous (the most specific physical sign of sin) to be cleansed. Above all, Jesus demonstrated His ability to give that eternal life which He promised—"I am the resurrection, and the life: he that believeth in me, though he were dead, yet shall he live" (John 11:25). Wonderful words, but are they within the power of Him who spoke them? When Jesus entered into the silent room where lay the corpse of Jairus' daughter, no human hope could expect more than tears of compassion. But beside that lifeless body stood the One who had created her, given her a soul, stretched out the heavens with His finger, brought forth all that is. So in that room the three disciples heard a quiet voice: "Little lamb"—a term of endearment, from the lips of Him by whom the worlds were made!—"I say unto thee, arise" (Mark 5:41). That quiet voice reached the remotest corner of infinite space, and at its command the soul returned, and the child lived again.

This is not strange, for when the same Being commanded, "Let there be light," had not the mighty beam burst forth?

No power of nature ("Even the winds and the sea obey him!"), no affliction of the body, no spiritual sickness, no dart of Satan—not even the awful one of death itself—can withstand the power or dispute the rule of this Jesus, a fact His deeds prove. ". . . the Son quickeneth whom he will" (John 5:21). "I am come a light into the world, that whosoever believeth on me should not abide in darkness" (John 12:46). "I and my Father are one" (John 10:30).

No wonder Paul says it is beyond the power of the imagination to conceive of the ultimate realm of such a king!

JESUS THE REDEEMER

The heart of the Gospel, the "good" part of the news of the Kingdom, is not that here is such a kingdom but that there is a way into it, a door of entry, a method for achieving citizenship—in short, a redemption. If this were not so, news of the eternal realm of which Jesus is King would be unbearably ironic, for no unrighteousness may enter into it, and none is righteous. "Because there is wrath, beware lest he take thee away with his stroke: then a great ransom cannot deliver thee" (Job 36:18). "God is angry with the wicked every day. If he turn not, he will whet his sword; he hath bent his bow, and made it ready. He hath also prepared for him the instruments of death" (Ps. 7:11*b*-13*a*).

"If he turn not . . . ." In eternity, there is, as it were, no room in which to turn. But the Gospel of the Kingdom tells us that in this life, in the dimension of time, eternity may be grasped. However, there is only one way to turn, which is to say "to repent." "Except ye be converted [*strepho,* to turn], and become as little children, ye shall not enter into the kingdom of heaven" (Matt. 18:3). Having turned, we face the Redeemer, who teaches what we need to know for our redemption. "Good and upright is the LORD: therefore will he teach sinners in the way" (Ps. 25:8). This verse is echoed in the New Testament: "And Jesus, when he came out, saw much people, and was moved with compassion toward them, because they were as sheep not having a shepherd: and he began to teach them . . ." (Mark 6:34).

Jesus phrased the teachings on redemption in various ways, to meet the specific needs of those who were ready to listen to Him—Nicodemus, the Samaritan woman, the Rich Young Ruler, Zacchaeus, the disciples who forbade the little children to come to Him; yet the summation is always the same: "Come unto me." ". . . He that believeth on me hath everlasting life" (John 6:47). As the child listens with complete responsiveness and belief, so must they listen who turn to Jesus. ". . . He that heareth my word, and believeth on him that sent me, hath everlasting life, and shall not come into condemnation; but is passed from death unto life" (John 5:24). The alternative is explicit: "But after thy hardness and impenitent heart [thou] treasurest up unto thyself wrath, against the day of wrath and revelation of the righteous judgment of God; who will render to every man according to his deeds" (Rom. 2:5, 6). "And who shall be able to stand?" (Rev. 6:17b).

No concept in all Scripture is richer in meaning or more central to the nature of God and of man's need than that expressed in the English verb "to redeem." This is expressed in the original tongues in a variety of words, each suggesting a slightly different dimension, a different facet of the truth. A modern dictionary gives as the chief meanings "to buy back," "to win back," "to liberate by payment," "to free by force," "to release from blame or debt," "to ransom," "to restore," "to reclaim." The force of two Hebrew words, *deputh* (Isa. 50:2) and *paraq* (Ps. 136:24) gives an additional dimension: "to separate," "to break off, to deliver."

Every meaning listed, and other implicit shadings, are directly relevant to man's need; and every action implied in the accomplishment of redemption is indicative of God's nature and work. The predicament is man's caused by his own rebellion; the solution, if there is to be one, must be totally God's. "Thus saith the LORD the King of Israel, and his redeemer the LORD of hosts; I am the first, and I am the last; and beside me there is no God" (Isa. 44:6). "I, even I, am the LORD, and beside me there is no saviour" (Isa. 43:11). "Fear not: for I have redeemed thee, I have called thee by thy name; thou art mine" (Isa. 43:1b). "I have blotted out, as a thick cloud, thy transgressions, and, as a cloud, thy sin: return unto me; for I have redeemed thee. Sing, O ye heavens; for the LORD hath done it . . ." (Isa. 44:22, 23).

Such words stud the Old Testament as diamonds a setting. They are as specific and "hard" as the warnings—the Lord "will not at all acquit the wicked" (Nah. 1:3); "Now consider this, ye that forget God, lest I tear you in pieces, and there be none to deliver" (Ps. 50:22). Except for the "shadowy" lessons of the ritual sacrifice of the Temple worship, "which was a figure for the time then present, in which were offered both gifts and sacrifices" (Heb. 9:9), no one of the Old Testament knew *how* the great promise of redemption could ultimately be accomplished in a way that would at once maintain God's immutable justice and yet clear (redeem) the sinner.

But once the cry of John the Baptist was heard—"Behold the Lamb of God, which taketh away the sin of the world!" (John 1:29)—everything began to fall into place. Every foreshadowing, every foretype, every prophecy, every promise of the Old Testament stood forth sharply, as if a mist had blown away from a blazing mosaic. Over and over, Jesus affirmed that His own coming and His redeeming works were in fulfillment of the Scriptures; that He was that same God who had said, "Look unto me, and be ye saved, all the ends of the earth: for I am God, and there is none else" (Isa. 45:22) ("He that hath seen me hath seen the Father"); that He alone has come down from heaven ("Ye are from beneath; I am from above: ye are of this world; I am not of this world. . . . If ye believe not that I am he, ye shall die in your sins"—John 8:23, 24); that He alone is the Good Shepherd as prophesied in the Scriptures:

"Behold, I, even I, will both search my sheep, and seek them out" (Ezek. 34:11); that He is the sole source of power ("For without me ye can do nothing"—John 15:5); and that there is no other saviour, no other redeemer—"No man cometh unto the Father, but by me" (John 14:6; Isa. 43:11).

And above all else, He revealed the manner in which the age-old promise of redemption should be fulfilled—that He, Son of God and Son of man, would go to Jerusalem at the time of the Passover, and "be delivered unto the chief priests, and unto the scribes; and they shall condemn him to death, and shall deliver him to the Gentiles: and they shall mock him, and shall scourge him, and shall spit upon him, and shall kill him; and the third day he shall rise again" (Mark 10:33, 34). In historical fact and in spiritual reality, the redemptive works foretold in detail throughout the entire Old Testament are, on Calvary, wrought, achieved, accomplished to the last detail, until on the cross He cried, "It is finished" (John 19:30). As He had declared: "The good shepherd giveth his life for the sheep. . . . No man taketh it from me, but I lay it down of myself. I have power to lay it down, and I have power to take it again . . ." (John 10:11*b*, 18). Therefore "ye know," writes Peter, "that ye were not redeemed with corruptible things, as silver and gold . . .; but with the precious blood of Christ, as of a lamb without blemish and without spot" (I Pet. 1:18, 19). And the praise will rise in heaven: ". . . for thou wast slain, and hast redeemed us to God by thy blood . . ." (Rev. 5:9).

The wholeness, the perfection, the total efficacy of this act, this atoning, redemptive death that He "once suffered for sins, the just for the unjust, that he might bring us to God" (I Pet. 3:18), is totally available to all who will accept. With equal (and fearful) force, rejection of this free redemption carries condemnation. "Of how much sorer punishment, suppose ye, shall he be thought worthy, who hath trodden under foot the Son of God, and hath counted the blood of the covenant, wherewith he was sanctified, an unholy thing, and hath done despite unto the Spirit of grace?" (Heb. 10:29). There is no other means of cleansing, "for though thou wash thee with nitre, and take thee much soap, yet thine iniquity is marked before me, saith the Lord GOD" (Jer. 2:22). But always the dark warning is illuminated by the bright promise: "If we walk in the light, as he is in the light, we have fellowship one with another, and the blood of Jesus Christ [God's] Son cleanseth us from all sin" (I John 1:7). The clarity of our knowledge as well as the perfection of the proffered redemption carries a burden of responsibility. "After such knowledge, what forgiveness?" asks T. S. Eliot, echoing Hebrews 2:3, "How shall we escape, if we neglect so great salvation . . .?" "If I had not come and spoken unto them," said Jesus, "they had not had sin: but now they have no cloak for their sin" (John 15:22). What that sin is He explains in declaring that a work of the Holy Spirit is to "reprove the world of sin . . . of sin, *because they believe not on me*" (John 16:8, 9).

Just as the Kingdom awaits final culmination and manifestation, though it is a present reality and the possession of every believer, so the work of redemption awaits completion and fulfillment, though each believer is in present possession of eternal life ("He that hath the Son hath life"— I John 5:12a). Even as the whole creation groans and travails, awaiting the consummation of God's plans, so "even we ourselves groan within ourselves, waiting for the adoption, to wit, the redemption of our body" (Rom. 8:23); for "we have this treasure in earthen vessels," suffering the ills of the flesh, but "knowing that he which raised up the Lord Jesus shall raise up us also by Jesus," and knowing, too, that "if our earthly house . . . were dissolved, we have a building of God, an house not made with hands, eternal in the heavens, . . . that mortality might be swallowed up of life" (II Cor. 4:7, 14; 5:1, 4). Until that Day of the Lord, the security of the redemption is absolute, for it is not in our feeble hands; rather, we "are kept by the power of God through faith unto salvation ready to be revealed in the last time" (I Pet. 1:5). "This is the Father's will which hath sent me," Jesus said, "that of all which he hath given me I should lose nothing, but should raise it again at the last day" (John 6: 39); "for by one offering he hath perfected for ever them that are sanctified" (Heb. 10:14). The stamp of possession of God the Holy Spirit is on every one of the redeemed, "whereby ye are sealed unto the day of redemption" (Eph. 4:30). "I give unto them eternal life; and they shall never perish, neither shall any man pluck them out of my hand" (John 10:28).

THE RESURRECTION

The assurance of redemption is precisely equated in Scripture to the fact of the resurrection. "Him God raised up the third day . . . through his name whosoever believeth in him shall receive remission of sins" (Acts 10:40, 43). For He "was raised again for our justification" (Rom. 4:24). "If Christ be not raised, your faith is vain; ye are yet in your sins" (I Cor. 15:17).

Little wonder, therefore, that of all that the apostles and early disciples taught, the core of unshakable conviction was the actual, physical, historical resurrection of the Lord. Over and over they asserted, as the ground and basis of their message, that "Christ died for our sins according to the scriptures; and that he was buried, and that he rose again the third day according to the scriptures: and that he was seen of Cephas, then of the twelve: after that he was seen of above five hundred brethren at once; of whom the greater part remain unto this present, but some are fallen asleep. After that, he was seen of James; then of all the apostles. And last of all he was seen of me also . . ." (I Cor. 15:3-8). Always they spoke as witnesses—"That which we have seen and heard declare we unto you . . ." (I John 1:3); "for we have not followed cunningly devised fables, when we made known unto you the power and coming of our Lord Jesus Christ, but were eyewitnesses of his majesty" (II Pet. 1:16).

There is equally little wonder that this fact should throughout all history have been the stumbling block of the secular realm and the point of attack from a world determined not to acknowledge this King, "even denying the Lord that bought them" (II Pet. 2:1). Christ's patience was remarkable toward those who, between His resurrection and His ascension, demanded more evidence; but He also made it clear to Cleopas and his companion on the road to Emmaus that the real barrier to belief is in the heart, not the head: "O fools, and slow of heart to believe all that the prophets have spoken" (Luke 24:25). This is that ignorance which is *willed,* of which Peter speaks (II Pet. 3:5), and also Paul, who describes unbelievers as "being alienated from the life of God through the ignorance that is in them, because of the blindness of their heart" (Eph. 4:18). For, in all truth, no intellectual or rational impediment stands between the most careful thinker and belief in the resurrection. The evidence is overwhelming, if it is truly and honestly examined. (As good a place as any for the secular-minded to start is with *Who Moved the Stone?* by Frank Morison [London, 1930, and many reprints, including paperbacks].) Therefore the most common protective gesture of the "willingly ignorant" is to walk quickly away, with a jest and a smile of superior wisdom—as happened to Paul in Athens: "When they heard of the resurrection of the dead, some mocked: and others said, We will hear thee again of this matter." And the consequence of this willed ignorance was the immediate departure of king's ambassador: "So Paul departed from among them" (Acts 17:32, 33). No one is forced into the Kingdom; no one is beaten until he says he believes; no one is deprived of his terrible right to go his own way, not even Judas, who was not forcibly expelled from the Last Supper but who rather heard the terrible, permissive word: "That thou doest, do quickly." And he "went immediately out: and it was night" (John 13: 27, 30). The alternative remains unchanged to this day: either the Inner Room of fellowship, faith, and light, or the darkness and loneliness of the night outside. Each soul freely chooses; none is compelled.

To try to retain Christianity without the resurrection is like trying to retain a definition with nothing to define. If Jesus did not rise, then He was not who He said He was; He did not do those mighty works His biographers say He did; His teachings are no better than the pious utterance of other mere humans; His promises are invalidated; His self-confidence was self-deception; and the apostles (who swore contrary to all this) were the most conscienceless deceivers in the history of the planet.

If all this were, despite its melancholy, inescapably taught by logic and historical research, then it would have to be accepted, no matter how grim. But, on the contrary, to accept it in even the most preliminary way is to embrace manifest logical absurdities and to do violence to the most elementary principles of historical scholarship.

This is not the place in purpose or in scope to attempt even a cursory survey of the evidences of the truth of the resurrection; but perhaps it is appropriate to note one contemporary line of skepticism that tries, futilely, to keep Christ and yet deny that He genuinely rose from the dead. Though centered in the "Bultmann school," it is better known in England and

America in the phrase of James M. Robinson, "a new quest of the historical Jesus," a movement sometimes now called "post-Bultmannian." This point of view (in over-simplified summary) declares that there was a real Jesus but that (as is demonstrably true of so many figures of mythical prowess) His nature and His work were gradually exaggerated, altered, and given fabulous dimensions by adoring writers, who step by step added wondrous deeds and swelling words to the record. So, for example, has it been with the story of King Arthur. It is up to the student of history to determine what actual core of humble truth lies behind the façade of fiction. This he does by unpeeling one layer of the fabulous after another from the real figure. Practitioners of this theory utter with confidence such judgments as, "clearly at later elaboration," or "palpably a combination of fabulous ingredients from the Fertility God myth."

The hitch is that records of the life of Jesus are utterly unlike those of any figure of myth. There *was no* gradual accretion of the miraculous. It is precisely the earliest (indeed, as now acknowledged, the contemporary) sources that are the most precise and inflexible in declaring the miracles and in insisting on the resurrection. The most wonderful deeds are precisely those preached by the apostles and other disciples to crowds who were in a position, had the claims been untrue, to hoot them to scorn. Indeed, it was by reminding the crowd of the miracles they had seen Jesus perform that the apostles compelled belief. The shout of triumph that Jesus was risen was made on the spot where it occurred, and in the presence of those who could instantly and effectually have scotched the claim once and for all had it not been true. Hundreds and thousands believed, and the Jewish and Roman authorities were unable to refute the specific, undaunted, repeated assertion of eyewitnesses that the Lord was alive, precisely as He had promised. Within a few weeks, a group of dispirited, defeated, frightened disciples became transformed into irresistibly courageous witnesses, willing to receive any punishment and torture, flatly refusing to deny what they knew to be true of their own physical experience: that their Lord was alive, victorious over death and hell, as He had declared.

These are the facts of history. The rational man must consider every possible hypothesis put forward to explain them and accept the one that is adequate. The "demythologizing" approach is neither faithful to the facts of history nor logically coherent. Honest skepticism must take recourse in a position once stated to the writer: "I agree that no hypothesis except the resurrection explains the facts; but I refuse to accept it, and I always will."

In sum, the resurrection, not the ethical teachings, was the earliest burden of the messages the apostles preached: "Him God raised up the third day, and shewed him openly; not to all the people, but unto witnesses chosen before of God, even to us, who did eat and drink with him after he rose from the dead" (Acts 10:40, 41); "to whom also he shewed himself after his passion by many infallible proofs, being seen of them forty days, and speaking of the things pertaining to the kingdom of God" (Acts

1:3). The presentation was unfailingly sober, factual, unchanging. Paul's manner was always to reason with his hearers "out of the scriptures, opening and alleging, that Christ must needs have suffered, and risen again from the dead . . ." (Acts 17:2, 3). And the aged John, seeing in his great vision a Being whose glory overwhelmed him, before whom he fell as one dead, felt with amazement a touch and heard a voice with which he had grown familiar years before: "He laid his right hand upon me, saying unto me, Fear not; I am the first and the last: I am he that liveth, and was dead; and behold, I am alive for evermore, Amen . . ." (Rev. 1: 17*b*, 18).

CONCLUSION

"Man is that great and true *amphibium,* whose nature is disposed to live, not only like other creatures in divers elements, but in divided and distinguished worlds: for though there be but one to sense, there are two to reason, the one visible, the other invisible. . . ." So wrote Sir Thomas Browne over three hundred years ago, memorably phrasing a truth he had learned from Scripture and from his own self-examination.

The reality of the visible is, by and large, the only reality to the modern temper, despite the teaching of science that visible matter and invisible energy are but two forms of a single "reality." Science, however, can teach us only of the intangible, not the spiritual, for "the natural man receiveth not the things of the Spirit of God: for they are foolishness unto him: neither can he know them, because they are spiritually discerned" (I Cor. 2:14). To discern the nature of the spiritual and to know that it is the only dimension within which to meet God, it is necessary for one to be taught of God, "giving thanks unto the Father, . . . who hath delivered us from the power of darkness, and hath translated us into the kingdom of his dear Son: . . . who is the image of the invisible God . . ." (Col. 1:12, 13, 15). We have no sure source of knowledge about the unseen world except in the words of Jesus, for "no man hath ascended up to heaven, but he that came down from heaven, even the Son of man which is in heaven. . . . He that cometh from heaven is above all. And what he hath seen and heard, that he testifieth . . ." (John 3:13, 31, 32).

Hence we walk by faith, not by sight, in earnest expectation and fervent hope; ". . . but hope that is seen is not hope: for what a man seeth, why doth he yet hope for? But if we hope for that we see not, then do we with patience wait for it. Likewise the Spirit also helpeth our infirmities . . ." (Rom. 8:24-26). "A little while, and ye shall not see me," Jesus told His disciples; "and again, a little while, and ye shall see me, because I go to the Father. . . . And ye now therefore have sorrow: but I will see you again, and your heart shall rejoice, and your joy no man taketh from you" (John 16:16, 22).

Such seemingly irreconcilable dualities as flesh and spirit, sin and righteousness, time and eternity, hell and heaven, creature and Creator, the world and the Kingdom of God, death and life are ultimately to be resolved only through a new creation, a new divine work, undertaken by that same Jesus by whom all things were made (John 1:3). It will not be by a blending of the warring ingredients into a kind of cosmic half-way-good mélange that the Kingdom will finally be set up. Nor is it by merely diminishing the power of death and sin that Christ has conquered; nor is it by extending time hugely into the future that life is made everlasting. It is by the creative "work" of God, of the kind that in the beginning flung out the heavens in space and breathed spiritual life into Adam and Eve. "My Father worketh hitherto," Jesus said, "and I work" (John 5:17).

The new creation begins with each redeemed soul. "Therefore if any man be in Christ, he is a new creature: old things are passed away; behold all things are become new" (II Cor. 5:17). The Kingdom is peopled, not with those who have been rehabilitated, but with those who have been reborn. ". . . except a man be born of water and of the Spirit, he cannot enter into the kingdom of God. That which is born of the flesh is flesh; and that which is born of the Spirit is spirit" (John 3:5, 6). "Whosoever believeth that Jesus is the Christ is born of God" (I John 5:1a).

The new creation will be culminated when the "heavens and the earth, which are now . . . kept in store, reserved unto fire against the day of judgment . . ." vanish; whereupon "we, according to his promise, look for new heavens and a new earth, wherein dwelleth righteousness" (II Pet. 3:7, 13). Paul gives a hint of a final, humanly unimaginable totality of glory, "when he [Jesus] shall have delivered up the kingdom to God, even the Father; when he shall have put down all rule and all authority and power. For he must reign, till he hath put all enemies under his feet" (I Cor. 15:24, 25).

If we at all believe what Jesus has taught us, the next "sign" the earth sees will be, not a king in disguise, renewing His offer of healing and pardon, but the "wrath of God . . . revealed from heaven against all ungodliness and unrighteousness of men . . ." (Rom. 1:18); "he shall smite the earth with the rod of his mouth, and with the breath of his lips shall he slay the wicked" (Isa. 11:4 b). Israel "shall look upon me whom they have pierced, and they shall mourn for him, as one mourneth for his only son, and shall be in bitterness for him, as one that is in bitterness for his firstborn. In that day shall there be a great mourning . . ." (Zech. 12: 10, 11). As for the world, as presented in John's vision, "The kings of the earth, and the great men, and the rich men, and the chief captains, and the mighty men, and every bondman, and every free man, hid themselves in the dens and in the rocks of the mountains; and said to the mountains and rocks, Fall on us, and hide us from the face of him that sitteth on the throne . . ." (Rev. 6:15, 16). Acknowledgment of His sovereignty, formerly refused by free choice, will then be enforced without choice, "that at the name of Jesus every knee should bow, of things in heaven, and things in earth, and things under the earth; and that every tongue should confess that Jesus Christ is Lord, to the glory of God the Father."

A NOTE ON BIBLIOGRAPHY

Theological writing, like other areas of modern scholarship, is suffering from acute hypertrophy. If wisdom were in direct ration to the bulk of published material, our age would be incomparably learned in the truth. Unhappily, this relationship does not hold true—though one must not be so cynical as to assert an inverse ratio. Insofar as the almost insurmountable body of scholarly writing may form a barrier between the seeker of truth and the Bible itself, it may be more productive of shadow than of light. This is the real danger, not that modern scholarship has in any way discredited the Bible. Indeed, the more one immerses himself in the writings that attempted to do so, the more one realizes the validity, on intellectual and all other grounds, of the traditional view of the Bible as unique, unlike all other books, precisely because it is God's Word and not man's. This article, therefore, has been deliberately written with almost total emphasis on what the Bible says. The writer is not unaware, it is hoped, of the latest developments of modern Biblical scholarship; but he is convinced that the conservative point of view of the Bible's integrity remains unshaken by anything to the contrary so far alleged.

The books listed below are of all shades of opinion. They are mentioned, not because it is felt that in all cases their positions are valid, but because they are representative. Nowhere in Scripture is it promised that "ye shall be guided in all things by the books scholars produce"; rather, Scripture promises that "the Comforter, which is the Holy Ghost, whom the Father will send in my name, he shall teach you all things . . ." (John 14:26).

A SELECT BIBLIOGRAPHY

6. JESUS CHRIST THE DIVINE REDEEMER

Donald M. Baillie, *God Was in Christ.* New York, 1948.

Joseph A. Baird, *The Justice of God in the Teaching of Jesus.* Philadelphia, 1963.

O. Sydney Barr, *From the Apostles' Faith to the Apostles' Creed.* Oxford and New York, 1964.

F. F. Bruce, *Are the New Testament Documents Reliable?* Grand Rapids, Michigan, 1954.

Emil Brunner, *The Mediator* (trans. by Olive Wyon). Philadelphia, 1947.

Oscar Cullman, *Christ and Time* (trans. by Floyd V. Filson). Philadelphia, 1964.

Alfred Edersheim, *The Life and Times of Jesus the Messiah* (2 vols.). New York, London, Toronto, 1950.

Werner G. Kümmel, *Promise and Fulfilment.* Zürich and Naperville, Illinois, 1956.

Charles M. Laymon, *Christ in the New Testament.* New York, 1958.

Gösta Lundström, *The Kingdom of God in the Teaching of Jesus* (trans. by Joan Bulman). Richmond, Virginia, 1963.

Thomas W. Manson, *The Teaching of Jesus.* Cambridge, 1951.

G. Campbell Morgan, *The Teaching of Christ.* New York, 1913.

Merrill C. Tenney, *The Reality of the Resurrection.* New York, 1963.

THE HOLY SPIRIT

Geoffrey W. Bromiley

Geoffrey W. Bromiley is professor of church history and historical theology at Fuller Theological Seminary, Pasadena, California. He previously was rector of St. Thomas' Church, Edinburgh, Scotland. Dr. Bromiley holds the B.A. and M.A. from Emmanuel College, Cambridge, and the Ph.D. and D.Litt. from the University of Edinburgh. He has written a number of books and has also edited and translated two major theological works: Karl Barth's Church Dogmatics *and Kittel's* Theological Dictionary of the New Testament.

7. *Geoffrey W. Bromiley*

THE HOLY SPIRIT

ONE OF THE greatest failures in Christian thought and practice has to do with the Holy Spirit. Far too often Christians have assumed that the Spirit and His operation are easier to understand than, say, the person and work of Christ. In almost every age, too little attention has been paid to pneumatology (the doctrine of the Holy Spirit), and this has resulted in a distortion of Christian doctrine and an impoverishment of Christian life and work.

Now, it is true that the economy of God's saving work of reconciliation and revelation does not lead to a concentration of interest on the Holy Spirit. In the objective fulfillment of the divine purpose, the leading role is played by the divine Son. Thus Jesus Christ is the primary content of the Gospel, object of faith, and theme of the Spirit's witness. In evangelism, theology, worship, devotion, and work, He rightly has the preeminence (Col. 1:18). The Spirit is self-effacing: "He shall take of mine, and shall show it unto you" (John 16:15).

Yet this does not mean that the Spirit can be taken for granted, or that He can be neglected with impunity. In fact, failure to see the proper relation between the Spirit and Christ is responsible for many of the worst shortcomings in this field. For one, the Spirit may be given a false prominence, as in the Montanist-enthusiast view that direct filling or inspiring by the Spirit is a higher stage of spiritual life, or in the rationalistic view (cf. Lessing's *Education of the Human Race,* §72ff.) that the age of the Son will yield to the supreme age of the Spirit. Again, separation of the Spirit and the incarnation can give rise to a false dichotomy between spirit and body, so that salvation becomes a purely "spiritual" matter and the wholeness of God's saving work is lost. This is the peculiar error of Gnosticism, with a parallel in the liberal denial of the resurrection of the body.

Thirdly, the Spirit may be set in a wrong anti-thesis to the letter (cf. Harnack's distinction between husk and kernel, *What Is Christianity?*, New York, 1903, p. 160), with grave consequences for the proper understanding and interpretation of Holy Scripture. Finally, belief in Christ and a correct regard for Scripture can be lifeless and ineffective if divorced from the sovereign and dynamic activity of the Spirit. This results in the sorry phenomenon of ossified orthodoxy.

An ancient principle holds that God's outward acts are undivided acts of the whole Trinity *(opera trinitatis ad extra sunt indivisa)* (cf. Bucan, *Institutiones Theologicae,* III, 14; cited in H. Heppe, *Reformed Dogmatics,* [first German ed. 1861], trans. by G. T. Thomson, London, 1950, p. 116). If this is true, then depreciation of the Spirit's role implies defective understanding, and distortion at one point leads to distortion at all points. In the doctrine of the Spirit, as in that of Father and Son, everything is at stake. This principle does not mean, of course, that there is not a special office of Father, Son, and Holy Spirit. The particular work of the Spirit, generally speaking, lies in the intimate area of subjective application. But this is a sensitive sphere, for, as modern existentialism shows, subjective application can easily be construed as subjectivization, which begins by swallowing up the objectivity of the Spirit and finally ends up, possibly in the name of the Spirit, with an anthropocentricity (self-centeredness) that is the mark of sinful man and the negation of all true knowledge of God (cf. Barth's trenchant criticism of Bultmann in his essay, *Rudolf Bultmann*).

The proper antidote to this, as to other errors on the right or the left, is to see the Holy Spirit in firm relation to God and His works according to the revelation of the Bible. Only in this light is it possible both to appreciate the reality of His person and to gain a true and balanced understanding of His ministry.

THE HOLY SPIRIT AND THE TRINITY

When we speak of the Holy Spirit, we refer, not to a vague essence, a world soul, a nebulous power, or a divine emanation, but specifically and distinctly to the third person of the triune Godhead.

It is true that the word "spirit" has a more general connotation in both secular and biblical usage. Thus the Hebrew *ruah* can be used for "wind," and it also denotes the spirit of man. The Greek *pneuma* is also a term for "wind," though rarely used in this sense in the New Testament (cf. John 3:8). As the breath of life in man, it can easily assume the sense of the human spirit. Indeed, one reads also of evil spirits.

It is also true that in the Bible the simple "Spirit" can be used instead of "Spirit of the Lord" or "Holy Spirit." Thus in Galatians 5 Paul can speak of walking in the Spirit, of the conflict between the flesh and the Spirit, of leading by the Spirit, and of the fruit of the Spirit. Here the content and context leave no doubt that the reference is to the Holy Spirit. In other passages, however, there can be a certain ambivalence. For instance, in Romans 8 one cannot always be sure whether Paul is speaking of our spirit or of the Holy Spirit.

But this does not mean that the two are ultimately one and the same. The very fact of ambiguity implies a fundamental distinction. This distinction is brought out in the many passages, both Old Testament and New, in which the Spirit is "my Spirit," "the Spirit of the Lord," "the Spirit of Christ," or, more commonly in the New Testament, "the Holy Spirit." The latter term seems to be based on Isaiah 63:10f. and Psalm 51:11 (cf. *Theologisches Wörterbuch zum Neuen Testament [TWNT]*, ed. by G. Kittel and G. Friedrich, I, 104ff.; in English, *Theological Dictionary of the New Testament [TDNT]*, trans. by G. Bromiley, Eerdmans, I, 103 ff.).

The phrase "Holy Spirit" is particularly well suited to bring out the deity of the Spirit, for already in the Old Testament the word "holy" is referred to the person of God. Indeed, it contains the innermost description of God's nature" (*TWNT,* I, 101; *TDNT,* I, 100). God Himself is the Holy Father in John 17:11, and Jesus is the Holy One of God (cf. John 6:69; Mark 1:24). In view of the distinctiveness imparted by this predicate, spirit in the absolute "is, in context, fully adequate to express the matter, especially on Hebrew soil" (*TWNT,* I, 105; *TDNT,* I, 104).

The deity of the Spirit is also expressed by the manner of His coming at Pentecost. As Jesus puts it, "I will pray the Father, and he shall give you another Comforter" (John 14:16). The Father sends this Paraclete, the Holy Spirit, in the name of Jesus to teach the disciples all things (v. 26). The Paraclete is sent by Jesus from the Father, and proceeds from the Father (15:26). His dwelling with and in the disciples is parallel to the fact that the Father and Jesus make their abode in them (14:23). In this whole complex, the Father, Son, and Spirit are presented in a unique relation that leaves us in no doubt that to have dealings with the Spirit, no less than with the Father and the Son, is to have dealings with God.

What is implied in these statements is brought out explicitly in the trinitarian formulas of the New Testament. In Matthew 28:19, the disciples are to baptize in the name of the Father, the Son, and the Holy Spirit. In Second Corinthians 13:13, Paul prays that "the grace of the Lord Jesus Christ, and the love of God, and the communion of the Holy Ghost" will be with his readers. A little more loosely, Paul in First Thessalonians 1:1 ff. speaks of "hope in our Lord Jesus Christ, in the sight of God and our Father," and of the coming of the Gospel in the Holy Spirit (cf. Col. 1:1ff.). Similarly, Peter in First Peter 1:2 refers to election by "God the Father, through the sanctification of the Spirit, unto obedience and sprinkling of the blood of Jesus Christ." Jude, too, has a trinitarian formulation when (vss. 20ff.) he speaks of "praying in the Holy Ghost, keep[ing] yourselves in the love of God, looking for the mercy of our Lord Jesus Christ unto eternal life." In First John 3, verses 21-24 link confidence toward God, belief in His Son, and the witness of the Spirit. In view of the development of this thought in First John 4 and 5, the inauthentic saying in 5:7 is not at variance with, nor a fanciful advance upon, the immediate context.

Three points that emerge from this survey of the New Testament data are: (1) The Holy Spirit is everywhere regarded as God; (2) He is God in distinction from the Father and the Son; (3) His deity does not infringe upon the divine unity. In other words, the Holy Spirit is the third person of the triune Godhead. This finds expression in three articles of the creed: I believe in God the Father . . . and in Jesus Christ . . . and in the Holy Ghost. It is also illustrated in the early practice of threefold immersion at baptism in the name of the Father, Son, and Holy Ghost (*Didach*, 7, 1; *Apostolic Tradition*, 21, 22).

The early Church did not find it easy to maintain balance among the three theses. Rather surprisingly, in view of the widespread polytheism of the pagan world, perhaps the least danger was tritheism. There are, it is true, loose phrases in some of the earliest writers. We also read that Dionysius of Alexandria was thought by his namesake of Rome to preach three gods, "dividing the sacred Monad into three substances foreign to each other" (cf. J. Stevenson, *A New Eusebius,* pp. 268ff.). But even if this were true—and Dionysius strenuously denied it—it was only an implication ("a pelting from afar with those two poor ill-fitting phrases of mine"), not a deliberate doctrine.

Denial of theses 1 and 2 has always been a more serious problem, corresponding as it does to the even more pressing Christological denial. Thus the failure to recognize the true deity of the Spirit is found in the various forms of subordinationism from Gnosticism to the so-called Tropici and Macedonianism (*ibid.,* p. 216, for a good summary see J. N. D. Kelly, *Early Christian Doctrines,* London, 1958, pp. 128ff., where Kelly rightly points out that the implication is a hierarchical polytheism). In the Gnostic schemes the Spirit seems to be an emanation, so that true deity is ruled out at once. In rather a different way, Origen reaches a similar conclusion in his speculations on the Trinity, for while he recognizes the unity of the three persons he does not accept their equal deity. "God the Father is superior to every being, the Son, being less than the Father, is superior to rational creatures alone, the Holy Spirit is still less" *(ibid.).* Arianism had a similar implication that was worked out by Aetius and Eunomius and came to fruition in Eustathius of Sebaste, the true leader of the so-called Macedonians, who did "not choose to call the Spirit God, nor presume to call him a creature" (see Kelly, *op. cit.,* pp. 255ff. on this whole question). Obviously if Jesus is not of one substance with the Father, no more is the Holy Spirit. As Basil of Caesarea points out in his work *On the Holy Spirit,* an attempt was made to show that the distinctions are biblical, especially through the use of different prepositions. But this sophistry was effectively dispelled in the writings of Cyril of Jerusalem, Athanasius, and Basil himself, who all contended for the true and necessary deity of the Spirit. Denial of the deity, which finds a new form in the modern evaporation of the Spirit into an impersonal force of influence, is a rejection of the biblical teaching that entails misunderstanding of the Spirit's person and misconception of His work.

Nevertheless, the modalistic overemphasis on unity at the expense of true trinity is an equal danger. How confusing this teaching can be is evident in the supposed view of Callistus of Rome, that the Father and Son are one and the same and that all things are full of the divine Spirit, who, incarnate in the Son, is not different from the Father (Stevenson, *op. cit.,* p. 164). Here is a mixture of the express patripassianism of Noetus (and Praxeas) and the more general Sabellian thesis that there is only one person of God manifested in the different modes of Father, Son, and Spirit. The point here is a rejection of the essential distinction of persons, which is no less integral a part of the biblical testimony than the deity of Son and Spirit, and which thus corresponds alone to the being of God as He has revealed Himself to be. It is true that, according to John 4:24, God is Spirit. This does not mean, however, that God is simply the Holy Spirit, or the Holy Spirit God. What it does mean is that the whole being of the triune Godhead is Spirit as distinct from created matter. The whole Godhead, and each person, is Spirit in this sense. But modalistic equation, or obliteration of the persons, is not implied.

The inter-relation of the Holy Spirit to the Trinity finds restatement along with the definition of the deity of Christ. Against all forms of subordinationism it is asserted that Son and Spirit are of one substance with the Father (Athanasius, Cyril of Jerusalem). Nevertheless, this is no vindication of modalism, for, as Basil pointed out, the divine unity cannot be subjected to mathematical ideas of unity. The fourth century learned to speak of three hypostases or persons within the deity, not in the tritheistic sense of three centers of consciousness, but also not in the weaker sense of three purely economic manifestations. From Nicaea and Constantinople on, the creeds sought to do justice to the essential biblical data along these lines, and a Reformation confession like the Anglican gives an excellent summary of the true teaching: "And in unity of this Godhead there be three persons of one substance, power, and eternity, the Father, the Son, and the Holy Ghost" (Art. I; for longer expositions see the Belgic, Arts. VIII-IX, and Second Helvetic, Art. III). The Holy Spirit, the third person in the triune Godhead, is Himself God.

What difference does this confession make? There are six main answers: (1) Any other account is a distortion of the normative biblical teaching. (2) On this confession alone we know God as He truly is, as He has shown Himself to be. (3) Only in terms of this definition is the Spirit's work known as a distinctive and yet also a divine work. (4) This understanding preserves us from transforming God's actions into cosmic or creaturely action, which involves the dissolution of theology in psychology and cosmology. (5) Appreciation of the innner wealth of the Godhead is safeguarded, in contrast to the sterility that results when God is seen only as a solitary monad. (6) The way is thus open for the true knowledge of the Spirit in His work.

THE HOLY SPIRIT AND CREATION

As noted already, all the outward operations of God are indivisible works of the whole Trinity. In Scripture, God the Father is presented primarily as the Creator of heaven and earth. This is why dogmatics usually present the Father as the fount of all things. It is also said, however, that by Jesus Christ, the Logos, all things were made (John 1:3), and there is a similar line of scriptural teaching that speaks of the Holy Spirit, the Lord and Giver of life, as the Creator. As the *Leiden Synopsis* puts it: "The Father of himself created the world through the Son and the Holy Spirit; the Son of the Father through the Holy Spirit; and the latter of the Father and the Son" (X, 9 [in Heppe, *op cit.,* p. 191]).

The first passage relating the Spirit to creation is Genesis 1:2, where it is said that the Spirit of God moved over the waters. This enigmatic verse has been variously interpreted. In view of 1:1 (unless this is treated as a general heading), it can hardly refer to original but formless matter that was given shape by the Spirit. Nor is there much to commend the odd suggestion of Karl Barth in his exposition in *Church Dogmatics* (III, 1, pp. 102 ff.) that the verse represents quasi-mythologically the dismissal of what God rejects to make way for creation by divine *fiat.* Perhaps the elements of truth behind these views are (1) that creation implies selection, and (2) that creation is also the impressing of order and purpose, not just the calling into being of formless matter. This leads us to the positive significance of the verse. The whole work, which has the wonderful universe as its end, stands under the sign not only of the will of the Father and the word of the Son but also of the moving of the Spirit. Creation is the work of the Spirit.

What is true of the cosmos in general is specifically true of man. For we read also in Genesis 2:7: "And the LORD God formed man of the dust of the ground, and breathed into his nostrils the breath of life." Now there is, of course, no express mention here of the Holy Spirit. But the reference to breathing and breath is a convincing indication of the Holy Spirit, in view of the fact that this is God's inbreathing. With this verse might be linked the well-known saying in Psalm 104:29, 30: "Thou takest away their breath, they die. . . . Thou sendest forth thy spirit, they are created." Also relevant is the fact that man's own "spirit" comes from God and finally returns to the God who gave it (Eccles. 12:7; Luke 23:46; cf. John 19:30). To be sure, Genesis 1:20 refers generally to moving creatures that have life, and there can be no doubt that the Spirit is active in all things as Creator. Nevertheless, the inbreathing of the breath of life would seem, along with the divine image and likeness of Genesis 1:26, 27, to constitute the distinctiveness of man within creation. This is why, to Ecclesiastes 3:19, 20, with its reference to physical death, there is rightly added the qualification of 3:21, the distinction between the spirit of man and the spirit of beasts. The Holy Spirit is at work in man in a distinctive way.

The first specific truth that emerges from the creative activity of the Holy Spirit is that of the sovereignty of God as the author of life. What

Jesus said of the Spirit's work in regeneration, "the wind bloweth where it listeth . . . ; so is every one that is born of the Spirit" (John 3:8), is no less true of ordinary generation, Creation could not and cannot emerge of itself. It had and has no ultimate control over the non-existent. It is certainly not self-existent. With every creature within it, it owes its being and its continuation in being, not only to the purpose of the Father and the authoritative *fiat* of the Son, but also to the transcendent breathing of the Spirit.

The participation of the Spirit in creation, however, is also an expression of the immanence of God in His works. As noted, animals as well as men are moving creatures that have life. They, too, have breath, "spirit." The physical life and breath are a pointer to the life and breath of God, without which they could not be. The intimacy is a reminder of the intimacy of the divine indwelling. Nevertheless, there is a clear safeguard against the identification of creature and Creator. Life can be withdrawn, and breath finally expelled. Creatures do not hold them in definitive possession. Similarly, God is in His works, but He is not identical with His works. Distinction remains between God Himself as life and breath, and the creature to which life and breath are imparted.

This is no less true of man. Inasmuch as God breathed into his nostrils the breath of life, one might say that God made him a participant in the Spirit. One cannot say, however, that man became an emanation or a part of the Spirit. Indeed, there is good reason to say, with Barth in *Church Dogmatics* (III, 2, pp. 344 ff.; cf. "Spirit" in *Baker's Dictionary of Theology*), that while man *is* body and soul, he *has* spirit. The only difficulty is that this way of putting it perhaps runs the very risk it seeks to avoid, namely, suggesting that there is a bit of God that comes into man and then returns to Him. The Spirit who gives life and breath is the transcendent Spirit who is also immanent, the immanent Spirit who is also transcendent. God dwells in His works but is also distinct from them. Just because they could not be without God, they are not God, and yet they stand in the most intimate relation to Him.

The more specific relation of the Spirit to man, by virtue of which one may not incorrectly speak of man's spirit, is a reminder that all that is good and noble in man and his works, all that is in accordance with His creaturely nature and purpose, is owed to the Holy Spirit. This is the truth that finds expression in the doctrine of what is sometimes called common grace. Notwithstanding man's fall and sin, creation and the new creation are not so distinct that the former is wholly the realm of the devil and the latter alone the sphere of the Spirit. To say this is not to engage in natural theology, for without the special work of the Word and Spirit, man is now excluded from the knowledge and salvation of God. It is to engage rather in a theology of creation. Even sinful man is still the creature of God. He is still the creature into whose nostrils God breathed the breath of life. Even sinful man can still do many things proper to his humanity. He can think high thoughts, write fine poems and music, make discoveries, establish law and order, cultivate the mind, stay the ravages of disease. To be sure, he will not do these things without the blight and curse of sin. But the fact that he can do them at all he owes to the Creator Spirit who has made him man.

At this point there are, of course, two special dangers. The first is Gnosticism, which identifies the Spirit's operation, not with the whole life of man, but solely with the intellectual or "spiritual" side. Now, it is true that man's special relation to God is linked with his being or having "spirit" in a way that other creatures are or have not. Nevertheless, to say this is not to disenfranchise other living creatures or even the inorganic world. By the Spirit, God is immanent in all His works, each after its kind. Man himself is both body and soul, and God's common grace is to man in his totality, not just to a special part of man that is exclusively or specifically from God. Indeed, the tendency of Reformed theology is to find the greatest distance from God, the most severe effect of the fall, "in spiritual and inward things" (*Leiden Synopsis,* XVII, 24 [Heppe, *op. cit.,* p. 365]).

The second danger is different, yet related. It is that of a natural theology, that, minimizing the fall, draws a straight line from the spiritual aspiration and achievement of natural man to the new life and knowledge in the Spirit that is the work of special grace. It is true that the breath of God is not immediately and definitely withdrawn from the sinner. It is true that the sinner, too, can think, speak, and do many things that bear the mark of the Spirit, that are even a distorted reflection of what may be known of God by His self-revelation in nature and conscience. But to know God in truth, to enjoy salvation, to be heir of eternity, to do that which abides, the sinner must receive new life and breath from above in a new creative work of the Spirit, (cf. the dictum of Keckermann [*Systema,* 263; Heppe, p. 364]: "Man cannot either know or love God savingly without the special grace of the Holy Spirit"). God has not abandoned fallen creation in the sense that there is nothing within it that is of the Spirit. But God's definitive purpose for creation, the perfection of His transcendent immanence, is not achieved without the new creation, the new breathing of the Creator Spirit.

THE HOLY SPIRIT AND CHRIST

The new man in whom the Holy Spirit puts forth His power afresh is the second man, the quickening spirit, the Lord from heaven (I Cor. 15:47f.). Unlike Adam, the first-begotten of the new creation is Himself Spirit (cf. II Cor. 3:17). He is in fact the second person of the Godhead, the Son of God, Himself God.

The fact that the new work of the Spirit is accomplished first in Jesus Christ, and that Jesus Christ is Himself God, is a reminder that prior to the relation of Son and Spirit on earth there is an eternal relation within the triune deity. Of this relation we hardly have the data to speak, and speculation avails little. The most that can be said is that it involves both richness of fellowship and intimacy of unity. Beyond that, the Church has been emboldened to say that, as the Son is eternally begotten of the Father, so there is an eternal procession of the Spirit from the Father (John 15:26). The western churches have added that this procession is also from the Son *(filioque)*. There are weighty considerations in favor of this. John tells us that the Spirit was sent by the Father in the name of the Son (14:26), and also that He was sent by the Son (16:7). The threefold order in the Trinity suggests that there should not be a direct jump to the Spirit that bypasses the Son. The triunity implies that in inward being as well as outward work, no person of the Trinity is without the other two. A necessary safeguard against such overemphases as Christomonism, Montanism, frozen orthodoxy, or uncontrolled inwardness is also afforded by the grounding of the strong soteriological link between Son and Spirit in an ultimate trinitarian relation. On the other hand, there is no need to be over-dogmatic here, for, as the *Leiden Synopsis* puts it, "some said, not unsuitably, that the Father breathes the Holy Spirit through the Son, and the Holy Spirit proceeds from the Father through the Son" (IX, 19 [Heppe, p. 131]). The main point is the link itself, not the precise mode of stating it.

The final trinitarian relation sheds a light, perhaps, on the Son's conception by the Spirit at the incarnation. This does not mean that the Holy Spirit is the Father of the incarnate Word, for the Spirit is the efficient, not the material, cause of the conception. But why does not the earthly birth of Jesus correspond to His eternal begetting? If the holy thing born of Mary is the Son of God, why does not God the Father come upon her? One simple reason is, of course, that the Son does not become such (again) at the incarnation. But there is also, perhaps, a reminder that even within the triune relationship there is no dispensability of persons. As Father and Spirit are not without the Son, so Father and Son are not without the Spirit.

There are, of course, other considerations. It is by the Spirit that the Godhead operates in the world. More specifically, the role of the Spirit is that of life-giver. It is thus supremely congruent that in the work of new creation God should act by the Holy Spirit. Nor is this just the ordinary work of the Spirit, as in all generation. Conception by the Spirit marks a break in the normal process of procreation. If Christ's human nature originates from the seed of Abraham and David, the man who is now born, though truly man, is the one who bears the image of the heavenly. His conception by the Spirit signifies that the new race will be filled with and directed by the Spirit. It is a sign that He is come from above, from God, in order that those who are from below might be raised up to God in Him. Although the Virgin Birth may not be a very prominent part of the apostolic preaching, in the light of the conception of the Spirit it is indispensable to Christ's person and saving work.

As Jesus Christ was conceived of the Spirit, so His whole life, work, and ministry was in the power of the Spirit. (For a fuller treatment see "The Spirit of Christ," *Essays in Christology for Karl Barth,* ed. T. H. L. Parker, pp. 135 ff.) The Spirit alighted on Him at His baptism. He was led by the Spirit into the wilderness. He taught by the Spirit, and spoke the words of God, for God gave not the Spirit by measure to Him. He claimed the Spirit's authority for His ministry. He healed in the Spirit. Finally, He offered Himself through the eternal Spirit without spot to God. Rather oddly, it is not explicitly stated that He was raised by the Spirit, but in the resurrection He was declared to be the Son of God with power according to the Spirit of holiness. Prior to His crucifixion He promised that the Spirit would come to be the Paraclete, and after His resurrection He breathed on His disciples and said, "Receive ye the Holy Ghost" (John 20:21). He also told the disciples to wait for the baptism and power of the Spirit (Acts 1:8). Begun in the Spirit, His ministry was accomplished in the Spirit, and then in its new form continued in the Spirit.

If Christ Himself sends the Spirit, and the Spirit comes in connection with His work, this means that the inter-relation between Word and Spirit does not end with the ascension. The incarnation of the Son took place to effect the objective work of revelation and reconciliation. But as the Spirit is active in and with this work, so Christ is active in and with the subjective work of the Spirit. Christ is, of course, at the right hand of the Father between the ascension and return. But He is also present now, and the Spirit is the intervening mode of this presence. Light is hereby shed on the vexed question of Christ's presence in word and sacrament. As the French Confession puts it in relation to the Lord's Supper (Art. XXXVI): "Although he be in heaven . . . by the secret and incomprehensible power of his Spirit he feeds and strengthens us with the substance of his body and of his blood."

The relation between Son and Spirit is also a reminder of the Spirit's role in revelation and reconciliation. The first aspect of this is that the incarnate life of Jesus is life in and by the Spirit. It is this in the old sense that all life is from the Spirit. The Son's solidarity with the race is thus assured by the conception of the Spirit no less than by the Virgin Birth, for in a general way all men are conceived of the Spirit. Nevertheless, the Son's life is in and by the Spirit in a new sense. Jesus is not just one man among others. He is the new man, the Lord from heaven, the first of a new race, which, in distinction from the fallen posterity of Adam, may enjoy the fullness of the Spirit. Conception by the Spirit does, of course, mean more than this. It implies the true and proper deity of Christ, which is no less essential to salvation than His humanity. In terms of humanity, however, it also signifies new humanity, though without severance from the old.

This humanity of Jesus is humanity for us. By identifying Himself with fallen man (Rom. 8:3), and also with the new spiritual body of resurrection, Jesus accomplishes in His person the death of the old man and the coming of the new. He does this in the incarnation, with its coming together of Son of God and seed of David. He does it supremely, however, in His death and resurrection, where the old man is brought to his end and the new man established as the true man. In Jesus, the Man who takes the place of other men, the work of the Spirit is also in a sense representative and substitutionary. Jesus effects in the Spirit for us that which, by virtue of this work, may be brought to fulfillment by the Spirit in us.

This work is not vicarious in the sense that it rules out the fulfillment by the Spirit in us. Already in Christ the old is indeed abolished and the new present. But we, who are of the old, are to have a place in the new. That we may do so is also the work of the Holy Spirit, whose present ministry is to cause us, too, to be born from above, to die to the old man, to be raised again in newness of life, not in addition to or in imitation of Jesus but in, with, and under His vicarious birth, death, and resurrection.

In sum, Christology is no less ineffectual than inconceivable without pneumatology, whether at the level of the "for us" or that of the "in us." Both are equally unthinkable, of course, without "Patrology," if we may so use the word. One cannot abstract Son from Spirit, or Spirit from Son, or both from Father. The work of revelation and reconciliation is the work of the triune Godhead therein reconciling and revealed.

THE HOLY SPIRIT AND SCRIPTURE

The relation of the Holy Spirit to Jesus Christ carries with it a relation to Holy Scripture, the divinely inspired record and interpretation of God in His saving word and work. This is stated in part in the third article of the Nicene Creed: "Who spake by the prophets."

The saving word and work of God covered many centuries and the most varied events. Men and women from the patriarchs to the apostles lived, spoke, and acted in fulfillment of the divine purpose. For the word and work of God to be known, believed, and understood in objective reality, it was necessary that there should be an authentic and authoritative account and exposition, and that this, being itself part of the word and work, bear the same divine endorsement. Holy Scripture is this record; its inspiration implies the endorsement.

It must be emphasized that Holy Scripture is itself part of the word and work, the revelation and reconciliation. This is why the word "witness" can be misleading when applied too exclusively or narrowly to the Bible. To be sure, Scripture is witness. Yet it is so in an internal, not an external, sense. The record is part of the work, the interpretation part of the word. Thus the prophets, moved by the Spirit, play an active role in events by the word embodied in their writings. Paul's writing of the epistles in exposition of the saving work of Christ is itself part of the divine work and word. Scripture does not stand apart as an additional, external factor that has only an instrumental role. *Mutatis mutandis,* it is evoked, guided, and empowered by the Spirit no less than the word or person of an Elijah, Isaiah, or John the Baptist. Thus, while the Scriptures are, in Calvin's phrase, "public records," God Himself "commanded his servants . . . to commit his revealed Word to writing" (Belgic Confession, Art. III).

The Bible does not greatly emphasize its own inspiration, but what is said is plain and definite. The Spirit's activity is particularly displayed at three levels. First, there is the word or act later recorded; for example, the spoken statements of the prophets with their "Thus saith the LORD." Then there is the recording or interpreting of the word or act, or a direct utterance in written form. This, too, is attributed to the breathing of the Spirit (II Tim. 3:16). Finally, there is the moving of the Spirit in the hearer or reader to give certainty of the truth of Scripture, illumination in saving understanding, and the principle of true interpretation: "The Holy Spirit is the only interpreter of Scripture." In the broad sense in which it covers all operations of the Spirit, inspiration may justly be used at all these levels so long as there is no one-sided concentration, but theologically it has been customary to apply the word more narrowly to the second level in terms of Second Timothy 3:16.

Scripture itself is silent about the nature of the Spirit's operation, so that what can be said is mostly negative. It is not possession or frenzy. The personalities of the authors are not overthrown. Inspiration is not divine dictation in the sense of a mechanical transmission of thoughts and words in which the writer's role is purely passive. On the other hand, this is not just the kind of inspiration that, on the basis of common grace, any author or scholar might enjoy. Analogically, the relation of Holy Spirit and human author is perhaps best understood in terms of Holy Spirit and incarnated Son, or of the divine and human natures in the one person of Christ. The Holy Spirit, from whom life comes, is the master of personal relations; we may confidently affirm that, as His work, the inspiring of Scripture is effected without either violence to the writers or prejudice to the finished work.

The fact that Holy Scripture is an inspired record implies the factual truth of the statements. God has spoken and acted, and His objective speech and action find authentication in Holy Scripture. But if this is true authentication, it must itself be authentic. If an absence of record would cast a haze over the finished words and deeds, so, too, would an untrustworthy record. A first implication of inspiration is genuine authentication (cf. Luke 1:1ff.). Without this (i.e., on the assumption that the factual biblical material is in part erroneous or even mythological), it is idle to speak of "inspiration" and "existential encounter" in the reader.

The fact that Holy Scripture is interpretation and speech implies the truth of the doctrine. There are many opinions about God and many interpretations of events, such as the birth and death of Jesus. If Scripture were not an inspired work, then it would be no more than an account of the interesting and perhaps admirable opinions and interpretations of great religious teachers. But the God who acts gives also His own speech and interpretation, and what He says about Himself and His work is authoritatively embodied in Holy Scripture. Inspiration implies not merely the authenticity of the facts but also the truth of the doctrine (cf. the twofold *authentia* of Turretinus, *Institutio,* II 4, 2: the *authentia historiae* and *authentia normae*).

Because the Bible is inspired speech as well as recorded, we may correctly refer to biblical propositions. These are not, of course, abstract propositions in the sense of theoretical statements constituting quasi-Euclidian demonstration. They have a point of reference in God. But they are still statements (propositions) about God, who He is, what He has done, the meaning and purpose of His work. As God is truth, so what is said under the Spirit about Him is also truth. The truth of the propositions is backed by the God who is both their object, for the truths are about Him, and their subject, for in the person of the Holy Spirit He is their author.

The inspiration of Holy Scripture is the ground of its infallibility and authority (cf. Westminster Confession, I, v). The former has two aspects: certainty in terms of truth and certainty in terms of efficacy. The Holy Spirit, both Spirit of truth and Spirit of power, invests Scripture with this twofold certainty. Authority is also twofold. It is normativeness for right belief about God and normativeness for the right response in human conduct. The Holy Spirit, Himself God, knows the deep things of God with a fullness and immediacy that alone can give a valid and definite norm both for knowledge of God and also for knowledge of His will for us. For this reason, on the basis of its inspiration, Scripture is rightly called the supreme rule of faith and practice.

Two final points must be made. First, the letter should not be divorced from the Spirit. This is the particular danger that threatens dogmatic orthodoxy or moral legalism. Rightly affirming an objective inspiration, literalism easily forgets (1) that Scripture's authority is truly that of the Spirit, (2) that the Spirit is the living Lord, (3) that Scripture is not normative truth and command by some quasi-magical quality imparted to it, and (4) that it cannot be equated directly with an ecclesiastical or academic system of belief or conduct. Scripture itself rightly has a warning against the disjunction that makes the letter a letter that kills. Evangelical theology makes the same point by pressing the inner testimony of the Spirit (cf. Belgic Confession, Art. V: "Especially because the Holy Ghost witnesseth in our hearts") and by making the final reservation that, for all the clarity of the letter, "without the Holy Spirit's aid a man cannot either rightly perceive Holy Scripture or be subject to it" (Riissen, *Compendium Theologiae,* I, 10 [Heppe, p. 41]; cf. Heidegger, *Corpus Theologiae,* XXI, 21 [Heppe, p. 517]).

On the other hand, we are also not to separate the Spirit from the letter. This is the error of much modern theology. In the name of the Spirit, Scripture has been revised or discarded as hampering and outmoded letter. The result has been a confusion of the Holy Spirit and the individual spirit, or the spirit of the age. Each man thinks and acts as the "spirit" moves. This spirit is, however, purely subjective. It is without objective reference. Now the Holy Spirit is indeed dynamic and sovereign, but He is not variable and capricious. He stands by the written Word He Himself has given. He may be recognized as the Holy Spirit, not merely by His freedom, but also by His committal to the letter. This does not mean that He is the letter's slave. It means that He takes the letter He has inspired and gives it life and power in illumination and application. The Holy Spirit is the Spirit of Holy Scripture.

THE HOLY SPIRIT AND THE CHURCH

The ministry of the Holy Spirit is in and through the Church. This is true by reason of the work in the members. But it is true collectively as well as individually. When Jesus promised endowment with power, it was a promise to a group. When power came on the infant Church, it was as they were all together in one place. If power lighted on each in particular, the descent was upon the whole body.

The Epistles as well as the Gospels and Acts connect this inter-relation of the Spirit and the Church with the promises and gifts of the ascended Lord (cf. John 14-16; Eph. 4:8 ff.; Acts 2:33). Because Jesus Christ Himself is so closely bound to His people, so is the Spirit of Christ. Corporate life in the body of Christ, to which believers are called, is life in the common Spirit. The Spirit means Christ Himself present in life-giving power and sovereignty. With one Father and one Christ, it is natural that there is reference also to one Spirit (Eph. 4:4 ff.).

Since Christ is the head of the body, one may justly say that this headship is discharged through the Spirit. In this connection the links between the Spirit and Christ and the Spirit and Scripture are of supreme importance. No error can be more disastrous than to try to ascribe to the Spirit a false autonomy, for this will give scope only to the individual spirit or the spirit of the group, whether in the form of *esprit de corps* or of clerical or intellectual domination. Neither pope, nor presbytery nor individual conscience is the vicar of Christ. This office is fulfilled by the Spirit ruling in living power by the Word.

As members of the Church are one in Christ, the Spirit is the bond of this fellowship. Love is shed abroad in the hearts of God's people by the Spirit (Rom. 5:5). They love one another in the Spirit (Col. 1:8). The graces of Christian life are the fruit of the Spirit (Gal. 5:22). The many members have different gifts, but all are gifts of one and the same Spirit (I Cor. 12:4 ff.). The fellowship for which Paul prays, along with the grace of Christ and the love of God, is the fellowship of the Spirit (II Cor. 13:14). The Church is a dwelling place for God, and God dwells there through the Spirit (Eph. 2:22).

The common life in the Church is a life in growth and edification. The great passages in Corinthians and Ephesians in which the Church is described as Christ's body make it clear that, while there is obviously individual edification, the great concern of the Epistles is with the edification of the community. The Church is to be edified, or to receive edification (I Cor. 14:4, 5). The body is to be integrated and to grow to the edifying of itself in love (Eph. 4:16). The gifts of the ascended Lord are given for the edifying of the body of Christ (Eph. 4:12). This work of edification, which consists both in extension and also in progress in Christian life, is accomplished (1) through men separated and called by the Spirit, and (2) through spiritual gifts.

Ministers are, of course, called and sent forth by Christ. But this calling is in and through the Holy Spirit. Even the disciples are not finally sent out until Jesus breathes on them and says: "Receive the Holy Spirit." They are to stay in Jerusalem until the outpouring of Pentecost. Paul, too, is commissioned by Christ (Acts 26:16), but his specific work is by the ordination (Acts 13:2, 4) and under the direction (Acts 16:6, 7) of the Holy Spirit. Hence Bucan rightly concludes that inward calling "takes place through the Holy Spirit" (*Institutiones Theologicae,* XLII, 35 [Heppe, p. 674]). The gift of individual ministries is ultimately comprehended in the supreme gift of the ministry of the Spirit by which believers are added and the community is strengthened.

The endowments that are given for the edifying of the Church are directly linked with the Spirit both in Acts 2 and in First Corinthians 12-14, where there is an enumeration and discussion. Paul states plainly here that all gifts are from one and the same Spirit, and he describes the gifts as spiritual in this sense. The reference is not so much to native talents, though these may also be dedicated to God and used by the Spirit to edification. What Paul has in view are special gifts of miracles, particularly healing, and utterance, particularly tongues, interpretation, and prophecy.

It is often asked whether these gifts were conferred only on the apostolic Church or whether they may be expected in any age. Three points may be made in this regard: (1) There are certainly expressed promises to the apostles that cannot necessarily be claimed by all Christians. (2) There is no way to bring the immediate gifts of the Spirit under ecclesiastical control—by ordination, for example. (3) Scripture does not explicitly restrict these gifts to the apostles or their day, and hence we have no ground on which to limit the sovereign disposing of the Spirit. A difficult problem of interpretation is involved here, namely, the use of New Testament precedents. It is a safe conclusion, however, that though we may not command or claim the *charismata,* or any specific *charisma,* the Spirit's donation may still be looked for as and when He Himself decides.

A second question is whether charismatic endowment is a second Christian blessing (often, and probably erroneously, associated with sanctification) without which one is not a complete Christian. Ought everyone to undergo an outpouring of the Spirit subsequent to initial repentance and faith? Several points may be noted: (1) There is a singularity to Pentecost as the first coming of the Spirit upon the Church. (2) Charismatic endowment may, as in the cases of Cornelius and Paul, accompany conversion. (3) There may be repeated filling with the Spirit (Acts 4:31), which does not have to be equated with charismatic endowment. (4) The total witness of the New Testament hardly supports a twofold-blessing schema, such as that represented by sacramentalists in baptism-confirmation, monastics in baptismal-monastic consecration, and certain evangelicals in conversion-sanctification or conversion-charismatic endowment (especially, in some cases, tongues). No one will resist prayer for the Spirit, or dismiss the possibility of His sovereign filling or endowment. But to impose a fixed pattern of operation at this point is surely to carry zeal to the excess where it brings only confusion, disruption, and disappointment.

The most valuable endowment is not necessarily the most spectacular. From Corinthian times, speaking with tongues has had a strange fascination for some, but Paul in his discussion of the hierarchy of gifts does not rate it very highly. Love is the greatest *charisma* of all. Without it, other gifts are futile, and love without other gifts can still be all-conquering. This gives us the clue to the criterion for assessing gifts. This criterion is edification. By this standard the most important of other gifts is prophecy —here surely, in the main, the forthtelling of God's Word. The reason is that God's work is done in and by the Word. The whole man is claimed for God, but understanding is of supreme importance. Neither visual perception nor emotional impress nor mere activity is adequate alone. If God's people are to grow, whether inwardly or outwardly, the ministry of the Word must be central. But this has to be the Spirit-filled Word, delivered by Spirit-filled men. In other words, the gift of prophecy is demanded.

Mention of the Word reminds us that there is another criterion— namely, Holy Scripture. No message, admonition, or revelation is genuinely of the Spirit unless it conforms to the primary record. Examples of supposedly spiritual utterances that are exposed by this rule may be found in the *Didache* (11, 7 ff.) and also in the sayings attributed to the Montanists (Epiphanius, *Haer,* 48 f.). In the *Didache,* the rule of edification is also broken. But even where it might appear to us that a message or action will edify the congregation, no spiritual gift is exercised, nor will there be authentic edification, if what is said or done is not according to Scripture. In this way spiritual gifts are safeguarded against arbitrary subjectivism or ecclesiasticism.

As noted, the upbuilding of the Church implies expansion as well as inner development. Both ministers and *charismata* serve to summon new believers as well as to strengthen the old. This means, however, that the Holy Spirit is active in, with, and by the Church in its fulfillment of the Great Commission. Indeed, the calling of men to faith in Jesus Christ, and their refashioning in the obedience of faith, is the supreme office and work of the Holy Spirit. Calling is the act of the Holy Spirit.

Thus in the parting discourses in John, the promises of the Spirit relate to the work of the Church as well as its life. Again, Pentecost is set wholly in the framework of evangelism, and leads at once to the first sermon and the first conversions. The story is the same in the rest of Acts and the Epistles. The first missionary journey (cf. also Philip) is ordained by the Spirit. Genuine success in Christ's work is impossible without the Spirit, by whom alone the deep things of God may be known. As John puts it in the third chapter of his Gospel, entry into the Kingdom is by the new birth from above, by the Spirit. The only effectual calling to the Church is calling in the Spirit.

This means that the community must be a community of the Spirit. It is this as it gives itself to the work of the Spirit in the power of the Spirit, not searching for relevance or adaptation but relying on the Word and Spirit. Prayer in the Spirit is also demanded. As Paul says in Romans 8:26, only the Spirit can enable us to pray as we ought, and the Spirit is Himself the Spirit of intercession. Working, preaching, and praying in the Spirit, the Church can say with confidence: "We are his witnesses of these things; and so is also the Holy Ghost" (Acts 5:32).

There are three important implications: (1) To enjoy the Spirit's presence and power, the Church must give itself to the task commanded. (2) It must not doubt the Spirit's adequacy. (3) It must not try—intellectually, ecclesiastically, financially, or in any other way—to substitute itself and its resources for the Spirit. Zechariah 4:6b—"Not by might, nor by power, but by my Spirit, saith the LORD of hosts"—might well serve as the Church's motto. This verse expresses its apparent weakness but also its real confidence, after the pattern of its Lord who lived, died, and rose again in the Spirit.

THE HOLY SPIRIT AND THE CHRISTIAN

What has been said thus far makes it apparent that the Holy Spirit stands related to the Christian in every aspect of life. The Holy Spirit is God; hence relation to God is relation to the Spirit. The Holy Spirit is Creator; hence natural life, the presupposition of salvation, is from the Spirit. The Holy Spirit is the Spirit of Christ; hence the work of salvation effected in Christ is the work of the Spirit. The Holy Spirit is the Spirit of Scripture; hence the word of truth and redemption derives from and is applied by the Spirit. The Holy Spirit is the Spirit of the Church; hence membership in the body of God's people, without which there is no Christian, implies an ineluctable relation to the Spirit. The Christian is the man for whom and in whom the work of the Spirit is accomplished.

The Spirit's work in the Christian is so vast and comprehensive that there can be no hope of covering every aspect. Perhaps it may best be summarized in terms of the new life-giving, the giving of eternal life in Jesus Christ. This yields three main divisions—the commencement, course, and consummation—in terms of the three aspects of the Spirit's operation: the evangelistic, ethical, and eschatological. To put it in another way, the Spirit is the Spirit of regeneration, renewal, and resurrection.

As natural life commences with a creative act, so too does the Christian life. This is the new birth of John 3. Beginning the Christian life can, of course, be described in other ways, such as conversion, new perception, response to the ministry of the Word, committal to discipleship. Taken alone, these might be understood as human possibilities for which there are parallels in other areas of life. But the Christian is convinced that beginning the Christian life has no parallels. It is unique and miraculous. This is implied in the fact that it is also and supremely the new birth, the new giving of life by the Spirit.

This truth has many ramifications in Scripture. There is a real sense in which the new birth is a fulfillment of the first birth. But it is a fulfillment in close relation to Jesus Christ in His Virgin Birth (see especially John 1:12, 13). The meaning of baptism is also apparent here, for while sacramentalist error should be avoided, the linking of water and Spirit cannot be ignored. Again, the centrality of the Word calls for attention. Those born of the Spirit are begotten of the Word, which is the Word of life (Jas. 1:18). This does not mean competition, for Spirit and Word are complementary. Regeneration takes place as the Word is faithfully presented in the power of the Spirit. In this sense, regeneration and effectual calling are in practice, one and the same, at least in the initial aspect of calling: "The first effect of calling is regeneration" (Burmann, *Synopsis Theologiae,* VI, iii, 1 [Heppe, p. 518]).

The fact that Christian life begins with this sovereign act of the Spirit also has important implications: (1) It destroys comparative religion at the root. (2) It rules out the Pelagian heresy that believes self-salvation is possible. "This beginning does not depend on the natural strength of the will, but is the beginning of grace alone" (Keckermann, *Systema Sacrosanctae Theologiae,* 263, 264 [Heppe, p. 521]). It also rules out the degenerate Arminianism that grants man the power of autonomous response to the Gospel. Although man is born, he does not bear himself. Even ministers of the Word can discharge only the function of midwife in this new birth. And they cannot discharge even this function if they do not present the given message.

Regeneration thus carries with it a certain abasement, but it also gives a strong assurance. It cannot be explained away or relativized. The deepest experiences, divorced from the Spirit, can be broken down, codified, compared, possibly evaporated. Failure to see this is the great error of the apparently promising apologetic of Schleiermacher, with this offer of a pragmatic inward citadel to cultured depisers. Now Christianity is undoubtedly empirical. But it cannot find authenticity at this anthropological level. Only when the Christian sees that he is grounded in God's work by Word and Spirit can he be sure that he is a Christian, that Christianity is authentic, and that it is exclusive and unique. For only then does he truly believe in the Holy Spirit, who in anthropological religion is taken for granted or reduced to the level of an explicable force. Right at the outset, this regenerating operation of the Spirit is a *sine qua non* that dethrones arrogance and establishes assurance.

The Spirit is also the Spirit of renewal. This is the process whereby the life of the regenerate is made new in conformity with Jesus Christ. It is the lifelong renovation that is the growing up of the Christian, the outworking in thought, word, and practice of the life received from the Spirit. It is the sanctification that is the product and consequence and also the goal and end of justification. The New Testament makes it abundantly clear that in every aspect, this work, too, is the work of the Holy Spirit.

Romans 8 is perhaps the classic passage here. It draws an antithesis between walking after the flesh and walking after the Spirit. The note of joy and triumph that rings through this whole section derives from the fact that the Spirit is life and power. The Christian has not just been given a fresh start and then left to work it out with a little assistance. He is given a new life, and his task is to live this life in the strength of the Spirit and in orientation to Jesus Christ crucified and risen. Since this is genuine renewal, there has to be a negative side, the putting off of the works of the man who was put to death in Christ, the denial of self, the mortification of sinful members and affections. But the accent is not on the dying with Christ. If the death is indispensable, the end is life. The Lord who died is now risen from the dead. Similarly, the Christian who died in and with Christ is risen in Him. Hence mortification is with a view to renewal. The old man is put off in order that the new man in Christ may live and grow—vibrant and positive, filled and impelled by the Spirit.

The antithesis between old and new means that there is conflict in the work of renewal. The carnal man, though crucified with Christ, is, in Luther's graphic phrase, unwilling to die. His death throes are dangerous and even violent. Galatians 5 expresses this as a mortal struggle between flesh and Spirit. Romans 8 should not mislead us here. Its assurance is justified, for the Spirit will not be defeated. But the conflict is real enough, and we are poor allies (or subjects) in the conflict. The fullness of victory is not yet. What we see is only the provisional fruit of the Spirit in His work of moral transformation. But this fruit is an installment, a down payment, a guarantee. We are sealed by the Spirit to the day of redemption. The Spirit's presence and work authenticate our regeneration, effect our progress in sanctification, and pledge the infallibility of final consummation.

Because God works in us by the Spirit, there are warnings in Scripture not to contend against the Spirit but to open the heart and life to Him. Ephesians 5:18 has the exhortation, "Be filled with the Spirit." Negatively, care must be taken not to grieve the Spirit (Eph. 4:30) and, even more seriously, not to quench the Spirit (I Thess. 5:19). Above all, one must not lie to the Spirit, pretending to obey His promptings but in fact circumventing them (Acts 5:1ff.). Since the reference, in the Epistles at least, is to true Christians, one can hardly assume that a complete crushing of the Spirit out of the life is at issue. But failure to work with the Spirit in renewal is serious all the same. It involves controversy with God, stultification of Christian life and service, and a harmful repression of the good, which is surely even more dangerous than the commonly censured repression of the bad!

Since renewal is a refashioning on the basis of Christ's vicarious death and resurrection, it is naturally a transforming into the likeness of Christ. This carries with it a fulfillment of the purpose of creation (the image of God), and the way is opened for a fruitful theology of creation within that of reconciliation, though the fall and sin of man rule out a straight line from the one to the other. The orientation to Christ, however, provides us also with the foundation, theme, and goal of Christian ethics. Indeed, it points us to the eschatological fulfillment as well, for we "are changed into the same image from glory to glory" (II Cor. 3:18; cf. v. 17).

This leads us to the third point: the Spirit is the Spirit of resurrection. Rather surprisingly, this thought is not greatly developed in Holy Scripture. God (the Father) raised up Jesus, and Jesus Himself is the quickening Spirit through whom we are to bear the image of the heavenly. Nevertheless, there are indications that the Spirit has also His function in the final life-giving. Thus even in First Corinthians 15, Christ defined resurrection in terms of Spirit, and the new bodies are to be spiritual. Again, in Romans 8:11 God quickens our mortal bodies by His Spirit. The testimony of Ezekiel 37, in its broader connotation, is to the same effect.

Two important truths are implied in the fact that resurrection is the Spirit's work. The first is that the consummation of God's work, like its commencement, is a miracle of divine grace and power. The second is that at the end, as at the beginning, we have to do with the whole Trinity. Although the divine persons have distinctive functions and offices, the totality and unity of God's work comes out with particular clarity here. As God the Father creates us by the Word and through the Spirit, so God the Father raises us again by the Word and through the Spirit. As the *Leiden Synopsis* puts it, "the resurrection of the dead [which cannot be accomplished by the virtue of any natural cause, LI, 22] is the action of God, Father, Son and Holy Spirit" (LI, 16). The triune God is one God from whom all men come, to whom all go, and in whom all believers find fulfillment.

CONCLUSION

The work of God by the Holy Spirit is His subjective, personal and intimate work in man. We may conclude briefly with three important warnings and three equally important assurances.

On the negative side, it is vital (1) not to forget the objectivity of the Spirit because of the subjectivity of His work; (2) not to think it possible to lie to the Spirit successfully; (3) not to give the lie to the Spirit by finally resisting or rejecting His testimony.

The third of these dangers is the most serious, for many theologians believe that this is the blaspheming of the Spirit for which there is no forgiveness: "This sin . . . is committed against the proper office of the Holy Spirit, which is to illumine our mind, engender faith, and sanctify us wholly to God" (Walaeus, *Loci Communes,* p. 285; cf. Heidegger, X, 73; Cocceius, *Aphorism,* VI, 11, 21 [Heppe, pp. 352ff.]). There can be no forgiveness for this, because definitive rejection of the Spirit's work is self-exclusion from the divine salvation.

Three other things need to be said, however, on the positive side: (1) If it is God who brings His work to fulfillment, there is no need to depend on self in its weakness and uncertainty. (2) We can also be sure that the work is done at the most inward and intimate level, with the guarantee of thoroughness and totality. (3) Finally, while the work of God is objective and comprehensive, it is also intensely personal: the

Creator God is Abba, Father, and the Saviour of the world is the Son of God who loved me and gave Himself for me.

If it is the office of the Spirit to be subjective executor of the divine salvation, it is obviously not enough merely to talk or write or read about the Spirit. His testimony is to be heeded, and the mind and heart and will should be opened to His gracious illuminating, regenerating, and sanctifying work. Therefore it is fitting for our study to close with the ancient prayer:

Come, Holy Ghost, our souls inspire,
And lighten with celestial fire.

Veni, Creator Spiritus.

A SELECT BIBLIOGRAPHY

7. THE HOLY SPIRIT

W. Barclay, *The Promise of the Spirit.* London, 1960.

K. Barth, *Church Dogmatics.* Edited and/or translated by G. W. Bromiley *et al.* Edinburgh, 1936———. I, 1: I, 2; IV, 3.

H. Berkhof, *The Doctrine of the Holy Spirit.* Richmond, 1964.

E. F. Harrison (ed.), *Baker's Dictionary of Theology.* Baker, 1960. "Spirit"; "Holy Spirit."

G. S. Hendry, *The Holy Spirit and Christian Theology.* London, 1957.

H. Heppe, *Reformed Dogmatics.* London, 1950.

J. N. D. Kelly, *Early Christian Doctrines.* London, 1958

G. Kittel and G. Friedrich (eds.), *Theological Dictionary of the New Testament.* Translated by G. W. Bromiley. Grand Rapids, 1964———. I, "Hagios"; V, "Pneuma."

A. Kuyper, *The Work of the Holy Spirit.* Grand Rapids, 1946.

B. Ramm, *The Witness of the Spirit.* Grand Rapids, 1959.

G. Smeaton, *The Doctrine of the Holy Spirit.* Edinburgh, 1882.

H. B. Swete, *The Holy Spirit in the New Testament.* London, 1910.
———, *The Holy Spirit in the Ancient Church.* London, 1912.

CHRIST AND HIS CHURCH

Marcus L. Loane

The Rt. Rev. Marcus L. Loane is Anglican Archbishop of Sydney, New South Wales, Australia. Before his consecration as bishop he was principal of Moore Theological College in Sydney. Bishop Loane is a graduate of the University of Sydney with the degrees of B.A. and M.A. and holds the honorary degree of D.D. from the University of Toronto. He has written extensively in the field of church history, and among his books are The Life of Archbishop Mowll, Sons of the Covenant, Pioneers of the Reformation in England, Life Through the Cross, Our Risen Lord, *and* The Place Called Calvary.

8.   *Marcus L. Loane*

CHRIST AND
HIS CHURCH

INTRODUCTION: THE MARKS OF THE CHURCH

Nicholas RIDLEY, who died at the stake on October 16, 1555, made a remarkable statement in his reply to one of the objections brought against his theology. "The holy, catholic or universal church," he said, "which is the communion of saints, the house of God, the city of God, the spouse of Christ, the body of Christ, the pillar and stay of the truth: this church I believe, according to the Creed; this church I do honour and reverence in the Lord. But the rule of this church is the Word of God, according to which rule we go forward unto life. 'And as many as walk according to this rule,' I say with St. Paul, 'peace be upon them and upon Israel, which pertaineth unto God.'

"The guide of this church is the Holy Ghost. The marks whereby this church is known unto me in this dark world and in the midst of this crooked and froward generation are these: the sincere preaching of God's Word; the due administration of the Sacraments; charity; and faithful observing of ecclesiastical discipline according to the Word of God. And that church or congregation which is garnished with these marks, is in very deed that heavenly Jerusalem which consisteth of those that be born from above. This is the mother of us all: and by God's grace, I will live and die the child of this church" (Nicholas Ridley, *Works* [Parker Society Edition, 1843], pp. 122, 123).

This fine statement of the Reformed doctrine of the Church, made under the stress of a critical examination, sums up the "marks" or "notes" that ought to distinguish the Church of God on earth. Ridley was not concerned at that moment with drawing a distinction between the "militant" and "triumphant" aspects of the Church or between its "visible" and "invisible" characters. He addressed himself to the question: How may we know the true Church in this world? This question was forced on him by the Reformation controversy with Rome, which had shaken Europe out of age-long spiritual slumber. The controversy still persists, and the issues at stake have been thrown up in a new form by the ecumenical movement toward organic reunion among Reformed churches.

"The marks whereby this church is known" were summed up in language reminiscent of Ridley's in Article XIX of the Church of England: "The visible Church of Christ is a congregation of faithful men, in which the pure Word of God is preached, and the Sacraments be duly ministered, according to Christ's ordinance, in all things that of necessity are requisite to the same." This new statement omits Ridley's reference to charity and discipline, and it limits the sacraments that must be ministered to those that were ordained by Christ Himself. Bishop H. C. G. Moule pointed out that a church must possess all the "notes" of reality though it may be lacking in the conditions of ideality. But the theologians of the Reformation made it clear that the two indispensable marks of the Church on earth are that the pure Word of God is purely proclaimed and that the two sacraments of the Gospel are duly dispensed.

Christ's Teaching About the Church

To consider in detail the later teaching of the New Testament on the Church is outside the scope of this essay; we are here mainly concerned with the teaching of Christ Himself in the gospel records. This teaching is surprisingly meager; the word *ekklesia* itself occurs in only two verses, both in one Gospel (Matt. 16:18; 18:17). F. J. A. Hort points out that this fact has led to the surmise that each phrase in which the word does occur must have been "thrust into the text in the Second Century in order to support the growing authority of the Ecclesia as an external power" (*The Christian Ecclesia* [Macmillan, 1897], p. 9). But there is no textual evidence to bear out this idea, and each verse in question must be allowed to stand.

The four Gospels commonly represent Christ as the Master in the midst of His disciples; His own teaching reveals Him as the King who rules over all His people or the Shepherd who knows all His sheep by name. There is hardly more than the most slender recognition of some outwardly organized form of the Church (Matt. 18:17), and this is in contrast with the recurring emphasis on the necessity of a personal commitment to Him. It was only toward the end of His life and after His resurrection that He gave clear-cut commands about the proclamation of the Gospel and the ministry of the sacraments. But there is very valuable material in the gospel records on two major aspects of the theme of Christ and His Church: the true nature of the Church He came to found, and the character of the unity He creates within that Church.

I. THE NATURE OF THE CHURCH

The first crucial question, that of the nature of the Church He came to found, comes up in the well-known account of His conversation with the disciples at Caesarea Philippi (Matt. 16:13-20). He had withdrawn to the foothills of Mount Hermon where He could be alone with the Twelve, and He asked them a question to test their insight: "Whom do men say that I the Son of Man am?" He did not ask what the rulers thought; it was all too plain that they thought Him an impostor. But the people had been full of wonder at His gracious teaching: what did they think? They all said that He spoke as one of the prophets, but there were some who were prepared to go further: "Some say that thou art John the Baptist: some, Elias; and others, Jeremias, or one of the prophets."

They were divided in their reaction, but the choice of names shows what they had marked in Him. One group identified Him with John the Baptist or Elijah the Tishbite. The names of these two men were linked because John had come in the power and spirit of Elijah. They had been men of steel; they were preachers of righteousness and repentance; they could rebuke kings to their face and stand alone against the world; and there were many who saw in Jesus another Elijah.

The second group identified Him with Jeremiah or one of the prophets. They may have had Hosea in mind as the other prophet. These prophets had been men of heart; they were preachers of compassion and tenderness; they could wish that their eyes were a fountain of tears to weep for the sins of Israel; and there were many who saw in Jesus another Jeremiah. Thus men saw Him sometimes as another Elijah and sometimes as another Jeremiah, for the prophetic character of both was manifest in His ministry.

The first question was meant to clear the ground for a second, much more direct question: "But whom say ye that I am?" The quiet record hides the dramatic and momentous character of this question. The great object in His training of the Twelve had been to lead them to a solid understanding of His identity with the Messiah foretold by the prophets, and their answer would now reveal to what extent they had really grasped the significance of His teaching. Simon Peter was the man who spoke in reply, though whether for himself alone or as spokesman of what was in the mind of all we cannot say. His resounding reply is well known: "Thou art the Christ, the Son of the living God."

This unfaltering and spontaneous reply had the highest value in Christ's calm and sober judgment. He had said so much that was in contradiction of the popular conception of the messianic ideal that this positive confession of faith made His spirit rejoice. Peter's words were a flash of insight that could have come from nowhere but above, and Christ at once replied: "Blessed art thou, Simon Bar-jona: for flesh and blood hath not revealed it unto thee, but my Father which is in heaven." He used the name *Simon,* the homely name by which Peter was known in the circle of his family and his companions, the name by which he was called when Andrew first brought him to Jesus. And He declared that this intuitive declaration of faith was the result, not of human wisdom, but of divine revelation. "No man knoweth the Son, but the Father;

neither knoweth any man the Father, save the Son, and he to whomsoever the Son will reveal him" (Matt. 11:27*b*).

The Crucial Text — Christ's Words to Peter

This provides the context for the saying that has become one of the storm-centers in all Christian history and that yet is vital to an understanding of the doctrine of the Church. The Lord addressed the disciple whose confession had caused such joy in an emphatic personal manner: "I say also unto thee that thou art Peter, and upon this rock I will build my church." His use of the name *Peter* is in contrast with His use of *Simon* but a moment before, and the remark is an undoubted reference to His saying of long before: "Thou art Simon the son of Jona: thou shalt be called Cephas, which is by interpretation, Peter" (John 1:42, RV). The word *Peter* means a stone, just as the King James version translates it, a piece of rock detached from the great mass of rock. The promise meant that Simon, the son of John, would in time become a man of granite. The promise was fulfilled, and his name was transformed when he avowed Jesus to be the Christ, the Son of God."

But it is not as though the Lord's saying ended with the confirmation of this new name; He went on to add a further saying that was full of word-play. "Thou art Peter *(petros)*, and upon this rock *(petra)* I will build my church." The word *petros* is masculine, the word *petra* feminine; but the play on words and the line of thought are clear. It is interesting to find the same kind of image in the first Epistle of Peter: "Ye also, as lively stones, are built up a spiritual house . . ." (2:5). The living stones and the spiritual house are an echo of the rock and the Church.

What Does "This Rock" Mean?

Thus the Church is likened to a house built up with living stones and "founded upon a rock," a house which cannot be shaken (cf. Matt. 7:24). But to what does "this rock" refer? It all depends on the application of the demonstrative pronoun. Perhaps a paraphrase will illustrate the point. "Thou wast Simon; thou art Peter: thou hast become a rock, and it is on this rock that I will build my church." But if it is meant to form a contrast, the sense will be: "Thou hast become a true living stone cut out of the rock; I am that rock on which I will build stones like thyself into my church."

One thing is clear: the meaning of these words cannot be resolved by the unanimous consent of the Greek and Latin Fathers. Origen held that "this rock" referred primarily, but not exclusively, to Peter; Augustine preferred the view that the rock was Jesus Himself. Chrysostom's theory was that "this rock" did not refer to a person at all but to the great confession of His deity. Many theologians since the Reformation have sided with Chrysostom (e.g., R. G. V. Tasker in *The Gospel According to St. Matthew*). But the force of the text (set out above) seems to confine the choice to the alternatives that "this rock" meant either Peter or Jesus Himself.

Reformed expositors have not shrunk from the first alternative. Thus F. J. A. Hort (*The Christian Ecclesia*) and B. F. C. Atkinson (*The Gospel According to Matthew*) have both held that Peter, with those for whom he spoke, was the rock to which Christ referred. This is perhaps the more natural conclusion. Nevertheless, there is much to be said for the second alternative. It fits the text itself and is in harmony with other New Testament teaching. The rock was a favorite metaphor for God in the Psalms and Prophets: "The LORD is my rock and my fortress" (Ps. 18:2; 31:3; 71:3). This idea was also linked with the rock from which living waters flowed for Israel in the desert. St. Paul boldly affirms: "That rock was Christ" (I Cor. 10:4*c*). Such a consistent metaphor in the Psalms, quite apart from the saying of Christ at Caesarea Philippi, made it easy for St. Paul to declare: "Other foundation can no man lay than that is laid, which is Jesus Christ" (I Cor. 3:11). Perhaps it is significant that St. Peter himself took up the Old Testament metaphor of the cornerstone and applied it with wholehearted devotion to Christ (I Pet. 2:6-8).

St. Paul, however, spoke of the cornerstone in a verse that may lend some support to the view that "this rock" points to Peter and those for whom he spoke: "Ye are built upon the foundation of the apostles and prophets, Jesus Christ himself being the chief cornerstone" (Eph. 2:20). St. John's vision of the City of God also includes this great image: "The wall of the city had twelve foundations, and in them the names of the twelve apostles . . ." (Rev. 21:14).

To reach any dogmatic conclusion about the Lord's saying is impossible, and we are left with a choice. St. Paul's comprehensive saying in the Ephesian epistle (2:20) takes in both points of view and shows that the human agents are the basal living stones that stand on Christ Himself. This idea was illustrated when the workers of the Palestine Exploration Fund found that at the southeast angle of the walls of Jerusalem, the great base stones were let into the rock, which had been cut into trenches for the purpose. Thus we may think of the Church as being built on the apostles as foundation stones that were let into the rock itself, "and that rock was Christ" (I Cor. 10:4*c*).

"The Gates of Hell"

The Lord at once followed up this statement with a further image: "The gates of hell shall not prevail against it." There has been much popular confusion over what this whole word picture is designed to convey. Some have thought that the gates of hell open for the host of evil to go out in battle array against the Church built on a rock like a fortress; some have thought of the Church as a mighty army that must go out from its fortress to storm the gates of hell. But neither interpretation is correct, for neither is based on true exegesis.

The word *gates* is weighted with a long Old Testament history. The gate of a city was the place where counsel was taken, judgment was given, justice was ordered, plans were made, and business was done (see, for example, Gen. 19:1; Ruth 4:1; II Sam. 15:2; 18:24). The word *hell* is

used in the King James Version to translate the word *hades,* and this refers simply to the place of unseen spirits. It speaks of the world of the
dead, but it implies neither good nor ill with regard to their lot in that
world.

Thus the combined image in this brief phrase "the gates of hell," taken
with the promise that they "shall not prevail," calls up a clear picture of
the hostile intrigues against the Church in that world of unseen spirits.
The promise is that the Church will not succumb, for it has the secret
of an immortal victory. This is as true for each member of that Church
as for the Church as a whole. When the French troops under Napoleon
took the city of Rome, they found engraved on the walls of a cell attached
to the Inquisition the words of one of its victims. We do not know his
name, but his words are worthy of remembrance: "Blessed Jesus, they
cannot cast me out of thy true church" (J. C. Ryle, *Holiness* [William
Hunt and Co., 1879], p. 319). It was a true record; the gates of hell
shall not prevail against the least member of that Church which stands
on the rock.

"The Keys of the Kingdom"

The next sentence is no less remarkable: "And I will give unto thee
the keys of the kingdom of heaven." This in effect equates the Church
that He would build with the kingdom of heaven. Before we turn to ask
what the keys of that kingdom are, we may remind ourselves of His teaching elsewhere about who may enter into it. This teaching is contained
in two crucial verses, each of which is one of the strongest statements He
ever uttered. The first was His reply to the ruler Nicodemus who came
to Him by night: "Verily, verily, I say unto thee, Except a man be born
again, he cannot see [cannot enter] the kingdom of God" (John 3:3, 5).
The other was His rebuke to the Twelve when He set a child in their
midst and told them: "Verily I say unto you, Except ye be converted,
and become as little children, ye shall not enter into the kingdom of
heaven" (Matt. 18:3).

To be born again, to be converted, is thus declared to be the one
essential condition for entrance into that kingdom. The emphasis in the
first phrase is on the work of God; it is through the mighty operation of
His Spirit that man is born again. The emphasis in the other phrase is
on the response of man; it is when man repents and believes that he turns
to God in authentic conversion. These two statements are so dogmatic
and so absolute that no ordinary preacher would dare to make them on
his own authority. They mean that no matter what else a man may have,
unless he has had this experience he cannot see the face of God. The
Son of God Himself has made it clear in these words of utter finality that
the only members of that kingdom, of that Church which He came to
found, are those who have been "born again," who have turned to God
in repentance and faith.

The phrase "the keys of the kingdom" refers us in picture language to
the need to unlock and throw open the gates of God's City for those who

may go in. Robert Barnes, who was much better versed in the great Schoolmen than most of the other early English Reformation divines, wrote a telling little tract to discuss what these keys mean. "Duns and all his scholars," wrote Barnes, "say that these keys be nothing else but an authority given to priests whereby they give sentence that heaven must be opened to this man and shut unto the other: so that heaven is opened and shut at the sentence of the priest. . . . Who could have invented such a doctrine but the devil himself? Who can speak greater heresy than this is?" (*Works* [Folio Edition, London, 1573], p. 257). The true key is "nothing else but the Holy Word of God whereby that we receive faith into our hearts. . . . This is the thing only whereby that our conscience is loosed and made free from sin" (p. 258). There is no other kind of key. "In that is all the might and power to loose our sins, and man is but a minister and a servant unto this Word" (p. 259).

Such were the keys that the Lord gave first to Simon Peter; how they were used is described by St. Luke in The Acts. It was Simon Peter who on the day of Pentecost opened the gates of the kingdom to the men of Israel as he proclaimed the word of life (Acts 2:41); it was Simon Peter who in the house of Cornelius opened the gates of the kingdom to the Gentiles as he declared the grace of God (Acts 10:44). But he who was the first to use those keys did but receive them in trust for others: "And they be the common treasure of the Church, and belong no more to one man than to another" (Barnes, *op. cit.,* pp. 261, 262).

"Binding and Loosing"

The Lord had yet one more promise to add: "Whatsoever thou shalt bind on earth shall be bound in heaven: and whatsoever thou shalt loose on earth shall be loosed in heaven." This promise was renewed in the same words and applied to all the Twelve on a later occasion (Matt. 18: 18). They all knew the kind of authority the ruler of a synagogue exercised among the Jews; "bind" and "loose" were rabbinical terms that had to do with rules and regulations for the conduct of the Jewish community. It was the same kind of authority that Christ conferred first on Peter and then on the Twelve: they had the right to take measures for the conduct of the Church's affairs and the exercise of its discipline. J. R. W. Stott sums it up with effective brevity: "It is by binding and loosing certain practices (declaring them lawful or unlawful) that the church can go on to bind those who disregard its teaching and loose those who . . . having disregarded it, repent" (*Confess Your Sins* [Hodder & Stoughton, 1964], p. 45).

The great masters of Reformation theology always linked this saying with that other saying of the Risen Lord in St. John's Gospel: "Whose soever sins ye remit, they are remitted unto them; and whose soever sins ye retain, they are retained" (John 20:23). But *remit* and *retain* were terms that went beyond rules and regulations for church discipline and church fellowship. They were concerned with the inner world of conscience, and they have a judgment value endorsed by a divine sanction.

They gave authority for the declaration of the terms of divine absolution or the fact of divine condemnation. Nothing beyond this well-defined right of declaration can be wrung from these words. It was the task of the Twelve, as it is ours, to declare in the Name of Jesus the grounds on which God will forgive and on which He must condemn; and this was the apostolic practice (see my book, *Then Came Jesus* [Marshall, Morgan & Scott, 1963], pp. 79, 80).

The church of Rome stakes its claim to universal authority on this famous passage. It holds that the words of Christ marked Peter out as the prince of the apostles and that Peter was the apostle who founded the church in Rome. The pope therefore sits on the throne of St. Peter and wears the triple crown as Christ's vicar on earth.

This is all quite untrue to the teaching of the New Testament. It was Peter who began to rebuke the Lord only a few moments after these words had been spoken and who heard in reply that most terrible indictment: "Get thee behind me, Satan; for thou art an offence unto me" (Matt. 16: 23*a*). The Twelve were to argue among themselves about which should be the greatest; there was no sign that they knew that Peter was to become their prince and chief (Matt. 18:1). Peter was quick to take the sword at Christ's arrest, and he sliced off the ear of Malchus. But he acted rashly and was told to put his sword back into its sheath (John 18:11). It was Peter who three times denied the Lord with oath and curse in the palace of the high priest, and then went out into the night to shed tears of wordless sorrow (Matt. 26:75).

Even after the great Pentecostal experience, Peter still was subject to criticism and sometimes to blame. Thus the church in Jerusalem took him to task over the baptism of Cornelius (Acts 11:1, 3). It was James, the brother of the Lord, not Peter, who took the chair and who summed up at the great council in Jerusalem (Acts 15:13). St. Paul was to withstand him face to face among the Christians in Antioch "because he was to be blamed" (Gal. 2:11). Peter himself wrote to "elders" simply as "an elder" (I Pet. 5:1). St. Paul never mentioned his name in the letters he wrote to and from the church in Rome, although he seemed anxious to speak of all in that church who were known to him. We may accept the legend that Peter was put to death as a martyr in that city, but it is clear that he did not found the church in Rome nor preside over it for twenty-five years.

To turn to the other extreme, what must be said of the Salvation Army? It exists to proclaim the Word but does not concern itself with the ministry of the sacraments. It sprang into being to meet the needs of the churchless masses in the great and growing cities of Queen Victoria's England. It did not claim to be a church, and it met with not a little popular obloquy. Let the following paragraph speak for itself:

> The Salvation Army is a fact. You are a good Churchman, and you think poorly of it, scornfully. You resent its schismatic origin and ungentlemanly methods. It is vulgar, blatant, ungrammatical, a mixture of perspiring enthusiasm and false quantities. It is the work partly of Mr.

W. Booth, you think, and partly of Beelzebub. You have a right to your opinion; but while its magnanimity is open to question, its insufficiency is certain. The Salvation Army is too large a fact to be thus interpreted. . . . [Its] limitations are clear; its theology is uproarious and questionable; its serio-comic and quasi-military jargon is to pure reason an impertinent absurdity; the harmonies of its brass bands are a subsidiary proof of original sin. But . . . droll, inadequate, corybantic if you like, it has yet shouted to English Christianity a true and forgotten watchword—spiritual quest of the outcast, apart from pecuniary or social aggrandisement; and with this cry, has caught the religious ear of the nation (Hubert Handley, *The Fatal Opulence of Bishops*, pp. 54, 55, 58).

Is the Salvation Army as such or the Roman Catholic Church as such to be identified with that Church which has been built on that rock? The answer in each case must be No, and for the same reason. The Church Christ declared He would found is not something institutional; it consists of individuals whose faith is stayed on Christ.

The Church Visible and Invisible

This must bring up the whole doctrine of the Church visible and invisible. To speak of the Church as invisible is as unpopular in some quarters today as to speak of "imputed righteousness" was twenty-five years ago. But the Reformation divines used this word without hesitation on the basis of the Scriptures. Richard Hooker's classic statement of this doctrine may be ignored; yet it need scarcely fear refutation (*Ecclesiastical Polity,* III, ii, 1). All is not Israel that is called Israel; neither is true circumcision a mere mark in the flesh. He is a Jew who is so in his heart, and true circumcision must be inward in the spirit. All men knew that Nathanael was an Israelite; the Lord alone knew with unerring certainty that he was one in whom there was no guile. It is only those who are born again, who have been converted, who are members of that true Church. Some are now in heaven and some on earth; and His is the only eye that can with absolute certainty discern who the members of that Church are. There are marks of grace by which they may be known; but our judgment is not infallible, nor did the Lord choose to delegate such judgment to another. Roman Catholics and Salvationists alike are true members of this Church, if the same essential conditions have been fulfilled; and each alike will be outside this Church, if those essential conditions are not fulfilled. This Church consists of "the blessed company of all faithful people" (*Book of Common Prayer,* 1662), both in this world and in the world beyond. Edward Bickersteth phrased it aptly in the Communion Hymn in which he speaks of the bread and wine as "sweet memorials" of Him until all the redeemed unite round His table on high:

> *Some from earth, from glory some,*
> *Severed only till he come.*

The visible Church as distinct from the invisible is the society of all professing Christians, organized for worship, orthodox in doctrine, and open to observation by all. The first stage is described in the memorable words about the converts on the day of Pentecost: "And they continued sted-fastly in the apostles' doctrine and fellowship, and in breaking of bread, and in prayers" (Acts 2:42). This was the stage when it was apt to speak of the church "in their house" (Rom. 16:5). A strong local church was the true product of the preaching of the Gospel and the gathering out of believers: there were the church in Jerusalem (Acts 2:47), "the church that was at Antioch" (Acts 13:1), "the church of God which is at Corinth" (I Cor. 1:2), and so on. And these local churches easily developed into something like a national church: there were "the churches of Galatia" (Gal. 1:2), "the churches of Macedonia" (II Cor. 8:1), "the churches of Asia" (I Cor. 16:19), and so on. The concept of such national churches was presently to develop into that of a universal church: "the church of God" (Acts 20:28).

The local church was to remain the great fundamental unit of all Christian fellowship in the apostolic era, while the concept of a national or universal church was to evolve with the passage of time. But it was clear from the outset that a man might belong to a local church here or there and yet have no part in the Church invisible (see Acts 8:21; II Cor. 13:5; Heb. 6:4-6). It was indeed to the local churches of Asia Minor, visible and organized, that the last words of the ascended, glorified Lord were spoken, and they make it abundantly clear that no church on earth can be identified absolutely with that Church whose members are known to God alone. Wheat and tares grow side by side in the same field; the Church in its visible character in this world must always be a mixture of the true and the false.

The church of Rome at length built up its vast monolithic structure with its claim to universal authority as though it were the one true Church of God on earth. This led to the revolt by the Reformation divines from the medieval concept of that universal authority, and an excessive emphasis on their doctrine of the right of private judgment led in due course to the fragmentation of national churches into denominational bodies. Such denominations came into being in order to preserve certain patterns of government and polity within the Church (Episcopal, Presbyterian, Congregational) or to safeguard certain doctrines in the ministry of the Word and sacraments (Methodist, Baptist, Church of Christ). Other bodies like the Quakers and the Brethren do not think of themselves as denominational at all. There are also fringe bodies like the Pentecostalists and Seventh-day Adventists that are vigorously denominational in organization and propaganda.

The whole idea of a denomination is a modern development resulting from a long historical process. One cannot say either that it is something laid down in the Scriptures or that it is wholly inconsistent with the Scriptures. The Lord Himself is in the midst where two or three meet in His Name, and His presence with His people means the Church is there. But all denominational bodies find that their true spiritual reason for existence is soon complicated by more earthly matters. They acquire a constitution with legal safeguards and limitations; they face problems that arise from ownership of property and the creation of trusts; they are involved in institutional and administrative work as a by-product of true Christian fellowship; and they try to secure theological continuity on a denominational basis. These things sometimes tend to encourage members to be loyal to a denomination as if the denomination were an end in itself. Thus all denominational bodies bear the marks of human imperfection and fall short of the true ideal.

The Church visible, organized, grouped in denominational bodies, has to address itself to questions of worship about which opinions may differ widely. Many arguments over liturgy and ritual, fellowship and discipline, have their roots deep in the soil of historical controversy and doctrinal conviction; and the only standard for a proper judgment in such cases is the teaching of Scripture. But other arguments may concern what are only matters of taste. St. Paul has laid down the golden rule that ought to govern all such matters in a local church when no theological or constitutional problems arise: "Let all things be done decently and in order" (I Cor. 14:40). Questions of liturgy or ritual may be indifferent if they are viewed alone; reverence and order are of cardinal importance in the worship of God.

Paul S. Rees has drawn attention to this argument in words that deserve to be pondered.

> Almost from the first century until this, from the days of the Apostles until now, the question of form versus spontaneity has had to be faced. The Church has its free Pentecostals and it has its formal Anglo-Catholics. Shall we say in a quick quotation from Kipling, "And never the twain shall meet"? Not if we are Pauline. The spiritually creative and the spiritually conventional are not sworn enemies. They only wage war against each other when each goes to excess and when each despises the other. . . . Flame without form gives you a volatile discipleship; it easily leads to emotional excesses and fanaticisms; but form without flame reduces Christianity to the fastidious properness of a corpse in a casket" (*The Keswick Convention* [Marshall, Morgan & Scott, 1956], p 140).

II. CHURCH UNITY ACCORDING TO JOHN 17

This leads to the second crucial question for which material is found in the Gospels, the question of the character of that unity which Christ creates within the Church built on the rock. This matter Christ dealt with in the prayer He uttered on the eve of His death (John 17:1-26).

It was that night on which He was betrayed. The bread and wine of the new Covenant had been shared at the Passover table, and the eleven disciples had heard the words of calm farewell. They had sung one of the psalms of David; then they had left the upper room. They had gone out through the silent streets and the city gates, over the brook Kidron, and on toward the Garden of Gethsemane. And the Lord had carried on His discourse as they went on their way beneath the light of a full moon. They heard Him speak of the vine and its branches, and then perhaps there was a pause. The whole party may have stood in wondering revery, in a silence that lasted until He was ready to speak again. Then He began to lift His heart to the Father, and the disciples listened as He engaged in a prayer of the most exalted character.

No other prayer that Christ uttered has been preserved in such detail or so clearly reveals the true quality of His fellowship with God. It begins in personal communion with the Father (John 17:1-5); it proceeds with a prayer for the disciples who were with Him (vv. 6-19); it is rounded off with intercession for all who will believe on Him (vv. 20-26). And the point of emphasis throughout this prayer is Christ's earnest longing for the absolute unity of His people. Scripture has no other passage so definite and emphatic in its teaching on this subject; and nothing was nearer to His heart as He moved through that night toward the cross.

The Unity of the Disciples

The first statement on this subject was in reference to the disciples. They were still in the world, while He was soon to go to the Father. These two facts were briefly stated (17:11*a*), then left without comment. But they introduced conditions that would create a new situation between the disciples and the Lord. Therefore He went on to lift up His heart in an address that combined reverence with tenderness: "Holy Father." "Keep through thine own name," He prayed, "those whom thou hast given me, that they may be one, as we are" (v. 11*b*). He asked that they might be kept through His "name," for that "name" is the region in which all true security consists. And they were to be kept "that they may be one, as we are." Preservation in all that His name stands for was the one sure ground for their safety and the only basis for their absolute unity.

"That they may be one, as we are." There is majesty in this conception. The phrase itself may be compared with something He said earlier: "I and my Father are one" (John 10:30). R. V. G. Tasker says in *The Gospel According to St. John* that this saying was often quoted in the Arian controversy by those who held that the Son is of one substance with the Father; and he goes on to say that it really seems to imply that the Father and the Son are one in will and purpose. This indicates that His prayer for the disciples was in the vein suggested by J. C. Ryle: "Keep them that they may be of one heart and one mind; that they may not be broken or weakened by quarrel or schism; keep them one as we are" (*Expository Thoughts on the Gospel of St. John* [Hodder & Stoughton, 1896], III, 212).

Bishop B. F. Westcott goes further still. In *The Gospel According to St. John* (John Murray, 1881), he insists that John 10:30 refers to oneness of essence. And this inherent unity between Father and Son in the Godhead is the pattern, or even the basis, for the essential unity of disciples or believers (cf. 17:22). This governs his exegesis of the words in this prayer: "That they may be one as we are." He sees this not merely as oneness in will and purpose but as oneness in nature itself. "As we are": the use of the plural pronoun is in Westcott's eyes a distinct claim that they were one in essence. The word "we" not only unites the Son with the Father but also asserts that their nature is one. Thus His prayer is for a harmony of nature, a fellowship in spirit, which can be known only where there is an authentic personal union of each with Christ Himself.

But caution is necessary; there can never be a literal unity between believer and believer such as there is between Father and Son. The ultimate unity in the Godhead is unique; it is beyond the reach of our experience. Yet, as H. C. G. Moule says, it is the "true analogue for our unity with one another in his Name" (*The High Priestly Prayer* [Religious Tract Society, 1908], p. 103). It is more than relatedness in the sense that one branch is joined with other branches as parts of the same vine; "it is oneness as the Father and the Son are one" (p. 104). It is so real and so profound that it has its kinship with that ultimate unity in the Godhead between Father and Son.

The Unity of Believers in All Ages

In Christ's prayer the unity of disciples now gives way to a yet larger concept—the unity of believers in all ages. Christ now treats the Church of the future as though it is at this moment present before His mind, and the oneness of the members of that Church now becomes the main underlying theme of this prayer. He treats the whole subject with an interest momentous beyond all words; and He reiterates it with decided emphasis. Each phrase adds some essential point to the whole and needs to be examined accordingly:

1. "That they all may be one" (17:21)
2. "That they may be one in us" (17:21)
3. "That they may be one even as we are one" (17:22).

The first phrase speaks of it as a unity of all: "That they all may be one." These words do not convey the hope that they might all become a mere unit, as when raindrops have been absorbed into one vast ocean. There is nothing here to suggest pantheism or to destroy the concept of personality. The words indicate a unity in which all the parts are perfectly related and yet remain distinct. The unity of the Godhead is a truth that consists with a variety of Persons; so the believing community may have many constituent members, but they are all centered in Christ. The spokes of a wheel all touch the rim at different points, but all the spokes meet in the hub. This is a unity that not only preserves the recognition of individual character but also transcends it.

The next phrase speaks of it as a unity similar to that of the Father and the Son:' "That they may be one in us, as thou, Father, art in me, and I in thee" (I have reversed the phrase order so as to bring out the point). This means that all those who believe on His Name are made one only because they have been joined to one Father and one Saviour; that is why they can be described as "one in us." There is oneness with one another only because there is oneness with God, who was "in Christ, reconciling the world unto himself" (II Cor. 5:19). And such unity with one another must then correspond in some mysterious sense to the words "thou in me . . . I in thee." Thus the clause as a whole points to a communion of saints that has its roots in the harmony of the Godhead; and this unity of believers with one another is as true and vital as the unity of the Father and the Son in the mysterious Triune Being of God Himself.

The last phrase speaks of this unity as one that transcends the limits of our understanding: "That they may be one, even as we are one: I in them, and thou in me." To be one "as thou art in me and I in thee" (17: 21) is to be one "even as we are one" (17:22); and such oneness is spiritual in quality and character. The Lord our God is one (Deut. 6:4), and He is a Spirit (John 4:24). The unity of believers with one another in Him pertains to a life that is hid with Christ in God; it belongs to those who are partakers of the divine nature. It represents that "unity of the Spirit" about which St. Paul speaks (Eph. 4:3). Words are inadequate to convey its meaning to our limited intellects. The Lord Himself traversed the same ground more than once so that the truth might be fully expressed: "Thou . . . in me, and I in thee" (17:21) . . . "I in them, and thou in me" (17:23). He is in us as He is in the Father; He is in us as the Father is in Him.

It is all summed up in the words: "That they may be made perfect in one" (17:23). These words do not refer to a local, organized congregation or an outward, visible community. The one essential point of reference in this prayer is clearly defined as "them which shall believe on me" (17:20). It is a prayer for all authentic believers, for all who share a "like precious faith" (II Pet. 1:1) in the Son of God. This means all those who are members of that body of which He is the Head, all who belong to that house which He came to build upon the rock. Any rupture of that mystical fellowship would be infinitely worse than a rent in the seamless raiment that He wore to the cross. Therefore He locked believers in the arms of prayer and prayed for their unity with one another, so that they might become "perfect in one."

We shall become "perfect in one" only when we arrive at that ultimate unity in which we shall all stand complete in Christ. How far was this ideal fulfilled among the first disciples? "When the day of Pentecost was fully come, they were all with one accord in one place" (Acts 2:1). It was upon a band of men who were of "one accord" that the Holy Ghost came down in authority and power. No finer picture of true Christian fellowship can be found than the one we see in the history of these disciples: "And they, continuing daily with one accord in the temple, and breaking bread from house to house, did eat their meat with gladness and singleness of heart, praising God, and having favor with all the people. And the Lord added to the church daily such as should be saved" (Acts 2:46, 47). Perhaps there has never been a finer seedtime in the life of the Church. St. Paul declared that his cup would be filled with joy if this experience could be renewed among the believers at Philippi and he poured out his heart with the loving exhortation: "That ye be like-minded, having the same love, being of one accord, of one mind" (Phil. 2:2).

Thus the inner essential unity of all those who believe in Christ found a clear, visible reflection in the glorious fellowship that came into being among the first converts. But this initial unity of heart and mind was not maintained when fresh converts began to form local congregations. Serious division was to develop in the Hebrew church at Jerusalem; party factions were to multiply in the Gentile church at Corinth. There was the clash of controversy in matters of doctrine; there was the need for separation in questions of conduct. St. Paul was to withstand Peter himself and separate from Barnabas as well in one early crisis. Such elements of division were to grow in number and strength with the passage of time, and no thoughtful person can think of them as though they were good in themselves.

But we need to discriminate between things that differ; confusing our terms can only result in fresh problems. Christian fellowship ought to transcend all the divisive elements of race, sex, class, or culture among those who are one in Christ Jesus (Gal. 3:28; Col. 3:11). All such Christian fellowship on earth helps to manifest the "communion of saints" and to reflect the true mystical unity of those who have been made "perfect in one" (John 17:23). But the only Church to which that unity in its perfection can be said to apply is the "invisible" Church, whose members share a heavenly heritage as "heirs of God and joint-heirs with Christ" (Rom. 8:17).

Ecumenism and Church Unity

Sixty years ago, David H. C. Read has observed, "only visionaries and romantics would have used the expression 'one world' " (*The Communication of the Gospel*, SCM Press, 1956). In the early years of the last world war, Wendell Willkie published a book with this as its title, *One World*. When it appeared, it gave tentative expression to what is now a growing and vital force in political affairs. The cold war has led the Western democratic nations to a widespread concern for some form of political federation that might make the world safe for peace and for freedom. The United Nations is the tangible evidence of this desire as well as the tacit promise of a yet more substantial unity. Its weaknesses are apparent to all, but it still aims at a lofty human ideal: to make all the kingdoms of the world live as one kingdom under the rule of men who are all of one mind.

This has its counterpart in the history of the denominational churches. In recent years, various movements for centralization or cooperation have been accelerated. The most prominent example was the formation of the Church of South India in 1947 through union of certain churches that had grown up through the work of denominational missionary societies.

But a still more significant fact has been the rapid development of the ecumenical movement. The World Council of Churches came into being at Amsterdam in 1948, and the International Missionary Council was in-

tegrated with it during the assembly at New Delhi in 1962. Many of the
leaders of this movement have now caught a vision of one great goal—
nothing less than the full organic reunion of all denominational churches
throughout the world. Indeed the large poster displayed at the Amsterdam
assembly set this out in plain terms: "One World, One Church."

There are regular denials that this is the official policy of the World
Council of Churches. But so many spokesmen of the movement have
made it clear that this is the goal on which their hearts are set that it
cannot be ignored. Their view is that Christian unity will be realized only
through surrender of independence by each denominational body. Those
who adhere to this concept of unity believe that Christendom has been
seriously weakened by the denominational system. The fact that denominational churches exist is to them a sin that ought to drive men to their
knees with honest regret. They think each should go into his own corner
and there repent for his own denomination's share in the present system.
Then all ought to work for the time when there will be one flock with one
Shepherd; and that, to them, means one world church.

Those who hold this view often quote the Lord's words of prayer:
"That they all may be one" (John 17:21). These great words are loosely
used to support popular theories of church reunion or ecumenical action
on the ground that they are opposed to all that is schismatic or divisive
in the visible and corporate body of all faithful people. But this is to lift
them right out of their context and to ignore the most elementary rules
of exegesis. There has never been a time when that true, inner, essential unity did not exist; invisible, mysterious, it is yet both fundamental
and real for all who have themselves been brought into union with Christ.
We cannot organize that unity by human methods; it is the creation of
divine goodness. All who believe on His Name shall "be made perfect
in one" (17:23); but this oneness can be achieved only on the level of
true personal commitment by faith to Christ. Apart from such a faith,
oneness in Christ is impossible and unity is a fiction.

Thus the oneness of which that prayer speaks has to do with the spirit
of the believing community and not with the body of an organized society.
Few words in Scripture are so regularly misquoted or so seriously mis-
applied by men who occupy positions of Christian leadership. It is hard
to escape the thought that those who are absorbed in the quest for organic
reunion among denominational bodies have made little effort to come to
terms with the original context or the primary intention of this prayer for
oneness. Conceivably, earnest effort may eliminate the elements of division
between this and that church; it might result in one body with one creed,
one liturgy, and one ministry. But the union of such denominational bodies
concerns the Church in its visible character on earth; it cannot be identified and must not be confused with the essential unity that now in fact
belongs to the true Church, which is invisible.

Emil Brunner asserts that the clerical element is always the victor in
the external reunion of the denominational churches, and "in the last re-
sort," he says, "such a movement must end with the victory of the most

ecclesiastical church—the Roman" (*The Misunderstanding of the Church* [Lutterworth, 1954], p. 112). An old cartoon depicts a shipwrecked and forlorn sailor on a raft in the rain, gazing down at a shark whose jaws are wide open with the gleeful hint that the sailor should come in out of the wet. This represents the attitude that the church of Rome has always taken toward the non-Roman churches; and the basic reason for this tremendous arrogance is that the church of Rome identifies herself alone with the true Church of God.

But the invisible Church of God cannot be identified with an organized, corporate church in this world, and true mystical unity is not the same thing as external reunion. That true mystical unity to which the Lord referred belongs to no outward body on earth; it is the great result of the unifying reality of God's presence in the hearts of all His people. No church on earth is so pure that there are not tares as well as wheat; but wheat and tares are not one and the same. Spiritual oneness is the experience only of those who are in Him just as He is in them. And this moving prayer on the eve of His death was that their unity might be manifest to all, so that "the world may believe that thou hast sent me" (17:21).

CONCLUSION: THE ONLY TRUE CHURCH

One must therefore conclude that the only true Church is that "spiritual house" (I Pet. 2:5) which the Lord Himself is still building on the rock that nothing can shake (Matt. 7:25); and that the true ultimate unity is found only among those who have been made "one in Christ Jesus" (Gal. 3:28) and are members of that "household of faith" (Gal. 6:10). Where is this Church, and where are its members? The Old Testament tells how the tribes of Israel would go up to Jerusalem, where God's glory was seen in the Temple. The New Testament develops this idea and pictures the Church as the unnumbered multitude of God's redeemed people who are gathered one by one in heaven around the Lord Jesus. Even here on earth our citizenship is in heaven, where He now is with whom we are yet to be (Phil. 3:20). This fact is superbly asserted in the letter to the Hebrews: "Ye are come unto mount Sion, and unto the city of the living God, the heavenly Jerusalem, and to an innumerable company of angels, to the general assembly and church of the firstborn, which are written in heaven, and to God the Judge of all, and to the spirits of just men made perfect, and to Jesus, the Mediator of the New Covenant . . ." (Heb. 12:22-24).

This Church therefore has a glorious destiny, for it is to gather round Jesus Himself in heaven. The true foretaste of this on earth is the fact that when two or three meet in His Name, He is then and there in the midst. The Church itself is the "habitation of God through the Spirit" (Eph. 2:22), and Christ dwells in the hearts of His people by faith (Eph. 3:17).

Scottish divines love to express this truth in their favorite metaphor of the burning bush as seen by Moses. They like to think of the fire as a symbol of God, and of the bush as a symbol of the Church. The bush

FUNDAMENTALS OF THE FAITH

was humble enough, yet not too humble for God to dwell in. It was poor enough, yet not too poor to burst into flame at His touch. God is in the Church, as the fire was in the bush; it is the shrine in which He burns, and that fire will never burn out. Samuel Rutherford summed it all up when he said that no man ever "yet saw the ashes of this fire" (A. A. Bonar, *Letters of Samuel Rutherford* [Oliphants, n.d.], p. 634).

The four adjectives in the historic creedal statements about the Church may be combined in one sentence: "I believe one (holy) catholic and apostolic church." These notes or marks of a true Church can be applied in their fullest meaning only to that "invisible" Church of which the Lord is the Head. That Church alone answers to the ideals of unity and sanctity; that Church alone is truly universal and apostolic. That Church is not identical with any one denominational body, nor with the sum total of such bodies; it is the Church of God built of living stones on that great rock which is Christ Himself. That rock may look at times as though it were shrouded in mist or lashed by storm; but it remains strong and steadfast, rooted in the everlasting stability of God Himself.

A SELECT BIBLIOGRAPHY

8. CHRIST AND HIS CHURCH

G. K. A. Bell, *Christian Unity: The Anglican Position.* Hodder & Stoughton, 1948.

C. Sydney Carter, *Reformation and Reunion.* Church Book Room Press, 1935.

R. A. Cole, *The Body of Christ.* Hodder & Stoughton, 1964.

A. C. Headlam, *The Doctrine of the Church and Reunion.* John Murray, 1923.

F. J. A. Hort, *The Christian Ecclesia.* Macmillan, 1897.

G. T. Manley, *Christian Unity.* Inter-Varsity Fellowship, 1945.

Stephen Neill, *The Unfinished Task.* Lutterworth Press, 1958.

Lesslie Newbigin, *The Reunion of The Church.* Student Christian Movement, 1948.

René Pache, *The Ecumenical Movement.* Dallas Theological Seminary, 1950.

A. M. Stibbs, *God's Church: A Study in the Biblical Doctrine of the People of God.* Inter-Varsity Fellowship, 1959.

J. R. W. Stott, *Confess Your Sins.* Hodder & Stoughton, 1964.

Henry Townsend, *The Claims of the Free Churches.* Hodder & Stoughton, 1949.

THE NEW BIRTH

Billy Graham

Billy Graham has preached to more than 50,000,000 people in person—and countless millions have heard or seen him by radio, television or film. General of the Army Dwight D. Eisenhower, former President of the United States, called him "an evangelist who can relate his basic spiritual beliefs to the tough problems of the day . . . ."

9. Billy Graham

THE NEW BIRTH

ALDOUS HUXLEY, in his *Brave New World,* devised a drug called "soma," which was intended to take all the rough edges from life. There is no doubt that if mankind is to be saved, something radical needs to be done quickly. Man stands on the brink of hell. The forces building up in our world are so overwhelming that man everywhere is beginning to cry out in desperation: "What must I do to be saved?"

Everything in our world seems to improve but man. In his essential moral nature, which governs his relationship to his fellow man, he steals, murders, lies, cheats, and brags. Since the beginning of time, he has remained essentially unchanged. The newspaper accounts of murder, rape, and brutality indicate that somewhere we have failed. After years of psychological study, Carl Jung said: "All the old primitive sins are not dead but are crouching in the dark corners of our modern hearts . . . still there, and still ghastly as ever."

Man is being forced to accept the reality of sin and the necessity of a new birth. Walter Lippmann said: "We ourselves were so sure that at long last a generation had arisen, keen and eager, to put this disorderly earth to right . . . and fit to do it . . . we meant so well, we tried so hard, and look what we have made of it. We can only muddle into muddle. What is required is a new kind of man."

We are beginning to recognize the inability of man over the centuries of futile religious, cultural, moral, and educational efforts to change his own heart. Man has labored ineffectually to achieve his moral goals and change himself by the improvement of his environment. Now we are disillusioned and know that somehow the change must come from within.

Man's Attempts to Change Himself

At present man is experimenting in what are called the behavioral sciences, including anthropology, psychology, and sociology, in order to discover the laws of human behavior. The trouble with these experiments is that they ignore the fact of human sin. According to the new sciences, sin is largely imaginary. Man is the product of his environment. He is the happy or unhappy product of a combination of genes and chromosomes. In this pseudoscientific sentimentality, a juvenile delinquent is merely underprivileged and a robber is simply maladjusted. In this philosophy we abandon the idea of sin and individual responsibility and blame everything but the offender. Therefore we have nothing to cure but man's environment in terms of bad housing, slums, poverty, unemployment, and racial discrimination, while the prime suspect, the individual, remains untouched and unchanged. Man himself and his behavior, according to this new science, are considered to be the result of natural selection.

Then there is man's attempt to change himself by chemistry. Scientists at present are deeply involved in the control of behavior by pharmacological agents. Professor B. F. Skinner of Harvard University said: "We are entering the age of the chemical control of human behavior. The motivational and emotional conditions of normal daily life probably will be maintained in any desired state through the use of drugs." At best, however, such drugs will provide only temporary changes either for better or worse, depending upon the nature of the administrator, with probable permanent damage to the brain.

THE POSSIBILITY OF THE NEW MAN

Jesus Christ demanded: "Ye must be born again" (John 3:7). He would never have given such a challenge, had it not been a possibility. Yes, man can be changed, radically and permanently, from the inside out. There is the possibility of a completely new man.

It is interesting that Jesus made this statement to Nicodemus, an upright and devout religious leader, who must have been stunned by it. If Christ had said this to Zacchaeus, who had cheated his way to the top of his own financial world—or to the woman at the well, who had had several husbands—or to the thief on the cross—or to the woman taken in adultery, it would have been easier to understand. We know that those persons needed changing. But Jesus said this to one of the great religious leaders of His time. Nicodemus fasted two days a week, spent two hours daily in prayer at the temple, tithed all his income, taught as a professor of theology at the seminary. Most churches would have been glad to have him; but Jesus said: "It is not enough. You must be born again." This implies that all men need the new birth, and it also implies that all men can be born again.

Dr. Wilbur M. Smith in a recent volume of *Peloubet's Select Notes* has given the following specific analysis of some aspects of the new birth: "What do we mean by a man being born anew, or born again? To be-

gin with, it means something tremendously radical. What we are by nature we are because of what we were when born. At birth our sex is
settled, the very frame of our body is already determined. No doubt our
very temperament, our capacities, our habits, our inclinations, are all
given to us at birth, at least fundamentally; indeed our very appearance.
To be born again at least implies an absolutely new beginning, not a
reformation of life, not a turning over of a new leaf, not the addition of
some one new attribute or aspect or capacity, but something so radical
that by it we are going to be something altogether different from what
we have been. Of course, anyone knows that we cannot be born the
second time physically. Therefore the reference here is spiritual, a rebirth
not of body, but of soul, and mind, and character. Again, we should
notice . . . the universal inclusiveness and absolute necessity for such a
miracle as this, if one is to be a member of the kingdom of God. No one
is excepted, and no one can substitute something else for this tremendous
reality."

To its own shame and to the detriment of society, the modern church
has to a large extent abandoned this message of the new birth. It preaches
social change, disarmament, and legislation; but it does not major in the
one thing that will solve the problems of our world—changed men. Man's
basic problem is spiritual, not social. Man needs a complete change.

The Bible refers many times to this change Jesus talked about. The
prophet Ezekiel said: "A new heart also will I give you, and a new spirit
will I put within you" (Ezek. 36:26). In the book of Acts, Peter called
it repenting and being converted. Paul speaks of it in Romans as being
"alive from the dead" (Rom. 6:13). In Colossians Paul calls it "[a putting off of] the old man with his deeds, and [putting] on the new man
which is renewed in knowledge after the image of him that created him"
(Col. 3:9, 10).

Thus the Bible teaches that man can undergo a radical spiritual and
moral change that is brought about by God Himself. The word that Jesus
used, and which is translated "again," actually means "from above." The
context of the third chapter of John teaches that the new birth is something that God does for man when man is willing to yield to God. As we
have already seen, the Bible teaches that man is dead in trespasses and
sins, and his great need is LIFE.

One day a caterpillar climbs up into a tree where nature throws a fiber
robe about him. He goes to sleep and in a few weeks he emerges a
beautiful butterfly. So man—distressed, discouraged, unhappy, hounded
by conscience, driven by passion, ruled by selfishness, belligerent, quarrelsome, confused, depressed, miserable, taking alcohol and barbiturates,
looking for escapisms—can come to Christ by faith and emerge a new
man. This sounds incredible, even impossible, and yet it is precisely what
the Bible teaches.

More than Reformation

This new birth is far more than reformation. Many persons make New
Year's resolutions only to break them because they do not have the

capacity to keep them. Man is ever reforming, but reformation at best is only temporary. Man's nature must be transformed.

A group of barbers at their annual convention decided to exhibit the value of their tonsorial art. They found a derelict on skid row, gave him a haircut, shave, and a bath; and they dressed him in new clothes of the finest tailoring. They had demonstrated to their satisfaction the worth of tonsorial excellence, but three days later the man was in the gutter again. He had been outwardly transformed into a respectable-looking man, but the impulses and drives of his inner being had not been changed. He had been powdered and perfumed, but not changed.

You can scrub a pig, sprinkle Chanel No. 5 on him, put a ribbon around his neck, and take him into your living room. But when you turn him loose, he will jump into the first mud puddle he sees because his nature has never been changed. He is still a pig.

Through the new birth the Bible teaches that man enters a new world. There is a new dimension of living. The change that comes over a man is expressed in the Bible in various contrasts: lust and holiness, darkness and light, death and resurrection, a stranger to the Kingdom of God and now a citizen. The man who has experienced the new birth is called a member of God's household. The Bible teaches that his will is changed, his objectives for living are changed, his disposition is changed, his affections are changed, and he now has purpose and meaning in his life. In the new birth, a new life has been born in his soul. He receives a new nature and a new heart. He becomes a new creation.

Nicodemus was puzzled by these statements of Christ, and he asked: "Can I enter into my mother's womb and be born the second time?" This was a natural response any one of us would have made. So much of what Nicodemus believed had been swept away. He was finding out that religion was not sufficient. The Law of Moses could not save him, because he was not really fulfilling its requirements. He had to be born again. He was told that no one could enter the Kingdom of Heaven without having eternal life, for nothing but "God-life" can exist there. He who has that life will be admitted. The great question is, Do I possess eternal life? If not, how do I get it? This is the most important question a man can ask or have answered.

The Bible tells of many men who have been changed by an encounter with Jesus Christ. There is the demoniac whose chains could not bind against the power of his seizures, but when he met Jesus he was changed and later was found in his home "clothed and in his right mind." No longer was he the prey of hallucinations. No longer was he in the grip of Satanic power. No longer had be the fears that had constantly beset him. No longer was he a menace to the community. He had become a changed man in character, dress, conduct, and even in environment (Luke 8).

There is Zacchaeus, who defrauded the people as a taxgatherer. When he met Jesus, all was changed. He proceeded to make restitution. "The half of my goods I give to the poor; and if I have taken anything from any man by false accusation, I restore him fourfold" (Luke 19:8).

Most of these encounters with Christ resulted in an instantaneous transformation. On the day of Pentecost there were three thousand who were born again that very day. In the morning they were lost, confused, and sinful. Before the day had ended, they had been born into the Kingdom of God. Each one had passed out of death into life (Acts 2:41).

A young man named Saul was on the road to Damascus to persecute Christians when he met Christ under the hot Syrian sun. He was never to be the same again. Over and over he referred back to that encounter. He was able to look back and speak about it years later, remembering the very day and the very moment when he met Christ (Acts 9).

The Philippian jailer had a similar experience. When he was gripped by fear, he cried out: "What must I do to be saved?" The Apostle Paul told him: "Believe on the Lord Jesus Christ and thou shalt be saved." Many modern psychiatrists might say that he was in no emotional state to make a permanent decision. Paul did not look at it that way, and he baptized the jailer that very night. The jailer then began to wash their wounds as a token of the new life he had received from God (Acts 16).

Any person who is willing to trust Jesus Christ as his personal Saviour can receive the new birth now. The early Methodist preachers were called the "now preachers" because they offered salvation on the spot. It is not something to be received at death or after death; it is to be received now. "Now is the accepted time; behold, now is the day of salvation" (II Cor. 6:2). God offers eternal life to anyone who will receive it.

HOW TO BECOME A NEW MAN

Some time ago during a question-and-answer session at Harvard Divinity School, a student stood up and asked me: "Can you tell me in plain and clear language what I must do to be saved?"

Over and over again I am asked that question at colleges and universities where I often lecture. Can the alcoholic, the thief, the murderer, the sex pervert be changed radically and made a new man? At a West Coast university a professor of science came to see me in my room at the Student Union, and he said: "You are going to be amazed at the ultimate question I am here to ask you." Then he told me a long story of his own inward struggle in moral, spiritual, and intellectual issues. "More and more," he said, "I have come to realize that my problem with Christianity is really not intellectual at all. It is moral. I have not been willing to meet the moral requirements of Christianity." And he added: "Here is my question: What can I do to receive Jesus Christ?"

When the governor of one of our states entertained us in his home, he asked to talk to me privately. We went into a back room, where he locked the door. I could see that he was struggling with his emotions, but finally he said to me: "I am at the end of my rope. I need God. Can you tell me how to find God?"

On another occasion when I visited a group of men on death row in a prison, a strong and intelligent-looking man listened to what I had to say. Then I asked the men if they would be willing to kneel down while

I prayed. Just before we knelt there, the man said: "Can you explain once again what I must do to be forgiven of my sins? I want to know that I am going to heaven."

These are precisely the same questions asked of Jesus Christ nearly two thousand years ago. These are the same questions asked of the Apostles as they proclaimed the Gospel throughout the Roman Empire. The questions indicate that man's inward spiritual longings have changed very little.

The rich young ruler came running to kneel before Christ, and asked Him: "Good Master, what shall I do that I may inherit eternal life?" (Mark 10:17). After Peter preached his great sermon at Pentecost, the Bible says that the people were "pricked in their heart, and said unto Peter . . . What shall we do?" (Acts 2:37). The African nobleman riding in his chariot across the desert talked with Philip the evangelist. Suddenly the nobleman stopped his chariot and said: "What doth hinder me?" (Acts 8:36). At midnight the Philippian jailer asked Paul and Silas: "Sirs, what must I do to be saved?" (Acts 16:30).

Twentieth-century man asks the same question that man has always asked. It is old, but it is ever new. It is just as relevant today as in the past.

Just what must one do to be reconciled to God? What does the Bible mean by such words as conversion, repentance, and faith? These are all salvation words, but so little understood.

Jesus made everything so simple and we have made it so complicated. He spoke to the people in short sentences and every-day words, illustrating His messages with never-to-be-forgotten stories. He presented the message of God in such simplicity that many could not understand what He said.

In the book of Acts the Philippian jailer asked the Apostle Paul: "What must I do to be saved?" Paul gave him a very simple answer: "Believe on the Lord Jesus Christ and thou shalt be saved" (Acts 16:30, 31). This is so simple that millions stumble over it. The one and only choice by which you can be converted is your choice to believe on the Lord Jesus as your own personal Lord and Saviour. You don't have to straighten out your life first. You don't have to make things right at home or in your business first. You don't have to try to give up some habit that is keeping you from God. You have tried all that and failed many times. In our crusades when I give the invitation to receive Christ, we sing the hymn entitled "Just as I Am," and you come to Christ just as you are. The blind man came as he was. The leper came as he was. Mary Magdalene with seven devils came as she was. The thief on the cross came as he was. You can come to Christ just as you are.

Conversion

The word "conversion" means simply "turning." From the beginning of the Bible to the end, God pleads with man to turn to Him (Prov. 1:23; Isa. 31:6; 59:20; Ezek. 14:6; 18:32; 33:9; Joel 2:12; Matt. 18:3; Acts 3:19; Heb. 6:1). However, it is impossible for man to turn to God to repent, or even to believe, without God's help! All you can do is call upon God to "turn" you. Many times in the Bible it is recorded that men did that very thing (Ps. 85:4; Song of Sol. 1:4; Jer. 31:18; Lam. 5:21). When a man calls upon God, he is giving true repentance and faith. That is why the Apostle Paul could say: "Whosoever shall call upon the name of the Lord shall be saved" (Rom. 10:13). The Bible never asks man to justify himself, to regenerate himself, to convert himself, or to save himself. God alone can do these things.

There are at least *two elements in conversion—repentance* and *faith.* Jesus said: "Except ye repent, ye shall . . . perish" (Luke 13:3). Repentance carries with it a recognition of sin involving personal guilt and defilement before God. It does not mean a cringing self-contempt. It is a simple recognition of what we are. We see ourselves as God sees us, and we say "God be merciful to me a sinner" (Luke 18:13). Job said: "I have heard of thee by the hearing of the ear: but now mine eye seeth thee. Wherefore I abhor myself, and repent in dust and ashes" (Job 42:5, 6).

Repentance

Repentance means also a change of feeling. This means a genuine sorrow for sin committed against God (Ps. 51). As Paul said in II Corinthians 7:9, 10: "Now I rejoice, not that ye were made sorry, but that ye sorrowed to repentance . . . for godly sorrow worketh repentance to salvation."

Repentance means also a change of purpose and carries with it the idea of an inward turning from sin by the exercise of the will. However, all you have to do is to be willing. God will help you.

Repentance is the launching pad where the soul is sent on its eternal orbit with God at the center of the arc. When our hearts are bowed as low as they can get and we truly acknowledge and forsake our sins, then God takes over and like the second stage of a rocket, He lifts us toward His Kingdom. The way up is down. Man got into difficulty when he lifted his will against God's. He gets out of trouble when he bows to the divine superiority, when he repents and says humbly: "God be merciful to me a sinner." Man's extremity then becomes God's opportunity.

Faith

The second element in conversion is *faith.* In order to be converted, you must make a choice. The Scripture says: "He that believeth on Him is not condemned, but he that believeth not is condemned already because he hath not believed in the name of the only begotten Son of God" (John 3:18). Now, who is it that is not condemned? It is he that believes. And who is condemned already? It is he that does not believe Then what must you do in order to be "not condemned"? The answer is simple. You must believe.

Now, of course, we must understand what this word "believe" implies. It means "commit" and "surrender." The Bible teaches that without faith it is impossible to please God. The Bible says: "He that cometh to God must believe that he is, and that he is a rewarder of them that diligently seek him" (Heb. 11:6). Believing is your response to God's offer of mercy, love, and forgiveness. God took the initiative. Salvation is all of God. When Christ bowed His head on the cross and said, "It is finished," He meant just that (John 19:30). God's plan for our reconciliation and redemption was completed in His Son. However, man must respond by receiving and trusting.

Faith is described in the Bible as "the substance of things hoped for, the evidence of things not seen" (Heb. 11:1). Faith is not just hanging on. It is laying hold of Christ, for Christ is the object of our faith. It is not simply a subjective feeling, but an objective act.

The most obvious thing about saving *faith is that it believes something.* It does not believe everything or just anything. It is belief in a person, and that person is Christ. Neither is faith antagonistic to reason or knowledge. Faith is not anti-intellectual.

Commitment

Faith is also commitment. Leighton Ford has said: "Belief is not faith without evidence but commitment without reservation." Belief involves the intellect. Desire involves the emotions. Commitment involves the will. Thus the whole man is involved in an act of proper faith. Faith is actually what we know, how we feel, and what we do about Jesus Christ. Thus faith becomes action, and the action is faith as commitment.

Dr. Ernest White points out that the first movement to be discerned in the process of conversion is conviction. This is done by the Holy Spirit. This will probably constitute a period of conflict, the type of conflict to depend largely upon the environment and temperament of the individual. Not all pass through the same kind of experience in the process of conversion.

In the sixteenth chapter of Acts there is the account of the conversion of two persons. One was Lydia, a businesswoman of the city of Thyatira, who was a worshiper of God and who went for prayer to the riverside where she heard Paul preach. She opened her heart, believed, and was converted without struggle or conflict. The other was the Philippian jailer whom we have already mentioned. He was thrown into panic when an earthquake put some of his prisoners into a position to escape. He rushed into the jail, drew out his sword to kill himself, when he heard the Apostle Paul's reassuring words. He called for a light and sprang in trembling to fall down before Paul and Silas. He asked: "Sirs, what must I do to be saved?" He heard from Paul the Gospel with the instruction to believe, and he rejoiced, believing in God. Here was drama, excitement, and crisis.

Emotion

With some persons there may be in conversion an emotional crisis, the symptoms of which are similar to those of mental conflict. There may be deep feeling and outbursts of tears and anxiety. There may be none of these things. There are those who experience little, if any, emotion. They accept salvation without any particular crisis of mind or emotion. They cannot, in fact, specify any definite time when they first entered into their knowledge of Christ. My wife is one of the finest Christians I have ever known, but she cannot pinpoint the moment of her conversion. Yet she is sure of her conversion because she knows Christ personally in the reality of daily life and service, and she has the joy of the Lord.

When Jesus described the new birth to intellectual, dignified Nicodemus, He said: "The wind bloweth where it listeth, and thou hearest the sound thereof, but canst not tell whence it cometh, and whither it goeth: so is every one that is born of the Spirit" (John 3:8). Jesus said it was like the movement of the wind, which sometimes is as imperceptible as a zephyr and at other times as revolutional as a cyclone. Conversion is like that, too — sometimes quiet and tender, sometimes uprooting and re-arranging the life under great emotional manifestation.

An Act of the Will

There is also volitional resolution. The will is necessarily involved in conversion. People can pass through mental conflicts and emotional crises without being converted. Not until they exercise the prerogative of a free moral agent and will to be converted are they actually converted. This act of will is an act of acceptance and commitment. They willingly accept God's mercy and receive God's Son and then commit themselves to do God's will. In every true conversion the will of man comes into line with the will of God. Almost the last word of the Bible is this invitation: "And whosoever will, let him take of the water of life freely" (Rev. 22: 17). It is up to you. You must will to be saved. It is God's will, but it must become your will, too.

Every week I receive scores of letters from those who say they have doubts and uncertainties concerning the Christian life. They wonder if they are Christians. They are not sure they have been converted. They think perhaps they have, but they have little of the joy of the Christian faith. Particularly is this true of those who did not have a crisis experience at the time of their conversion. At the turn of the century, Professor Edwin Starbuck, a leader in the field of psychology, observed that Christian workers generally were recruited from the ranks of those who had had a vital, dramatic conversion. In other words, they had a clear concept of what it means to be converted. They had experienced it.

Much of the philosophy of modern religious education has been based on the idea that a person can become a Christian by a process of education. Therefore, we have herded into the church tens of thousands of people who have never had a personal encounter with Jesus Christ. Great numbers of so-called Christians have missed this "encounter experience" with Christ, having had in its place only religious training.

Rarely do we conduct a crusade without having some seminary students or even pastors make a profession of conversion. In one recent crusade sixteen clergymen came forward to receive Jesus Christ as Saviour. Many of these men had been trained theologically, but some of them had never had a genuine encounter with the person of Christ. To one of the most religious men of His day, Jesus said: "Ye must be born again" (John 3:3). Nicodemus could not substitute his profound knowledge of religion for spiritual rebirth, and neither can we.

The ugly larva in its cocoon spends months in almost unnoticeable growth and change; but no matter how great that growth may be, there comes a moment when it passes through a crisis and emerges a butterfly. The weeks of silent growth are important, but they cannot take the place of that experience when the old and the ugly are left behind and the new and the beautiful come into being.

It is true that there are multitudes of Christians whose life and faith testify that consciously or unconsciously they have been converted to Christ. They may not know the exact hour. It is my opinion, however, that this may be the exception rather than the rule. Whether they can remember the time or not, there was a moment when they crossed over the line from death to life. You cannot tell the exact moment when night becomes day, but you know when it is daylight.

Dr. Donald Grey Barnhouse once said: "It is not presumption for me to say that I am just as sure that I shall be in Heaven as I am sure Jesus Christ will be there. If any percentage of my doings had a part in it, then it would be presumption; but when I say that my doings, the 2 percent or the 50 percent or the 80 percent . . . are all set aside, and God's 100 percent of righteousness is my salvation, then surely boasting is excluded." As Paul wrote: "Where is boasting then? It is excluded. By what law? of works? Nay: but by the law of faith" (Rom. 3:27).

Assurance

There are three ways that I may know that I have eternal life: objectively, because God's Word says it; subjectively, because of the witness of the Spirit within; and experimentally, because little by little as time goes on I can see the experimental working of God in my life. It is a slower process than I would like, but it is a process. Therefore I can say: "I know."

How to Receive Christ

The question that comes to many minds is this: Just what must I do actually to receive Christ? I wish it were possible for me to wrap it up in a neat little formula and hand it to you, but that is impossible. As I have already suggested, each person's experience is different from all others. Just as there are no two snowflakes alike, there are no two experiences with Christ exactly the same. However, there are certain guidelines in the Bible that will help to guide you to accept Jesus Christ as your Saviour. Therefore, let me summarize what you must do.

First, you must recognize that God loved you so much that He gave His Son to die on the cross. "For God so loved the world, that he gave his only begotten Son, that whosoever believeth in him should not perish, but have everlasting life" (John 3:16). "The Son of God . . . loved me, and gave himself for me" (Gal. 2:20).

Second, you must repent of your sins. Jesus said: "Except ye repent, ye shall . . . perish" (Luke 13:3). He said: "Repent . . . and believe" (Mark 1:15). As John Stott, pastor of All Souls Church in London, wrote: "The faith which receives Christ must be accompanied by the repentance which rejects sin." Repentance does not mean simply that you are to be sorry for the past. To be sorry is not enough; you must repent. This means that you must turn your back on sins.

Third, you must receive Jesus Christ as Saviour and Lord. "But as many as received him, to them gave he power to become the sons of God, even to them that believe on his name" (John 1:12). This means that you accept God's offer of love, mercy, and forgiveness. This means that you accept Jesus Christ as your only Lord and your only Saviour. This means that you cease struggling and trying to save yourself. You trust Him completely, without reservation, as your Lord and Saviour.

Fourth, you must confess Christ publicly. Jesus said: "Whosoever therefore shall confess me before men, him will I confess also before my Father which is in heaven" (Matt. 10:32). This confession carries with it the idea of a life so lived in front of your fellowmen that they will see a difference. It means also that you acknowledge with your mouth the Lord Jesus. "If thou shalt confess with thy mouth the Lord Jesus, and shalt believe in thine heart that God hath raised him from the dead, thou shalt be saved" (Rom. 10:9). It is extremely important that when you receive Christ you tell someone else about it just as soon as possible. This gives you strength and courage to witness.

It is important that you make your decision and your commitment to Christ now. "Now is the accepted time . . . now is the day of salvation" (II Cor. 6:2). If you are willing to repent of your sins and to receive Jesus Christ as your Saviour, you can do it now. At this moment you can either bow your head or get on your knees and say this little prayer that I have used with thousands of persons on every continent:

O God, I acknowledge that I have sinned against Thee. I am sorry for my sins. I am willing to turn from my sins. I openly receive and acknowledge Jesus Christ as my Saviour. I confess Him as Lord. From this moment on I want to live for Him and serve Him. In Jesus' name, Amen.

If you are willing to make this decision, if you have to the best of your knowledge received Jesus Chirst, God's Son, as your own Saviour, then according to the preceding statements of Scripture, you have become a child of God in whom Jesus Christ dwells. Altogether too many people make the mistake of measuring the certainty of their salvation by their feelings. Don't make this serious mistake. Believe God. Take Him at His word.

THE DYNAMICS OF THE NEW MAN

In the third century, Cyprian, the Bishop of Carthage, wrote to his friend Donatus: "It is a bad world, Donatus, an incredibly bad world.

But I have discovered in the midst of it a quiet and holy people who have learned a great secret. They have found a joy which is a thousand times better than any of the pleasure of our sinful life. They are despised and persecuted, but they care not. They are masters of their souls. They have overcome the world. These people, Donatus, are Christians . . . and I am one of them."

If you have repented of your sins and have received Christ as Saviour, then you, too, are one of them.

Forgiven and Justified

The moment you were converted to Christ, several dramatic things happened, whether you were aware of them or not. *First, your sin was forgiven.* "In whom we have redemption through his blood, even the forgiveness of sins" (Col. 1:14). "Your sins are forgiven you for his name's sake" (I John 2:12). Throughout the New Testament we are told that the one who receives Christ as Saviour also receives immediately, as a gift from God, the forgiveness of sin. The Bible says: "As far as the east is from the west, so far hath he removed our transgressions from us" (Ps. 103:12). The only reason our sins can be forgiven is, of course, because Jesus Christ paid the full penalty for our sins on the cross. He was "delivered for our offences" (Rom. 4:25).

However, God's forgiveness goes much farther than the forgiveness of sin. God not only forgives, He justifies. This means that man is actually without guilt in God's sight. As someone has said: "I am justified, and it is just-as-if-I'd-never-sinned." My secretary often uses an erasable bond, a chemically treated paper from which errors can be erased without blemish. God treats our hearts with the chemistry of His grace and erases the errors so that we are without spot and without blemish in His sight.

Every person who puts his trust in Jesus Christ stands guiltless before God. He is cleared of every charge. It is not a matter of feeling; it is a fact. You can apply Galatians 2:16 to yourself: "Knowing that a man is not justified by the works of the law, but by the faith of Jesus Christ." Justification and forgiveness are God's free gifts. They involve absolutely no merit on man's part; all is of God. They are His unmerited favor. Forgiveness and justification are transmitted to us through faith.

In these days of guilt complexes, perhaps the most glorious word in the English language is "forgiveness."

A man serving a life sentence for murder escaped from the Oklahoma State Penitentiary. The warden offered the fugitive 1,500 dollars to present himself at the gate of the prison, but there was a catch to the offer. The reward was to be earned and saved by the escaped prisoner through his working in the prison. "If he comes, we will see that he does not get out again," said the warden. "Justice must prevail."

How different is the offer God makes to all fugitives from divine justice. There is no catch to His offer. "Let the wicked forsake his way . . . and let him return unto the Lord . . . for he will abundantly pardon" (Isa. 55:7). Civil justice seeks to catch the criminal. Divine justice is intent on setting him free. Justice has been satisfied by the death of Christ. All who present themselves to God in faith and repentance will be received, not as fugitives, but as sons of God "justified from all things" (Acts 13:39).

Adopted

Second, the new man is adopted. "To redeem them that were under the law, that we might receive the adoption of sons" (Gal. 4:5). The moment we receive Christ as Saviour, we receive the divine nature of the sons of God. We are now placed in the position of a joint heir with Jesus Christ. "Having predestinated us unto the adoption of children" (Eph. 1:5). We have now all the rights of a son. All things in the Kingdom are now ours to enjoy.

My friends, Roy Rogers and Dale Evans, have adopted several children. Once I asked them if they gave the same rights and privileges to their adopted children as they gave their real children. They were shocked by my question and said: "Of course, we do. They are ours as much as the ones who were born to us. They have all the rights and privileges of our own flesh and blood." We, too, have been adopted into the family of God, with all the rights and privileges of sonship.

The Holy Spirit

Third, the new man is indwelt by the Spirit of God. Before He ascended into Heaven, Jesus Christ said: "And I will pray the Father, and he shall give you another Comforter, that he may abide with you for ever; even the Spirit of truth . . . ye know him; for he dwelleth with you, and shall be in you" (John 14:16, 17). During His lifetime on earth, Christ's presence could be experienced only by a small group of men at any given time. Now Christ dwells through the Spirit in the hearts of all those who have received Him as Saviour. The Apostle Paul wrote to the Romans: "But ye are not in the flesh, but in the Spirit, if so be that the Spirit of God dwell in you" (Rom. 8:9). Later he wrote to the Corinthians: "Know ye not that ye are the temple of God, and that the Spirit of God dwelleth in you?" (I Cor. 3:16).

The Holy Spirit is given to every believer—not for a limited time but forever. Were He to leave us for one moment, we would be in deep trouble.

With some disdain and contempt a lady said to a clergyman to whom she had listened: "You are not abreast of the spirit of the age." The minister replied: "You are quite right, I am not abreast of the spirit of the age. But I do have within me the Holy Spirit of this age."

Walter Knight tells the story about a little boy who had recently received Christ. "Daddy, how can I believe in the Holy Spirit when I have never seen Him?" asked Jim. "I'll show you how," said his father, who was an electrician. Later Jim went with his father to the power plant where he was shown the generators. "This is where the power comes from to heat our stove and to give us light. We cannot see the power, but it is in that machine and in the power lines," said the father.

"I believe in electricity," said Jim.

"Of course, you do," said his father, "but you don't believe in it because you see it. You believe in it because you see what it can do. Likewise you can believe in the Holy Spirit because you see what He does in people's lives when they are surrendered to Christ and possess His power."

Thus, by faith you accept the fact that you are indwelt by the Spirit of God. He is there to give you special power to work for Christ. He is there to give you strength in the moment of temptation. He is there to produce the supernatural fruits of the Spirit, such as "love, joy, peace, longsuffering, gentleness, goodness, faith, meekness, and temperance" (Gal. 5:22, 23). He is there to guide you over all the difficult terrain you must cross as a Christian.

Sometimes when I go to Europe to preach I like to go by sea, and I enjoy the five days on the ship. On one of my voyages Captain Anderson of the *United States* took me down to see the ship's gyroscope. He said, "When the sea is rough the gyroscope helps to keep the ship on an even keel. Though the waves may reach tremendous proportions, the gyroscope helps to stabilize the vessel and maintain a high degree of equilibrium." As I listened, I thought how like the gyroscope is the Holy Spirit. Let the storms of life break over our heads. Let the enemy Satan come in like a flood. Let the waves of sorrow, suffering, temptation, and testing be unleashed upon us. Our souls will be kept on an even keel and in perfect peace when the Holy Spirit dwells in our hearts.

Strength to Resist Temptation

Fourth, the new man has the possibility of victory over temptation and sin. "There hath no temptation taken you but such as is common to man: but God is faithful, who will not suffer you to be tempted above that ye are able; but will with the temptation also make a way to escape, that ye may be able to bear it" (I Cor. 10:13).

The Bible teaches that the new man is to "abhor that which is evil" (Rom. 12:9) and to "put off concerning the former conversation the old man, which is corrupt according to the deceitful lusts" (Eph. 4:22). We are told also to "make not provision for the flesh, to fulfill the lusts thereof" (Rom. 13:14).

However, the great problem is, How do we do it? Where do we get such a capacity and such strength?

This new capacity and this new strength come from the Holy Spirit, who lives within every true believer. It is not the result of our own struggling against temptation. It is the life of God within us. He lives in our hearts to help us to resist sin. It is our job to believe and to yield to Him. The Christian life from this point on is to be lived through the activity of faith. Faith is the shield of our defense against Satan (Eph. 6:16), and this faith enables us to overcome the evil world around us (I John 5:4).

The Bible teaches us that as Christians we can become "more than conquerors" (Rom. 8:37). The strength for our conquering and our victory is drawn continually from Christ. The Bible does not teach that sin is completely eradicated from the Christian in this life, but it does teach that sin shall no longer reign over you. The strength and power of sin have been broken. The Christian now has resources available to live above and beyond this world. The Bible teaches that whosoever is born of God does not practice sin (I John 3:6-9). It is like the little girl who said that when the devil came knocking with a temptation, she just sent Jesus to the door.

Thus in Jesus Christ the new man is actually a new man. What does it mean to be a new creature or a new person? Let it be said at once that the new man is not the old man improved or made over. He is not even the old man reformed or remodeled, for God does not make the new out of the old nor put new wine in old bottles. The new man is Christ formed in us. As in the creation, we were created in the image of God. In the new creation, we are re-created in the image of Christ. Paul said: "For whom he did foreknow, he also did predestinate to be conformed to the image of his Son" (Rom. 8:29). This new man is not the product of psychological change. According to psychiatrist Ernest White, Christian conversion "has permanent results in the depths of the personality and sets a man forward on the path of sanctity. Psychological treatment can bring about a rearrangement of the mental and emotional pattern, but it does not introduce a new power into the life."

The new man is actually Christ in the heart, and Christ in the heart means that He is in the center of our being. The Biblical use of the word "heart" symbolizes the whole realm of the affections. Into this area Christ comes to transform our affections, with the result that the things for which we formerly had affection pass away, and the things for which we now have affection are new and of God. If Christ dwells in the heart, it means that He dwells also in the mind with its varied function of thinking and self-determination. In the process of change into a new creature when Christ indwells the heart, the human personality is neither absorbed nor destroyed. Instead it is enriched and empowered by this union with Christ.

The New Man Not Perfect

There is one problem that Christians face immediately upon conversion. Some people get the idea that they become perfect right away, and then they find themselves tempted, in conflict, and even on occasion yielding to temptation. Many of them become filled with confusion, frustration, and discouragement. They say the Christian life is not what they thought it was going to be. The Bible does teach that we can become mature, but that does not mean that we are ever flawless. Ernest F. Kevan says: "The perfect Christian is the one who, having a sense of his own failure to attain, is minded to press toward the mark" (Phil. 3:14).

The Bible teaches: "For the flesh lusteth against the Spirit, and the Spirit against the flesh: and these are contrary the one to the other: so that ye cannot do the things that ye would" (Gal. 5:17). It teaches that there is a spiritual conflict in the heart of every true believer. It is true that the Christian possesses a new nature, but the old nature is still there.

It is now up to us, day by day, to yield to the reign and control of the new nature, which is dominated by Christ. Because we are a new creation for whom all old things have passed away and all things have become new, we no longer practice sin.

We may fall into sin, but we hate it. The new nature commits no sin; but when the Christian sins, it is because the old nature has been yielded to for a moment. And when the Christian sins he is miserable until the sin is confessed and fellowship with God is restored. This is the difference between the believer and the unbeliever. The unbeliever makes sin a practice, and the believer does not make a practice of sin. He abhors it, and rather than live in the former lawlessness, he seeks to abide by the commands of God. Thus Paul says: "Who walk not after the flesh, but after the Spirit" (Rom. 8:4). It means that we are to be submissive to the new nature, to the Holy Spirit who indwells us. "Neither yield ye your members as instruments of unrighteousness unto sin: but yield yourselves unto God, as those that are alive from the dead, and your members as instruments of righteousness unto God" (Rom. 6:13).

New Standards

We are to feed the new nature on the Word of God constantly, and we are to starve the old nature, which craves the world and the flesh. We are told to "make not provision for the flesh" (Rom. 13:14). We are told to "present your bodies a living sacrifice, holy, acceptable unto God" (Rom. 12:1).

From now on our choices are made from a new perspective and a new dimension. When we are living up to the full privileges and powers of our new life in Christ, sin loses its control over these choices and dispositions. The Christian is under the domination of Christ and consequently lives according to new standards with a new power.

In London, England, an alcoholic was placed under the care of a psychiatrist who soon gave up because the alcoholic was getting no better. During our meetings at the Harringay Arena, the alcoholic was invited to attend. He listened in wonderment to the Gospel messages. "Maybe there is some hope for me," he thought. One night when the invitation was given, he went forward with several others. He was converted, and a new power came into his life. That night before he went to sleep, he reached as usual for the nearby bottle of liquor; but something—or rather, Someone—restrained his hand. Getting out of bed, he took the bottle and emptied it down the drain. When he awakened in the morning, through habit he reached again for his usual morning bracer. It was not there, but there was no sense of disappointment.

The man called his psychiatrist and said: "You have lost a patient. Christ has saved me from drink. I am a new man." The psychiatrist said: "That sounds fine. Maybe I can find help where you found it. I am not an alcoholic, but I have my own needs and problems." The psychiatrist began, too, to attend the meetings, and he, too, accepted Christ as his Saviour.

One year later in the lobby of a fashionable London hotel both the psychiatrist and the former alcoholic testified to the saving power of Jesus Christ. Christ had kept them both.

New Orientation

The reason we as new creatures experience the passing away of old things and the beginning of new things is fivefold. *First, the new man has a new orientation.* Before conversion, he was oriented to the world and its materialistic, secular pursuits. Now he is oriented to Jesus Christ with the higher ideals of Christian life.

New Motivation

Second, the new man has a new motivation. Before conversion the motives for life were centered around his wills and appetites. He wanted what he wanted to do, to get, and to be. It was sometimes good and sometimes bad, but it was usually away from God. Now his motivation is God's will. This is the highest possible motive in life, and as long as we are inspired and activated by this motivation we act in the character of the new creatures we are.

New Direction

Third, the new man has a new direction. Before conversion the direction of life was away from God. It was easy for him to do wrong. It was natural for him to sin. Now his life takes on a new direction. "We all had our conversation in times past in the lusts of our flesh . . . and were by nature the children of wrath, even as others. But God, who is rich in mercy . . . hath quickened us together with Christ" (Eph. 2:3-5).

We now move in the direction of God's will. New and different emotions flood our hearts. We find sinful practices unattractive and even abhorrent. We move in the direction of righteousness and godliness. We think God's thoughts after Him. We move with the mind of Christ, and we are free from the enslavements of the natural mind. We are free from envy and resentments, and become more gracious and kind as He was.

New Growth

Fourth, the new man will experience a new growth spiritually and morally. One can imitate the Christian life by religious effort, but one can always detect an artificial flower. There is a difference between a spiritually natural growth of Christian principle and a moral copy of it. One is growth; the other is accretion. Jesus said: "Consider the lilies how they grow" (Luke 12:27). How do they grow? They grow organically and spontaneously, automatically, without trying or struggling or fretting, just as we grow physically without conscious effort.

One of my sons said once: "I am going to be big like Daddy," and he stretched himself up. But his effort did not make him a fraction taller.

The moment you receive Christ you start out as a spiritual baby. "As newborn babes, desire the sincere milk of the word, that ye may grow thereby" (I Pet. 2:2). A child may be born into a wealthy home and thus become the possessor of good parents, brothers and sisters, houses and lands; but at the time of his birth, the main point is not that he be informed of all these wonderful things. There are other important matters that must be taken care of first. He must be fed because he is hungry and needs to grow. He must be protected because he has been born into a world of many enemies. In the hospital room he is handled with sterilized gloves and kept from outsiders, so that he will not fall victim to any of the myriads of germs waiting to attack.

You have become a child of God. You have been born into His family as a baby. This is a strategic moment in your life, and there are two or three things that will help to strengthen you for the battle ahead and to keep you safe from the wiles of Satan, the enemy of your soul.

1. It is important that you build up your soul by *reading the Scriptures.* If you do not have a Bible, get one as quickly as possible and begin reading the New Testament. "Wherewithal shall a young man cleanse his way? by taking heed thereto according to thy word" (Ps. 119:9). "Thy word have I hid in mine heart, that I might not sin against thee" (Ps. 119:11). So I challenge you to read and to memorize portions of the Word of God.

Satan will do everything in his power to keep you from reading the Bible and to defeat you in your new-found Christian life. In the past you may not have been attacked viciously by Satan, but now he has seen you take the step that angers him more than any other. You have renounced him and joined the ranks of those who believe in the Son of God. You are no longer Satan's property; you belong to the One who has bought and paid for you with a price—the price of His blood on the cross. You may be sure that Satan will attempt to trouble you. His attacks assume many forms, and you can overcome them only as you use the weapon that God has provided. "Take . . . the sword of the Spirit, which is the word of God" (Eph. 6:17). Not only is the Word of God an offensive sword; it is a defensive shield to ward off the darts of the enemy (Rom. 10:17; Eph. 6:16).

Therefore, it is vitally important for you to study the Scriptures. When Christ in the wilderness was tempted three times by the devil, He met each temptation with Scripture, saying: "It is written" (Matt. 4). If Jesus Christ found it necessary to thwart Satan's attacks by quoting the Scriptures, how much more you need this mighty weapon.

2. It is important that you *learn to pray.* Jesus said: "Men ought always to pray" (Luke 18:1). Again He said: "Hitherto have ye asked nothing in my name: ask, and ye shall receive, that your joy may be full" (John 16:24). The Apostle Paul went so far as to say: "Pray without ceasing" (I Thess. 5:17). Since you have made your decision for Christ, you may now address God as Father. In the beginning you will not be able to pray very fluently, yet it is important that you begin immediately. The first prayer you pray may be something like this: "O Father, thank You for saving my soul. I love You. In Christ's name, Amen." It may be just that simple, but you will find that soon you will

be praying about everything. Soon your prayers will be constantly in your subconscious. This is when you begin to "pray without ceasing."

3. It is important for you to have *fellowship with other Christians.* God does not intend for you to live the Christian life alone. You need to be in the fellowship of a church. "Not forsaking the assembling of ourselves together" (Heb. 10:25). If you separate a live coal from the others, it will soon die out. However, if you put a live coal in with other live coals, it will be a glow that will last for hours. There may be a Bible class or prayer group in your community that you know nothing about. You can soon find your way into all kinds of Christian fellowship that will give you new friendships and will strengthen your faith.

You are now a member of a world-wide brotherhood that spans every national, racial, and linguistic barrier. I have walked down jungle trails in Africa where I met fellow Christians; and immediately we were brothers even though we were separated by language, race, and culture. One of the great joys of my life has been to travel around the world and meet thousands of Christians in every country.

New Social Concern

Fifth, the new man should have a new social concern. This will affect your family relationships, your business relationships, your attitude toward your work, and your attitude toward your neighbor.

The whole difference between the Christian and the moralist lies right here. The Christian works from the center, the moralist from the circumference. One is an organism in the center of which is a living germ planted by the living God. The other is crystal; very beautiful it may be, but only a crystal. It lacks the vital principle of growth.

You will understand that God is interested in the great social issues of our day, such as immorality, destitution, racial problems, and crime. The Apostle James said: "Faith without works is dead" (James 2:20). Our good works testify that we have received Christ. We are to visit the sick, to visit the prisoners, to give friendship to the lonely and to try to get those who are estranged back together again. We will try to point wasted lives to new values. We will go out of our way to show kindness, courtesy, and love to persons of another race. We will be willing to suffer, to be persecuted, to take abuse and ridicule from a hostile world, which does not understand our motives.

It is an exhilarating experience to live the new life with Christ within me enabling me to live it. As a man was riding along in his Ford, suddenly something went wrong. He got out and looked at the engine, but he could find nothing wrong. As he stood there another car came in sight, and he waved it down to ask for help. Out of a brand-new Lincoln, stepped a tall friendly man who asked: "Well, what's the trouble?" "I cannot get this Ford to move," was the reply. The stranger made a few adjustments under the hood and then said: "Now start the car." When the motor started, its grateful owner introduced himself and said:

"What is your name, sir?" "My name," answered the stranger, "is Henry Ford."

The one who made the Ford knew how to make it run. God made you and me, and He alone knows how to run your life and mine. We could make a complete wreck of our lives without Christ. When He is at the controls, all goes well. Without Him we can do nothing.

THE REFORMED
DOCTRINE OF
SANCTIFICATION

Cary N. Weisiger III

Cary N. Weisiger III is pastor of the Menlo Park Presbyterian Church, Menlo Park, California. He holds the A.B. degree from Princeton University and the Th.D. from Westminster Theological Seminary. His previous pastorates were in Pennsylvania, Virginia, and Georgia, and he also served for three years as a college teacher in India. In 1955 he traveled around the world, preaching and visiting in seven countries. Since 1961 he has been a member of the United Presbyterian Church delegation to the Consultation on Church Union.

THE REFORMED
DOCTRINE OF
SANCTIFICATION

ANYONE WHO tries to expound sanctification for discriminating readers should enter a plea for charity. Many people who have written about the subject have done so in a mood more quarrelsome than sanctified, or else their views have provoked unsanctified hostility. John Wesley brought lightning and thunder down upon his head because of his distinctive teaching on this subject. Sanctification, however, whether as a doctrine or as an experience, aims at a good Christian life.

The warfare Christians must wage is not with one another but with sin. If we disagree about sanctification, as many Christians do, let us do so charitably and with openness of mind to one another's insights. Christian instinct should tell us that sanctification does not belong in the arena of sectarian polemics.

THE MEANING OF THE TERM

In a broad sense sanctification means God's act of setting apart a people for Himself and for mission to the world. The activity of God always comes first in biblical formulation.

Deuteronomy 7:6 and 11 provides a basic clue to what sanctification is: "For you are a people holy to the LORD your God; the LORD your God has chosen you to be a people for his own possession, out of all the peoples that are on the face of the earth. . . . You shall therefore be careful to do the commandment, and the statutes, and the ordinances, which I command you this day" (RSV used throughout this essay). The Israel of the old covenant was a nation set apart for God and His purpose. To be sure, some in Israel who cherished the setting apart to God were apt to forget the purpose and to bask in privilege. But Israel's failure did not annul the divine intention.

John 14, 15, and 16 contain a rich treasure of truth about sanctification. At the heart of this passage are these words: "You did not choose me, but I chose you and appointed you that you should go and bear fruit and that your fruit should abide . . ." (15:16). Jesus chose *His* disciples. They did not choose Him until they were chosen by Him. Then, as the whole New Testament makes clear, Jesus sent them out in mission to the world. The old covenant was fulfilled and amplified with a distinct glory in the new covenant and in its people, the Church of Jesus Christ.

With these things in mind we can understand why Paul could call the Corinthian believers "sanctified." He remembered his first visit there, his rejection by the Jews, and the comforting vision in the night in which the Lord said, "Do not be afraid, but speak and do not be silent; for I am with you, and no man shall attack you to harm you; *for I have many people in this city*" (Acts 18:9, 10, italics added). The church at Corinth was, therefore, "the church of God . . . sanctified in Christ Jesus, called to be saints . . ." (I Cor. 1:2). When Paul wrote to the Corinthians, they were carnal, self-centered, immature, schismatic, and unruly in their passions. Nevertheless, from God's point of view—that is, from the stance of divine call and intention—they were "sanctified."

In theological formulation the term "sanctification" has a precise meaning. In the words of the Shorter Catechism, it is "the work of God's free grace, whereby we are renewed in the whole man after the image of God, and are enabled more and more to die unto sin and live unto righteousness."

The pervasive teaching of the New Testament is that God's purpose cannot be fulfilled nor His mission accomplished unless believers have formed in them the character of Jesus Christ. This is why Paul wrote the Corinthians in such vehement protest against their contradiction of their high calling: "Do you know that you are God's temple and that God's Spirit dwells in you? If anyone destroys God's temple, God will destroy him. For God's temple is holy and that temple you are" (I Cor. 3:16, 17).

What Paul wrote to the Corinthians collectively he also reinforced by individual application in his rebuke of immorality. "Do you not know that your body is a temple of the Holy Spirit within you, which you have from God? You are not your own; you were bought with a price. So glorify God in your body" (I Cor. 6:19, 20). The holy call to sanctification means that a Christian's body is the sacred residence of the Spirit of God because Christ paid the price of sacrifice to secure that body as His own. The demand of sanctification is for a complete and practical realization of Spirit-residence that controls the whole person.

In His farewell words (John 14, 15, and 16), Jesus sought to comfort His disciples; but even then He warned them about the necessity for a cleansing discipline: "I am the true vine, and my Father is the vinedresser. Every branch of mine that bears no fruit, he takes away, and every branch that does bear fruit he prunes, that it may bear more fruit" (John 15:1, 2). It is impossible for a believer to fulfill His Lord's choice without the pruning that cuts away unholy impulse and habit.

Sanctification, whether taken in its elective sense or in its more precisely ethical sense, finds its root significance in separation. Sanctification basically means holiness or separation from all that negates God's majesty and will. God is holy because He is far above all creaturely limitation and rebellion. In this separation from the finite and the fallible, God is holy, and there is none like Him. Hence the cherubim cry, "Holy, holy, holy is the Lord of hosts" (Isa. 6:3), and because an earth with finite, fallible creatures cannot hide the immense power of that outshining holiness, the cherubim also exclaim, "the whole earth is full of his glory."

God's work of sanctification, whether in elective call or in ethical effect, never makes us infinite. We cannot be partakers of His glorious essence. But by His whole saving work in Christ and by His fatherly discipline "we may share his holiness" (Heb. 12:10). That is to say, in some measure we fulfill His call and we reflect His character as Christ is formed in us. This is the great end of sanctification, and it will be gloriously consummated when "we shall see him as he is" (I John 3:2).

THE PERILS OF DESCRIPTION

So far our discussion has been in an area where Christians enjoy large agreement. Sanctification means God's act of covenant choice whereby He sets apart a people to accomplish His mission in the world. But it also means God's work by which His people develop a Christlike character as they do God's will. As we proceed further, we shall encounter difficulties.

The hazards of describing sanctification in detail find an illustration in what is for me and for many other people a favorite and frustrating form of exercise. I refer to golf. Since I was twelve I have been working off and on at my game. I have taken lessons from professionals. I have watched them in the pressure of big tournaments. I have read many books and articles.

From all this dedicated research two facts emerge. The professionals can do marvelous things with a golf ball. With reasonable variation, their execution is uniformly good. But their description of how they do it has an amazing and sometimes bewildering variety.

Since I myself am seeking to be sanctified, I shall resist the temptation to dazzle my readers with impressive documentation from Percy Boomer, Bobby Jones, Tommy Armour, Sam Snead, Cary Middlecoff, Ben Hogan, Byron Nelson, Bobby Locke, Arnold Palmer, and others. And if any of my readers are, like the late Mr. Churchill, fond of higher pursuits like bricklaying and painting, sharing his scorn for those who waste their lives chasing little white balls, I shall say: "You, sir, are not yet sanctified!" Golf for the Christian is a challenge to, if not a means of, grace.

In any case, one professional puts all his emphasis upon golf as a left-sided game (if you are a righthander). Another says that you must hit the ball hard with your right hand. One expert cautions against hitting too hard and favors emphasis upon rhythm and timing. Another says he grew up learning to slug the ball as hard as he could. In the midst of this and much other advice, the ordinary golfing mortal must somehow learn to execute a swing with proficiency. Probably the best thing he can do is to pick a good swinger of his own size and copy him.

So in sanctification the literature is full of claims and counterclaims. Romanists live and move in a merit theology. Calvinists and Puritans expose the dark root of remaining sin. Wesley and his successors urge some kind of perfectionism. We need to keep checking our descriptions against biblical norm and to remember that our descriptions may not yet have reached perfection, though in this life we should seek it.

I offer an example of contradictory description. Writing in the *Christian Century,* Charles Malik says:

> . . . The life of the spirit, which is life in Christ Jesus, is a life of intense suffering and struggle. . . . We struggle on at least six fronts. We struggle, first, on the front of the world and its temptations, this world which is so exciting, so colorful, so seductive, so sweet, that we are always in danger of losing ourselves in it and forgetting about Jesus Christ. We struggle, second, against our own memories, those strange whisperings in the dark which ever want to keep us captive to themselves. We struggle, third, against our sweet natural tendency to be lazy and slothful, to covet more than we need, to expect from life more than we give it. We struggle, fourth, against our inveterate pride, that creaturely raising of ourselves above ourselves, that blasphemous pitting of ourselves against God, that pitiful refusal to let go in humor, in brokenness and in tears. We struggle, fifth, against our daily fall in the worship of things and objects — the worship of ourselves, our possessions, our country, our culture. . . . Finally, we struggle daily against the devil himself; the devil who always lures us by the three temptations of security, magic and power. . . . The besetting temptation of the life of the spirit is simply to quit . . . ("The Gospel and the Life of the Spirit," copyright 1961, Christian Century Foundation; reprinted by permission from the August 23, 1961, issue of the *Christian Century*).

One can detect a Puritan accent in this eloquent man of Eastern Orthodox tradition.

In contrast, Charles G. Trumbull, editor for many years of the *Sunday School Times*, wrote in "The Life that Wins":

> There is only one life that wins; and that is the life of Jesus Christ. Every man may have that life; every man live that life. . . . There were once great fluctuations in my own spiritual life, in my conscious closeness of fellowship with God. Sometimes I would be on the heights spiritually; Sometimes I would be in the depths. . . . Victories [were] interspersed with crushing and humiliating defeats. . . . It was about the middle of August that a crisis came. I was attending a young people's missionary conference, and was faced by a week of daily work for which I knew I was miserably, hopelessly unfit and incompetent. . . . The first evening that I was there a missionary bishop spoke to us on the Water of Life. He told us that it was Christ's wish and purpose that every follower of his should be a wellspring of living, gushing water of life *all the time* to others. . . . The next morning, Sunday, alone in my room I prayed it out with God. . . . If there was a conception of Christ that I did not have . . . I asked God to give it to me. . . . God, in his longsuffering patience, forgiveness and love, gave me

what I asked for. He gave me a new Christ—wholly new in the conception and consciousness of Christ that now became mine. . . . At last I realized that Jesus Christ was actually and literally within me. . . . I have learned that, as I trust Christ in surrender, there need be no fighting against sin, but complete freedom from the power and even the desire of sin.

In this description of a complete, once-for-all break with sin, one hears a genuine Wesleyan accent.

So there is the contradiction sharply stated. You fight and never quit; you stop fighting because there is no desire to sin. There is much of this contrast in Christian literature. In my conviction, the fault lies mainly in description, and description is powerfully influenced by temperament, habit, and type of experience. The Malik who is so conscious of struggle is looking to Christ but is peculiarly sensitive to what is worldly, fleshly, and demonic in and around him. The Trumbull who is so aware of victorious trust is peculiarly conscious of a sanctifying development in his life that outshines ambiguities and defeats. I know of no synthesis that effects a complete reconciliation between the teaching of the Reformers and their successors and the teaching of Wesley and his successors. Personally, I stand in the line of the Reformers, although I confess that I need the positive emphasis and bracing challenge of the Wesleyans.

A BASIC PASSAGE

The farewell discourse of Jesus in John 14, 15, and 16 prepared His disciples for life after His departure. The words are comforting because they contain so much that is essential to sanctified living. They reveal (1) the unique mediatorial position of Jesus, (2) the gift of the Spirit-Counselor, (3) the necessity of faith and loving obedience for fruitful fellowship with Jesus, (4) the discipline of the Father, and (5) the hatred of the world.

In this Johannine report we find no access to God except through Jesus Christ. He is "the way, and the truth, and the life"; no one goes to the Father except by Him (14:6). To know Jesus is to know the Father. To see Jesus is to see the Father. Both the words and the works of Jesus are proof that He was in the Father and the Father was in Him. Faith in Jesus, who so perfectly mediates the Father, means a potential for accomplishment greater even than that realized by Jesus in the days of His flesh. Immense possibilities in prayer open to those who ask in Jesus' name. All of this is vital to a proper understanding of sanctification because it centers our attention upon Jesus Christ. We look to Him all the time for everything that helps us experience and manifest goodness.

So far so good. But what if Jesus were taken from His disciples? What were they to do then? Who would help them and make the mediatorial presence of Jesus a living reality? Jesus anticipated these questions in the minds of His desolate followers by announcing the gift of the Spirit-Counselor. He would be with the disciples forever, and they would be aware of His companionship and indwelling (14:16, 17). The sadness caused by Jesus' departure is to be modified by the comforting assurance of His resurrection appearances (14:18, 19). "In that day" (14:20) refers to the effect of those appearances and to the assurance that the Spirit-Counselor would bestow. As a result, the disciples would recognize a triple indwelling—the Son in the Father, the disciples in Jesus, and Jesus in the disciples (14:20). Loving obedience to Jesus would bring a sense of being loved and a special manifestation of Jesus (14:21). Both the Father and Jesus would make their home with those who are lovingly obedient (14:23). The experience Jesus was describing for His disciples was the experience of intimacy and fellowship that the Spirit-Counselor would bring.

There is always a danger that the spiritual and mystical may become uncontrolled and too subjective and so result in states of mind prompted by fleshly impulse and imagination. Therefore the Spirit-Counselor was to teach all things, especially with reference to what Jesus had said. The words of Jesus would be brought to remembrance (14:26) and would provide an objective check to unspiritual fancy. This is confirmed in 15:26. The Spirit of truth would bear witness to Jesus. Any spirituality that is not Christocentric is spurious. Here is a warning to those who love strange and novel cults, who separate sanctification from justification.

The departure of Jesus is advantageous for His followers because of the advent of the Spirit-Counselor. Jesus before leaving could be physically in one place; later He would be spiritually in every place (16:7). The Spirit-Counselor would do a persuading work in the world, bringing conviction about sin, righteousness, and judgment (16:8-11). So His operation would be upon believers and unbelievers. The unbelievers would see their sin in not believing in Jesus, their erroneous idea of righteousness, and the evident falseness of worldly judgment and rule that had condemned Jesus.

As for believers, the Spirit of truth would guide them into all truth (16:13). This is certainly a promise about the veracity of the New Testament and all church tradition that is agreeable to it. The Spirit's authority would not be His own but would evidently be that of the Father and the Son. He would be the Spirit of new prophecy, and He would glorify Jesus Christ (16:13, 14). Again we find that the Spirit's work is Christocentric. In other words, the realization of the Spirit's truth and efficacy is a personal realization of the Christ of the Gospel. Normally, openness to the Spirit's teaching will lead to a disciplined study of the New Testament. This in turn will lead to a better understanding of Jesus Christ. This, finally, will have a dynamic spiritual effect upon the believer. Or, in other words, this will be a potent influence in sanctification.

There can be no sanctification, however, apart from moral realities. Sanctification divorced from ethics is like leukemia. The white cells of piety devour the red cells of moral reality. This is why Jesus insisted upon faith and loving obedience. "Truly, truly, I say to you, he who believes in me will also do the works that I do; and greater works than these will he do, because I go to the Father" (John 14:12). 'If you love me, you

will keep my commandments" (14:15). "He who has my commandments and keeps them, he it is who loves me . . ." (14:21). "If a man
loves me, he will keep my word . . ." (14:23). (See also 14:24; 15:10;
15:12-14, 17). Some people are by temperament more mystical than
others and after prolonged study and thought may commit themselves to
personal or social action that will be a proper expression of the Spirit's
leading. Others are by temperament more practical; after indignant and
active response to some evil in themselves or society, they may find themselves led to an appreciation of the Spirit's presence and power. In either
case the Spirit is doing His work, and that work *must* have an essentially
ethical quality.

The allegory of the vine and branches in 15:1-11 confirms the necessity
of a believing and loving obedience. The recurring imperative to the
disciples is "abide." Said Jesus, "Abide in me, and I in you. As the
branch cannot bear fruit by itself, unless it abides in the vine, neither can
you, unless you abide in me. . . . He who abides in me, and I in him,
he it is that bears much fruit. . . . If a man does not abide in me, he is
cast forth as a branch and withers. . . . If you abide in me, and my words
abide in you, ask whatever you will, and it shall be done for you. . . .
Abide in my love" (15:4-7, 9). The allegory also introduces the idea of
the Father as the vinedresser. He cuts away the unfruitful branches and
prunes the fruitful ones so that they may bear more fruit. Jesus' treatment
of this aspect of sanctification is brief here, but it concerns a discipline of
God that may go on for years as a painful necessity. The sproutings of
self-will in pride, sloth, anger, jealousy, gluttony, lust, and avarice may
be so stubbornly recurrent that the Father must repeatedly use the knife
of hard circumstance. Paul's temptation to pride was so strong because
of the many revelations granted him that he had to endure an unremoved
thorn in the flesh.

Thus our Lord's farewell words reveal that His disciples receive no
exemption from struggle. While they enjoy access to the Father through
the Son and receive the gifts and graces of the Spirit, they live in the
"oughtness" of faith and obedience and under a loving but firm discipline.
Even more they must be prepared for the hatred of the world. We find
this developed in the section 15:18–16:4. The opening verses of the section provide the key: "If the world hates you, know that it has hated
me before it hated you. If you were of the world, the world would love
its own; but because you are not of the world, but I chose you out of the
world, therefore the world hates you" (15:18, 19). Sanctification takes
place always in the midst of antagonism. Sooner or later a faithful witness to Christ and His righteousness evokes the hostile reaction of the
world. Christians do not have to try to be irritating; their witness will at
times be irritating because men cannot endure the light. Men love darkness rather than light when their deeds are evil. No doubt this opposition
is used by the Father with beneficial effect in sanctification. Suffering for
Christ purifies. It refines essential purpose and lasting values more clearly.

It refines motivation. It urges consistency in living. It confirms attachment to Christ. It constrains dependence upon the Spirit's resources.

ANOTHER BASIC PASSAGE

Whereas the farewell discourse chapters in John are more personal and intimate, chapters 6, 7, and 8 of the Romans letter are more doctrinal and apologetic. In preceding chapters Paul has established the absolute freeness of saving grace. "All have sinned and fall short of the glory of God" (3:23). "While we were yet helpless, at the right time Christ died for the ungodly. . . . God shows his love for us in that while we were yet sinners Christ died for us. . . . The grace of God and the free gift in the grace of that one man Jesus Christ abounded for many. . . . The free gift following many trespasses brings justification" (5:6, 8, 15, 16).

Paul then finds that justification by grace through faith poses at least three problems. One is ethical, the second is legal, and the third is psychological.

Knowing that his insistence that where sin increased, grace abounded over it, makes him vulnerable to a very serious ethical charge, Paul states the matter boldly: "What shall we say then? Are we to continue in sin that grace may abound?" (6:1). He answers his question with a most emphatic negative: "By no means! How can we who died to sin still live in it?" (6:2). He then appeals to the significance of baptism. The sacrament signifies union with Christ of a kind that means death and life. The baptizand is buried with Christ in death and raised with him in resurrection so as to walk in newness of life.

Paul does not get sidetracked into questions of religious formalism or spiritual immaturity on the part of the baptizand. He assumes the genuineness of the baptismal experience and expounds its significance. Baptism is "into Christ." It means "we have been united with him in a death like his" and that "we shall certainly be united with him in a resurrection like his" (6:5). The verses following through 6:10 make clear the absolute death that has occurred so that the believer is freed from sin and lives with Christ to God. Paul even says that we must in unqualified fashion consider ourselves "dead to sin and alive to God in Christ Jesus."

If Paul had ended his discussion here, we would most certainly be constrained to take the perfectionist position. But in the verses 2 through 23, we find a situation of moral tension in which the baptizand lives and in which he is to respond to such strong imperatives as: "Let not sin therefore reign" (v. 12), "Do not yield your members to sins" (v. 13), "Yield yourselves to God" (v. 13), "So now yield your members to righteousness for sanctification" (v. 19). Although these imperatives indicate a moral exertion that makes it impossible to believe that the desire and possibility of sinning are extinct, they rest upon such a complete internal change wrought by divine grace in the baptizand that a libertine response to grace ("let us continue in sin that grace may abound") becomes impossible.

This, then, is Paul's answer to the ethical problem posed by the doctrine of salvation by grace alone.

In Romans 7:1-6, Paul teaches that union with Christ in death and resurrection means also death to the law and a "new life of the Spirit" (v. 6). The illustration in verses 1-3 of a widowed woman is not to be pressed beyond the one point that a death means freedom for a new relationship. The illustration is like a single-pointed parable. It is not an allegory enforcing several points, for allegorical interpretation breaks down. Captivity to the law was legalism. The captive lived under the condemnation of law, and his efforts to keep the law were nullified by the power of sinful passions. As Emil Brunner points out, "Through Jesus Christ man has been placed on a different ground, he has a new position, a position in Christ and therefore in the righteousness of God . . ." (*The Letter to the Romans: A Commentary,* Westminster, 1959, p. 45). This position means a new relationship, and service in the power of a new life.

In verses 7-12 Paul treats the nature of the law. Is it evil? By no means. It gives a man knowledge of his sinfulness. It condemns a man to death. Although Paul does not say in this paragraph that the law shuts a man up to repentance and faith in Christ, this appears to be in his thought. So, for this reason if for no other, "the law is holy, and the commandment is holy and just and good" (v. 12). I am convinced that one cannot find disparagement of the law in the New Testament. Our Lord and Paul found fault with various forms of legalism—abuses or misapplication of the law—but they extolled the law itself (Matt. 5:17-19; Rom. 7:12).

Romans 7:13-25 is a famous exegetical battleground. I shall touch briefly the primary teachings as I understand them. Verses 13 and 14 say in effect: "Whatever you do, don't blame the law; blame sin or the sinner, but don't blame the law; the law is spiritual, that is, of the Spirit of God." At verse 15 Paul states significantly, "I do not understand my own actions." In what follows I understand Paul the Christian to be speaking, and I believe that he is using popular language to describe the conflict he feels between contrary impulses. It seems very clear to me that only a regenerate man can have such intense longings to will and to do what is right and to delight in the law of God. It also seems that it is a mistake to look here for profound psychological analysis, for this leads to strange divisions of the person in conflict—divisions that involve all sorts of difficulties. For instance, if verse 17—"So then it is no longer I that do it, but sin which dwells within me" is pressed too far, one may get the peculiar dichotomy of Abraham Kuyper with a regenerated, sinless central self and a peripheral sin-controlled self. If Paul's language is taken in a popular sense, then the good impulse within the Christian may be called the "inmost self," "the law of the mind," and "the mind," while the evil impulse may be called "sin," "the flesh," and "another law at war with the law of the mind."

Meanwhile, Paul gives a hint of something better than wretched conflict in verses 24, 25a: "Wretched man that I am! Who will deliver me from this body of death? Thanks be to God through Jesus Christ our Lord!" He then proceeds in Romans 8 to set forth the triumph of a higher law, "the law of the Spirit of life in Christ Jesus" (v. 2). This operating principle enables those who are justified in Christ Jesus to fulfill the moral law (v. 4) and to rise above the operating principle of sin and death (v. 2). Paul then describes many of the gifts and graces of the Holy Spirit, who is supremely the Agent of sanctification.

To sum up: (1) The ethical problem of grace disappears when we understand that grace not only justifies but also procures radical inner change. (2) The legal problem disappears when the nature and purpose of the law are understood together with the vindicating fulfillment of the law that occurs in the new life of the Spirit. (3) The psychological problem is eased when the Christian understands that his mind, which can be absorbed in the flesh or in conflict, is rather to be absorbed in Jesus Christ and in the enablements of the Spirit. Of this conflict Calvin says: "The pious heart therefore perceives a division in itself, being partly affected with delight, through a knowledge of the Divine goodness; partly distressed with sorrow, through a sense of its own calamity; partly relying on the promise of the gospel; partly trembling at the evidence of its own iniquity . . ." (*Institutes of the Christian Religion,* III, ii, 18). He adds: "For the invariable issue of this contest is, that faith at length surmounts these difficulties."

THE SPIRIT AS A GIFT

To many who are well instructed in the doctrines of grace it will seem quite obvious to say that the Holy Spirit as the chief Agent of sanctification is a gift of God. He was poured out upon the Church when Jesus was glorified as the supreme gift of grace.

Only by much struggle did I come to see this. I had been reared on the Bible and the Shorter Catechism. I memorized the latter as a boy to earn a bicycle. Yet when I went to Princeton University I lacked a clear understanding of the Spirit's place in my daily life. I encountered there the tag end of the Oxford Group, for President Hibben had asked Frank Buchman to leave the campus several years before. Through this fellowship I learned about seeking to be sensitive to the Spirit's leading in daily details. This scared me at first, but I risked it and kept at it. In the middle of my senior year Dr. Sam Higginbottom wrote from Allahabad, India, asking me to be a short-term teacher at the Agricultural Institute there. I was cleared by the Presbyterian Foreign Board and sailed in June, 1931, four days after receiving my B.A. degree. On the way I spent about two weeks at the Oxford Group houseparty in Oxford, England.

After being in India about a year I got all bogged down spiritually. I longed passionately for a life of greater assurance and power. I found no help in the vast religio-cultural systems of Hinduism and Islam. They were essentially fatalistic and had no Mediator of salvation, and in my reading and observation I found no emancipating hope for sinners. I was seized by a pervasive doubt about the inspiration of the Scriptures.

At the same time I came across some literature of the Keswick movement in England and eagerly devoured this. It seemed that if I could have some shatteringly clear experience of the Holy Spirit, I would find the solution to the problems of weakness and uncertainty. For some reason, probably stupidity, I confided in no one and struggled alone.

My misery increased. While doubt grew to the point where I thought of abandoning Christianity completely, I somehow got the notion that I had to earn the Holy Spirit. God could not give me the Spirit unless I had a better record. So each day I looked back at the previous day for some hope of convincing goodness, but I saw nothing adequate to meet God's approval. I did foolish, desperate things like walking down a deserted road in the dead of night to show God I was in earnest. Once in a rage of despair I threw my Bible across my dormitory room, crying out, "God, You don't want me to have the Holy Spirit!" As far as I know, God never got very excited about my tantrums.

One day, when I was emotionally and spiritually in the abyss, I asked myself in thought: "What has the death of someone two thousand years ago got to do with me?" The answer came like a flash: "Jesus died for me." It had overwhelming power. I did not feel thrilling emotion but rather a deep assurance. "Yes," I said to myself, "that is true." My reading took me to John 6 and the memorable answer Peter gave to Jesus' question, "Will you also go away?" Peter said, "Lord, to whom shall we go? You have the words of eternal life" (vv. 67, 68). I made a decision. Although there were difficulties in the Bible, I would stand upon the Scriptures as inspired and true until I found a better place to stand.

This led to another decision. I reasoned that I could not believe in Jesus Christ without the help of the Holy Spirit. Further, God had promised the Spirit to those who received His Son. So I began to live a day at a time in the belief that the Spirit was a gift of grace as much as the Son my Saviour. I had no special feeling except one of fitness and peace. Since then I have never doubted that any good thought, feeling, or accomplishment of mine was a result of the Spirit's prompting. In five pastorates my chief aim and prayer has been that God would establish my parishioners in faith in Jesus Christ and in the promises of the Gospel, by the power of the Holy Spirit, and that this faith would work out in practical expressions of grateful obedience.

Looking back upon my misguided struggles, I agree heartily with G. C. Berkouwer when he says in his admirable book *Faith and Sanctification:*

> Indeed, nearly all the problems of sanctification are bound up with the question of this "transition" from justification to sanctification. One of the complaints which assail us constantly is that sanctification is being cut loose, or abstracted, from justification. And if it be true that a wedge has been driven between them, the church is certainly in mortal danger of slipping into moralism, with its attendant self-conscious pride or its nagging uncertainties (Eerdmans, 1952, p. 20).

The moment I depend upon my record as meritorious, I have forsaken the grace-faith way of salvation. I then expose myself to the possibilities of arrogance, exaggeration, hideous dishonesty, shallow understandings of sin and righteousness, blindness to moral ambiguities in myself and in most of life's situations, and racking uncertainty as to whether I have ever done enough. The New Testament requires me to trust in the grace of God alone. Christ Jesus is my justification and sanctification, and it is the Holy Spirit who makes Him real and efficacious to me from day to day and for all time. Let Paul speak. "Did you receive the Spirit by works of the law, or by hearing with faith? Are you so foolish? Having begun with the Spirit, are you now ending with the flesh?" (Gal. 3:2, 3). I thank God for the gift of the Spirit, earned for me by Jesus Christ.

THE SPIRIT OF ENLIGHTENMENT

Calvin stressed the intimate connection between Christ and the written Word on the one hand and, on the other, the Spirit-bestowed ability in a believer to understand and have certainty. ". . . The Holy Spirit is the bond by which Christ efficaciously unites us to himself" (*Institutes* III, i, 1). Again, ". . . till our minds are fixed on the Spirit, Christ remains of no value to us; because we look at him as an object of cold speculation without us, and therefore at a great distance from us" (III, i, 3). Does this mean that a Spirit-touched believer has a short-cut to a knowledge of the Bible and of Christ? No. ". . . The knowledge of faith consists more in certainty than in comprehension" (III, ii, 14). But the believer is truly dependent upon the Spirit to appropriate saving truth. ". . . Nothing is effected by the word, without the illumination of the Holy Spirit" (III, ii, 33). Calvin appeals to Ephesians 1:13 to point out that the Spirit acts as a seal. Therefore, what the mind imbibes must by the Spirit be transfused in the heart (III, ii, 36).

All this leads us to appropriate the work of the Spirit in the believing heart by and with the word of Scripture. The Spirit who guided the writing of the New Testament attests its truth. Christ's promise was of the Spirit of truth, not a spirit of error. "When the Spirit of truth comes, he will guide you into all the truth; for he will not speak on his own authority, but whatever he hears he will speak, and he will declare to you the things that are to come" (John 16:13). Here is a promise that is basic to apostolic and New Testament faith. Whatever we do with questions of source material, literary construction, and exegesis of the New Testament, we may not and dare not forget this promise. Either it was a guarantee of the truthfulness of the New Testament, or there is no guarantee. Thus radical revisionists who disfigure and deny the substance of the New Testament are destroyers of the truth that saves and sanctifies.

In my judgment one of the greatest statements ever made about the Christian faith outside the Bible occurs in chapter I, paragraph 10, of the Westminster Confession of Faith: "The Supreme Judge, by whom all controversies of religion are to be determined, and all decrees of councils, opinions of ancient writers, doctrines of men, and private spirits, are to be examined, and in whose sentence we are to rest, can be no other but the Holy Spirit speaking in the Scripture." If anyone thinks that exegesis of the Bible involves hopeless difference of interpretation and confusion, let him listen to the testimony of ecumenical scholars after an Ecumenical Study Conference at Wadham College, Oxford, in 1949: "In our study together we have used Jeremiah 7:1-15 as a test case in discovering the extent of agreement in the application of hermeneutical principles. We have found a measure of agreement that surprised us all" (*Biblical Authority for Today, A World Council of Churches Symposium,* ed. by A. Richardson and W. Schweitzer, Westminster, 1951, p. 240). The statement is signed by the following: C. T. Craig, United States; V. E. Devadutt, India; C. H. Dodd, England; W. Eichrodt, Switzerland; G. Florovsky, United States; J. Marsh, England; G. Mayeda, Japan; D. L. Munby, England; A. Nygren, Sweden; N. W. Porteous, Scotland; A. Richardson, England; E. Schlink, Germany; G. Stachlin, Germany; W. Schweitzer, Switzerland; O. S. Tomkins, England; T. F. Torrance, Scotland; L. J. Trinterud, United States; and G. E. Wright, United States.

It was significant when the definitive statement of membership in the World Council of Churches was changed to include the phrase, "according to the Scriptures." The statement now reads: "The World Council of Churches is a fellowship of churches which confess the Lord Jesus Christ as God and Saviour according to the Scriptures and therefore seek to fulfill their common calling to the glory of the one God, Father, Son and Holy Spirit." Christ, the Scriptures, and the Spirit of truth are inseparably joined, and the believer lives in the power of a new life as he consciously keeps these together.

Some of those present at the Consultation on Church Union in Oberlin, 1963, testified to their sense of the Spirit's presence. In any case, fifty-four representatives from six denominations agreed on the "unique authority of the Holy Scriptures and made a distinction between tradition and Tradition in the churches, Tradition only being that element in the life of the Church which is a result of the Spirit's guidance and nourishment and which agrees with Scripture. The consultation issued the following statement:

> The six churches represented in the Consultation on Church Union recognize and acknowledge that the Holy Scriptures of the Old and New Testaments have a unique authority. . . . The members of the Consultation are agreed that there is a historic Christian Tradition. . . . By Tradition we understand the whole life of the church, ever guided and nourished by the Holy Spirit . . . in the Church. Scripture and Tradition are found together (*Digest of Proceedings of the Consultation on Church Union for 1962 and 1963,* ed. by George L. Hunt [Box 69, Fanwood, N.J.], pp. 44, 45).

The danger in exalting Tradition is that it may contradict and displace Scripture. It becomes the corrupt tradition of men against which Jesus warned. Ecumenical discussion and negotiation will nullify the written Word of God whenever it accords Tradition equal status with the written Word or permits Tradition that does not have the endorsement of the written Word to become normative or binding on Christian conscience.

THE SPIRIT OF FREEDOM

One of the vexing problems of sanctification is the relation of the Christian to the law. If Christians "are not under law but under grace" (Rom. 6:14) and "love is the fulfilling of the law" (Rom. 13:10), what has the Christian to do any more with the law? One may argue, as many have, that the Christian has passed beyond the law. Brunner, in an effort to solve this problem, distinguishes between law and commandment. (See G. C. Berkouwer, *Faith and Sanctification,* Eerdmans, 1952, pp. 168-72.) The law is provisional and only "an oblique expression of the will of God." The believer breaks through this outer shell to find the will of God, which is never expressed in general terms and external prescriptions but is a commandment for a particular, concrete situation and comes as a momentary hint. Brunner seeks to escape the bondage and coercion of legalism, but his distinction is not supported in the New Testament. The Christian may use the law gratefully as a guide. He may see the law as a gift of grace, and because a new love for God has been shed abroad in his heart by the Holy Spirit, he wants to keep the law—not out of compulsion but out of grateful affection. The freedom of the Christian is a freedom from the slavery of sin to the service of God. His freedom is from condemnation under a Judge into acceptance with a loving Father; hence fear is gone because it is displaced by love. He aims to observe the law not to establish a proud record but to please his Saviour, and his confidence is not in legal exactness but in grace that forgives imperfections. This was the view of the Reformers. It found expression in confessional statements like those of Heidelberg and Westminster, which have long expositions on the Christian and on the Ten Commandments.

Brunner is better when he states in his commentary on Romans 6:15-23: "Freedom from the law does not mean freedom from God but freedom for God. . . . Man is made in such a way that he must always be obedient; the question only is: obedient to whom? . . . Either he obeys God, or he obeys sin . . .." *(The Letter to the Romans,* Westminster, 1959, pp. 53, 54).

Barth says: "It is not simple obedience that is legalistic" (*Church Dogmatics IV,* Part II, T. and T. Clark, 1958, p. 542). Barth protests against any sophisticated pseudo-obedience that pretends to hear the call of Jesus but ends up ignoring the form of action obviously demanded by Jesus.

Take as an example of the place of law in the life of a Christian the challenge of the civil-rights movement. Unquestionably, many white Christians in the United States sought to love their Negro neighbor in personal relationships but were blind to the social implications of neighborly love. It was not loving to acquiesce in the subjection of the Negro to all sorts of humiliating denials. Then, to the shame of white Christians, the United States Supreme Court in the school decision of 1954 jolted the churches into taking a second look at American ways. Along with this came the bus boycott by Negroes in Montgomery, Alabama. White Christians had to reconsider such basic teachings as the law of neighborly love and the golden rule. The simple fact is that white Christians have had to confess that they have not loved God with all their heart, soul, mind, and strength, and their neighbor as themselves.

It is not legalism for white Christians to seek a fresh start, late as it is, toward fulfilling the law of love and remembering all things that Christ has commanded. The best hope for all Christians, white and Negro, is faith in the grace of God, which forgives and reconciles, and humble reliance upon the Holy Spirit to discover ways and means whereby they may do the will of Christ.

It may be too late for the civil-rights movement to have any consistent motivation in Christian theology. Joseph R. Washington, Jr., has pointed out that love and nonviolence may work together but cannot be fused (*Black Religion,* Beacon Press, 1964, p. 8). The root of love is in God, theologically interpreted. The root of nonviolence is in philosophy. "[Martin Luther] King borrowed more than nonviolence from Ghandi. He accepted his syncretic spirit, and it is as though Socrates, Thoreau, Hegel, and Jesus were all dumped together into one philosophical bowl like tossed salad." Washington continues: "Obviously, the honeymoon with love has given way to a pragmatic emphasis upon justice. The religion of love is no longer at the center of the nonviolent movement. Instead of reconciliation and the Man on the Cross, there is the cup of endurance running over" (p. 12). Again, he says: "There is a new religion among Negro students, but not a renewal of faith. The religion is that of belief in direct mass action as the shortest distance to equality" (p. 17). The call is for white Christians to sit beside the Negro and share with him in the richness of Christian faith and life. Otherwise a folk religion that consists only of racial unity for freedom and equality will in the end reveal its barrenness and lack of theological rootage.

My freedom as a Christian consists in a glorious series of new beginnings. From every failure to do the will of Christ I turn again to the throne of grace. I may live not in the burden of condemnation but in the release of justification. And the power of ever-fresh starts is in a personal relationship with Christ, established and vitalized by the Holy Spirit. My efforts to do better are not pitiful, moralistic striving to live up to a code but openness to living out a life. In all of this the law serves to keep me humble and to save me from a shallow analysis of the moral situation and my responsibility in it. I am driven to prayer. I have to ask God to do in, with, and through me what I cannot do of myself. The Spirit of freedom leads me in a daily adventure with the living God wherein I have wholesome respect for His moral principles as the expression of His will but wherein my devotion is to the Person behind the principles.

THE SPIRIT IN THE CHURCHES

While the work of the Holy Spirit is upon and with individuals, His work always relates individuals to a fellowship. The moving of the Spirit in the Book of Acts is social. He came upon the gathered group on Pentecost (2:1-4). He fell upon Gentiles as Peter preached the Gospel to Cornelius and his company (10:44). He came upon the Ephesian disciples as Paul led them from the baptism of John into baptism in the name of the Lord Jesus (19:1-6). In the Spirit's operation, the singular turns into the plural.

The Ephesians letter establishes the binding character of the Spirit's work, so that Christians must ever be "eager to maintain the unity of the Spirit in the bond of peace" (4:3). After all, "there is one body and one Spirit" (4:4). All the imperatives that follow these basic statements presuppose that Christians live and grow in a fellowship. Not in isolation but in group experience are believers to put off the old nature, put on the new nature, put away falsehood, and be careful not to grieve the Holy Spirit of God (4:22, 24, 25, 30). Christians are commanded to "be filled with the Spirit, addressing one another in psalms and hymns and spiritual songs" (5:18, 19).

Here is the true ecumenism. The Spirit constrains Christians to seek fellowship with all who are born of the Spirit. The late Samuel M. Shoemaker was distinguished among ministers of old-line churches in the United States by his burning zeal for the life and power of the Spirit among inert, conventional and moribund church members. He said once that true Christians will act like quicksilver on a table top. They will run together. One of his catchy slogans was: "Get changed; get together; get going." And his idea of getting going was to live "in the stream of the Spirit." "Another great experience of the Holy Spirit," he said, "is the way he brings unity and fellowship . . . this unity above freedom and dissent, above diversity of personality and function . . . a quiet inward pressure upon people that lowers the tone of voices, stills the clamor of opinionated convictions and reminds everyone of the Higher Will that should prevail" (*With the Holy Spirit and With Fire*, Harper, 1960, p. 33). Again he says: "The Holy Spirit seems able to do His best work in a group" (p. 40).

Lesslie Newbigin says in *The Household of God* that he feels the absence of Pentecostals in ecumenical discussion. Since the Church is the community of the Holy Spirit, those who have especially sought His gifts and graces have a contribution to make to other Christians. Writing a defense of the South India scheme of union, Newbigin says: "The Church is the one temple of the one Holy Spirit"; "factions and divisions are the signs of a relapse into carnality, into life after the flesh" (*The Reunion of the Church*, SCM Press, 1960, p. 52).

The difficult problem of structured and visible ecumenism is to achieve a union of churches that is the result of the Spirit's urging and not of man's contriving by the sacrifices of cherished truth. In spite of the problem, it appears that Christians should take advantage of the new openness in our time to discover the leading of the Spirit. This is certainly true for those churches that agree on God's grace-faith way of salvation.

Presumably all Christians who belong in any way to the Reformation long for renewal. Few take issue with the admission that the churches are sick and need a new filling of life and strength. Shoemaker was right when he wrote: "What we are feeling for, imagining, longing for, really praying for, is a world-wide awakening under the power of the Holy Spirit" (*With the Holy Spirit and With Fire,* Harper, 1960, p. 10). Again he wrote: "The mark of the true Church is always the presence and power of the Holy Spirit" (p. 23). Even if we qualify that statement to read "a" mark, we must confess that the Church of the Book of Acts throbbed with a power that expanded and energized in astonishing ways ordinary people with ordinary abilities. In the same vein Newbigin has written: "If we would ask the question 'Where is the Church?', we must ask 'Where is the Holy Spirit recognizably present with power?' " (*The Household of God,* Friendship Press, 1954, p. 95).

One of the leaders in the tongues movement among the older denominations is Harold Bredesen, pastor of the First Reformed Church of Mount Vernon, New York. After hearing him speak of his experience in glossolalia at a meeting for ministers in Palo Alto, California, I read carefully the issue of *Trinity* magazine dated Trinitytide 1962. I found joyous testimonies from Episcopalians, Lutherans, Methodists, Presbyterians, and others in its pages. An article by Lewis Holm quotes an appraisal of this recent movement by R. A. Daehlin, present of the Rocky Mountain District of the American Lutheran Church. Daehlin refers to Paul's appeal for a balanced understanding of charismatic gifts in First Corinthians 12-14. The granting of these gifts is "God's business and entirely as he wills and chooses." Daehlin continues:

> Proof of the Spirit's presence and power is best demonstrated in the experience of being forgiven through faith in Jesus Christ, in living in his Word, demonstrating the "fruits of the Spirit" (Gal. 5:22), for herein is the upbuilding of the church. Prophecy should be encouraged, coveted, sought, striven for. Tongues should not be promoted and encouraged in this way, but should not be forbidden, and they must be interpreted when used in the Christian assembly. We should not "quench the Spirit" (I Thess. 5:19) and neither should we "grieve the Spirit" (Eph. 4:30) . . . (*Trinity,* Trinitytide, 1962, pp. 42, 43).

The Holy Spirit cannot be manipulated. His ways are mysterious. But He can be prayed for (Luke 11:13). The churches in our time desperately need a fresh visitation of His life and power. In penitence, in charity where some cherish one way or doctrine or gift that is different from ours, and in ecumenical breadth, we need to ask God to grant to the churches in fuller measure the One who sanctifies.

GROWTH TOWARD PERFECTION

Luther's famous maxim—*simul justus, simul peccator* (at the same time righteous and a sinner)—has always been taken seriously in the Reformation tradition. Luther wrote: "Sin remains in us until the end of our life, as we read in Galatians 5:17: 'The flesh lusteth . . .' " (*Commentary on Romans,* trans. by J. T. Mueller, Zondervan, 1954, p. 84). Calvin wrote: "On this subject all sound writers are agreed—that there still remains in a regenerate man a fountain of evil, continually producing irregular desires, which allure and stimulate him to the commission of sin (*Institutes,* III, iii, 10). And again he wrote: "We maintain, there-fore, that sin always exists in the saints, till they are divested of the mortal body" (*ibid.*). And, sin, "though it ceases to reign, . . . continues to dwell in them" (III, iii, 11).

The challenge of John Wesley led to a great divide within the Reformed tradition on the subject of sanctification. One of Wesley's successors today has said:

> We believe that entire sanctification is that act of God, subsequent to regeneration, by which believers are made free from original sin, or depravity, and brought into a state of entire devotement to God, and the holy obedience of love made perfect. It is wrought by the baptism with the Holy Spirit, and comprehends in one experience the cleansing of the heart from sin and the abiding, indwelling presence of the Holy Spirit, empowering the believer for life and service (H. Orton Wiley, *Christian Theology,* Beacon Hill Press, 1960, II, 466).

In all discussions of this subject there are two key words—"sin" and "perfection." Albert C. Outler maintains that Wesley's position has been consistently misunderstood. Wesley's idea of perfection did not come from the Latin *perfectus,* meaning "faultless." It came rather by way of Marcarius from the Greek *Teleōsis,* meaning "fullness." Says Outler:

> [There may be a] conscious certainty, in a present moment, of the fullness of one's love for God and neighbor. . . . This is not a state, but a dynamic process. . . . There is no level of Christian achievement from which pride or self-will may not topple us. . . . Perfection is the fulfillment of faith's desire to love God above all else and all else in God, *so far as conscious will and deliberate action are concerned* (*John Wesley,* ed. by Albert C. Outler, Oxford, 1964, p. 31).

Normally, he adds, the gift of perfect love is deferred until death.

Even if one limits sin to conscious voluntary states and qualifies perfection as a mood of fullness experienced from time to time, he finds that Wesley has successors who will not be satisfied with these descriptions. For them entire sanctification is a second work of grace and brings complete deliverance from sin.

However, it seems that most theologians today who regard themselves as children of the Reformers keep sanctification closely bound to justification and cannot find in the Scriptures a doctrine of a second work of grace. Furthermore, most of them steadfastly hold that sanctification is not the experience of a moment but a lifelong process or development. Berkouwer says:

> The Scriptures always speak of sanctification in the existential sphere of faith. Paul speaks of "perfecting holiness in the fear of God" (II Cor. 7:1). Holiness is never a "second blessing" placed next to the blessing of justification. . . . Our completion is only realized in Christ (Col. 2:10) "for by one offering he hath perfected for ever them that are sanctified" (Heb. 10:14). The exhortation which comes to the Church is that it must live in faith out of this fullness; not that it must work for a second blessing, but that it must feed on the first blessing, the forgiveness of sins" (*Faith and Sanctification,* Eerdmans, 1952, p. 64).

John Murray says cogently:

> Paul's references to mortification are striking because of the contexts in which they occur. In the contexts, the once-for-all death to sin and the translation thereby to the realm of new life in Christ are in the forefront. No place might appear to be left for mortification of sin. It is not so. "But if by the Spirit ye put to death the deeds of the body, ye shall live" (Rom. 8:13; cf. Col. 3:5) (*Basic Christian Doctrines,* ed. by Carl F. H. Henry, Holt, Rinehart and Winston, 1962, p. 230).

One of the interesting ways to read Barth's section on sanctification in his *Church Dogmatics* is to take consecutively all the fine-print comments on Calvin. For the most part, Barth is highly appreciative of the great Reformer. He does find, however, an overemphasis on mortification at the expense of vivification. I think this criticism is justified and is one that any reader of Puritan devotional works and biography may well bear in mind. To bemoan and bewail "the flesh" which will always be "the flesh" falls short of New Testament confidence and joy.

While strict Calvinists and confirmed Wesleyans may never reach complete agreement, they may move closer together when the Calvinists emphasize newness of life in the Spirit and the Wesleyans moderate their descriptions of sinlessness, the second blessing, and perfection.

How, then, do Christians grow toward perfection? In many ways:

By an enlarged appreciation of Christ's death and resurrection both for justification and sanctification;

By living from day to day in an attitude of entire dependence upon the grace of God, realizing more and more that all goodness comes from Him;

By honest confession of all known sin and a humble recognition that even our confession needs to be confessed as inadequate, for Paul moved from a consciousness of being worthy as an apostle to an awareness of being less than the least of all saints to a confession that he was chief of sinners;

By emphasis upon grateful obedience and service, for holiness, like happiness, seems to come when one is not preoccupied with it but is chiefly concerned with Christ and the needs of people;

By trust that God will persevere with poor, imperfect believers and will even release His power through them;

By enlarged charity toward all who are of the household of faith, and toward even the most vicious and vile in the world who have missed the way to God;

And by a developed longing for eschatological deliverance and fulfillment when sin shall finally drop away and service shall ever be full of joy and glory.

SUMMARY

To sum up the matter:

1. Sanctification is God's work. He chooses sinners, justifies them freely by His grace in Christ Jesus, and operates in and with them to achieve His purpose in and for the world.

2. Our descriptions of sanctification call for humility and charity.

Temperament and type of experience, plus denominational conditioning, affect our understanding of the Scriptures and our formulations of doctrine.

3. Sanctification is Christocentric. The Holy Spirit is the chief Agent within believers, whose required response is faith and obedience. Sanctification takes place within the discipline of a loving Father and in a hostile world.

4. Sanctification is based upon the renewing work of the Holy Spirit. It is a subjective realization of the death and resurrection of Christ. The Holy Spirit will not permit a Christian to live in the flesh but will hold the law before him as a reminder and guide of what God wants him to be. The Christian should be primarily absorbed, not with his flesh nature or with moral tension and conflict, but with Christ and all the gifts and graces of the Spirit.

5. The Holy Spirit is as much God's gift to a believer as Christ is.

6. The Holy Spirit makes Christ and the Scriptures vital and helpful to Christians, and He is thereby the supreme guide to truth in this ecumenical day.

7. The freedom the Holy Spirit brings is deliverance from sin to the service of God. The Spirit helps Christians keep on the wholesome road of the law of love as this pertains to a contemporary issue like racial justice, and helps them make their way safely between legalism and lawlessness.

8. The Spirit baptizes believers into the body of Christ. Spiritual experience is corporate. All Christians should pray today for a fresh visitation of the Spirit upon the Church of Christ.

9. Calvinists and Wesleyans should seek to understand each other, for, after all, they have a common goal—perfection in Christ. No Christian may dare to do less than press on toward perfection.

A SELECT BIBLIOGRAPHY

10. THE REFORMED DOCTRINE OF SANCTIFICATION

Karl Barth, *Church Dogmatics IV, The Doctrine of Reconciliation,* Part Two. Edinburgh: T. and T. Clark, 1958.

G. C. Berkouwer, *Faith and Sanctification.* Grand Rapids, Michigan: William B. Eerdmans Publishing Company, 1952.

John Calvin, *Institutes of the Christian Religion.* Philadelphia: Presbyterian Board of Christian Education, 1935.

Carl F. H. Henry (ed.), *Basic Christian Doctrines.* New York: Holt, Rinehart and Winston, 1962.

Lesslie Newbigin, *The Household of God.* New York: Friendship Press, 1954.

Albert C. Outler (ed.), *John Wesley.* New York: Oxford University Press, 1964.

Samuel M. Shoemaker, *With the Holy Spirit and With Fire.* New York: Harper & Brothers, Publishers, 1960.

H. Orton Wiley, *Christian Theology II.* Kansas City: Beacon Hill Press, 1960.

HEAVEN OR HELL?

Fred Carl Kuehner

Fred Carl Kuehner is dean and professor of biblical languages at the
Theological Seminary of the Reformed Episcopal Church, Philadelphia,
Pennsylvania. He is also special lecturer in New Testament at Westminster Theological Seminary, Philadelphia, Pennsylvania. Dr. Kuehner holds the A.B. from the University of Pennsylvania, the B.D. and
D.D. (hon.) from the Reformed Episcopal Seminary, the Th.M. from
Westminster Theological Seminary, and the Th.D. from Eastern Baptist Theological Seminary. He has also worked in the field of Semitics
at Dropsie College.

11. *Fred Carl Kuehner*

HEAVEN OR HELL?

DEATH IS THE most democratic institution on earth. It comes to all men, regardless of color, education, wealth, or rank. It allows no discrimination, tolerates no exceptions. The mortality rate of mankind is the same the world over: one death per person. The only exception we know of are Enoch and Elijah, both of whom were taken up into the presence of God without dying, and those believers who, living at the time of the return of Christ, will be transformed without passing through death.

"It is appointed for men to die once." With this scriptural verdict there can be no dissent. But the immediately following statement in Hebrews 9:27—"and after that comes judgment"—opens the door to a thousand questions. What follows death? What is man's state after he has left this life? Is there a heaven for the right, a place of everlasting bliss, where they will enjoy endless communication with God? Is there a hell for the wicked, a place of eternal banishment from the presence of God? Are the souls of the wicked (or of all men) annihilated at death? Or may we hope that all men, Judas Iscariot included, and all demons, even Satan himself, will at length be restored and returned to the good graces of their Creator? Questions like these might have haunted Hamlet when he said:

> *To die; to sleep;*
> *To sleep, perchance to dream; ay, there's the rub;*
> *For in that sleep of death what dreams may come,*
> *When we have shuffled off this mortal coil,*
> *Must give us pause . . .*

AFTER DEATH — JUDGMENT

The idea of a final tribunal, a Great Assize before which all men must appear and at which they will be assigned their eternal destiny, did not, of course, originate in the ghoulish depictions of medieval artists and writers. Behind them lies the source of this awesome concept: the joint testimony of the Old and New Testaments. When the writer of the Epistle to the Hebrews refers to a post-mortem judgment, he is not introducing some novel idea. Earlier in the letter he placed "eternal judgment" as the final item in a catalogue of "elementary doctrines of Christ" consisting of such tenets as repentance from dead works, faith toward God, baptism, ordination, and the resurrection of the dead (Heb. 6:1, 2). Since "eternal judgment" occupies a place among the six basic articles of Christian faith, it is not surprising to discover references to it throughout Scripture.

In the Old Testament God is repeatedly designated as the God of judgment who as "the Judge of all the earth" will "do right" (Gen. 18: 25), who "will judge the world with righteousness, and the peoples with his truth" (Ps. 96:13), and who "will bring every deed into judgment, with every secret thing, whether good or evil" (Eccles. 12:14). That judgment will make an eternal distinction between men, for "many of those who sleep in the dust of the earth shall awake, some to everlasting life, and some to shame and everlasting contempt" (Dan. 12:2).

These prophetic intimations come to final expression in the New Testament. What were once seed thoughts, germinal and incomplete, now appear in full maturity in the teaching of Jesus Christ and of His apostles.

Never were there words as solemn and as searching as those in which Jesus warned of the judgment to come. In twelve out of thirty-six of His parables He depicts men as judged, condemned, and punished for their sins. In one, the parable of the rich man and Lazarus, He draws back the veil on the conditions of men in the hereafter to show the rich man in torment, suffering an anguish that has no relief and no end, confined to one side of a chasm that is forever unbridgeable (Luke 16:19-31).

Some of Jesus' sternest teaching on divine retribution appears in. the Sermon on the Mount. Commenting on the consequences of hatred, He warns of the impending "hell of fire" (Matt. 5:22). Later, speaking of the adulterous implications of a lustful look, He pleads with men to make every kind of sacrifice, to surrender eye, arm, foot, rather than be cast into hell (Matt. 5:27-30). Then, comparing a man's life to a tree, He declares, "Every tree that does not bear good fruit is cut down and thrown into the fire" (Matt. 7:19). And, anticipating the superficial adherents who would be among His followers, He tells of a day when their pious protestations will not avert His awful rejection: "I never knew you; depart from me, you evildoers" (Matt. 7:23). Finally, in describing the fool whose house, built on the sand, collapsed when the winds and the rain beat against it, Jesus warns of the possibility of a great and irrevocable tragedy overtaking the human soul (Matt. 7:24-27).

Elsewhere in the Gospels, Jesus' teaching sounds the same deep note of judgment. The terms He employs to warn of that impending crisis are, to be sure graphic, symbolic, figurative; but they are nonetheless terribly real. He speaks of unquenchable fire, of outer darkness, of the undying worm, of the weeping and gnashing of teeth, of the resurrection of judgment, of the judgment of hell, of perdition, of many stripes.

In His last public teaching, as He sat on the Mount of Olives, Jesus outlined the details of the last judgment in His parable of the sheep and goats. To one class of men, those on His left hand, He as the Son of Man, will say, "Depart from me, you cursed, into the eternal fire prepared for the devil and his angels." Concluding that parable with a description of this punishment, Jesus said, "And they will go away into eternal punishment, but the righteous into eternal life" (Matt. 25:46).

The doctrine of the last judgment occupies a significant place elsewhere in the New Testament, though not as pervasively as in the four Gospels. Paul summarizes his view in Second Thessalonians 1:6-9: "God deems it just to repay with affliction those who afflict you, and to grant rest with us to you who are afflicted, when the Lord Jesus is revealed from heaven with his mighty angels in flaming fire, inflicting vengeance upon those who do not know God and upon those who do not obey the gospel of our Lord Jesus. They shall suffer punishment of eternal destruction and exclusion from the presence of the Lord and from the glory of his might." As did Jesus, the Apostle describes the punishment as "eternal" and its nature as "exclusion from the presence of the Lord." Thus the "destruction" is not annihilation but endless ruin in separation from Christ.

Peter, in his second epistle, speaks of fallen angels who are "cast . . . into hell" and of God's keeping "the unrighteous under punishment until the day of judgment" (II Pet. 2:4, 9). Jude writes in the same vein, saying that "the angels that did not keep their position but left their proper dwelling have been kept by him in eternal chains . . . until the judgment of the great day" (Jude 6). And in the last book of the Bible, John portrays the visions he saw of the last day. Those who worship the beast and his image "shall be tormented with fire and brimstone . . . and the smoke of their torment goes up for ever and ever; and they have no rest, day or night, those worshippers of the beast and its image" (Rev. 14:9-11). In a final apocalyptic scene, John sees "the dead, great and small, standing before the throne, and books were opened. Also another book was opened, which is the book of life. And the dead were judged by what was written in the books, by what they had done. . . . If any one's name was not found written in the book of life, he was thrown into the lake of fire" (Rev. 20:12-15).

In a world created and governed by a sovereign and holy God, there must be judgment, or else the very fabric of the spiritual universe is torn to shreds. But Scripture calls it God's "strange work" (Isa. 28:21, KJV); He takes no delight in it, and in the fullest way possible He extends His mercy that it may triumph over judgment.

And where in human history do we see the fullest expression of the mercy and judgment of God? At the cross of Christ. There, in the sufferings and death Jesus Christ underwent in dealing with our sins, we behold unveiled the divine love. This is the love the New Testament writers perceived when they looked at the cross. And for this reason they rarely speak of the love of God without in the same sentence referring to the cross of Christ and to our deliverance from the guilt into which our sins had plunged us (John 3:16; Rom. 5:8).

But more than the love of God is revealed at the cross. There we see, unsheathed, the implacable hostility of God's wrath against sin—past, present, and future. There at the cross God judged sin in Christ, having imputed our guilt to the Redeemer; Christ was our substitute and the bearer of our sin in His own body on the tree. The cross, therefore, is also a judgment, a divine execution of wrath upon sin, and is as such a precursor of the last judgment, when history, as we now know it, will be brought to a close.

ETERNAL RETRIBUTION

A judgment without the possibility of retribution is inconceivable. In a court, the accused is charged with breaking a law. If he is found guilty, the court decrees an appropriate punishment. Such punishment has in it a clear penal, retributive element, designed to satisfy the law.

Divine judgment may fall upon the sinner in innumerable temporal guises, such as the gnawing unrest of a guilt-ridden conscience, the accelerated loss of health and life, and the punishment administered by human courts. Against these temporal aspects of divine retribution, most of us raise little or no opposition. Such expressions of punishment, we agree, are consistent with human convictions and experience.

But transfer the concept of punishment from temporal to eternal categories, refer to everlasting punishment in hell, and the climate of the discussion changes. The silence with which any serious treatment of the subject is greeted, the reticence even of evangelicals to preach on hell and everlasting punishment, the modern resurgence of universalism (the belief that all men will ultimately be saved) in Protestant theology, and the frequent, glib use of the word "hell" in ordinary language, not only that of the street but also that of government, news media, and literature—these are the varied reactions that the doctrine of eternal retribution evinces today. The Russian theologian Berdyaev, feeling the pulse of modern thought, rightly diagnosed the ailment: "It is remarkable how little people think about hell or trouble about it. This is the most striking evidence of human frivolity" (*The Destiny of Man,* Scribners, 1937, p. 338).

"Hell," a word subjected to much perverted use in common profanity, is a biblical term that occurs more often in the teaching of Christ than elsewhere in Scripture. Noting this fact, William Shedd writes, "The strongest support of the doctrine of Endless Punishment is the teaching of Christ, the Redeemer of man. . . . The mere perusal of Christ's words when he was upon earth, without note or comment upon them, will convince the unprejudiced that the Redeemer of sinners knew and believed that for impenitent men and devils there is an endless punishment" (*The Doctrine of Endless Punishment,* Scribners, 1887, p. 12). To establish this, Shedd takes three pages to quote the words of Christ, citing such passages as Matthew 7:22, 23; 10:28; 11:23; Mark 9:43-48; Luke 9:25; 12:9, 10, 46; 16:22, 23; John 5:28, 29; 8:21.

In the desire to set aside Christ's clear-cut teaching on eternal retribution, men have resorted either to open rejection of its validity or to subtle reduction of its language. Nels F. S. Ferré, for example, says that the doctrine of the Second Coming "completely shut out the living God, embracing and reconciling all men with His eternal time and power," and substituted the concept that "all mankind would be extinguished or tormented forever except the few who would escape punishment through faith in the merits of Jesus." He adds: "It seems doubtful that Jesus ever taught such a doctrine" (*The Sun and the Umbrella,* Harper, 1953, p. 33). Ferré deliberately overstates traditional teaching on eternal retribution by grotesquely contrasting the "all mankind" and "the few" and by employing the word "extinguished," a term not found in the Gospel or in historic Christian theology. Thus by a brusque wave of the hand he dismisses not only a conspicuous element in the teaching of Jesus but also the catholic witness of the Church.

Other men, less bold than Ferré, have attempted to modify the meaning of the temporal terms Jesus used, to reduce their solemn impact. Formerly F. W. Farrar and others insisted that the retribution, rather than being "eternal," was temporary, lasting but for an age. Today, J. A. T. Robinson speaks of "eternal" in a vertical sense, having it describe not an endless spiritual state but rather "the eternal seriousness of the choice before man."

But will the New Testament words for "forever" and "eternal" accommodate these interpretations? Does not the use of these terms for the eternity of God mean that they cannot be taken to imply a limited duration? God is said to be "the King of ages, immortal, invisible, the only God" (I Tim. 1:17); glory is ascribed to Him "forever" (Rom. 11:36); and He is blessed "forever" (II Cor. 11:31). Moreover, their frequent use in the New Testament in reference to the never-ending "age to come" and to "eternal life" indicates that *aion* and *aionios* must have the significance of unlimited time. Thus, James Barr can say in his *Biblical Words for Time:* "The cases of *aionios* refer fairly uniformly to the being of God or to plans and realities which, once established by him, are perpetual or unchanging."

Christ, in the parable of the sheep and goats, clearly defines *aionios.* To those at His left hand the Son of Man says, "Depart from me, you cursed, into the eternal [*aionios*] fire prepared for the devil and his angels" (Matt. 25:41). This "eternal fire" He further describes as "eternal punishment" in the concluding statement of the parable: "They [the 'cursed,' those rejected by the judge] will go away into eternal punishment, but the righteous into eternal life" (v. 46). Here the phrase "eternal" [*aionios*] punishment" is balanced by the phrase "eternal [*aionios*] life," both states being permanent and final. It is impossible to remove the thought of "eternal" from one occurrence of the word *aionios* without taking the same liberty with its counterpart. Whatever is the duration of the "life" is the duration of the "punishment."

And this is not the only place in the New Testament where *aionios* is used to define the duration of man's ultimate destiny. Fifty-one times it describes the happiness of the righteous, and seven times the punishment of the wicked. No wonder W. R. Inge declared in *What Is Hell?*, "No sound Greek scholar can pretend that *aionios* means anything less than eternal."

HELL—THE PLACE OF PUNISHMENT

The Old Testament offers but little information about the eternal destiny of the individual, and most of this is concerned with the future of the righteous rather than of the wicked. *Sheol,* the place to which both godly and ungodly are said to go after death, is depicted as an abode of shadowy, limited existence, but existence nonetheless. Later, in noncanonical Jewish literature, we meet with the idea of compartments within *sheol,* areas designed separately for the wicked and the righteous, in which each experiences a foretaste of his final destiny (Enoch xxii. 1-14).

Even the etymology of the Hebrew word *sheol* is uncertain. Some scholars derive it from a verb meaning "to ask" (suggesting either an insatiable pit always asking for more souls or a place where one may ask after an oracle). Others find its origin in a root meaning "hollow" and make it refer to a hollow, deep place under the earth.

Although the Old Testament information is meager, says Harry Buis, its meaning is clear:

> The Old Testament clearly teaches a life after death, commonly in the form of an existence in Sheol, where good and evil alike share a similar dreary fate. However, there are also passages of inspired hope in a better life beyond death for the believer, a life of glorious fellowship with his God. Although there is in these passages no direct teaching with regard to the eternal punishment of the unbeliever, there is the beginning of a differentiation between the lot of the unbeliever and that of the believer (*The Doctrine of Eternal Punishment,* Baker, 1957, p. 12).

In Greek literature the underworld, or realm of the dead, was known as *hades.* This is the word that the translators of the Septuagint (the Greek Old Testament) used to render *sheol* in almost every instance of its appearance. *Hades* also appears in the New Testament. In the parable of the rich man and Lazarus it indicates the place of the rich man's torment (Luke 16:23). It is the word denoting Satan's kingdom in its opposition to the Church in the statement, "The gates of *hades* shall not prevail against it" (Matt. 16:18). And it is the word representing the prison of Satan and the wicked in John's apocalyptic vision: "Death and Hades gave up the dead in them. . . . Death and Hades were thrown into the lake of fire" (Rev. 20:13, 14).

This last reference (along with others) strongly suggests that *hades* is an intermediate state of punishment for disembodied spirits, a place to eventuate, after the last judgment, in "the lake of fire." Elsewhere in the

New Testament the final and eternal place of punishment, where persons in the body are to be incarcerated, is called *gehenna*. This term, which occurs twelve times in the New Testament, all but one of them in the teaching of Christ, is never named in connection with the torment of the present intermediate state. It is Christ who speaks of "the *gehenna* of fire" as equivalent to "eternal fire" into which men may be "thrown," in contrast to entering into "life" (Matt. 18:8, 9). He further explains it to be "the unquenchable fire . . . where their worm does not die" (Mark 9: 43-47). It is Christ also who warns the Pharisees with the words, "You serpents, you brood of vipers, how are you to escape being sentenced to *gehenna?*" (Matt. 23:33). He instructs His own disciples, telling them to "fear him who, after he has killed, has power to cast into *gehenna*" (Luke 12:5). Calling for the most extreme sacrifice in the effort to avoid *gehenna,* He tells His hearers that "it is better that you lose one of your members than that your whole body be thrown into *gehenna*" (Matt. 5: 29, 30). And it is Christ who exposes the consequences of hatred in the words, "Whoever says, 'You fool!' shall be liable to the *gehenna* of fire" (Matt. 5:22), a warning interpreted later by His apostle in plain terms: "Any one who hates his brother is a murderer, and you know that no murderer has eternal life abiding in him" (I John 3:15).

There is no question that these passages, teaching as they do the reality of a place of eternal punishment, present profound problems to our mind. Much in our nature rises in revolt and horror against such a doctrine. Yet we ought not to compound the difficulties by insisting that the terms Christ used in describing *gehenna* be pressed to their full literal significance. Christian doctrine has never demanded that "the unquenchable fire" be interpreted as "a fiery oven" where "the flames do now rage and glow" and that "the view of the misery of the damned will double the ardour of the love and gratitude of the saints in heaven" (Jonathan Edwards). The Church has never formally taken the position that "in order that nothing may be wanting to the happiness of the blessed in Heaven, a perfect view is granted them of the torture of the damned" (Thomas Aquinas). Nor has the Church in its creedal formulations even remotely declared that "in fire exactly like that which we have on earth thy body will lie, asbestos-like, forever unconsumed, all thy veins roads for the feet of Pain to travel on, every nerve a string on which the Devil shall for ever play his diabolical tune of hell's unutterable lament" (Charles Spurgeon).

Such grotesque literalism is not an interpretation of Scripture but a caricature. Protestant theologians have repudiated such macabre use of terms that are obviously metaphorical. Calvin, commenting on Matthew 3:12, says:

> Many persons, I am aware, have entered into ingenious debates about the eternal fire, by which the wicked will be tormented after the judgment. But we may conclude from many passages of Scripture, that it is a metaphorical expression. For, if we must believe that it is real, or what they call material fire, we must also believe that the brimstone and the

fan are material. . . . We must explain the fire in the same manner as the worm (Mark 9:44, 46, 48) and if it is universally agreed that the worm is a metaphorical term, we must form the same opinion as to the fire.

Charles Hodge, the great Princeton theologian, echoes Calvin, saying:

> There seems no more reason for supposing that the fire spoken of in Scripture is to be a literal fire, than that the worm that never dies is literally a worm. The devil and his angels who are to suffer the vengeance of eternal fire, and whose doom the finally impenitent are to share, have no material bodies to be acted upon by elemental fire (*Systematic Theology,* Scribners, 1876, III, 868).

And Louis Berkhof summarily declares, "A great deal of the language concerning heaven and hell must be understood figuratively" (*Reformed Dogmatics,* Eerdmans, 1941, p. 736).

None of these statements advocating a symbolical interpretation of such terms as "fire" and "worm" denies the reality of hell as a place of eternal retribution. None minimizes the misery and the doom of those who are eternally separated from hope, from Christ, from God. None attenuates the remorse and suffering that will be the lot of those under the penal judgment of God. Hell, as Christ Himself refers to it, is an awesome reality.

In the end, discussion of this doctrine must not rest on human feelings, nor should it be removed from the whole subject of the character of God, the nature of evil, and the requirements of justice. This is the tack taken by C. S. Lewis in his reply to five objections raised against the doctrine of eternal punishment (*The Problem of Pain,* Macmillan, 1944, chap. 8). We summarize the objections and Lewis' replies:

1. Is not retributive punishment an idea wrong in itself? No, says Lewis. All punishment is basically retributive, not reformatory or deterrent. We have strictly no *right* to punish merely for reformatory and deterrent purposes. Unless a man deserves to be punished, we ought not to make him suffer. Nothing can be more immoral than to inflict suffering on a man who does not deserve it for the purpose either of improving him or deterring others. (See also Leon Morris, *The Cross in the New Testament,* Eerdmans, 1965, pp. 385 ff.). Furthermore, what else can God do with a man who has always lived a hellish life? God cannot condone this evil. To condone it would amount to treating evil as if it were good.

2. Is not "eternal damnation" for "transitory sin" a gross disproportion? No, say Lewis. A man's life is always long enough for it to become set in its direction. If a million chances were necessary for a man to do good, God would provide them. But they would make no difference in a wicked man's essential choice of self over God.

3. Is not the description of the pains of hell merely metaphorical? No, says Lewis. None of the images Christ used to describe hell—punishment, destruction, banishment should be used to the exclusion of others, but all of them agree on something "unspeakably horrible."

4. How can the saints in heaven have pleasure if they know there is a single human soul still in hell? If this idea is true, says Lewis, then man is more merciful than God.

5. Is not God defeated in His purpose if a single soul is ultimately lost? In a sense, yes, says Lewis; but this was the chance God took in "creating beings with free wills." Those in hell are there of their own volition, refusing, even while being punished, to give up the selves they have chosen above God.

Most of these arguments can be strengthened, and all of them need the buttressing of divine revelation. In the light of scriptural testimony we dare not reduce hell to the status of "a remedial, terminable retribution" (Farrar). Nor can we conceive of it as a Roman Catholic purgatory, "a pedagogic cleansing process" (Brunner). Nor may we imagine it to be, of all things, "a means of grace," a place of a second (and successful) chance (Ferré). Hell, in Scripture, is never viewed in temporary terms; it is an ultimate and eternal place of punishment.

ROADS BYPASSING HELL

From the time of Origen, the Alexandrian Church Father (185-254), there have been attempts to bypass the scriptural teaching on eternal punishment. One such evasive route is annihilation. Advocates of this view say that only the righteous will live forever. The wicked will be judged, condemned, and destroyed, put out of existence. This view, a form of which is also known as conditional immortality, has not found acceptance in the Church. It circulates largely among the sects, as, for example, the Seventh-day Adventists and Jehovah's Witnesses. In Scripture, all the references to the punishment of the impenitent are of such a nature that they cannot be applied to a state of annihilation. The figures employed by Christ—everlasting fire, the undying worm, eternal darkness—have no meaning if punishment is annihilation. Moreover, the parallel in Matthew 25:46 between eternal life and eternal punishment cannot be maintained if the fate of the wicked is cessation of being.

Another detour taken to avoid the implications of Christ's words on eternal punishment is universalism, the belief that all of God's creation will ultimately be redeemed. Origen himself envisioned the final restoration of all men to holiness and blessedness, a hope he extended to Satan and all other demonic spirits. To Origen the fires of hell were remedial, not penal, and were limited in duration, not eternal. In the end, after sufficient purging, the devil himself will be saved and God will be "all in all."

At the second Council of Constantinople (553) the Church condemned Origen's views, and since then none of the major branches of the Christian Church—Roman, Eastern, and Protestant—has held to universalism. Not until the Reformation did the universalism controversy break out again, in the teachings of the Anabaptists. Chapter 17 of the Augsburg Confession (1530) formally condemned the Anabaptists, "who believe

that there will be an end of punishments of the damned and the devils."
In the nineteenth century new impetus came to the universalist position.
In Germany Schleiermacher, who taught that God elected all men, gave
the weight of his tremendous influence to it. In England, Thomas Erskine,
Andrew Jukes, and (with reservations) F. W. Farrar promoted the view.
In America a denomination came into being specifically to advance uni-
versalism as a doctrine. The Universalist Church (which in 1961 merged
with the Unitarian Church) began in New England with the preaching of
John Murray (1741-1815), who for a time had been a Methodist preacher.
Today the Unitarian-Universalist Association numbers about 164,000
members.

Nineteenth-century poets probably did more than any formal theological
work to move opinion toward universalism. Tennyson, Browning, Faber,
Whittier, and Longfellow all expressed a hope in a redemptive love that
would ultimately embrace all mankind in its bosom. Tennyson's *In
Memoriam* provided the movement with its well-known caption—"the
larger hope":

> *The wish, that of the living whole*
> *No life may fail beyond the grave,*
> *Derives it not from what we have*
> *The likest God within the soul?*

> *I stretch lame hands of faith, and grope,*
> *And gather dust and chaff, and call*
> *To what I feel is Lord of all,*
> *And faintly trust the larger hope.*

THE NEW UNIVERSALISM

Today, as we move toward the close of the twentieth century, universalism appears with a new face, one made welcome in most of the major
denominations. It no longer hugs the shadows as an outlaw of Christianity
but finds its way into the best of ecclesiastical circles. The Confession of
1967 of the United Presbyterian Church tends to make room for universalism, if not actually to endorse it. For example, it affirms a second
coming of Christ but makes no mention of hell. It speaks of Christ's
role as judge but omits reference to eternal retribution as a possible consequence of His verdict.

The new universalism comes to expression also in the thrust of the
new evangelism. If "all men are doomed to be saved," then evangelism
is not the winning of men to Christ. Men need only to be informed that
they are in fact redeemed and ought to begin enjoying the felicity of the
Kingdom of God sooner. The evangelist, therefore, is no longer burdened
with the task of soliciting the response of individual men and women to
repent and in faith to say yes to Jesus Christ. The missionary is not concerned to bring Christ to Asia or Africa, for Christ, the universal Saviour
of all men, is already there. The new breed of evangelist and missionary

goes forth to announce the universal lordship of Christ and invites men to acknowledge it in their lives.

It takes no great amount of reflection to conclude that, if all men are finally saved, it makes little difference whether they are reached with the Gospel now or never. Why bother promoting the cause of foreign missions? Why call young people to a life of Christian witness overseas? Why pray for the salvation of the lost, if indeed there are no lost? Why ask for mission contributions, if the money can more profitably be used for social uplift? Why disturb people in their beliefs or lack of beliefs? Who cares whether their practices are shameful, their worship idolatrous, their religion hideous? Universalism's attack on missions is instantaneous and devastating. It strikes at the nerve of all Christian witness, killing the sense of urgency, deadening the feeling of responsibility, and anaesthetizing the impulse of concern. It is the modern restatement of the first lie, "Ye shall not surely die" (Gen. 3:4).

THE THEOLOGY OF THE NEW UNIVERSALISM

Two enticing appeals have opened the door to the new universalism. One is theological and the other is biblical. The voices making these appeals sound new, fresh, and modern, but what they offer is old and timeworn.

The theological appeal focuses on the redemptive character of God's love and the victory of the cross. Nels Ferré sees God's nature as radical love, a love that will pursue every man until every man is redeemed. In *Evil and the Christian Faith* he says, "God has no permanent problem children," for in love He will "put the screws" on every man until he comes to acknowledge God as his Father. Indeed, God could not be God, nor heaven be heaven, if one of God's creatures were excluded from His presence. "Love so amazing, so divine" must triumph in the end in the reconciliation of all mankind.

Emil Brunner takes the same theological tangent. For him, the scriptural statements concerning hell and retribution do *not* refer to objective facts about the hereafter; the Bible uses them merely to challenge us to decision and action. Furthermore:

> God confronts man with the unequivocal demand that he should recognize and endorse the prior decision which God has already made concerning him by electing man to belong to Himself. . . . The doctrine of forgiving Grace — the doctrine of justification — finds its crown in a proclamation of universal redemption (*Eternal Hope,* London, 1954, pp. 177, 178, 182).

To this optimistic hope, Ethelbert Stauffer adds his voice: "God's irresistible grace and will is destined to overcome the most obdurate opposition. . . . None is to remain outside" (*New Testament Theology,* Macmillan, 1955, p. 223).

The most forceful impetus behind the new universalism is the theology of Karl Barth. To be sure, Barth nowhere directly teaches universal sal-

vation. Nor does he say, in so many words, that no men are to be forever lost and that all will be forever with God in glory. Yet he will not
divide men into the saved and lost. Instead, he considers all men as both
lost and saved. Thus Barth allows the possibility that elect are lost, in-
congruous as that may seem. All men are reprobate in Christ, who is
the only reprobate. All men are elect in Christ, who is the elected man.
In Christ, God chose death and rejection for Himself and life and acceptance for mankind. And since all men are in Christ, "election is God's
decision concerning all and for all as the decision of the gracious God who
is *for* man" (G. C. Berkouwer, *The Triumph of Grace in the Theology
of Karl Barth,* Eerdmans, 1956, p. 265).

For Barth, therefore, the reconciliation that takes place in Jesus Christ
is actually the reconciliation of all men of all times and all places—*objectively,* at least. Because the objective elements of *reconciliation*—
justification, sanctification, and calling—concern all men equally, there
is no difference between the Christian and the non-Christian. Whatever
differences there may be, come about because of the individual or subjective aspects of reconciliation. These differences, according to Barth,
are chiefly a noetic concern. The Christian is different because he knows
and acknowledges that he is reconciled; the non-Christian does not know
it—yet.

Clearly, Barth's theology leaves scarcely any room for the biblical insistence on faith. Whereas Scripture calls on men to believe and be saved,
Barth's emphasis on objective universalism reduces the seriousness of
unbelief as guilt and removes the urgency from the Church's mission to
urge lost sinners, "Be reconciled to God."

Serious dangers are imbedded in the theology of the new universalism.
For one thing, there is such an exclusive emphasis on the love of God
that all other divine attributes seem subordinated or even eliminated. The
apostle who said, "God is love," also said in the same epistle, "God is
light," thereby stressing the absolute holiness of God (I John 1:5; 4:8).
Scripture depicts God as manifesting His redeeming love in the salvation
of believers but also as exhibiting His holy justice in pronouncing the
condemnation of unbelievers. There is what W. M. Clow called "the
dark line in God's face."

Universalism also ignores the consideration that continued impenitence
throughout eternity involves never-ending retribution. It refuses to face
the fact that divine judgments, however severe and repeated they may be,
however mingled with longsuffering and common mercies, nevertheless fail
to secure the repentance of the wicked. Indeed, we may well abandon
the hope that the prodigal will come to himself in a day of mercy at
some remote stage of eternity after accumulated aggravations of trans-
gression. For, as a contemporary British theologian has tersely put it,
"God has no more to show to Judas than was shown to Judas in the
course of his life in this world."

Even more dangerous are the extreme statements made by neouniver-
salists regarding the sovereignty of God, statements that skirt perilously

close to mechanistic determinism. How can this conclusion be avoided when such statements as these are made: "God's will is destined to overcome the most obdurate opposition" (Stauffer); "God will make our own way so self-punishing that at last we come to our better selves" (Ferré); "How should the feeble creature in its defiance of God, its 'no' to God, show itself to be stronger than God? Must God be content with a situation in which He . . . is obliged to accept a second-best solution?" (Brunner)? Even a Calvinist would demur from making such statements. He would refuse to say that God forces men to be saved. He recognizes the reality of what F. W. Robertson called "God's terrible permission"— His allowing a man to deny Him to the point of self-destruction.

UNIVERSALISM'S BIBLE

Universalists, from Origen to the present, have appealed to certain texts of Scripture in support of their view. Six of these passages seem to predict the ultimate salvation of the entire human race. Christ said, "I, when I am lifted up from the earth, will draw all men to myself" (John 12:32). Peter spoke of "the times of restitution of all things" (Acts 3: 21, KJV). Paul declared that "one man's act of righteousness leads to acquittal and life for all men" (Rom. 5:18). God's purpose, he wrote in another place, is to "unite all things in him [Christ], things in heaven and things on earth" (Eph. 1:10). The same apostle declared that Christ shall reign until "all things are put in subjection under him" (I Cor. 15: 22-28) and "every tongue [shall] confess that Jesus Christ is Lord" (Phil. 2:9-11).

Two passages of Scripture announce God's benevolence toward all men. Paul declared that God "desires all men to be saved and to come to the knowledge of the truth" (I Tim. 2:4). And Peter affirmed that "the Lord is . . . not wishing that any should perish" (II Pet. 3:9).

A group of five passages indicate that the cross of Christ has reference to all men. "God was in Christ reconciling the world to himself" (II Cor. 5:19). God designed through Christ to "reconcile to himself all things, whether on earth or in heaven" (Col. 1:20). "The grace of God has appeared for the salvation of all men" (Titus 2:11). Christ came into the world "so that by the grace of God he might taste death for every one" (Heb. 2:9). And, finally, Christ's death provided a propitiation for "the sins of the whole world" (I John 2:2).

We seem to hear a grand note of universal restoration echoing in these passages. Yet when we compare Scripture with Scripture, bringing within view the full orbit of divine revelation, we are compelled to conclude that the Bible does not teach universal salvation. All these passages stand in contexts that contain references to the judgment of God against certain souls. John 12:32, for instance, must be seen in the light of the dual destiny announced in verse 25: "He who loves his life loses it, and he who hates his life in this world will keep it for eternal life." Ephesians 1:10 is followed by the statement that "we were by nature children of wrath, like the rest of mankind" (2:3). Two verses after Acts 3:21 ("the time of restitution of all things") we read of a warning against certain people who shall be "destroyed from the people." And if Philippians 2:11 predicts that every tongue shall confess the lordship of Christ, Philippians 3:19 asserts that the end of those who are the enemies of the cross of Christ shall be "destruction."

These passages, moreover, are open to more likely explanations than that which sees in them universal salvation. The words "all" and "whole" in not a few of them refer rather to the universal offer of the Gospel. Christianity, as Paul points out in his Areopagus address, lays emphasis on the *one* risen Saviour, for the *one* human race, in view of the *one* divine judgment (Acts 17:22-31). As a world faith, Christianity operates in two ways: it excludes all other faiths as competitors, and it includes all men in its offer—"to *every one* that believeth." For this reason the Church has a universal mission—"to make disciples of *all nations*"; a universal message—"God . . . commands *all men* everywhere to repent"; and a universal Messiah—"Christ Jesus . . . gave himself as a ransom for *all*."

The two texts that tell of God's desire that all men be saved are precise in the verbs they employ: "desire" and "wish"—not "will" or "purpose." Thus they point, not to God's purpose to save all men, but to His benevolent desire toward the human race, as shown in His provision of a Redeemer and offer of salvation. And when Paul says, "As in Adam all die, so also in Christ shall all be made alive" (I Cor. 15:22), he is speaking of persons previously described as "those . . . who have fallen asleep in Christ" (v. 18)—those who by spiritual birth belong to Christ, as by their natural birth they belonged to Adam.

Particularly significant is the statement in Second Corinthians 5:19. When Paul declares that "God was in Christ reconciling the world to himself," he adds immediately what this involved: God's "not mounting their trespasses against them." The reconciliation, therefore, is defined in terms of the non-imputation of trespasses, the trespasses that are not reckoned to men were reckoned to Christ: "For our sake he made him to be sin who knew no sin, so that in him we might become the righteousness of God" (v. 21).

But are we to assume that the word "world" implies that Christ was the Sin-Bearer for all men indiscriminately? No, for the context indicates that some men are reconciled and some are not as yet reconciled. "God, who through Christ reconciled *us* . . . , gave *us* the ministry of reconciliation. . . . *We* beseech *you* on behalf of Christ, be reconciled to God" (vv. 18, 20, italics added). It is evident that, as B. B. Warfield says:

> There is the need for men to respond to the divine grace; . . . reconciliation is not something which is carried through independently of men's reaction. While it is true that, in some sense, reconciliation can be thought of as something offered to man on the basis of Christ's work, yet it cannot be thought of as availing in the case of any individual man until he

himself has become reconciled to God (*The Plan of Salvation,* Eerdmans, repub. 1942, pp. 70, 71).

Indeed, all these "universalist" passages, however they may be individually interpreted, must be considered in the light of the urgent call to repentance and faith so prominent throughout the New Testament. Only "he who believes in the Son has eternal life; he who does not obey the Son shall not see life, but the wrath of God rests upon him" (John 3:36). God "justifies him who has faith in Jesus" (Rom. 3:26). "This is the testimony, that God gave us eternal life, and this life is in his Son. He who has the Son has life; he who has not the Son of God has not life" (I John 5:1, 12). "Without faith it is impossible to please him. For whoever would draw near to God must believe that he exists and that he rewards those who seek him" (Heb. 11:6). The Gospel is "the power of God unto salvation to every one who has faith" (Rom. 1:16). There can be no mistaking Scripture's insistence that no man gains salvation through the victory of the cross until he turns from his sin and believes the Gospel.

There is a true universalism in the New Testament—not only of the worldwide proclamation of the Good News but also of the cosmic triumph achieved by Christ in His cross and resurrection. For Christ's redemptive work accomplished more than the salvation of individuals. The cross and empty tomb laid the groundwork for the redemption of mankind, the world, and the universe. For this reason Scripture speaks of Christ as coming to save the world, accords Him the title of "the Saviour of the world," and declares that God purposed "through him to reconcile to himself all things, whether on earth or in heaven, making peace by the blood of his cross" (Col. 1:20). Such statements do *not* mean that all men without exception will be saved; they mean that "the human race attains the goal for which it was created, and sin does not snatch it out of God's hands: the primal purpose of God with it is fulfilled; and through Christ the race of man, though fallen into sin, is recovered to God and fulfills its original destiny" (B. B. Warfield, *The Plan of Salvation,* p. 103).

TODAY IS THE DAY

Heaven or hell?—these are the alternatives the Word of God sets before the human race. By its warnings, threats, invitations, and commands, it urges men to recognize the decisiveness of this life. It permits no cavalier view of life, or of death, or of destiny. Instead, it insists on the inevitable fact that a man shall have what he has chosen, that "whatsoever a man soweth, that shall he also reap" (Gal. 6:7). It further declares that "now is the acceptable time" and that "now is the day of salvation" (II Cor. 6:2).

If Christ told His contemporaries, "you will die in your sins unless you believe that I am he" (John 8:24), it is unthinkable that a follower of His should take an indifferent attitude toward the issues of life. If the Apostle Paul sought to persuade men, prompted as he was by "the terror of the Lord," it is difficult to see how a preacher of the Gospel can be unconcerned for the salvation of the lost.

Today's generation needs to be told what the New Testament teaches about hell and the awful reality of eternal punishment. Admittedly, this task is not congenial; but it is necessary. It must be done not sadistically but seriously. And the task is not only to preach but also to pray with a heart of love for the lost. Coupled with the message of judgment must be the glorious offer of eternal life through faith in the redeeming work of Christ. We must call men to repentance, off the path that leads to hell, and on to the way that leads to life everlasting.

A SELECT BIBLIOGRAPHY

11. HEAVEN OR HELL?

Loraine Boettner, *Immortality*. Grand Rapids: Wm. B. Eerdmans Publishing Co., 1956.

Emil Brunner, *Eternal Hope*. London: Lutterworth Press, 1954.

Harry Buis, *The Doctrine of Eternal Punishment*. Grand Rapids: Baker Book House, 1957.

William Hendriksen, *The Bible on the Life Hereafter*. Grand Rapids: Baker Book House, 1959.

C. S. Lewis, *The Great Divorce*. New York: Macmillan Company, 1946.
———, *The Problem of Pain*. New York: Macmillan Company, 1944.

James Martin, *The Last Judgment*. Grand Rapids: Wm. B. Eerdmans Publishing Co., 1963.

Reinhold Niebuhr, *The Nature and Destiny of Man*. New York: Charles Scribner's Sons, 1943.

Heinrich Quistorp, *Calvin's Doctrine of the Last Things*. London: Lutterworth Press, 1955.

Hermann Sasse, *"aion, aionios," Theological Dictionary of the New Testament*, I, Gerhard Kittel, ed. Trans. by Geoffrey W. Bromiley. Grand Rapids: Wm. B. Eerdmans Publishing Co., 1964.

William G. T. Shedd, *The Doctrine of Endless Punishment*. New York: Charles Scribner's Sons, 1887.

Geerhardus Vos, *The Pauline Eschatology*. Grand Rapids: Wm. B. Eerdmans Publishing Co., 1952.

THE SECOND
ADVENT OF CHRIST

Wilbur M. Smith

Wilbur M. Smith is professor emeritus of English Bible at Trinity Evangelical Divinity School, Deerfield, Illinois. He was educated at the Moody Bible Institute, Chicago, and the College of Wooster, Ohio, and was awarded the D.D. degree by Dallas Theological Seminary. Dr. Smith was ordained to the Presbyterian ministry in 1922 and served churches in Ocean City and Baltimore, Maryland; Covington, Virginia; and Coatesville, Pennsylvania. He became a faculty member of the Moody Bible Institute in 1938 and remained there until 1947, when he went to Fuller Theological Seminary as one of its charter professors. In 1963 he became professor of English Bible at Trinity Evangelical Divinity School. Dr. Smith is known for his many books and articles on the Bible, such as Therefore Stand *and* This Atomic Age and the Word of God. *He is an expert in religious bibliography. Since 1933 he has edited the annual volumes of* Peloubet's Select Notes *on the* International Sunday School Lessons.

12.   *Wilbur M. Smith*

THE SECOND
ADVENT OF CHRIST

T HE IDEA of the return to this earth of the founder of a world religion is utterly contrary to the thinking of Western man in a day when even the idea of a life to come is repudiated. Any discussion of it therefore requires careful examination of the documents in which it is initially set forth. Yet before investigating the literary data, we should remind ourselves of the basic points involved in the very phrase "the Second Advent of Christ."

These words refer, of course, to the same Lord Jesus Christ who once appeared on this earth in the most crucial and far-reaching event in human history. For it was in this advent that Jesus lived the one perfect and absolutely holy life among men. It was in this advent that He made possible the remission of sins and the reconciliation to God of those who were enemies and the enemies of His Father. It was in His First Advent that, by His resurrection, He gave man a hope that does not fade away but will be consummated in our own resurrection and inheritance in glory. It is through Jesus Christ in His First Advent that we come to know the truth of God as Father. It was because of His advent and ministry that the Church of Christ, which is His body, was made possible. Even the unbelieving world bears constant testimony to the profound importance of the First Advent: it uses a chronology based upon Christ's entrance into history.

Professor A. M. Fairbairn has not exaggerated the case in saying:

> The greatest problem in the field of history centers in the Person and Life of Christ. Who He was, what He was, and how and why He came to be it, are questions that have not lost, and will not lose, their interest for us and for mankind. The problems that center in Jesus have this peculiarity;

251

they are not individual but general — concern not a person but the world.
. . . No other life has done such work, no other person been made to
bear such transcendent and mysterious meaning. . . . He is the permanent object of human faith, the pre-eminent subject of human thought
(*Studies in the Life of Christ,* 1880, pp. 1, 2).

The concept of the Second Advent is wholly divorced from any thought
of a second Saviour or another prophet. It is Christ who is pre-eminent
in both advents, one the inevitable consummation of the other.

In the second place—and this, too is axiomatic, but nevertheless important—the Second Advent is exclusively concerned with this earth on which
the human race exists. It is not a second appearance of an incarnate life
ending in a redeeming death on some other planet, but refers exclusively
to a coming back to this same earth on which our redemption was wrought
out in the first half of the first century of our era. The word *advent,* of
course, implies a coming *to,* and this has for a necessary corollary a coming *from.* Christ was received up into heaven at the time of His ascension,
and He will at His Second Advent return from heaven (see Acts 1:11
and I Thess. 4:16).

There are similarities between the Second Advent and the First, and
there are also contrasts. The angel said to the apostles at the time of
our Lord's ascension, "Ye men of Galilee, why stand ye gazing up into
heaven? This same Jesus, which was taken up from you into heaven,
shall so come in like manner as ye have seen him go into heaven" (Acts
1:11). This implies that the return of our Lord will be personal, involving His own visible presence. It is not to be understood merely as an
eschatological movement, or merely as a time of judgment or consummation. It is not something directed from heaven to marshal the forces
of evil for a final conflict, though this will indeed take place. It is the
literal, visible, personal return to this earth of Jesus of Nazareth.

On the other hand, while the First Advent was, we might say, local,
the Second will have immediate world-wide effects. Not only will the
inhabitants of Jerusalem "look unto [him] whom they have pierced"
(Zech. 12:10), but, as St. John informs us, "every eye shall see him, and
they also which pierced him: and all kindreds of the earth shall wail because of him" (Rev. 1:7). This can only be the meaning of such a statement as: "For as the lightning, that lighteneth out of the one part under
heaven, shineth unto the other part under heaven; so shall the Son of
man be in his day" (Luke 17:24). Francis Pieper is not wrong, then,
in saying that Christ's coming will be so sudden that "Europe will not
be able to flash the word of his coming to America" (*Christian Dogmatics,*
1953, III, 516, n. 30). Our Lord in His First Advent came in weakness;
He will return in power. He came in humility; He will return in glory.
He came to die, making atonement for sin; He will come the second time
to judge the world and to rule.

It is hardly necessary to add that no such thing as a third coming of
Christ, or a series of comings, is hinted at in Scripture. There are only
two advents—one past, the other future. The consummation of the pro-

gram of God for the redemption of mankind involving the end of history and the beginning of eternity, the victory of righteousness and the judgment of unrepentant sinners, will be brought to pass in this one single future event. The Second Advent of Christ will never be followed by the advent of some other messenger of God, for there is no other God and no other Son of God. It is given unto all men once to die, and after that comes the judgment. Christ once died for all; after this will come His final judgment of the world, at a time appointed by God.

Some say that the Bible does not speak of a Second Advent, but that is incorrect. Not only did our Lord Himself say, "I will come *again,* and receive you unto myself" (John 14:3), but we are told, with a specific chronological reference, that "unto them that look for him shall he appear the second time" (Heb. 9:28).

Before turning to the great events that will take place at our Lord's return, let us look at the Greek words used in the New Testament for the idea of the return. First of all, there is the word *parousia,* which means basically "presence" and is so translated in such a phrase as "his bodily presence" (II Cor. 10:10). This word is often used to refer to the coming of some person to visit a church or Christian community, as in St. Paul's phrase, "my coming to you again" (Phil. 1:26). St. Peter uses it when speaking of the first coming of our Lord (II Pet. 1:16). This is the word frequently found in the comprehensive statements of St. Paul about the Second Advent (I Cor. 15:23; I Thess. 2:19; 3:13; 4:15; 5:23). It was this word that came to the lips of the inquiring disciples when they privately asked our Lord, "What shall be the sign of thy coming?" (Matt. 24:3). *Parousia* often appears in the Latin version as *adventus,* from which, of course, our word "advent" derives (see the Latin text of such verses as Matt. 24:3 and II Pet. 1:16). This word *parousia,* which does not appear in the pastoral epistles, is used by St. Paul in one passage to refer to the coming of Antichrist (II Thess. 2:9) but generally refers, as we have seen, to the Second Coming of our Lord, as in Second Thessalonians 2:1, 8. And St. James, in one of his rare passages concerning our Lord, also uses it, twice admonishing us to be patient in waiting for the coming of the Lord (5:7, 8). St. John uses the word in exhorting us that, if we abide in Christ, we will "not be ashamed before him at his coming" (I John 2:28). *Parousia* has been carried over directly into the English language, so that in scholarly literature the Second Advent is often called "the Parousia."

Another word that occasionally appears in passages about the Second Advent is *epiphaneia,* meaning "appearance." This occurs in the New Testament only in references to Christ's appearances on this earth. Arndt and Gingrich say that "as a religious technical term it means a visible manifestation of a hidden divinity, either in the form of a personal appearance or by some deed of power by which its presence is made known." Trench says this word "was already in heathen use, constantly employed to set forth those gracious appearances of the higher powers in aid of men. If God is to be immediately known of men, He must in some shape or another appear to them, to those among whom He has chosen for this honor. Epiphanies must be Theophanies as well (Gen. 18:1; Josh. 5: 13-15; Judg. 13:3)." The word is used in the Old Testament to denote God's making His face to shine upon His people. In the New Testament it is sometimes used of Christ's First Advent (as in II Tim. 1:10 and, in verbal form, Titus 2:11 and 3:4) but more often refers to the Second Advent (I Tim. 6:14; II Tim. 4:1, 8; Titus 2:13). Like *parousia, epiphaneia* has been brought over into the English language, so that we speak of the Epiphany. And in the Latin text it too is translated *adventus*.

A third word is *apokalypsis,* the "revelation" of something that was hidden. It is most commonly used in reference to the Second Advent by the Apostle Peter (I Pet. 1:7, 13; 4:13), and in its verbal form (II Thess. 1:7). *Apokalypsis* also has been brought over into the English language, not in reference to our Lord's advent but, in the form "apocalypse," as a name for the last book of the New Testament. Milligan helpfully remarks that "the substantive in the New Testament is applied exclusively to communications that proceed from God or Christ, or to the divine unveiling of truths that have been previously hidden." "Thus the whole of salvation history in both Old Testament and New Testament stands in the morning light of the revelation which will culminate in the Parousia" (Oepke in Kittel, III, 585).

Another word is used extensively by our Lord in His Olivet discourse in reference to the Second Advent: *erchomai,* "to come" or "to arrive." It sometimes refers to the coming of false christs (Matt. 24:5), but generally to the return of Christ, whether in parabolic teaching or in direct assertation (see, for example, Matt. 24:30, 39, 42, 44; 24:6, 13, 31, and parallel passages in Mark and Luke). This is the word used by St. Paul when he says that by partaking of the Lord's Supper, "ye do show the Lord's death till he come" (I Cor. 11:26). As with the other words we have been considering, this one may refer to such a simple matter as the journey of a man from one city to another, as Paul's sailing from Paphos to Perga, or, much later, Iconium (Acts 13:13, 51). And like the other three words, *erchomai* is sometimes used in reference to the First Advent of our Lord (I Tim. 1:15; I John 4:2). It is the word used in the last reference to the Second Advent in the New Testament Scriptures, where our Lord announced to the Apostle John, "Behold, I come quickly" (Rev. 22:7). And it is used in the original Greek text of the Apostles' Creed in the declaration that "Christ shall come to judge the quick and the dead."

To sum up our study of these particular words: All four are sometimes applied to the movements of men from one place to another. They are used to refer to the First Advent and also to the Second Advent. No one word in the New Testament refers exclusively to the Second Advent, nor is any one of these four we have looked at, when transposed into the English language, used exclusively for the Second Advent. Efforts to distinguish various periods of the Second Advent by these separate words have not proved satisfactory.

ACCOMPANYING PHENOMENA

Although a great deal of attention has necessarily been given to the actual *consequences* of the stupendous event of the return of Christ, seldom do we find a satisfying treatment of the phenomena that our Lord and the apostles informed us will attend the return. We may well begin with our Lord's own words in the great Olivet discourse: "They shall see the Son of man coming in the clouds of heaven with power and great glory. And he shall send his angels with a great sound of a trumpet" (Matt. 24:30, 31; see also Mark 13:26, 27; Luke 21:27). In somewhat similar language, our Lord declared to the high priest on the day of His trial, "Hereafter shall ye see the Son of man sitting on the right hand of power, and coming in the clouds of heaven" (Matt. 26:64; Mark 14:62).

Clouds often accompany divine manifestations. At the time of the giving of the Decalogue, we are told that "it came to pass on the third day in the morning that there were thunders and lightnings, and a thick cloud upon the mount, and the voice of a trumpet exceeding loud" (Exod. 19:16). At the time of the giving of the second table of laws, when Moses went up into the mount, "the LORD descended in the cloud, and stood with him there, and proclaimed the name of the LORD" (Exod. 34:5). When the tabernacle was finished, "a cloud covered the tent of the congregation, and the glory of the LORD filled the tabernacle. And Moses was not able to enter into the tent of the congregation, because the cloud abode thereon, and the glory of the LORD filled the tabernacle" (Exod. 40:34, 35). Even in these descriptions of events so long ago, we find three terms later used by our Lord in reference to His Second Advent—clouds, glory, and trumpet. At Christ's transfiguration, "behold, a bright cloud overshadowed them: and behold a voice out of the cloud which said, This is my beloved Son, in whom I am well pleased; hear ye him" (Matt. 17:5; cf. II Pet. 1:17). At His ascension, "a cloud received him out of their sight" (Acts 1:9).

Our present age of aerial transportation helps us understand what it means for our Lord to come upon the clouds. And what other aerial phenomena will be directly related to such an event? Will He come riding on a planet, or in a rainstorm or snowstorm? His coming might be as lightning strikes, from the east to the west, but He is not to come on a streak of lightning. And so penetrating will be His glorious person that He will be seen through the clouds, which will be, as it were, His footstool. There is no ground for abandoning a literal interpretation here, or for saying, as does Paul Minear, that "to insist on this sort of literalness would destroy faith in the invisible." This is exactly the point. Christ's parousia will involve not invisible things but visible ones. The reference to clouds is repeated in the classic statement of the Apostle Paul that all who are in Christ "will be caught up . . . in the clouds, to meet the Lord in the air" (I Thess. 4:17). So also the word of the Apocalypse, "Behold, he cometh with clouds; and every eye shall see him" (Rev. 1:7).

In the affirmation that He would come with power, or, as Mark's Gospel reads, "with great power" (Mark 13:26), the Second Advent is set in striking contrast to the First. He first came as a helpless Babe, and the Holy Family had to flee to Egypt to escape the wrath of Herod. He was even "crucified through weakness" (II Cor. 13:4). His entire incarnate life was lived under the laws of the Roman Empire. He subjected Himself to the verdicts of the rulers of this earth. But when He comes the second time, to subdue all the powers of this world, human and satanic, He will exercise omnipotent power in every realm of this world in which we live, and reign with undisputed authority.

One expression our Lord uses in describing the phenomena accompanying His return deserves a whole volume of interpretation. It is that He will come with "great glory." Sometimes this is expressed as His glory (Matt. 25:31 and Luke 9:26). At other times, He speaks of this accompanying glory as that of His Father (Matt. 16:27; Mark 8:38; Luke 9:26). Bernard Ramm, in his fine treatment of this subject of glory, gives us as good a definition as this inexhaustible word permits:

> The glory of God is the excellence, beauty, majesty, power and perfection of his total being. It is the completeness, the wholeness, and therefore the utter desirability of God. It is the appeal, the fascinating power, the attraction which he exerts over men. The man so affected by the glory of God returns glory to him by praise and adoration. Thus glory is not only a totality-character of God but something which the creature returns to the Creator (*Them He Glorified*, 1963, p. 22).

This idea, like that of the clouds, goes back to that overwhelming manifestation of God at the time when His Presence entered into the holy of holies. In the Old Testament the glory of God is basically related to the concept of kingship—first, as a summary of the magnificence attending an Oriental king, and then in reference to God Himself, who is called "the King of glory" (Ps. 24:7-10). How appropriate the word is when ascribed to the coming of the King of kings! Even at the beginning of Christ's ministry, St. John said that they beheld His glory, "glory as of the only begotten of the Father" (John 1:14). Our Lord could even speak of the glory He had with the Father before the world was (John 17:24). The body in which He was raised was a body of glory (Phil. 3:21). At the time of His ascension He was taken up into glory (I Tim. 3:16). And His statement that He would come in "great glory" is, of course, the origin of the assertion of the Apostle Paul that believers are to be found "looking for that blessed hope, and the glorious appearing of the great God and our Saviour Jesus Christ" (Titus 2:13).

That our Lord will be accompanied by angels at His return does not need elaboration. Early in His ministry He referred to the time when He would come "in his own glory, and in his Father's, and of the holy angels" (Luke 9:26). His statement is echoed by St. Paul, who speaks (II Thess. 1:7) of the time when "the Lord Jesus shall be revealed from heaven with his mighty angels."

In the definitive passage in the First Letter to the Thessalonians, another group of phenomena are particularly emphasized. "The Lord himself shall descend from heaven with a shout, with the voice of the archangel, and with the trump of God: and the dead in Christ shall rise first" (I Thess. 4:16). The word translated "shout" is frequently used in classical Greek of a command in battle. "It is not stated by whom the shout in the present instance is uttered, perhaps by an archangel, more probably by the Lord himself, as the principal subject of the whole sentence" (George Milligan, *St. Paul's Epistles to the Thessalonians,* 1908, p. 60). An archangel is mentioned only one other time in the New Testament, in Jude 9, and here again the idea is only an enlargement of our Lord's own words that in His return He will be accompanied by angels. Trumpets are often heard in times when God is revealing Himself in some unusual manner. This was true, for example, at the giving of the law (Exod. 19:16). Trumpets are also mentioned in descriptions of great prophetic events, as in Isaiah 27:13 and Zechariah 9:14.

THE WITNESS OF THE CREEDS

From the earliest formulation of creeds down through the great creedal statements of the Reformation, the return of Christ has been a basic theme. It is briefly summarized in the Apostles' Creed in the words, "He ascended into heaven, and sitteth on the right hand of God the Father Almighty; from thence He shall come to judge the quick and the dead." The larger Nicene Creed declares that "He shall come again with glory to judge both the quick and the dead: whose kingdom shall have no end." The Athanasian Creed is even more detailed: "He sitteth at the right hand of the Father from whence He shall come to judge the living and the dead, at whose advent all men are to rise again with their bodies and render an account of their own deeds."

J. N. D. Kelly, the leading authority of our day on the early creeds of the Church, has reminded us that during the second century "the theory that the returned Christ would reign on earth for a thousand years came to find increasing support among Christian teachers" (*Early Christian Doctrines,* 1958, p. 465). Elsewhere Kelly has said that "though the thought of His exaltation and lordship was no doubt present, it was the promise of His coming again to judge the living and the dead which loomed largest and most impressive in the catechumen's consciousness" (*Early Christian Creeds,* 1950, p. 125).

The fourth of the profoundly influential Thirty-Nine Articles of the Church of England reads as follows: "Christ did truly rise again from death, and took again His body, with flesh, bones, and all things appertaining to the perfection of man's nature; wherewith He ascended into heaven and sitteth until He return to judge all men at the last day." In the Heidelberg Catechism, Question 52 is: "What comfort is it to thee that 'Christ shall come again to judge the living and the dead'?" And the answer is: "That in all my sorrows and persecutions, with uplifted head I look for the very same person, who before offered Himself for my sake, to the tribunal of God, and has removed all curse from me, to come as judge from heaven: who shall cast all His and my enemies into everlasting condemnation, but shall translate me with all His chosen ones to Himself, into heavenly joys and glory."

Although the Westminster Confession of Faith does contain elaborate statements about the resurrection of the dead and the last judgment, these epochal events are not specifically said to be brought about by the Second Advent of our Lord, though that is implied. But at the conclusion there is a final exhortation in which the Second Advent is announced: "So will He have that day unknown to men, that they may shake off all carnal security and be always watchful, because they know not at what hour the Lord will come, and may be ever prepared to say 'Come, Lord Jesus, come quickly.' " The Larger Catechism (Question 56) is more specific regarding the Second Advent: "Christ is to be exalted in His coming again to judge the world in that He, who was unjustly judged and condemned by wicked men, shall come again at the last day in great power, and in the full manifestation of His own glory and of His Father's with all His holy angels, with a shout, with the voice of the archangel, and with the trumpet of God, to judge the world in righteousness."

What a boon it would be to the entire Church of Christ if the great truths of these confessions were enunciated and expounded once again from the thousands of pulpits in Christian lands! How seldom, one fears, do millions of Christians give thought to what their own Church testifies concerning the return of the Lord Jesus.

THE SEQUENCE OF EVENTS

To discuss the two advents of our Lord even briefly brings one to the very difficult question of what is to occur when the Lord returns and in what order the events will take place. One of the most distinguished Dutch theologians of the nineteenth century, J. J. Van Oosterzee, rightly said:

> All that the Gospel tells us of the premundane glory of the Son and of the majesty of His earthly appearing is but little in comparison with that which it proclaims to us of His glory in the day of the future. But how difficult at the same time to enter upon a field in which, more than in any other, one is only too easily lost in arbitrary conjectures, and is so soon inclined to decide that which Scripture has left undecided; to calculate that which it indicates as one day to be effected or to doubt that which does not in every respect harmonize with . . . the present view of the world. . . . We regard it as impossible *before* the day of fulfillment to determine with infallible certainty what in the promises of Scripture concerning the things of the future is *mere* imagery and what is *more* than imagery. But the more do we esteem it our solemn duty to add nothing to, and also to take nothing from, that which is here told us concerning the secrets of the coming age (*The Person and Work of the Redeemer*, n.d., pp. 449-51).

No student can be expected to construct a chronology, even of just the main prophetic events to be introduced by the return of our Lord, that will satisfy all believers. One aspect over which opinions vary widely is the millennium. Many in the Church, true believers, reject the whole concept of a millennium and the rule of Christ on this earth. Other Christians who do believe in a millennium are divided into two groups— those who look for the Church to bring it about, and those who consider a millennial era possible only when Christ returns. Of those holding the latter view, some believe Christ may come at any time, others that the Church must go through some period of tribulation, and still others that the Church at the end of the age must go through all the tribulation, after which the Lord will return. Some give no place at all to a future existence of Israel on this earth; others believe that the unfulfilled Old Testament promises to Israel are still valid. And there are some who become dogmatic in insisting upon two future comings of Christ—one for believers and one for the world. Many readers will disagree with some aspects of the following discussion.

Before we consider, with provoking brevity, the major events connected with our Lord's return, let us recall six passages in the New Testament that set forth a series of future events, a kind of a calendar of prophecy. This is fundamentally true of the Olivet discourse, which speaks of three eras: before the tribulation, during the tribulation, and after the tribulation. Then there are the two summaries of prophetic events in the classic statement of Paul about the resurrection, First Corinthians 15:20-28 and 51-54. First Thessalonians 4:15-17 is the well-known summary of events relating to the rapture of believers at the time of the Second Advent, and Second Thessalonians 2:3-12 unfolds a series of future events in relation to the doom of Antichrist. Finally, on almost the last page of the Scripture (Rev. 20:1-12), we have a series of eight events to follow after the battle of Armageddon, extending to the last judgment. Every event that will occur as a result of the return of our Lord must be assigned its chronological place within the framework of these six passages.

The Resurrection of Believers

Hardly any student of the New Testament would deny that the first event to take place at the coming of the Lord will be the resurrection of believers, clearly set forth by St. Paul in these words: "For if we believe that Jesus died and rose again, even so them also which sleep in Jesus will God bring with him. For this we say unto you by the word of the Lord, that we which are alive, and remain unto the coming of the Lord shall not prevent them which are asleep. For the Lord himself shall descend from heaven with a shout, with the voice of the archangel, and with the trump of God: and the dead in Christ shall rise first: then we which are alive and remain shall be caught up together with them in the clouds, to meet the Lord in the air: and so shall we ever be with the Lord" (I Thess. 4:14-17).

The words of George Milligan about this passage are apt:

> The resurrection of *all* men does not here come into view. All that the
> Apostle desires to emphasize, in answer to the Thessalonians' fears, is that
> the resurrection of "the dead in Christ" will be the first act in the great
> drama of the Parousia, to be followed by the rapture of the living saints
> (*St. Paul's Epistles to the Thessalonians*, 1908, p. 60).

To my mind, the resurrection of our bodies involves just about the greatest
exercise of divine power of any event in the history of the universe, greater
even than creation. It is the hope set forth by St. Paul and St. Peter in
passages we have already considered (I Cor. 6:14, 15, 23 ff.; I Pet. 1:3, 4).
Like so many other prophetic themes found in the New Testament epistles,
this one derives from the earlier utterances of our Lord (John 5:25-29;
6:39, 40, 44).

In the fifteenth chapter of First Corinthians, Paul sets forth four truths
regarding the body Christians will have in glory: It will be identical with
the earthly body (though care must be taken in defining *identical*); it will
have the qualities of incorruptibility, beauty, and power; it will be a spiritual body, in contrast to our present natural bodies; it will be like the body
of the Lord Jesus. There will be a similarity between the bodies we now
have and those of the resurrection. We shall be with Him in our resurrection bodies, and we shall recognize one another. The body that suffered death because of sin will be raised from the dead. Here a mystery
arises. Around what will this resurrection body be built? If the stalk of
wheat comes from a living germ buried in the ground, is there some hidden
germ of our own being around which Christ will build our resurrection
bodies? This was the view William Milligan set forth in *Resurrection of
the Dead* (Edinburgh, 1894).

At the judgment of believers there will be a reckoning according to
what they have done on earth as followers of the Lord Jesus. St. Paul
refers to this when he says, "For we must all appear before the judgment
seat of Christ; that every one may receive the things done in his body,
according to that he hath done, whether it be good or bad" (II Cor. 5:
10; see also Eph. 6:8). It is then that "of the Lord [we] shall receive the
reward of the inheritance" (Col. 3:24). "When the chief Shepherd shall
appear, ye shall receive a crown of glory that fadeth not away" (I Pet.
5:4; consider also the profound parabolic teachings of our Lord, e.g.,
Matt. 16:27; 25:19).

The Subjection of Earthly Powers to the Returning Christ

The New Testament presents different aspects of the Lord's return in
power. One of these is, of course, His coming down from heaven to confront the federations of kings determined to make war against the Lamb,
and their overwhelming defeat in the battle of Armageddon (Rev. 19:11-
21). It may well be that this confrontation of the rebellious earthly powers
by the Lord of glory is referred to in First Corinthians 15:24-28, a passage too often ignored in discussions of the Second Advent: "Then cometh
the end, when he shall have delivered up the kingdom to God, even the
Father; when he shall have put down all rule and all authority and power.

For he must reign, till he hath put all enemies under his feet. The last enemy that shall be destroyed is death. For he hath put all things under his feet. But when he saith, all things were put under him, it is manifest that he is expected, which did put all things under him. And when all things shall be subdued unto him, then shall the Son also himself be subject unto him that put all things under him, that God may be all in all."

What a new world there will be when the wicked powers are all subdued unto Christ! Paul's eloquent words give us some conception of the vast consequences that will follow the return of our Lord in power. Something of what this means is seen also in Second Thessalonians 2:8-11, here quoted in the vivid Phillips translation: "When that happens the lawless man will be plainly seen—though the truth of the Lord Jesus spells his doom, and the radiance of the coming of the Lord Jesus will be his utter destruction. The lawless man is produced by the spirit of evil and armed with all the force, wonders and signs that falsehood can devise. To those involved in this dying world he will come with evil's undiluted power to deceive, for they have refused to love the truth which could have saved them. God sends upon them, therefore, the full force of evil's delusion, so that they put their faith in an utter fraud and meet the inevitable judgment of all who have refused to believe the truth and who have made evil their playfellow."

With the overthrow of these ruling powers will begin the righteous reign of Christ upon this earth, to which the Old Testament prophets continually pointed and of which the New Testament also speaks.

Since the return of Christ will have such vast consequences, it is simply impossible to identify it with the fall of Jerusalem, as some have done. This event was rather the slaughter and enslavement of a million Jews and the destruction of the holy city. And Christ was not there. The Apostle John, writing his epistles twenty years *after* the destruction of Jerusalem, was still looking for the coming of the Lord. Nor is the return of Christ to be identified with the coming of the Holy Spirit, for Christ said that if *He* did not go away, the Holy Spirit would not come. Neither is the Second Coming to be interpreted as the appearance of a universal church, or an increase of world-wide culture, or the spread of democracy.

Immediately after the battle of Armageddon will apparently come the doom of the beast and the false prophet, who will be "cast alive into a lake of fire burning with brimstone" (Rev. 19:20). It is at this period that there must take place the destruction of the man of sin, Antichrist himself, who "opposeth and exalteth himself above all that is called God, or that is worshipped; so that he as God sitteth in the temple of God, showing himself that he is God . . . whom the Lord Jesus shall consume with the spirit of his mouth, and shall destroy with the brightness of his coming" (II Thess. 2:4, 8).

The Righteous Reign of Christ

Whether we believe in a literal millennium or not, we cannot deny that both the Old and the New Testament clearly set forth a time when

Christ Himself will reign upon this earth, when righteousness will prevail, when the enemies of Christ will be subdued, when all rule and authority and power will be subjected to Christ. This will culminate in the deliverance of creation from the bondage of corruption into the liberty of the children of God (Rom. 8:21). This is no doubt the period to which our Lord Himself refers when He speaks of the time "in the regeneration when the Son of man shall sit in the throne of his glory" (Matt. 19:28). Here the Greek word translated "regeneration," which is similar to the one used of individual regeneration (I Cor. 4:16; Col. 3:10), is defined by Thayer as "that signal and glorious change of all things in heaven and earth for the better, that restoration of the primal and perfect condition of things which existed before the fall of our first parents." I have always believed that this period of peace, of righteousness, of abounding joy, of deliverance from crime, fear, and the violence of nature, is that of which the angel spoke to Mary when he said that the one to be born of her "shall be great, and shall be called the Son of the Highest: and the Lord God shall give unto him the throne of his father David: and he shall reign over the house of Jacob for ever" (Luke 1:32, 33; see also Isa. 9:7; 16:5; Jer. 33:17; 23:5; Amos 9:11; Zech. 12:8, 9).

The Last Judgment

It is most significant, though sometimes tragically forgotten, that both Christ Himself and the Apostles relate the Second Advent to the Judgment, at one period of this event or another. Early in His ministry Christ, speaking of those cities of Judea and Galilee that refused to hearken to His message, prophesied that their punishment "in the day of judgment" would be greater than that which awaited Sodom and Gomorrah (Matt. 10:15; 12:41, 42; 11:22-24). This theme often reappears in our Lord's eschatological parables (e.g., Matt. 21:40; 25:19). There is involved in this final judgment "the harvest [at] the end of the world" (Matt. 13:39), at which time the angel will sever the wicked from the just (Matt. 13:49, 50).

Both St. Peter and St. John refer to "the day of judgment" (I Pet. 2:9; I John 4:17), and St. Jude, to "the judgment of the great day" (v. 6). This, of course, is that time of which St. Paul so frequently speaks, "the day when God shall judge the secrets of men by Jesus Christ" (Rom. 2:16; I Cor. 4:5; I Tim. 4:1). The Apostle pointed to this coming and inevitable day in his great address to the Athenian philosophers, when he said that "God hath appointed a day, in which he will judge the world in righteousness by that man whom he hath ordained; whereof he hath given assurance unto all men, in that he hath raised him from the dead" (Acts 17:31). This last great judgment is unfolded before us in apocalyptic terms—and properly so—at the end of the canonical Scriptures, where the Judge is seen sitting on a great white throne (Rev. 20:11-15).

One word that Paul attaches to the judgment of which he speaks in the Athenian address has for some reason been almost wholly ignored in modern theological works, though it is constantly identified with judgment in both Old and New Testaments. That word is *righteousness*. Again and again the Psalms declare that God "will judge the world in righteousness." In fact, one whole section of the 119th Psalm is devoted to the righteousness of God in judgment. It begins: "Righteous art thou, O Lᴏʀᴅ, and upright are thy judgments. Thy testimonies that thou hast commanded are righteous and very faithful. My zeal hath consumed me, because mine enemies have forgotten thy words. Thy word is very pure; therefore thy servant loveth it. I am small and despised; yet do not I forget thy precepts. Thy righteousness is an everlasting righteousness, and thy law is the truth." So too the prophets frequently declare that it is "the Lᴏʀᴅ of hosts who judgeth righteously, who trieth the heart and the mind."

Since God has appointed Christ the Judge of all mankind, and since this judgment, like all divine judgments, must proceed according to righteousness, how harmoniously perfect is the revelation of Christ in the New Testament as "Jesus Christ the righteous," or, in the words of the Apostle Paul, "the righteous Judge." He came to "fulfill all righteousness" and "is made unto us the very righteousness of God," and in His holy death He displays for all eternity the righteousness of God. In the midst of the bold judgments of the Book of Revelation, John says that he heard the angel of the waters saying, "Thou art righteous, O Lord, which art, and wast, and shalt be, the Holy One, because thou hast judged thus" (16:5).

Throughout the Word of God there is one unified testimony to the truth that the judgment of the souls of men at the throne of Christ is *final.* It is determined by what a man does on this earth. All the Scriptures testify that for each man there will be only one period of trial. Judgment does not occur when a man dies; all the wicked are awaiting judgment. Contrary to the unscriptural doctrine of purgatory, nothing one generation can do will result in any alteration in the conditions of the souls of any of the dead of any preceding generation.

There is an absolute finality to the return of Christ and the accompanying events. Our Lord frequently used the words "end of the world" (Matt. 13:49; 28:10). Over and over again He spoke of "the last day" (John 6:39, 40, 44, 54; 11:24; 12:48). In the Olivet discourse we find the clause "then shall the end come" (Matt. 24:14). Sometimes the biblical writers use a simple phrase: "the day" (Rom. 2:16), "the great day" (Jude 6), "the day of the Lord" (I Thess. 5:2; I Cor. 1:8), or, as we have seen, "the day of judgment." No doubt, some of these phrases are to be identified with specific eras in the vast consequences of the Second Advent, but with all of them there is the note of finality. All things are summed up in Christ. He is the beginning and also the end, the first and the last. The destiny of the human race and the future of the whole universe are determined by their relation to the glorious victories of the Lord Jesus Christ.

In these troubled decades, scores of writers are attempting to foresee what may be ahead for our world—economically, politically, scientifically.

Even some contemporary histories of European civilization conclude with chapters suggesting what is ahead. But very few of these writers even hint at the most important of all such future events for the human race, the Second Advent of Christ, which will bring this historical era to a close. What secular man sees on the horizon is, after all, only a human guess. But the Christian looks with absolute certainty for the return of his Saviour, Jesus Christ, because that event was announced by the Teacher who came from God, was reaffirmed by the apostles, is a major theme of divine revelation, and has always been believed by the universal Church. Ultimately and inevitably, because Christ is the only begotten Son of God, the Redeemer and Judge of mankind, all things must be summed up in Him.

WHEN WILL CHRIST RETURN?

In His great prophetic discourse on the Mount of Olives, Christ clearly declared in reference to His return that "of that day and that hour knoweth no man, no, not the angels which are in heaven, neither the Son, but the Father" (Mark 13:32; Matt. 24:36). Later in the discourse He repeated His warning several times. Yet despite these and similar warnings, some men in every age of the Church have foolishly attempted to construct chronological schemes for the sequence of future events, with dates attached. These schemes are invariably futile and only confirm the impossibility of deriving any such conclusion from the data of the Scripture.

On the other hand, there *are* such things as signs of the times. Christ, after enumerating numerous phenomena that would occur between His First and Second Advents and especially toward the end of this age, exhorted His disciples and the generations that would follow them: "Ye, when ye shall see all these things, know that it is near, even at the doors" (Matt. 24:33). To be sure, many distinguished servants of God through the ages have felt convinced that they themselves were living at the end of the age. This belief was expressed as early as the fourth century, by Lactantius. In the Middle Ages there was a great literature known as "The Fifteen Signs Before Doom's Day." Martin Luther, commenting on Luke 21:25-36, went into great detail about his own conviction that he was at the end of that age. And there have been and are more modern writers of the same persuasion. Their error does not, however, prevent us from considering some of the phenomena that the New Testament says will mark the end of the age, and from looking at present events and movements to see whether they seem to be setting the stage for the return of Christ.

Confining ourselves for the moment to the Olivet discourse, we note that one phenomenon marking the end of the age will be lawlessness (Matt. 24:12), culminating in the appearance of the Lawless One (II Thess. 2:7, 8). Despite the advanced state of our culture, our age seems to be the most lawless one the world has known—at least, for the last four centuries. In St. Luke's account of the Olivet discourse, one sentence in particular seems to be a vivid description of what we now see happening around the world: "Upon the earth distress of nations, with perplexity; the sea and the waves roaring; men's hearts failing them for fear, and for looking after those things which are coming on the earth" (Luke 21: 25, 26). Our Lord, who taught a Gospel of peace and love, nevertheless predicted that down through the ages there would be "wars and rumors of wars . . . for nation shall rise against nation, and kingdom against kingdom" (Matt. 24:6, 7). It is estimated that more than *one hundred million* people have been killed in wars on this planet in the last sixty years. Our century has seen the first two wars that could accurately be called world wars, and during the last forty years there has hardly been a day when the front pages of our newspapers have not carried something about war somewhere on earth.

Christ spoke also of false prophets and false messiahs. In my opinion we have not yet had a great manifestation of this fearful deception, though there are already many false cults. Yet in a day when unbelief seems to be increasing throughout Christendom, these words of our Lord seem particularly applicable: "When the Son of man cometh, shall he find faith on the earth?" (Luke 18:8).

There are those who do not believe there is any particular future for Israel; yet one cannot ignore our Lord's words that "Jerusalem shall be trodden down of the Gentiles, until the times of the Gentiles be fulfilled" (Luke 21:24). Since the passage seems clearly to declare that the day will come when Jerusalem will not be trodden down by the Gentiles, a corollary would seem to be that the city would return to the custody of the Jews—and this has now happened.

In Christ's comparison of conditions on earth during the days of Noah with conditions that will prevail at the end of this age (Matt. 24:37-39), the emphasis is not on immorality, unbelief, drunkenness, or anarchy, but on a secular civilization without God. This is the way our contemporary civilization is drifting.

The Book of Revelation, though it does not give precise details, in several passages predicts not only a number of groups of united nations but ultimately one great world-wide sovereignty, with evil forces in authority, called "the kingdom of this world" (Rev. 11:15, RSV). As the kings of the earth go out to make war "against the Lamb," they "have one mind, and shall give their power and strength unto the beast" (Rev. 17:13).

Happily there is a prediction in the Olivet discourse pointing to victories for the Gospel: "The gospel of the kingdom shall be preached in all the world for a witness unto all nations; and then shall the end come" (Matt. 24:14; Mark 13:10). Let us not forget that this "gospel of the kingdom" is exactly what St. Paul was preaching at the end of his ministry (Acts 28:31). Christ's words do not even hint that the nations will all be converted but affirm that they will all have a witness in their midst. Think of the great number of agencies that have arisen to help make this possible—the great outburst of missionary activity since Carey, the vast translation work of the Bible societies, the tremendous outreach of religious radio and recordings. Oscar Cullman speaks of the relation of missionary activity to faith in the Second Advent. "The missionary work of the Church," he says, "is the eschatological foretaste of the kingdom of God, and the biblical hope of the 'end' constitutes the keenest incentive to action" (quoted in Gerald H. Anderson, ed., *The Theology of the Christian Mission*, 1961, p. 43).

In this discussion of conditions in our times, this comment by a well-known secular historian is significant:

> The new age bears another and more ominous gift for the historian, one that has not been conspicuous in historical writings since the works of the Christian fathers. This gift is the element of the catastrophic. The Church fathers, with their apocalyptic historiography, understood the dramatic advantage possessed by the storyteller who can keep his audience sitting on the edge of eternity. The modern secular historian, after submitting to a long cycle of historicism, has at last had this dramatic advantage restored. The restoration, to be sure, arrived under scientific rather than apocalyptic auspices. But the dramatic potentials were scarcely diminished by placing in human hands at one and the same time the Promethean fire as well as the divine prerogative of putting an end to the whole drama of human history (C. Vann Woodward in the *American Historical Review*, LXVI, No. 1 [October, 1960], p. 19; see also the profound discussion in Toynbee's monumental *Study of History*, IX, 119, 289, 343-49).

We do not know, of course, exactly when Christ will return. Yet unless I, along with many other Bible students, misinterpret the prophetic Scriptures after years of studying them, it seems certain that the drift of the word in our desperate age is nothing less than the setting of the stage for the climax of human history, determined by and concluded through the Second Advent of Christ. Emil Brunner has said:

> Nowhere in the New Testament do we find any expectation that in the course of the centuries mankind will become Christian, so that the opposition between the world and the Church would be overcome in historical time. But the contrary is true: the Christian community or Church will be a minority until the end, and therefore the battle between the dark powers and the powers of Christ goes on until the day of judgment. If there is any truth in the apocalyptic pictures which we find in the New Testament, we have to say even more. The apocalyptic visions are unanimous in depicting the end of time, the last phase of human history before the coming of the day of Christ, as a time of uttermost tension between light and darkness, the Church and the world, Christ and the Devil (*The Scandal of Christianity*, 1950, p. 110).

Perhaps God will yet arrest these profound, seemingly irresistible movements toward an abyss and grant us a world revival. But if this is not to happen, then we seem to be near the end.

THE BLESSED HOPE

Down through the ages the Church has always referred to the Second Advent of the Lord as the great *hope* of all believers. St. Paul speaks of it as "that blessed hope" (Titus 2:13). Indeed, the Second Advent of our Lord is involved in all the important New Testament passages refering to the Christian's hope. Sometimes it is called "the hope of glory" (Col. 1:27), sometimes "the hope of eternal life" (Titus 1:2 and 3:7), sometimes "the hope of righteousness" (Gal. 5:5). St. Paul speaks of "the hope which is laid up for you in heaven" (Col. 1:5). In the well-known passage at the beginning of his First Epistle, St. Peter reminds us that God, according to His great mercy, "hath begotten us again unto a lively hope by the resurrection of Jesus Christ from the dead, to an inheritance incorruptible, and undefiled, and that fadeth not away, reserved in heaven for you . . . salvation ready to be revealed in the last time" (I Pet. 1:3-5). Then he exhorts his readers to "be sober, and hope to the end for the grace that is to be brought unto you at the revelation of Jesus Christ" (1:13). It is significant that in the writings of the Apostle Paul alone, the noun "hope" appears twenty-eight times, and in verbal form twenty-one times.

Hope in itself takes in three main ideas. In the first place, it must have reference only to things yet to come; we may rejoice in the past, or regret it, but we cannot hope for anything that has already taken place. Second, we speak of hoping only for something that is desirable, something we should like to have or like to see take place. Finally, any hope worth talking about must refer to something within the realm of possibility. You and I do not hope to be millionaires, even though we might like to be. None of us hopes to live hundreds of years. Our Lord's return is gloriously desirable; it is the ultimate perfection of every holy longing. And it is a reality for us—not just a desirable possibility, not a dream or fantasy, but something guaranteed by promises centered in Christ. Emil Brunner begins his volume *Eternal Hope* with these words:

> What oxygen is for the lungs, such is hope for the meaning of human life. Take oxygen away and death occurs through suffocation, take hope away and humanity is constricted through lack of breath; despair supervenes, spelling the paralysis of intellectual and spiritual powers by a feeling of the senseless and purposelessness of existence. As the fate of the human organism is dependent on the supply of oxygen, so the fate of humanity is dependent on its supply of hope.
>
> It is scarcely necessary to prove that Western humanity of today, at least in Europe, has entered a phase when it is feeling an acute and distressing need of breath through the disappearance of hope. Everyone is becoming aware of this, to a greater or less degree, and if anyone is not aware of it he can find the proof of it in contemporary literature and philosophy (*Eternal Hope,* 1954, p. 7).

St. Peter speaks of this hope as a *living* hope. How many of our human hopes have had to die! But the biblical hope is a living hope, because it centers in the living Christ and thus can never be extinguished. In this hope are involved the resurrection of the body, beholding of the Lord in His glory, fellowship with believers of all ages, and everything else attending inexhaustible experience of eternal life—life in Christ. Moreover, this hope transcends the individual. It is a hope that will be consummated in the new heavens and a new earth "wherein dwelleth righteousness" (II Pet. 3:13). Christians have a right, then, to hope for a final state of this earth, when, following judgment, crime and sin and shame and death itself will be put away because of the righteous Son of God, and there will not even be a whisper against God or His Son.

A corollary of the hope of the Christian is the hopelessness of the unbeliever. The hope of a reign of righteousness is at the same time the announcement of the doom and destruction of the enemies of God, including the nations that rebel against Him. The hope of Marxism is a communistic world brought about by human effort. The hope of the Christian is a righteous world brought about by the omnipotence of the Redeemer. Ultimately our hope is not in democracy, the United Nations, peace treaties, culture, or science, but in the coming of the Lord Jesus. How tragically futile was the statement made by Woodrow Wilson before the United States Senate in 1919: "the League of Nations is the only hope of mankind."

The words of British scholar J. E. Fison are even more apposite today than when they were written thirteen years ago: "The time is short. The rival eschatology of Karl Marx is in the field. It is high time that the Christian Church awoke to the situation and either honestly abandoned hope or else proclaimed the Gospel of the Advent of hope" (*The Christian Hope,* 1954, p. 28). And the leading authority on Marxism in America, Dr. Bertrand D. Wolfe, has strongly reaffirmed this thought:

> In an age prepared for by nearly two thousand years of Christianity with its millennial expectations, when the faith of millions has grown dim and the altar seems vacant of its image, Marxism has arisen to offer a fresh, antireligious religion, a new faith, passionate and demanding, a new vision of the Last Things, a new Apocalypse, and a new Paradise. Like the Apocalypse of the Bible, the Revolution is a day of judgment when the mighty shall be humbled and those of low degree exalted. It is the beginning of a Millennium (the very word is the same), a new thousand-year reign of historyless history (*Marxism,* 1965, p. 369).

SOME ETHICAL IMPLICATIONS OF THE SECOND ADVENT

Of the many passages in the New Testament referring to the Second Advent, there is hardly one that does not in itself or in its context insist upon the influence such a hope ought to have on our inner spiritual life, on the mood of our souls, the joy of our hearts. Sometimes the exhortation is very simple, as when in the Olivet discourse our Lord said, "Therefore, be ye also ready: for in such an hour as ye think not the Son of man cometh" (Matt. 24:44). By being ready, of course, He meant living so as not to be ashamed at His coming. These words were echoed by St. Paul, who reminded the Philippians that their citizenship was in heaven, "from whence also we look for the Saviour, the Lord Jesus Christ" (Phil. 3:20). Our mood as we wait for the Lord to come should be one of patience, as St. Paul and St. James remind us. "The Lord direct your hearts into the love of God, and into the patient waiting for Christ" (II Thess. 3:5). "Be patient therefore, brethren, unto the coming of the Lord. Behold, the husbandman waiteth for the precious fruit of the earth, and hath long patience for it, until he received the early and latter rain. Be ye also patient; stablish your hearts: for the coming of the Lord draweth nigh" (James 5:7, 8).

This waiting, however, is not to be a time of idleness. The parables of the pounds and the talents, as well as other parables, vividly set forth the obligation to labor for the Lord until He shall return from the far country into which He has gone. The command of the nobleman was, "Trade with these till I come" (Luke 19:13, RSV). Moreover, there is hardly a stronger passage exhorting Christians to be constant in work than that which concludes Paul's magnificent resurrection chapter: "Therefore, my beloved brethren, be ye stedfast, unmovable, always abounding in the work of the Lord, forasmuch as ye know that your labor is not in vain in the Lord" (I Cor. 15:58).

Not only are we to be diligent in the Lord's work, while we patiently wait for Him, but we must "live soberly, righteously, and godly, in this present world; looking for that blessed hope, and the glorious appearing of the great God and our Saviour Jesus Christ" (Titus 2:12, 13; the same language is found in First Thessalonians 5:8). The conduct believers are to have while they wait for the Lord's return is summed up in a word often used by St. Paul that has almost escaped the attention of our contemporary age: unblameable. One passage will be sufficient: "To the end he may establish your hearts unblameable in holiness before God, even our Father at the coming of our Lord Jesus with all his saints" (I Thess. 3:13).

The similar words of the Apostle John written at the end of that century are well known: "Beloved, now are we the sons of God, and it doth not yet appear what we shall be: but we know that, when he shall appear, we shall be like him; for we shall see him as he is. And every man that hath this hope in him purifieth himself, even as he is pure" (I John 3:2, 3).

A SELECT BIBLIOGRAPHY

12. THE SECOND ADVENT OF CHRIST

Gerald H. Anderson, *The Theology of the Christian Mission.* New York: McGraw-Hill Co., 1961.

Emil Brunner, *Eternal Hope.* Philadelphia: Westminster Press, 1954.

————, *The Scandal of Christianity.* Richmond: John Knox Press, 1965.

A. M. Fairbairn, *Studies in the Life of Christ.*

J. N. D. Kelly, *Early Christian Creeds.* New York: McKay Co., 1960.
————, *Early Christian Doctrines.* New York: Harper & Row, 1959.

George Milligan, *St. Paul's Epistles to the Thessalonians.*

Francis Pieper, *Christian Dogmatics.* St. Louis: Concordia Publishing House, 1953.

Bernard Ramm, *Them He Glorified.* Grand Rapids: Wm. B. Eerdmans Publishing Co., 1963.

Bertram D. Wolfe, *Marxism.* New York: Dial Press, 1965.

THE GLORIOUS DESTINY
OF THE BELIEVER

Merrill C. Tenney

Merrill C. Tenney is dean of the graduate school and professor of
Bible and theology at Wheaton College. With the degrees of Th.B.
(Gordon College), A.M. (Boston University), and Ph.D. (Harvard),
Dr. Tenney is ordained to the Baptist ministry. He previously was
pastor of the Stores Avenue Baptist Church in Braintree, Massachu-
setts, and a faculty member at Gordon College. He has served as
chairman of the Education Commission of the National Association
of Evangelicals and president of the Evangelical Theological Society.
Among Dr. Tenney's books are Galatians: The Charter of Christian
Liberty, The New Testament: A Survey, and Interpreting Revelation.
He edited The Zondervan Pictorial Bible Dictionary.

13. *Merrill C. Tenney*

THE GLORIOUS DESTINY
OF THE BELIEVER

A GLORIOUS destiny for man is inherent in Christianity. The Christian faith includes the certainty that the God who delights in His creation purposes perfection for that creation. Mankind is either a biological accident that conferred upon senseless matter the dubious blessing of consciousness without significance, or the product of a creative will that designed it to enjoy a self-conscious life capable of continuing growth and enduring usefulness. The Christian faith proclaims the second alternative and assures all believers that they are destined to glory, not to extinction.

This concept of personal destiny is peculiar to the revelation of the Scriptures or to those religions derived from the Judeo-Christian tradition. None of the other great religions or philosophies speaks with assurance about man's future. For example, Hinduism, the traditional belief of hundreds of millions, conceives of destiny as the wheel of existence, by which the soul passes through successive transmigrations until at last it is absorbed into Nirvana. As the raindrop falls into the ocean, losing its identity but not its existence, so the soul will finally be resolved into the universal being, formless and undefinable. Consciousness will be obliterated; and as desire fades into oblivion, all passion and pain will cease. Buddhism also, with its implicit denial of the living God, holds no hope of ultimate personal destiny.

The Greeks had a more strongly individualized idea of destiny. They believed in the survival of the individual soul after it was freed from the confines of the body. Yet their mythology represented the after-life as a cold, shadowy existence, devoid of cheer and progress, but with the persistence of personality. The present life was good; the future was either frightening to contemplate or too uncertain to be a cause for concern. Some Greek philosophers argued convincingly for survival in another world. But even they were skeptical at times. Socrates, the most original thinker of his age, after defending himself confidently before the judges who condemned him to death, remarked, "And now it is time to go, I to die, and you to live; but which of us goes to a better thing is unknown to all but God" (Plato, *Apology,* 41D). Despite his argument for immortality, he remained unsure whether life or death is better.

In the century when Christianity was born, the average citizen seemed to have lapsed into despair. Epitaphs on contemporary tombs all too often carry the cynical inscription, "I was not; I became; I am not; I care not" (see S. Angus, *The Environment of Early Christianity* (Scribners, 1920, p. 104). The Stoics, who disciplined their emotions more rigorously than the common herd, looked on existence as a predicament that could be escaped by suicide when it became too wearisome or futile.

Into the darkness of that depressed and despairing world shone the Gospel of Christ. God's redemptive purpose, revealed through the utterance of the prophets and culminating in the historical person of Christ, provided a firm foundation for both personal and corporate expectation of destiny.

The divine utterance in Genesis 3:15—"I will put enmity between thee and the woman, and between thy seed and her seed; it shall bruise thy head, and thou shalt bruise his heel"—is the first intimation of destiny in the Bible. Man's disobedience to the initial command of God not to eat of the tree of knowledge of good and evil had brought the sentence of death and expulsion from Paradise. Reduced to self-conscious shame, he was alienated from his Maker. His resources and privileges were drastically curtailed, and he was banished from the pleasant and fruitful life in the garden to wring a living from the earth by the sweat of toil. But God gave one encouraging word. He promised that the seed of the woman would overcome the tempter that had led man astray and introduced disaster and death.

This promise was the foundation for all further revelation of the future, for it stated the divine objective and defined the means for its achievement. The reversal of evil implied a restoration of the glories forfeited by disobedience; the "seed of the woman" indicated that reconciliation would be effected by some member of the human race. Once the divine purpose had been declared, a sure basis of hope was established.

Old Testament prophecy has relatively little to say about the individual destiny of the believer. It is chiefly concerned with the people of God as a corporate body. The various stages of development in the divine purpose for the group were marked by solemn agreements called "covenants," by which God sought to reach an accord with men that would permit a further disclosure of His attitude and intentions. Each of these covenants involved a new selective process defining more narrowly the line of "the seed," and each marked an advance toward the designated goal.

The covenant with Abraham, initiated by calling him out of a pagan civilization into a nomadic life in Palestine, involved separation from idolatrous worship and devotion to personal fulfillment of the divine will. God promised Abraham that his posterity would inherit a land, that they would be multiplied as the dust of the earth, and that they would descend from a son born to him and Sarah, despite their advanced years. Thus Abraham's faith was focused on the destiny of a people rather than on his own happiness or greatness.

The promise given Abraham remained as the hope of the patriarchs and became the inspiration of Moses. When God summoned Moses to become the deliverer of His people, He identified Himself as "the God of Abraham, the God of Isaac, and the God of Jacob" (Exod. 3:15). Under Moses' leadership the chosen seed emerged from Egyptian slavery into nationhood. The covenant of the law revealed at Sinai imparted to them a new concept of the unity and sovereignty of God that set them apart from all other nations. It established a fundamental moral standard loftier than that of surrounding paganism, and although features of its ritual were analogous to observances in other religions, the emphasis of its teaching was unique. It stressed love, not fear, righteousness more than ritual.

The main purpose of the law was educative, not restrictive. It emphasized strongly the sovereignty of God over human life. He became the sole center of worship, for the first commandment states, "Thou shalt have no other gods before me" (Exod. 20:3). His power to preserve and to destroy was plainly asserted: ". . . visiting the sins of the fathers upon the children unto the third and fourth generation of them that hate me, and showing mercy unto thousands of them that love [him] and keep [his] commandments" (20:5, 6). His righteousness and power were stressed so that the people would be ready to fulfill the purpose for which He had called them out of Egypt. The promised land lay before them; but if they were to take possession of it, they had to be morally and spiritually capable of administering it. The law was intended to provide the standards for establishing the commonwealth through which the Messianic hope could be realized. As Paul said, "The law was our schoolmaster to bring us unto Christ . . ." (Gal. 3:24). Although the law was silent about the future life, it contained a latent eschatology, for its avowed intent was to prepare a people for fulfilling a divine destiny.

The establishment of the Davidic kingdom introduced a new element of political solidarity and purpose. The conquest of Palestine by the twelve tribes had been slow and incomplete. The period of the Judges was characterized by anarchy, for "every man did that which was right in his own eyes" (Judg. 21:25). Under Saul the kingdom was unwisely administered, and ill-concealed dissension between the northern and southern sections prevailed. Under David the conflicting elements were united and the plan of God reaffirmed. To the doctrine of the "seed" was added, in God's pledge to David, the concept of royal succession. "When thy days be fulfilled, and thou shalt sleep with thy fathers, I will set up thy seed after thee, which shall proceed out of thy bowels, and I will establish his kingdom. He shall build a house for my name, and

I will establish the throne of his kingdom for ever" (II Sam. 7:12, 13).

The theocracy of the law was strengthened by the introduction of the kingdom. The king became God's visible representative whose commands conveyed the knowledge of the divine will. Although many of the kings of Judah were recreant or rebellious, the kingship was still part of the covenant. The tribes were fused into a political unit under the Davidic rule; the nation became one worshiping people, and the expectation of Messianic sovereignty over the world began to appear. The second Psalm voiced this hope clearly:

> Why do the heathen rage,
> And the people imagine a vain thing?
> The kings of the earth set themselves,
> And the rulers take counsel together
> Against the Lord, and against his anointed.
>
> . . . .
> Then shall he speak unto them in his wrath.
>
> . . . .
> Yet have I set my king
> Upon my holy hill of Zion.

This psalm contrasts the political anarchy of a rebellious humanity with the orderly rule God desires and says He will elevate His chosen representative to the throne of the world. The son of David, who represents the line of the chosen seed, is destined to become the universal sovereign.

The same general idea appears in later prophecy. Isaiah, who witnessed the decline of Judah, predicted that a shoot out of the stock of Jesse would become the ruler of the earth, and that He would judge the poor with righteousness and administer justice for the meek (Isa. 11:1-4). Jeremiah, who prophesied during the last fateful years when Judah was carried into exile by the Babylonians, spoke of the "righteous Branch" of David's line who would ultimately "reign as king, and deal wisely, and . . . execute justice and righteousness in the land" (Jer. 23:5, ARV).

Echoes of individualized aspiration for eternal life appear occasionally in the Old Testament. David, in lamenting the death of his infant son, said, "I shall go to him, but he shall not return to me" (II Sam. 12:23b). Job, speaking from the anguish that illness and ostracism brought upon him, declared (19:25, 26):

> For I know that my redeemer liveth,
> And that he shall stand at the latter day upon the earth:
> And though after my skin worms destroy this body,
> Yet in my flesh shall I see God.

The Prophet Isaiah anticipated a resurrection, for he announced that in the day of Jehovah, "Thy dead men shall live; together with my dead body shall they arise. Awake and sing, ye that dwell in dust: for thy dew is as the dew of herbs, and the earth shall cast out the dead" (Isa. 26:19). The prophecy of Daniel is even more explicit: "Many of them that sleep in the dust of the earth shall awake, some to everlasting life, and some to shame and everlasting contempt" (Dan. 12:2).

These hints of individual destiny are amplified in the teaching of the New Testament. John the Baptist, whom the Gospel of Matthew (Matt. 3:3) identified with "the voice of one crying in the wilderness" mentioned by Isaiah the prophet (Isa. 40:3), issued a call to repentance and faith in the coming Messiah. He introduced Jesus to his disciples as "the Lamb of God, which taketh away the sin of the world" (John 1:29). The attention of the people of God was thus directed toward the person of Jesus Christ, in whom the preceding covenants found an enduring fulfillment. He was peculiarly the "seed of the woman," because He was born of a virgin. He was the descendant of Abraham, Isaac, and Jacob (Matt. 1:1, 2) and heir to their covenant rights. He was the scion of David and legitimate successor to his throne (Luke 1:32, 33).

In Christ there is established also the new covenant, which deals with inward holiness as well as with outward privileges. Jeremiah defined its nature: "This shall be the covenant that I will make with the house of Israel: After these days, saith the Lord, I will put my law in their inward parts, and write it in their hearts; and I will be their God, and they shall be my people" (Jer. 31:33). The former covenants had depended on the obedience of the people to a set of external conditions and had failed because of human inability to meet them. This covenant would change the inner life of the people, so that obedience would be spontaneous and complete.

The writer of Hebrews provides the explicit connection between the prophecy of Jeremiah and its fulfillment in Christ by calling Him "the mediator of a better covenant, which was established upon better promises" (Heb. 8:6), and by quoting Jeremiah's words to substantiate his statement. Jesus undoubtedly referred to this covenant when He told His disciples at the last supper that the cup of which they partook was the new covenant in His blood shed for them (Luke 22:20). The divine assurance of blessing is perpetuated through Christ's death and resurrection, which offer greater hope than the former covenants.

THE INDIVIDUAL DESTINY OF THE BELIEVER

In progressive revelation the biblical teaching of the individual destiny of the believer reached its fullest development after the Exile. At the time of the Exile, when family ties were ruptured and the national structure of Israel was dissolved, each person had to decide for himself whether he would continue to worship the God of his fathers or conform to the standards of the surrounding paganism.

Ezekiel dealt with the problem when he remonstrated with Israel for disclaiming personal spiritual responsibility. The people had taken refuge behind a current proverb, "The fathers have eaten sour grapes, and the children's teeth are set on edge" (Ezek. 18:2). The exiles blamed the sins of their fathers for their plight and shifted the guilt of their misdeeds to the preceding generation. Ezekiel asserted that each man was answerable for his own sins and that "the righteousness of the righteous shall

be upon him, and the wickedness of the wicked shall be upon him"
(18:20). The rise of this individualism prepared the way for the apostolic witness to Christ, which calls for individual repentance and faith.
The believer's destiny cannot be taken for granted because he belongs to a
particular family or nation; it hinges upon his own relationship with God.

But this new relationship cannot originate with man himself, because
man is irretrievably lost apart from the intervention of God. He cannot
escape the heritage of evil inherited from his ancestors. Individual perversity and corruption of society unite to create a pressure that impels
him toward sin. Circumstances and habit aggravate this, making him the
victim of his own shortcomings and errors. Man cannot avert the dis-
illusionment that slowly engulfs him as he realizes his entanglement with
sin, nor can he turn aside the penalty of death that is its logical consequence. Alienated in spirit and shamed in the presence of a righteous
God, man can neither improve his own condition nor justly expect any
remedy for it.

God, however, by the new covenant in Christ, has provided reconciliation for those who will accept His terms. Jesus said, "He that heareth
my word, and believeth on him that sent me, hath everlasting life, and
shall not come into condemnation; but is passed from death unto life"
(John 5:24). Being liberated from guilt and condemnation, the believer
is introduced to a new life freed from the oppression of fear and failure.
He can anticipate the future with joy rather than dread; he can expect
glory rather than shame.

Accompanying the new freedom granted the believer is fellowship with
God. Salvation means more than emancipation from oppression and
punishment; it restores the relationship that disobedience destroyed. Christ
intended to make His disciples His eternal companions in the realm to
which He went when He left the earth. In His intercessory prayer on
the eve of the cross, He petitioned the Father that His disciples might
be with Him and behold His glory (John 17:24). He expected that they
would be elevated from the oppressive and hostile atmosphere of the
world into the eternal glory that was His by right and that He desired to
share with them.

This transition is no sudden introduction into an exalted state but the
culmination of a process. During their discipleship, Jesus' followers had
enjoyed His fellowship, though imperfectly because of their own limitations. But He intended to expand their horizons and enlarge their vision
so that they could enjoy a more intimate companionship with Him than
they had previously known.

The clearest statement Jesus made about the believer's destiny is the
familiar promise, "In my Father's house are many mansions: if it were
not so, I would have told you. I go to prepare a place for you. And
if I go and prepare a place for you, I will come again, and receive you
unto myself; that where I am, there ye may be also" (John 14:2, 3). The
ultimate goal is the Father's abode—a place of purity, peace, joy, and
light. Just as in the patriarchal system the families of sons and daughters

were incorporated into one household and lodged under one roof, so in the household of God there will be ample room for all believers. No longer strangers to God, they will be part of His family; no longer wanderers, they will have a permanent habitation. They will feel at home with Him, because they will be with Christ. Whatever one thinks about the location, Jesus was unmistakably predicting that the believer's final destiny is the presence of God.

One of the believer's glories will be his triumph over the temptations and opposition encountered along the way of life. Harassed by confusing problems that beset him from every side, he often loses sight of his true goal and finally succumbs to lethargy because he feels that the struggle is unavailing.

In contrast to this attitude of futility, the Scriptures enjoin persistence. The letters to the seven churches of Asia in the Apocalypse of John were written to Christians living in prominent centers of heathenism and engaged in desperate conflict with its evils. To encourage them, a promise was included in each letter "to him that overcometh." The divine message guaranteed that the victor should "eat of the tree of life" (Rev. 2:7), "not be hurt of the second death" (2:11), "eat of the hidden manna and . . . [receive] a new name" (2:17), "[have] power over the nations" (2:26), "be clothed in white raiment" (3:5), "[become] a pillar in the temple of . . . God" (3:12), and "sit with [Christ] in [his] throne" (3:21). Each of these figures of speech, whether positive or negative, sounds a note of triumph. The toil of life does not end in meaninglessness or defeat; in spite of losses and failures, it culminates in success.

The promises extended to the overcomers in these seven letters not only are specially relevant to their immediate circumstances but also reflect a complete restitution of what man lost when he fell from the favor of God. Because of his sin, he was debarred from the tree of life that symbolized the source of all spiritual vitality. Now by the grace of God the overcomer may partake of it freely and enjoy the fullness of all that God can supply. Whereas the first man was told that in the day he sinned death would overtake him, redemption exempts the believer from "the second death." The curse that compelled man to forage for his food and to contend with thorns and weeds will be superseded by the blessing of a "hidden manna," the gift for which he need not labor. Instead of conflict and subjection, the believer will enjoy the exercise of authority over the nations. The nakedness of which Adam and his wife became conscious will be covered with the "white garments" of God's righteousness. And instead of banishment from the divine presence, man will have a permanent place in the worship of God as a "pillar" remains in the structure of a temple. The ultimate triumph will be to sit down with Christ in His kingdom, sharing His exaltation and rulership.

The destiny of the believer is not limited to his spiritual achievements and privileges; it also includes a physical transformation. A salvation that nullified only the spiritual aspect of death would be incomplete. Man is a unit, and his material body is no less important than his spiritual nature.

As a part of God's creation, man's body was designed to be the instrument of man's mind and to express his personality. Permanent destruction of this instrument by death would be a disastrous loss.

The present body may be afflicted with weakness or racked by disease. Tyrannical appetites may demand gratification that contravenes the highest standards God has set, so that the flesh becomes man's master instead of his servant. Yet the body is not inherently evil, nor should we regard it merely as a prison from which death brings a welcome escape. Its limitations are not the necessary concomitants of physical life but rather the results of sin, which has corrupted it.

The Scriptures describe our flesh as "the body of our humiliation" (Phil. 3:21, ARV). Weakness prevents the accomplishment of the work that requires physical strength. As energy declines with age, physical resources fail to equal the skills experience has developed. Like a rusting machine, the body ceases to be useful. Then comes death and burial.

God promises to transform the body of humiliation into the likeness of the body of Christ's glory, which could transcend the limitations of the flesh and could never be subject to death. "It is sown in corruption; it is raised in incorruption: it is sown in dishonour; it is raised in glory: it is sown in weakness; it is raised in power; it is sown a natural body; it is raised a spiritual body" (I Cor. 15:42b-44a). The Lord Jesus Christ was able to appear and disappear from human sight, instantly, to enter a locked room, and yet He was subject to all the criteria of sense that confirmed His physical reality. In similar fashion, His followers will possess bodies that demonstrate the perfection of God's new creation.

Paul's phrase, "a spiritual body," does not suggest an intangible or ethereal entity. By contrast with the preceding adjective "natural," it implies a body that will be subject to the control of spirit rather than of animal appetites and nature. It will express the spiritual aspirations of its possessor far better than the present mechanism of flesh ever could.

The writers of the New Testament affirm unanimously that the occasion of this prospective transformation will be the second advent of Christ, who will return to complete the work He began during His earthly ministry. Paul set forth this principle by saying that, after being "reconciled to God by the death of his Son, . . . we shall be saved by his life" (Rom. 5:10). Since the impartation of life follows the effect of death, Paul must mean that an even richer experience awaits the believer who has been reconciled to God. As Christ emerged from the grave into a new sphere of victory, so the believer will share with Him the completeness of eternal life.

Different facets of this destiny are described by the authors of the New Testament in a variety of images. Peter, whose first epistle refers in every chapter to the death of Christ, speaks of "an inheritance incorruptible, and undefiled, and that fadeth not away, reserved in heaven for you, who are kept by the power of God through faith unto salvation ready to be revealed in the last time" (I Pet. 1:4, 5). Then he says that the proof of their faith will be rewarded "at the appearing of Jesus Christ."

The figure of an inheritance is appropriate, denoting a benefit not available immediately but guaranteed to the prospective recipient. He has every right to expect that he can claim it at the proper time, because it cannot be denied him. Furthermore, the inheritance of which Peter speaks cannot decay or be defiled by misuse; nor can it be devaluated by the passing of time. This inheritance corresponds to the new body described by Paul, for it is incorruptible, free from uncleanness, and everlasting as an unfading wreath.

In similar fashion the writer of Hebrews links the destiny of the believer with the return of the Lord by saying that "Christ was once [for all] offered to bear the sins of many; and unto them that look for him shall he appear the second time without sin unto salvation" (Heb. 9:28). "Salvation" in Hebrews denotes the completeness of forgiveness and of new life under the new covenant. It implies soundness or wholeness, since the process of regeneration beginning with a person's initial relation to Christ must be perfected by the final transformation of the resurrection. The figure of "appearance without sin" as applied to Christ is drawn from the ministry of the Jewish high priest. On the day of atonement he entered into the Holy of holies beyond the veil with an offering of blood to atone for the sins of the people. They waited breathlessly outside the sanctuary for his reappearance, knowing that if he was not accepted he would be stricken dead. When he did appear, they were assured that the offering was accepted and their salvation accomplished. Just so will the return of Christ indicate that He has completed His work of reconciliation and that His people are secure.

The Johannine writings confirm this teaching, adding the glorious assurance of personal transformation. "Beloved, now are we the sons of God, and it doth not yet appear what we shall be: but we know that, when he shall appear, we shall be like him; for we shall see him as he is" (I John 3:2). The nature of that future event is established by the use of "appear" in John 21:1, where Jesus "showed himself" (or "appeared") to His disciples at the Sea of Galilee after the resurrection. He talked with fishermen, prepared a meal for them, and was so obviously identical with the Lord they had known that they dared not question His reality. The effect of the objective manifestation of the glorified Christ will be the transformation of the saints of God, living or dead, into His likeness.

The Pauline teaching on individual glorification is contained in First Thessalonians and First Corinthians. The letter to the Christians at Thessalonica was written to an infant church that had just suffered the death of some of its members. Evidently they had cherished the hope that the Lord's imminent coming would prevent such a tragedy. They feared that the dead would be excluded from the blessings the living would enjoy at the Parousia: the old concept that death ended all hope still possessed them.

In offering consolation, Paul assures them that the believer's hope transcends the unbeliever's despair. At the coming of the Lord, he says, the dead will rise first, and then the living will be translated from earth to dwell with Him forever. Paul's purpose was to relieve the emotionally distressed rather than to satisfy the intellectually curious. For this reason he did not undertake here any detailed discussion of the nature of the resurrection.

The fifteenth chapter of First Corinthians was written from a different standpoint, as a defense of the resurrection against those who had denied its reality. It is therefore more argumentative and goes into detail. Paul begins his discussion by establishing the historical fact of Christ's resurrection, which both the Thessalonians and the Corinthians accepted. Then he goes on to show how the doctrine of the believer's resurrection, which the Corinthians questioned, was founded on this promise. The major portion of his argument in this chapter is compressed into one sentence in the parallel statement of First Thessalonians: "If we believe that Jesus died and rose again, even so them also which sleep in Jesus will God bring with him" (I Thess. 4:14).

At the conclusion of First Corinthians 15 Paul declares the transformation of the believer to be a "mystery," a truth not previously disclosed in the course of the divine revelation. Although the doctrine of the resurrection was latent in the Abrahamic covenant, it was not self-evident to readers of the Old Testament. Jesus had said that "the God of Abraham, and the God of Isaac, and the God of Jacob" is "not the God of the dead, but of the living" (Matt. 22:32). Only through Christ Himself, however, were the implications of this statement explained. Paul's dictum that "flesh and blood cannot inherit the kingdom of God" does not mean that humanity must be permanently excluded from God's presence; quite the contrary, the burden of his contention is that life shall triumph over the corruption and humiliation of death.

While the burden of the fourth chapter of First Thessalonians is consolation, the burden of the fifteenth chapter of First Corinthians is victory. The teaching in First Thessalonians was meant to allay sorrow, that in First Corinthians to counter frustration and a sense of futility. Because life seemed meaningless, the Corinthians were inclined to adopt the philosophy, "Eat and drink, for tomorrow we die" (I Cor. 15:32b). The assurance of resurrection and reward is cited as a stimulus to persist in labor, since the results will endure to eternity.

In both Thessalonians and Corinthians, Paul uses a striking military metaphor to convey the idea of the believers' transformation. He pictures an army camped in bivouac. Most of the soldiers are wrapped in their cloaks or blankets, asleep on the ground, while a few sentries remain on guard. Unexpectedly the general arrives in camp late at night and orders the army to move to another location. The trumpets sound an alarm, the sleeping soldiers rise, break camp, and shoulder arms, the contingent on duty swings into line, and the entire army marches away on another campaign. When the Lord returns, He will call all believers to Himself by a shouted command, and this trumpet will sound the last reveille. The dead will be raised from their bivouac, the living will be translated, and the entire group will enter into the kingdom introduced by the advent of Christ.

THE CORPORATE DESTINY OF BELIEVERS

Believers are related to one another not only through their individual vertical relation to Christ but also horizontally, through the new society redemption has created, represented in the New Testament by the Church, the Kingdom, and the City of God. These three are not related nor are they exactly synonymous.

The Church consists of those.who have put their faith in Christ and who are associated together for witness and worship. This term usually denotes local assemblies in various places, but it may also denote the universal body of believers (Acts 20:28; Eph. 1:22, 23) that transcends space and time.

"Kingdom of God" echoes the concept that originated with the Old Testament theocracy, though it was modified and expanded in the teaching of Jesus. Primarily it refers to the domain of God, whether spiritual or material, that was designed as the basis for the kingdom of Israel but failed to be fulfilled. Both John the Baptist and Jesus declared that this kingdom was "at hand" (Matt. 3:2; 4:17). Long disputes have arisen over its nature. Is the Kingdom identical with the Church, or with the dominion of the Gospel over the spiritual nature of man? Is it an external social order that will be slowly introduced as the ethical standards of Jesus permeate existing civilization? Or is it a period of rule still future, to be inaugurated by the return of Christ in person? Is it the advent of a new age that will gradually and imperceptibly replace the present order, or will it come by a cataclysmic judgment at the end of time?

No one simple answer is adequate to exhaust the content of the term "the Kingdom." As George E. Ladd has shown, the fundamental meaning of the biblical concept is *rule* or *authority,* and consequently it may be applied in several ways. It comprises the eternal sovereignty of God over the universe, His specific command over individual lives, and the future dominion over the world that will be established by the return of Christ (George E. Ladd, *The Gospel of the Kingdom,* Eerdmans, 1959, pp. 19-23).

The Gospels make it plain that the Kingdom of God was announced as imminent by John the Baptist, and that it was initiated in the person of the King, Jesus Christ, who enunciated its principles and yet regarded its final manifestation as future. In essence, the Kingdom came in His person; its full realization will come when He returns.

The City of God is the final abode of the servants of God and the consummation of His redemptive purpose. In this usage the word "city," translated from the Greek *polis,* has a broader meaning than our English term. We usually use "city" to refer to a place where buildings, transportation facilities, commerce, and industries are concentrated. But here the word refers primarily to the organization of the people, and only second-arily to material features.

The City of God is the future climax, for it is the restoration of an organized society, purified and centered about God and Christ. The Church, no longer a suffering and witnessing body, will be absorbed into the total number of the redeemed. The Kingdom, from which all enemies shall have been expelled and which shall have established universal do-minion, will be surrendered by Christ to the Father, "when he shall have put down all rule and all authority and power" (I Cor. 15:24). Both will be united in the City of God, which will become the eternal residence of the Church and the capital of the Kingdom.

THE CHURCH

The Epistle to the Ephesians, which affords the fullest discussion of the Church in the New Testament, describes it by three apt metaphors. The first is the body of Christ (Eph. 1:23). Just as the human body is the vehicle by which a man can express his feelings and accomplish his work, so the Church is the means by which Christ reveals Himself to the world. The Church is thus a living organism rather than a machine. The vital force of the Holy Spirit connects each member with the Head, who im-parts His life to the members. The gifts of the Spirit empower the mem-bers to carry out the functions of the body harmoniously. Each discovers his proper place in relation to the others as he participates in the unified activity of the whole.

This cooperative effort gives significance to every participant, because his contribution is needed for the perfect functioning of the body. How-ever inconspicuous he may be, he is indispensable; if he does not fulfill his mission, every other member may be handicapped. And if the entire body functions smoothly, every member shares in the success it attains. The destiny of usefulness is both individual and social. In the unified activity of the body, every member shares in the eternal life of the Head.

The second figure is that of a building, drawn doubtless from Paul's memory of the numerous shrines that graced the public squares in the cities of the Roman empire, especially the great temple of Artemis at Ephesus. All the engineering skill and artistry the ancient world could command was built into its temples, some of which took decades, if not centuries, to construct. Likewise the Church is the product of God's wis-dom and power, built on the foundation of the apostles and prophets, with Christ Himself as chief cornerstone of the entire structure (Eph. 3:20-22). It is an eternal tribute to its Architect, as the Taj Mahal perpetuates the ingenuity, skill, and artistic tastes of its designer. The believer finds his destiny as a product of God's handiwork, fashioned of crumbling human clay, yet transformed into a part of the eternal temple.

Temples often consisted of a complex of buildings united in one archi-tectural plan. Perhaps Paul had this in mind when he spoke of "each several building" (2:21, ARV). It is the believer's privilege to share in the unity of groups belonging to all nations, races, and ages. His destiny is inextricably involved with others of like faith. He is not isolated but rather is integral to the structure God is building.

The Church is intended to be the "inhabitation of God through the Spirit." God, as Paul said, does not dwell in temples made with hands, but by His Spirit He inhabits the hearts of men and makes His presence felt wherever true worshipers gather together. Within the Church, God is manifested to the world, and thus each believer becomes a means of this manifestation. God purposed that now the manifold wisdom of God might be known by the Church (3:10), but this purpose is not exhausted by its present function. The benediction that ends the first section of Ephesians says, "Unto him be glory in the church by Christ Jesus throughout all ages, world without end" (3:21). The believers will be a permanent exhibit of God's redemptive craftsmanship.

The third metaphor applied to the Church is that of a bride. The term is not equated with the Church directly, but the analogy is unmistakable. "Husbands, love your wives, even as Christ also loved the church, and gave himself for it; that he might sanctify and cleanse it with the washing of water by the word, that he might present it to himself a glorious church, not having spot, or wrinkle, or any such thing; but that it should be holy and without blemish" (Eph. 5:25-27).

In this analogy the emphasis is laid upon the purity of the Church. "Loved with everlasting love," the Church, the collective society of all believers, has been chosen by Christ for intimate association with Him. His redemptive death has sanctified her, so that He may ultimately present her to Himself purged of all blemishes and stains. At present she is far from perfect, for her members are often sinful, undisciplined, careless, and forgetful of Him. By the discipline of the Word, by the precepts imparted by revelation and enforced by the inward compulsion of the Holy Spirit, He will remove all disfigurements until the Church stands clean and spotless before Him.

The believer in Christ is destined to share in the blessings and privileges of the Church as a whole. He is part of the body that expresses Christ, a part of the building that enshrines Him, and a part of the bride that receives His love and care. Eternal vitality, eternal indwelling, and eternal love are His heritage through the Church.

THE KINGDOM OF GOD

The Kingdom of God, as previously noted, has many phases. The essential image of the Kingdom is probably a legacy from the Davidic covenant of the Old Testament, which promised an enduring physical reign to David and to his descendants. At the annunciation of Jesus' birth, the angel declared to Mary: "He shall be great, and shall be called the Son of the Highest: and the Lord God shall give unto him the throne of his father David: and he shall reign over the house of Jacob for ever; and of his kingdom there shall be no end" (Luke 1:32, 33).

Entrance to this Kingdom is attained by the new birth. "Except a man be born of water and of the Spirit, he cannot enter into the kingdom of God," said Jesus to Nicodemus (John 3:5). Although His statement was negative, it clearly implied that those who have experienced the new birth become members of His Kingdom. Since the new birth relates to the present state of believers, the Kingdom must also have a present existence. Its fundamental character is spiritual; it is not primarily a social or political organization. Essentially it consists of all regenerate disciples of Christ, though the sphere of sovereignty may extend beyond their number. It is the nucleus of those who have pledged complete allegiance to Christ in this world, and on whom He can depend for support in the exercise of His authority.

The Kingdom need not necessarily be visible in order to be real. During the last World War, when several European nations had been overrun by invaders, they maintained governments in exile. Their leaders resided outside the country but still commanded the allegiance of their people, even though the people were in territory that was under the enemy's domination. Similarly the Kingdom of God is composed of those who cherish Christ as invisible Lord of their lives, even though they may reside in the territory controlled by "the god of this world." The invisible Kingdom will appear in its true nature when its King returns to inaugurate His rule and assert His royal rights.

In the enigmatic parable of the sheep and the goats, which deals with the establishment of the Kingdom, one point is clear: The righteous shall inherit the kingdom prepared for them from the foundation of the world (Matt. 25:34, 46). Jesus equated the inheritance of the Kingdom with eternal life and promised that the righteous would share in the fruits of His final victory.

The nature of the triumphal reign of the righteous is indicated in a challenge offered to those who conquer evil in this life: "He that overcometh, and that keepeth my works unto the end, to him will I give power over the nations: and he shall rule them with a rod of iron; as the vessels of a potter shall they be broken to shivers . . ." (Rev. 2:26, 27).

The discipline of present Christian experience is intended to prepare believers for future responsibility. The establishment of Christ's Kingdom over the earth will necessitate the exercise of remedial authority that He will assign to His followers. Without the discipline of temptation and without the character of holiness, they will be unfit for the responsibilities that rulership entails. Christ has chosen them to participate with Him in His work of judgment and reconstruction, but He cannot so use them if they have not proved themselves worthy.

THE CITY OF GOD

As the Church represents the worshiping and witnessing group of believers, and the Kingdom the conquering and ruling believers, the City of God depicts the final destination of the redeemed. Although utopia has been the dream of many social reformers, it has not been attained, because a sinless society cannot be achieved by sinful men. In the divine economy, God has planned a community that will be realized when the Church's witness is complete and when the Kingdom has established the divine rule upon the earth.

The desire for such a society began when man first felt the alienation and loneliness that followed his separation from God. To compensate for his rejection by his fellow men, Cain built a "city" for himself and his descendants, and after the Flood the descendants of Noah attempted to erect Babel in order to preserve their unity and establish their prestige. Both these enterprises lacked divine sanction and therefore failed, but they were symptoms of the human craving for a social, economic, and political organization that would ensure security and prosperity. No human effort to realize this goal has yet succeeded. Babylon, Athens, Rome, and all the capitals of the modern financial and political world are doomed to change, decay, and oblivion. The "Great Society" will not be a human creation, though working conditions may be improved, transportation accelerated, education increased, and leisure time multiplied. The "city which hath foundations" (Heb. 11:10, 16) has been the quest of all earnest seekers since time began, but its builder and maker must be God Himself.

The believer thus becomes a member of a new, divinely created state. The Apocalypse speaks of "the names written in the Lamb's book of life" (Rev. 21:27) as the roster of its citizens. Paul, in writing to the Philippian church, says, "Our citizenship is in heaven" (Phil. 3:20, ARV), or, as Moffat renders it, "We are a colony of heaven." While abiding here, we are like a colony in a distant land, whose privileges and protection are assured by the country to which they belong. Although we may be non-residents, our citizenship is in the homeland, and we expect to return there in due time. The believer's true home is the City of God; he is only a sojourner in this world.

The City of God is not modeled after the cities of men. It is called Zion, or the New Jerusalem, after the city of David (Heb. 12:22; Rev. 21:2). Throughout the period of the United and Divided kingdoms and through the dreary years of Babylonian captivity, Jerusalem was the cherished focus of national life. When the exiles of Israel were commanded by their captors to entertain them with songs of their homeland, they replied (Ps. 137:4-6):

> How shall we sing the Lord's song in a strange land?
> If I forget thee, O Jerusalem,
> Let my right hand forget her cunning.
> If I do not remember thee,
> Let my tongue cleave to the roof of my mouth;
> If I prefer not Jerusalem above my chief joy.

To this day, when an orthodox Jew celebrates the Passover, he says: "This year, here; next year, in Jerusalem." Wherever he may live, he still regards Jerusalem as his capital and his home.

The devotion that the true Jew showed to Jerusalem while still in the hands of its captors is the model for the believer's loyalty to the City of God. "Here have we no continuing city, but we seek one to come" (Heb. 13:14). The impermanence of existing social systems precludes confidence in any of them as the final state of mankind. Only the government of heaven can assure the lasting stability and satisfaction a Christian craves, because nothing less than God's plan can meet his spiritual standards.

The description of the eternal city given in the Apocalypse is likewise modeled on Jerusalem. Whether it be understood literally as a material city with a specific geographical location, or whether the dimensions and description are regarded as figurative, is not very important. The fact remains that God has provided a rest for His people, "the city of the living God, the heavenly Jerusalem," where are "an innumerable company of angels, . . . the general assembly and church of the firstborn, which are written in heaven, and . . . God the Judge of all, and . . . the spirits of just men made perfect" (Heb. 12:22). Scripture depicts the New Jerusalem as an Oriental city with external walls, foundations, and gates, filled with buildings that gleam like jewels. Just as the white stucco walls of Jerusalem gave it a blinding brightness under the noonday sun, so the shining battlements of the New Jerusalem make it a source of lights for the nations that surround it.

The description in Revelation is both positive and negative, for the City of God is distinguished by the features it has and also by those it lacks. Its first and most obvious characteristic is the glory of God (Rev. 21:11), the incandescent radiance that symbolizes the divine presence. God is always represented as appearing in brilliant light. Moses saw Him in the bush that glowed with flame and yet was not consumed (Exod. 3:2). The fiery cloud that descended on the Tabernacle at its dedication (Exod. 40:34) and later on Solomon's Temple (II Chron. 7:1) indicated that God has condescended to dwell with His people in a singularly intimate way. Although He can be called omnipresent, at times He can manifest Himself more directly. The City of God will enjoy a fuller sense of His nearness than has previously been known.

The city has twelve gates, three on each side, directed to the four points of the compass and named for the twelve tribes of Israel. They offer universal access for all people through the provision promised in the Old Testament revelation, which was given that all the families of the earth might be blessed. God's mercies are not exclusively for any one class, nor are they restricted to any racial, cultural, or economic levels. All believers will be welcome.

The twelve angels at the gates (Rev. 21:12) are the guardians, who exclude those not entitled to enter and welcome those for whom the city has been prepared. They contrast with the cherubim of Eden, who were stationed at the gate with flaming swords to bar the return to the tree of life.

The twelve foundations, bearing the names of the twelve apostles (21:

14), indicate that the City of God is the ultimate goal of the Church, as the gates suggest its connection with Israel. The apostles on whose testimony the structure rests are honored as charter members of the New Jerusalem from the new dispensation.

The river of life (22:1) recalls the rivers that traversed Eden with their life-giving water. Flowing from the throne of God, the source of all life and power, it offers a plentiful supply to all who will partake.

The throne of God (22:1) speaks of God's central sovereignty and power. When the conflict with evil is ended, He is still undisputed master of the universe and victor over the powers of darkness. In the City of God, righteousness is finally triumphant.

The negative characteristics of the believer's destiny are just as significant as the positive, because they accentuate the contrast between his future and the existing conditions in which he lives. At least seven things are missing from the city of God that are common to all earthly cities.

The city contains no temple. In every center of population in the time when the Apocalypse was written, there was at least one shrine built in honor of the local deity. Rome was so filled with places of worship that a contemporary satirist said one could find a god there more easily than a man. Temples with their priesthood, ritual, and sacrifices express a human outreach for God; when He reveals Himself directly, they become superfluous. No indirect method of worship will be needed, for His servants shall see His face (Rev. 22:4).

Neither sun nor moon will be needed to provide light. These luminaries were created by God to give light to the earth; but their radiance is secondary because they are the products of His power, not Deity itself. The light of the city will be His own splendor shining directly within it.

The gates will never be closed. In the Oriental cities, the great gates were always shut and locked at night to protect the inhabitants from bandits. After dusk, a person could enter only if he had a pass to show at the small, carefully guarded postern gate. The gates of the City of God will remain open because the presence of God will protect it and because nothing evil will be allowed inside or outside its walls.

Nothing unclean can abide within its borders. The ancient cities generally lacked sanitation. Garbage and refuse accumulated in the streets, and the gutters served as sewers. These conditions prevailed at the time the Apocalypse was written. But the city of God will tolerate no filth. Presumably the word "uncleanness" has a moral rather than a physical meaning, though the imagery is drawn from physical conditions. The community God establishes will be free from corruption.

There will be no curse upon the earth, for there will no longer be any need to limit its productiveness. When the first man sinned, God declared that he would reap weeds and briars instead of profitable crops, and that he would be compelled to struggle for his living against drought, floods, wind, hail, pests, and parasites. God knew that without a struggle to challenge him, man would degenerate faster and devote all his energies to evil. The hardships of making a living would deter him from the decay of idleness and stimulate him to engage in useful industry. With the advent of a new race made righteous through faith in Christ, the ban will be lifted, and believers will no longer be compelled to battle against hostile elements. Since the eternal city will be inhabited only by those who have been redeemed, God will remove the restrictions that were introduced to check evil and will permit the enjoyment of full production. Not work but unavailing toil is a curse. In the restored Eden, the effort expended will be matched by the returns.

There will be no night within the eternal city. Street-lighting was unknown in the ancient world. The dark corners and alleys were the haunts of bandits and thugs who made nocturnal travel dangerous, if not impossible. Householders seldom ventured from their homes after nightfall unless accompanied by armed servants. Under the cover of darkness, crime flourished and work ceased. The perpetual illumination of the presence of God will brighten the heavenly city, and in its light the inhabitants will enjoy freedom from fear.

The abolition of death will ensure an eternal future to the dwellers in the City of God. With no death to interrupt labor, there can be unlimited growth in knowledge and achievement. Death interrupts progress, because the time necessary to educate one generation to take the place of another retards the development of ideas and sometimes makes the thinking of one generation incomprehensible to the next. Men with the ripest experience and wisest judgment are removed at the time when they should be contributing the most to their associates. Were they capable of living for ever, their enlarging experience would enable them to accomplish more, and their growing mental powers would build a superior civilization.

God purposely limited human life because of sin; if death did not cut short the wickedness of any generation, it would degenerate until the world's evil made existence intolerable. Although death is the penalty of disobedience (Gen. 2:17; Rom. 6:23), it is nevertheless a merciful provision to prevent the unending expansion of moral corruption. With evil eliminated, God can bestow everlasting life upon His servants so that they will enjoy the privileges and knowledge that were the original heritage of humanity. The City of God will be the final society, in which men can grow to the stature God first intended them to have.

All the blessings a believer can anticipate are conditioned upon his relation to Christ. Christ is the center of the new world. The New Jerusalem is called "the Lamb's wife" because it is so dear to Him. The apostles whose names are inscribed on its foundations are apostles "of the Lamb." His presence renders a temple unnecessary; His brightness is its illumination. The roll of its citizens is "the Lamb's book of life," and its government is "the throne of God and of the Lamb." His service will be the occupation of its inhabitants, and in His victory they will achieve their eternal triumph.

With this picture the New Testament ends. Language is inadequate to express the wonders that await the servants of God, who are heirs of the future. If the language of Revelation can to any extent be taken literally, it depicts a state of being that transcends anything mankind has experienced. If it is only symbolic of the future, that future must be so glorious that no adequate concept of it can be formed and no speech can convey its meaning.

The City of God is the goal of the total redemptive process. Not only does God seek to restore what was ruined by sin; He also creates a new world better than the one that was lost. The destiny of the believer is not simply a return to the first bliss of Eden, with the potential of repeating the sins and consequent miseries of the past; it is rather a better world founded upon the redemption that insures a permanent deliverance from evil and a fuller comprehension of God's character.

The fall of man brought into focus the love of God that was manifested in His concern for sinners, and the persistence of His purpose that maintained the development of revelation. That revelation culminated in Christ, in His voluntary participation in human life through the frustration and suffering of the cross and in the anticipatory demonstration of His victory in the resurrection. The meaning of this salvation is perpetuated in the City of God. The very title of Christ, "the Lamb," recalls His sacrificial death. The "river of life" is a constant reminder of the inexhaustible life He imparts to believers. The calamity that necessitated redemption may eventually be forgotten; the new joys redemption creates will abide forever.

A SELECT BIBLIOGRAPHY

13. THE GLORIOUS DESTINY OF THE BELIEVER

William R. Alger, *A Critical History of the Doctrine of a Future Life.* Philadelphia: Geo. W. Childs, 1864. Old but exhaustive.

René Pache, *The Future Life.* Translated by Helen I. Needham. Chicago: Moody Press, 1962. Deals with total destiny of the believer.

Bernard Ramm, *Them He Glorified.* Grand Rapids, Mich.: Wm. B. Eerdmans Publishing Co., 1963.

Ulrich E. Simon, *Heaven in the Christian Tradition.* New York: Harper, 1958. From moderate liberal standpoint; a historical summary.

Wilbur M. Smith, *The Biblical Doctrine of Heaven.* Chicago: Moody Press, 1968. Full summary of Biblical teaching on the concept of heaven.